Military Force
and
American Society

the text of this book is printed
on 100% recycled paper

Military Force
and
American Society

Edited by
Bruce M. Russett and Alfred Stepan

HARPER TORCHBOOKS

Harper & Row, Publishers
New York, Evanston, San Francisco, London

MILITARY FORCE AND AMERICAN SOCIETY

First HARPER & ROW edition published 1973.

LIBRARY OF CONGRESS CATALOG CARD NUMBER: 72–84236

STANDARD BOOK NUMBER: 06–139365-7

designed by Ann Scrimgeour

Contents

INTRODUCTION

The Military in America:
New Parameters, New Problems,
New Approaches

Bruce M. Russett and Alfred Stepan

During the thirty years after World War II . . . Americans devoted much attention to the expansion of Communism (which in fact expanded very little after 1949), and in the process they tended to ignore the expansion of the United States influence and presence throughout much of the world in terms of aid, investment, bases, trade patterns, deployment and commitments. Future historians will, I think, view the Soviet Union, China and the United States as expansionist powers during this period, but they will view the U.S. as a highly successful expansionist power and the other two as frustrated expansionist powers.

Samuel P. Huntington [1]

The Fact of Role Expansion

Daniel Bell observed that "the social and economic map of the U. S. has been redrawn more in the past twenty years by the influence of defense and defense spending than by any other single factor."[2] In this book we consider the causes and effects of an expanding political role for the American armed forces and

[1]"Political Development and the Decline of the American System of World Order," *Daedalus,* 96 (Summer 1967): 927–28.
[2]"Notes on the Post-Industrial Society," *The Public Interest,* 7 (Spring 1967): 107.

the increasing reliance by civilians on military methods. We are concerned about an expansion of the armed forces in two senses: the enormous enlargement of military forces and military expenditures over previous non-wartime standards, and the expansion of the military into roles previously performed by civilians or not performed in the political system at all.

Some factual information documenting the armed forces' enlargement is first in order. Before World War II active-duty military personnel amounted to about 330,000 men, less than 1 percent of the working-age male population. Virtually all those men were stationed in the continental United States or in American possessions. Military expenditures totaled less than $1.3 billion, or about $1.8 billion including veterans' benefits. Even the larger figure amounted to less than 20 percent of the federal budget and approximately 2 percent of the gross national product. Military research and development expenditures could be counted in the low millions. The nation had no foreign allies and virtually no foreign military bases. A combination of distance and relatively primitive technology gave the country a sense of security from foreign attack; the military aircraft of the day typically had a combat radius of but a few hundred miles and in any case could carry only a ton or so of high explosive bombs. Foreign threats were far away and a major attack on the Western Hemisphere promised to carry early warning. Domestically, by the late 1930s the nation seemed to have recovered its political stability, and there were no major calls for army action against civil disturbance.

The post-World War II period looks very different to anyone who sets it in longer perspective. In 1970, for example, American armed forces numbered about 3.2 million men, or 6 percent of the male labor force. More than one million uniformed men were stationed abroad, in countries on every continent. In addition over one million civilians were employed directly by the Defense Department. The military budget hovered around $75 billion; with veterans' benefits ($10 billion) and interest on the largely war-incurred national debt ($17 billion), payments on past, current and presumed avoidance of future wars accounted for over 61 percent of the money appropriated by Congress. Together those figures totaled more than 10 percent of the gross national product—five times the pre-World War II level. Military research and development costs totaled $8 billion and reached into virtually every university and large corporation. The United States could count forty-one formal military allies and during the cold war period had carried out military assistance programs to more than fifty nations. Military assistance and military export sales (described by then-Secretary McNamara as "an integral and essential part of our collective defense and overall foreign policies") amounted to about $2 billion. Military threats, both given and received, were immediate. Bombers and missiles could reach halfway around the globe carrying payloads whose explosive power equaled 100 million times that of a prewar bomber. Missiles could deliver their warheads in less than thirty minutes, and with but a few minutes warning even to the super-alert. For cases where the presence of armed men, rather than mere destructive force, was required, whole divisions could be airlifted across the ocean in less than a day.[3]

Skills and attitudes also changed. Most American cold war leaders had been political or military officials during the years of World War II; for their generation warfare constituted a heroic epic in the destruction of tyranny. That victory through force of arms, combined with the fact of an enormous American military capability during most of the post-World War II period, fed a confidence in the tools and concepts of force, coercion and deterrence in foreign policy. Military-political research centers were set up to create a new scholarly expertise in strategic questions. Thus emerged the intellectual outgrowth of the material growth of the American military—a great corpus of civilian analysts who thought easily and readily in military terms.

However necessary for national security military expansion may have seemed, however circumspect officers may have been in trying to defer to civilian authority, the facts of an enormous change are inescapable. For those of less than middle age who

[3]Documentation on these matters can be found in such places as U.S. Bureau of the Census, *Statistical Abstract of the United States, 1970* (Washington, D.C.: Government Printing Office, 1970); U.S. Bureau of the Census, *Historical Statistics of the United States, Colonial Times to 1957* (Washington, D.C.: Government Printing Office, 1960); Institute for Strategic Studies, *The Military Balance, 1970–1971* (London: Institute for Strategic Studies, 1970); and *Statement of Secretary of Defense Robert S. McNamara before the Senate Armed Services Committee on the Fiscal Year 1969–73 Defense Program and 1969 Defense Budget* (Washington, D.C.: Government Printing Office, 1968).

know history as the span of their adult lifetimes, the change may not be obvious, but by any perspective extending more than thirty years, we have a new world. Furthermore, the expanding military expenditures, manpower and technological sophistication have unavoidably produced changes, perhaps of equal magnitude, in the American political system.

The speed, range and size of modern weapons have transformed traditional diplomacy. Because the potential of major-power attack is always present, because the capability of American military intervention floats almost everywhere on the seven seas, the military instruments of national influence are always considered alongside the traditional economic and political instruments. Civilian leaders are preoccupied with questions of potential violence, internationally and nationally; they have incorporated military leaders into the highest planning levels of foreign and even domestic policy. New institutional structures have been created to direct the use of force in international affairs. The National Security Act of 1947 established the Joint Chiefs of Staff and the National Security Council. It also founded the Central Intelligence Agency with its combination of economic, political and paramilitary functions. Other institutions, such as the National Security Agency, employ both military and civilian personnel for intelligence gathering and policy execution. The National Security Council deals not only with overt problems of military and foreign policy but with domestic concerns as well, under the principle that strong instruments of foreign policy require a large, stable domestic base. American presidents' increasing reliance on the National Security Council and its staff, instead of on the State Department, means that an organization with a strong military orientation has replaced an overwhelmingly civilian institution as the central advising organ for American foreign policy.

The role of military men overseas has expanded also. Nearly half of recent American foreign aid has taken the form of military assistance. Until recently economic and military assistance were "packaged" together in the same appropriations bills; economic aid was more palatable to Congress if its apparent contribution to military security was emphasized. American military men have been employed as mediators with the elites of the less-developed countries. Both American civilian and military leaders warmly embraced the new doctrine that the military advisor should be an activist soldier-statesman in such fields as preventing insurgency, administrative reform and nation building. This is accentuated by recent American expectations (not entirely fulfilled) of a great effort by the communist powers to initiate revolutionary warfare in Latin America and around the Eurasian littoral. As the fear of direct nuclear or conventional attack by the Soviet Union lessened, it was replaced by the fear of Maoist fish in a peasant and proletarian sea.

Nor has military role-expansion been limited to American overseas activities. Many essentially civilian programs have been justified in the name of national security; the national security label has doubtless contributed, properly or not, to the volume of such pork-barrels as the interstate highway program, strategic material stockpiles, the space program, shipbuilding and the merchant marine, some agricultural subsidies and, yes, the National Defense Education Act. And while the rhetoric of these programs has contributed to the sense of national priority for military matters, more direct expansions of the activities of military men themselves are also apparent. Project 100,000 of the Defense Department, to induct and train many young men who would otherwise be passed over by the draft, brought the armed forces into a new health and education role. The same was true for Project Transition, designed to give useful civilian skills to those about to be discharged from military service. Selective Service itself brought the armed forces into new functions and of course utterly changed the expectations of every healthy, young American male from what they would have been in the 1930s.

Demands for riot control and maintenance of domestic security in a period of national unrest have had great impact on the professional military of this country. First the National Guard, and then the regular army, have been deeply engaged in riot control. A number of the best army combat units have spent much of their training time preparing for domestic missions. In 1968 the army was put under orders to be prepared to send as many as 10,000 men simultaneously to each of twenty-five cities in the event of major riots.[4]

Intelligence gathering about civilian activities and policy plan-

[4] *New York Times*, 24 December 1970, 22:2.

ning for dealing with civil unrest have followed. For example, in 1968 an official army document was widely disseminated to units stationed in the United States. It shows how army leaders perceived that their service had become profoundly concerned with domestic American policies:

The current civil disturbance situation dictates a change in the degree to which the army must seek advance information concerning potential and probable trouble areas and troublemakers. . . . [It] must know in advance as much as possible about the wellsprings of violence and the heart and nerve causes of chaos.[5]

Army officers did not necessarily seek these tasks. On investigating the program of military intelligence gathering about civilians, Assistant Secretary of Defense Robert F. Froehlke decided that civilian officials had ordered a "reluctant" military to conduct investigations in specific communities, but once involved, "the military over reacted."[6]

Thus what it means to be a military man has changed enormously over the past few decades, and with it the American political system has also changed. The soldier must take on tasks that were unknown, certainly to him and perhaps to anyone, thirty years ago. Moreover he expects to take on those tasks, and civilians expect him to do so. The result is a new force in the political system and new strains on the role-conception of the military man himself.

It is almost impossible to establish the precise mechanisms by which this role-expansion occurred. Some observers would largely blame the enthusiasms of the military men themselves, usually willing, even anxious, to take on a new job and do it well. Certainly there is a reluctance, evident in tasks as well as budgets and manpower levels, to give up a capability once it has been acquired, whether or not the original need still exists. Such bureaucratic inertia or "ratchet effects" are not limited to the military. Moreover, it must be recognized that there is a strong civilian component behind military role-expansion. Civilian personnel seem all too willing to defer to military "expertise" regarding questions at the margin or indeed to select military instruments on their own initiative. When civilians try a task and

[5] *New York Times*, 1 March 1971, 34:2.
[6] *New York Times*, 19 February 1971, 12:2.

fail, it may well seem natural to let the army have a try. Civic action, intelligence gathering and riot control are distasteful operations for most civilians anyway; civilian officials often prefer to have someone else do them, and the obvious someone else is the military.

Furthermore, there are often symbiotic effects between military activity and civilian benefit. The ramifications of mutual support implied by the term "military-industrial complex" are too obvious to require noting for any reader of this book. But they are not limited to the exchange of economic benefits. And as one of the contributors to this book notes so well, the ideological impetus for militant anticommunism in this country has been provided fully as much by civilians as by soldiers. Observers of the American political system must be alert not just for military usurpation of formerly civilian functions, but must equally be self-conscious about the types of roles civilians give to the army. There is a pull as well as a push. Civilian abdication of responsibility, as well as military aggrandizement, must be watched.

It is of course true that the past year or two, at least, have brought some diminution in the size of the military establishment. Military spending as a proportion of the gross national product has now dropped to the lowest level since the beginning of the Korean War. Military manpower has been cut sharply, and may fall even more dramatically under the impact of a new volunteer army. These changes must be recognized, though, as we emphasized earlier, by a perspective that looks farther back, to the late forties or before World War II, the military establishment is still extremely large. And even the reduction, accompanied by rising antimilitary sentiments in.parts of the populace, can have the effect of further politicizing the military. As the cold war consensus evaporates, as a large proportion of the population becomes resentful toward recent American foreign policy, military men have to work harder to generate political support for their activities. Furthermore, in the effort to avoid being again drawn into counterinsurgency wars they cannot win, military men understandably seek the capacity to make their own judgments about the political appropriateness of their activities. In this sense the civilians responsible for a foreign policy that has failed also are responsible for the politicization of the military that has sprung from that failure.

Doubtless the policy recommendations of military men at times have been more liberal or more humane than the recommendations of civilians. In applauding such occasions, it is tempting to welcome such military inputs to the political process. But the perspectives of military men, like the perspectives of other groups of people, must diverge from those of various civilians. Military officers are members of a bureaucratic organization, with distinct interests and responsible to their institutional superiors. Political leaders are ultimately responsible to their electorate, and cannot forget to compare their actions with those they perceive their constituents as desiring. No amount of educating military men to broaden their perspectives can erase this difference. To replace civilians with military men in policy-making positions, even when the military inputs may appear temporarily more pleasing, is to court long-term trouble.

New Approaches to New Problems

The articles that follow are the fruit of a series of formal and informal sessions held almost weekly for the last year at Yale University. The participants were scholars and military officers— often the same individuals were both. We quickly perceived that the traditional concerns of "civil-military relations" were much too narrow to permit an understanding of military role-expansion as just reviewed. For example, a major focus of the old literature was how to insure that military officers would obey the orders given them by civilians or how to prevent unauthorized military action. Such concerns lead to a profound misconceptualization of civil-military problems. They do not lead us to ask whether civilians are militarizing society. They do not lead us to ask what determines the *kind of orders* civilians give to the military, what determines the roles that both civilians and military conceive to be appropriate to the armed forces. In this light the questions of military obedience and military initiative become much more complex.

Similarly, the idea of a "military-industrial complex" also is much too restrictive. It assumes, really by definition, the importance of economic interests in promoting military activities. By so doing it directs attention away from such an impetus as ideology.

Material interest may be important, perhaps even it is control-ling, but analysts must not simply assume its importance before carefully examining other forces.

Thus the traditional concepts are useful in part, but very limi-ted. In this book we wanted to begin to broaden both the focus of analysis and the variety of methodological tools that could be brought to bear. Questions about the role of the military in the American political system are so central and so complex that we must be deliberately eclectic in our methodological approaches. For this volume some problems seemed best explored from the perspective of the participant-observer, others by rigorous quan-titative methods and still others by the analysis of symbols and ideology. The volume begins with an examination of attitudes and socialization within the military, then broadens to the study of the attitudes and behavior of major civilian political actors in regard to defense issues, and finally expands the scope of inquiry to explore the underlying ideological assumptions that explain or sustain new American patterns of civil-military relations.

The first two articles examine the impact of the new missions and roles of the military on the behavior of military officers and on the theory of military professionalism. For over fifteen years Samuel Huntington's classic work on military professionalism has been widely accepted as both an accurate description of and a prescription for the role of military officers in American society. Indeed, the very concept of military "professionalism" has been one of the major theoretical themes of the entire scholarly litera-ture on civil-military relations.

According to this theory the specialized skills needed by the military to carry out the mission of external defense are such that the vocation of officership "absorbs all their energies and fur-nishes them with all their occupational satisfactions."[7] Indeed, the functional specialization needed for external defense meant that it was "impossible to be an expert in the management of violence for external defense and at the same time skilled in either politics or statecraft or the use of force for the maintenance

[7]See, Samuel P. Huntington, "Civilian Control of the Military: A Theoretical Statement" in *Political Behavior: A Reader in Theory and Research*, eds. H. Eulau, S. Eldersveld, and M. Janowitz (New York: Free Press, 1956), p. 381.

of internal security. The functions of the officer become distinct from that of the politician and policeman."[8]

Thus a major argument of this view of traditional military professionalism is that professionalism contributes to civilian control precisely because military men are so preoccupied with the requirements of military specialization that they are apolitical. "Civilian control is thus achieved not because the military groups share in the social values and political ideologies of society, but because they are indifferent to such values and ideologies."[9]

Prima facie, however, it has seemed to us that when the new roles and missions of the military are taken into consideration, the content and consequences of professionalism have radically changed from the classic view described above. Instead of functional specialization focused on external defense, we now see military professionalism focusing on an increasingly broad range of subjects designed to analyze, prevent and combat insurgency abroad and at home. Whereas the traditional theory sees military professionalism as engendering apolitical attitudes, the new professionalism appears implicitly and often explicitly to politicize the officer corps.[10] This theme is examined in the first two essays of this book.

The participant-observer approach is an especially valuable way to explore the implications of the new content of military professionalism for the American officer corps. James Dickey holds a graduate degree in international relations and is an active-duty major in the army. He has performed political-military duties in Vietnam, and in the United States was attached to a combat unit much of whose time was devoted to training for domestic riot control. In an unusual and personal article Dickey explores some of the tensions created within the officer corps by the missions of the new professionalism.

To gain historical perspective on long-term trends of military

[8]Samuel P. Huntington, *The Soldier and the State: The Theory and Politics of Civil-Military Relations* (New York: Vintage Books, 1964), p. 32.

[9]Huntington, "Civilian Control of the Military," p. 381.

[10]Alfred Stepan initially formulated this argument with the developing world in mind but some of the same processes can be discerned in the United States; see his, "The 'New Professionalism' of Internal Warfare and Military Role-Expansion," in A. Stepan, ed., *Authoritarian Brazil: Origins, Policies, and Future*, (New Haven, Conn.: Yale University Press, 1973).

professional concern with political issues, Major Raoul Alcalá and Clarence Abercrombie, III, carried out an extensive analysis of the curricula at the major army schools of the United States, as well as the contents of influential army-related journals. The time period examined was from 1920 to 1970. Their data clearly indicate that since 1954 there has been a rising political content in the curricula and thought of these organs of military socialization and opinion. Alcalá, like Dickey, now teaches at West Point.

Because so much of the American military's role-expansion since World War II has been supported, and indeed often originated and ordered, by two of the major civilian branches of government, namely the executive and the legislature, it is necessary to expand the scope of the inquiry to include civilian policymakers. Though it ought to be clear that an examination of the behavior and attitudes of key civilian actors in regard to defense issues should have a high priority among research tasks for behavioral social scientists, a study of the literature indicates that few analysts have tailored quantitative techniques in such a way as to carry out relevant research. The articles by Jong Lee and Wayne Moyer are attempts to explore important substantive problems while at the same time indicating ways in which scholars can profitably apply advanced behavioral methods to clarify complex relationships that are almost impossible to demonstrate by more traditional methods.

Jong Lee, in a highly original article, uses such techniques as factor analysis, multidimensional scaling and content analysis to determine the underlying constellations of issues and concerns that executive policymakers see as closely related or mutually opposed, and to determine which domestic issues are downgraded when national security issues are given a high priority. He then shows the interaction between foreign crisis and military expenditure and how military spending has hindered economic growth. Wayne Moyer, a professor at Grinnell College and former navy lieutenant commander, applies roll-call scaling and multiple-regression analysis to examine the attitudes and behavior of congressmen in regard to defense issues. He generates strong evidence that ideological factors are more powerful than constituency pressures emanating from the military-industrial complex in determining congressional voting patterns.

Moyer's article, as well as informal discussions among group members, led us to the conclusion that to study the role of the military in America it is necessary to go beyond the study of the behavior of national political leaders, to the study of the underlying attitudes, problem-solving styles and especially the ideology of the American people. The role of ideology has been inadequately studied by conventional scholars of civil-military relations. As a result, many of the more interesting formulations of the problem have come from the writings of political activists, journalists and polemicists. Douglas Rosenberg is a doctoral candidate in political science at Yale and has been active in the peace movement. In this book he makes an important attempt to integrate the normative and ideological dimensions of the problem of civil-military relations into a study of how beliefs and values have contributed to expanding the role of military force in American society.

The annotated bibliography which closes this volume grew out of our discovery that the study of the new parameters of the role of the military required the use of sources that lay outside the standard academic literature. While these essays were being written, we made an extensive inventory of both traditional sources and the more obscure and difficult-to-obtain military writings. Because the polemical literature is often rich in information, formulations and critical interpretations, this widely scattered literature was also culled closely. New approaches to new problems require a new bibliography. The result was an annotated and unorthodox listing containing many little-known items organized under new rubrics, essential for exploring the new civil-military relations.

Part 1
POLITICIZATION
OF THE
MILITARY

A Personal Statement

Major James S. Dickey, U.S. Army

The phrases "identity crisis" and "search for a purpose in life"
have become clichés in 1972 America. Even so, they appear to fit
the American army officer of the last decade and will probably be
even more appropriate in the foreseeable future. Prior to the
Kennedy Administration, an army officer could pick up a copy of
Samuel P. Huntington's *The Soldier and the State*[1] and find a model
which defined his professional role and his relationship to the
society he was sworn to defend and with which, at least superfi-
cially, he could identify. Even now the Huntington model has
tremendous intrinsic appeal. A highly professional, apolitical
army, working diligently to counter threats to the nation's
security from "armed forces operating from outside its institutional and territorial confines" and subjecting its will to the policies of the constitutionally elected leadership is certainly a
felicitous concept. In Huntington's model civilian control is best
assured by allowing the army to develop its own values and ethos
based on discipline—a necessarily antidemocratic value. Huntington calls it "objective control." But objective control has now
lost any relevance it might once have had. For better or worse,
army officers have become involved in ever-expanding political
roles: domestically and within foreign nations. Role-expansion
disturbs me as a professional army officer and raises doubts in my
mind about the benefits (or dangers) to society of the new definitions of military professionalism which are inherent in the accomplishment of these new roles.

[1]Samuel P. Huntington, *The Soldier and the State, The Theory and Politics of Civil-
Military Relations,* (New York: Vintage Books, 1957).

Let me make clear that I feel the United States Army does not and will not pose a threat to take over American society in any time I can see. Neither is this article a call for the army officer to return to a strictly circumscribed role of fighting wars—a role which is rooted in myth in any case. I speak as an individual who grew up as the son of a regular army officer, went to the United States Military Academy and served as a regular officer for my entire adult life. My interests are common to many junior officers. The questions are many. How did this process of role-expansion come about? Given this process, what new definitions of military responsibility and expertise need to be made. Are these new definitions objectionable to an officer concerned with the army's proper subordinate role to civil and civilian society? If they are objectionable, what can be done about it and by whom?

It is not true that the army's original mission was solely to defend against foreign armed aggression. The army has had a role in internal security since the time of the American Revolution.[2] In frontier times protection of settlers and dealing with the Indians required direct (political) involvement with civilians. In recent years the army has become more involved with civil disturbances. It has always performed this role, but until the mid-nineteen sixties the probability of such activity appeared so slight that it is difficult to fault Huntington for excluding it from his list of security functions in which the military is or should be involved.

Nor is the army officer oblivious to Huntington's third (situational) aspect of security, which involves the "threat of erosion resulting from long term changes in social, economic, demographic and political conditions tending to reduce the relative power of the state."[3] If the army officer is performing a function which is vital to the survival of his country, he must have some feeling that the country is worth protecting. Thus he must have made a personal decision that the goals and values of that nation are approximately congruent with, or at least not inimical to, his own. For that reason he is willing to subordinate his individuality to the protection of those goals and values. If those values should

[2] Examples abound: the Whisky Rebellion, the Pullman Strike, the Bonus Marchers, etc.
[3] Huntington, *The Soldier and the State*, p. 1.

change, he has more than a slight interest in both the change and the process of the change. Changes in situational security may vitiate the officer's whole purpose in adhering to the military profession. For example, the collusion of two branches of government to destroy the effectiveness of the third would create a novel domestic situation and possibly one to which the officer, as a student of the Constitution, could not accede. It may not be the army's role to change society; but if society changes, the bedrock upon which the officer's commitment rests may turn to quicksand. Historically, General Walker's "Pro-Blue" program in the 24th Infantry Division showed that at least one officer felt the army had an operational role in affairs affecting situational security. Two quotations from articles by military officers, one in a national daily and the other in a service journal, show a degree of topical interest in situational security:

. . . Communist strategy aimed at defeating the United States not on the battlefield but on the home front has succeeded.[4]

[It is the military's duty] to safeguard within the military profession the attributes of patriotism and loyalty in a day when God is banned from the public schools and the National Anthem is used as a riot control device at football games.[5]

None of this is particularly new or particularly startling. It certainly does not point to an American Boulanger's arrival in the near future. But suddenly one reads in the press of army intelligence's surveillance of political figures, of the effect of military officers' thinking on Vietnam policy, of Green Berets tracking down Bolivian revolutionaries and of a school at Fort Bragg which trains army officers to advise foreign counterparts on all aspects of their counterparts' jobs (which in not a few cases involves running the countries' governments).[6] All of these sound like missions which civilian organizations or men should handle; but the army has been or is doing them.

Role-expansion has occurred, and, I would hypothesize, it will continue to occur because the army is operationally oriented and

[4]MG Thomas A. Lane, "The Right to Intelligence," *New York Times*, 11 January 1971, p. 31.
[5]Carl M. Guelzo, "As We Should See Ourselves," *Infantry*, November–December 1965, p. 59.
[6]See discussion in Ward Just, "Soldiers," *Atlantic*, November 1970, pp. 70–81.

because key civilian decisionmakers think that the army has the capability to handle such missions in a relatively speedy and efficient manner. The process feeds upon itself. A mission, domestic or international, needs to be accomplished. The army has the manpower and resources immediately available. The army will therefore be given the mission. Given the mission, the army must build up expertise to accomplish it. Once the army has built up the expertise and the crisis is past, it is more cost-effective to leave the army with the mission than to turn it over to another organization which should more appropriately accomplish it on a regular basis. The army is also the logical candidate to accomplish new missions in related fields when the need arises. And since these missions have become increasingly political, the army inexorably gains operational political expertise and roles. This process is reversible from within the military only with great difficulty. The difficulty arises because of the way the goals, values, institutions and recent historical experiences of the United States Army operate upon the members of the officer corps.

The regular army officer's oath of service requires him to "uphold his country's Constitution against all enemies foreign and domestic."[7] This is his "mission" in both the strictly military sense and in the more amorphous sense of a calling. Protection of the nation is his overriding concern—his duty. But duty is a nebulous concept. At one level duty means "Instant and Unquestioned Obedience at All Times."[8] At another level it is faithfulness to his oath to the Constitution. The myriad problems inherent in the resolution of these two concepts of duty are most obvious when reading General of the Army Douglas MacArthur's statement:

For example, I notice in existence a new and heretofore unknown and dangerous concept that the members of our armed forces owe primary allegiance and loyalty to those who temporarily exercise the authority of

[7]Department of Defense, *The Armed Forces Officer*, (Washington, D.C.: Government Printing Office, 1950), p. 1.

[8]An aphorism displayed on a bulletin board in an orderly room at West Point in 1956. Jack Engeman, *West Point: The Life of a Cadet*, (New York: Lothrop, Lee and Shepard, 1956), p. 42. Such signs are made at the direction of the superintendent or commandant and reflect his views.

the executive branch of government, rather than to the country and its Constitution which they are sworn to defend.[9]

The officer then is the servant of the Constitution and of the nation at large. He cannot abdicate his responsibility to check his orders against the ultimate law to which he has sworn his oath, i.e., against a criterion of constitutional lawfulness. In theory all orders which protect the Constitution are by definition lawful and should be obeyed. But here further problems arise. The Constitution embodies a humanitarian concept concerning the treatment of man which must necessarily impose a constraint on actions to protect it. Compounding the problem, Nürnberg legitimized punishment for "crimes against humanity"—a concept which could see the officer charged by peoples of a foreign nation for his being overzealous in performing his primary duty. It is, therefore, obvious that even at the most basic level, the officer is left with serious problems to resolve. In a normal career an officer may never have to deal with such problems. But for some the problems appear in bold relief. MacArthur, in pursuing a higher perceived duty, disobeyed his orders; men executed or imprisoned for war crimes apparently obeyed theirs.

The concept of honor is intertwined with that of duty throughout an officer's career. He swears his oath, thereby involving his personal honor. Thereafter, he becomes honor-bound to obey lawful orders. He is also honor-bound to disobey unlawful orders. At West Point honor has almost absolute paramountcy over duty in a cadet's day-to-day life. On guard a cadet might not report a friend for an infraction of regulations; but if either's honor is somehow involved (and the system often makes it so), a report is made and not begrudged. Honor violators are expelled for even the most minute infraction. Duty (or regulations) violators, except in extreme cases, are given confinement or less serious punishments.

The concept of honor is, however, most important in the officer's career specifically when duty conflicts arise. An officer cannot object from his position within the service once a decision has been made or a mission given (he may do so prior to the render-

[9]Richard H. Rovere and Arthur M. Schlesinger, Jr., *The General and The President and the Future of American Foreign Policy,* Farrar, Straus and Young.

ing of the decision or the giving of the mission). Expeditious accomplishment of the mission demands this philosophy. If one feels that one cannot reconcile one's orders to one's duty to the Constitution, then one is, in my opinion, honor-bound to resign. An appreciation of the legitimacy of civilian control embodied in the Constitution allows no other recourse. Resignation, however, is a draconian step for an officer who contemplates a career in the army, and the punishment for failure to obey lawful orders is severe. In addition, no training, socialization or statutory authority exists orienting an officer toward exercising this option. Thus, for most of an officer's career one's honor is rationalized as doing one's duty. For internal organizational and bureaucratic reasons and because of the army's reward system, the narrowest sense of duty—obey orders—wins out on a day-to-day basis.

Obeying orders is crucial for mission accomplishment. Unless the army successfully performs its primary mission, the nation cannot survive. Given this, both duty and honor are ultimately caught up in the concept of winning. Reinforcing these imperatives for winning is the perception that the legacies of Nürnberg, the Katyn Forest, the Yamamoto Trial and the massacre of Batista's officer corps in Cuba have destroyed the concept of defeat with honor. The officer of a losing army can quite possibly expect to go to the gibbet in disgrace as a war criminal. Thus, winning becomes all important, and everything must be dared for the win. Given these pressures, even tieing becomes unacceptable.[10]

The drive for mission accomplishment and winning runs deep. There may be reason for not accomplishing a mission but never an excuse. Not accomplishing a mission is failure. Therefore, from the beginning of an officer's career, the army is checking him against a standard of accomplishing missions, preferably in spite of circumstances which would favor failure. From "pass that inspection" to "take that hill" to "win in Vietnam," the only criterion is favorable results. With winning the only standard, the imperatives for honor start to erode. False paperwork is made out to "cover" in an inspection. Overly optimistic intelligence forecasts are given. Hanging over the officer's head is the knowledge that the mission is there to be accomplished, and if he cannot accomplish it, the immediate reaction of his superior will not be

[10]Witness the reception of a tie at an Army football game.

to wonder why but to look for someone who can. One's tickets to success (laudatory efficiency reports) are based on good results, not good attempts that end in failures. This obsession with mission accomplishment is, I feel, crucial to any understanding of the growth of the army's expanded role in domestic and foreign politics in the post-World War II era.

Other factors assisting the army's move into politics and policy making are the "Soviet threat" and revolutionary warfare, foreign and domestic. Prior to World War II, no viable land threat existed, or at least America's commitments were such that the army had little justification in demanding large defense forces in being. In the postwar era, perceptions of the Soviet threat made such forces more necessary. Under the Constitution the size and composition of standing forces are domestic political matters. The political process, however, is slow and, in affairs of military procurement and programs, subject to stresses which tend to introduce inefficiencies. The military might feel that the United States needs a new bomber now, but the bomber must wait until the decision is made as to whether it will be built in California or Texas or elsewhere. If the national security mission of the military has moved from the realm of preparation for mobilization to preparation for active operations, the national security mission demands more active proselytization in the political sphere for vital programs. The consequences of remaining professionally aloof are too great for the security of the nation. The sentiment, pervasive through much cold war military writing, is that "if war is too important to be left solely to the generals, defense is too important to be left to the civilian strategists."[11]

Expertise in domestic political affairs has become a growing requirement in the years since World War II, and the army has had to determine the best way of gaining it. Direct entry into domestic politics via elections is unlawful, but an officer may legally study the political process. Senior officers were therefore sent to civilian universities for graduate schooling in the social sciences.[12] Concurrently, the army's elite was receiving more and more information on foreign and domestic political matters at

[11]George E. Lowe, "The Importance of Being Professional," *Army,* January 1966, p. 54.
[12]Department of the Army Pamphlet 600–3.

the senior service colleges.[13] A year's study at a civilian university will now be allowed some officers in lieu of war college level military schooling.[14] Thus, politics has become part of an officer's professional training. As the army gained political training and expertise, it increased its capability for employment in political roles. Political activity was even greater in international affairs, where World War II had legitimized a role in foreign nations' domestic politics and in United States foreign policy. This institutionalization of interest and activity in foreign and domestic political and societal affairs increases the chances of spillover of military activities and impact into the civilian sector. Before noting specific examples of this linkage, I shall discuss how this model operates in the field of foreign affairs to make the manner and imperative of this spillover clearer.

In foreign affairs the doctrine of revolutionary war has led the army to become interested in the domestic political affairs of numerous foreign nations. Vietnam provides the perfect example of how this process occurs, and Vietnam provides the model for the future. Originally, the Military Advisory Group, Vietnam, was responsible primarily for support of and assistance to the Vietnamese military forces, while the Agency for International Development (AID), the United States Information Service (USIS) and the Central Intelligence Agency (CIA) provided separate assistance, at least at the province level and higher. As Vietnamese political leaders are, in general, military officers, a situation arose wherein, of all these disparate advisory teams at province level and higher, the military was the largest and most professionally congruent with their military (and political) counterparts. More importantly, at district level the *only* advisor was a military officer, who was responsible to the sector (province) military advisor. If AID, USIS or other civilian advisors wanted anything done or checked at the operational level, the U. S. military advisor, who was supposed to cooperate, was the only man to work through.

[13]See John W. Masland and Lawrence I. Radway, *Soldiers and Scholars: Military Education and National Policy* (Princeton, N.J.: Princeton University Press 1957); Edward L. Katzenbach, Jr., "The Demotion of Professionalism at the War Colleges," *U.S. Naval Institute Proceedings,* March 1965 and Comments; June 1965, pp. 110–115; September 1965, pp. 112–116, for studies on this subject.

[14]"Some Army War College Selectees Will Go to Civilian Colleges (sic)," *Army Times,* 2 December 1970, p. 3.

The fact that only the military advisors went to the lowest level gave the military group the greatest capability of accomplishing missions on a regular, continuing, day-in and day-out basis. Thus, indicators of success from the field for essentially civilian agencies were provided by military men who collected information based on their own perception of priorities and on the realization that their true superior, and therefore the individual to be satisfied was their military superior. In 1967 to foster efficiency the entire advisory effort was merged into one organization. While before, an American officer might, especially at district level, be involved in all aspects of Vietnamese life, political, social, cultural, etc., now the system was institutionalized so that he *must* become involved in all these aspects. If the Vietnamese war is at heart an internal political struggle and the military officer is given the mission of advising in all phases of the struggle, he must therefore be aware of internal, domestic Vietnamese politics as well as military affairs. Ultimately, there are few facets of Vietnamese life about which the army officer must not be an expert and in which he must not become involved.

Given the mission in Vietnam and the existence of potential Vietnams everywhere, the army has learned the obvious lesson that it had best be prepared for similar missions wherever and whenever the need may arise. Again expertise is needed to prepare properly for any future mission, and an institution has been created to assure that such expertise is generated—the Military Assistance Officers Program (MAOP).

MAOP is designed to prepare the American military advisor to work with a foreign military counterpart. An appreciation of the actual and potential characteristics of underdeveloped nations given in the 1967 Internal Defense Development Planning Guide, prepared by the school where MAOP training is now conducted, reflects the Vietnam experience directly:

The officers in most cases exceed their civilian counterparts in administrative skill. In many nations military officers are used to establish new government administrative agencies or to revamp inefficient organization.

The level of technical skill usually is greater among professional military personnel than among the population as a whole. They have been exposed to technology, logistics and training in modern organization. This training gives the military man a modern outlook which is not often an outstanding characteristic of civilian elites.

The military since it represents a force in being is responsive to the direction of the national government and can be employed in remote areas where it would be extremely difficult to recruit a civilian organization.[15]

If, as in numerous underdeveloped nations, the American military advisor's foreign counterpart is or may be in control of the nation's political, cultural and/or social institutions, then the advisor should be prepared to assist him in a sizeable proportion of those activities. Contingencies prepared for become capabilities which may be exercised.

John Steward Ambler in *Soldiers against the State*[16] showed the backward linkages which existed between the French army's involvement in "foreign" politics and deeper political involvement at home. The real and potential parallels between the French experience and the American are too obvious to be ignored. Fighting or advising for his country abroad, any army officer must feel support from the nation back home. The soldier is overseas at the direction of his country's political leadership. If the American public is dissatisfied about political policy that sent soldiers overseas, the officer inevitably feels that the public should not complain about the army but about the political leadership. It is also up to the leadership to recognize its command responsibility entirely to absorb any criticism. If the leadership does not, the corporate feeling fostered within the service will result in efforts to exonerate itself. If the criticism continues and the motivation is political, it is not improbable that the army will fight back in political terms. This reasoning is not far-fetched. Witness a comment by an army officer connected with the MAOP school, quoted from a series by Ward Just in a recent issue of *Atlantic:*

We are victimized. We are called upon to take abuse from the press and the public for decisions in which we have taken no part. So we must have men on our staff who have all the tickets, and who are going to make their recommendations in military terms, and in other terms too. The political terms. We want a voice in our own destiny.[17]

[15]Just, "Soldiers," p. 73.
[16]John S. Ambler, *Soldiers against the State: The French Army in Politics,* (Garden City, N.Y.: Doubleday, 1968).
[17]Just, "Soldiers," p. 77.

Other spillover effects are equally obvious. A general in Just's article speaks of a desire to become involved in civic action in America. ". . . hell, maybe we could build a few dams or bridges here. . . ."[18]—a thought echoed by a cadet at West Point.[19] The army has its own lobbying organization, the Association of the United States Army, which has its own organ, *Army*, "a professional publication devoted to the advancement of the military arts and sciences and representing the interests of the entire U. S. Army."[20] Finally, the army has been drawn into the fabric of American civil life and domestic political affairs by direction.

The army's frontier and strikebreaking role was mentioned earlier. In the 1930s the army was charged with overseeing the activities of the Civilian Conservation Corps and thus became involved in supervising the activities of American civilians in an atmosphere wherein the work was forced in nature. In the McNamara years and since, the army has been charged with making soldiers of men who for mental, physical or medical reasons were unfit for military service (The New Standards Program, formerly Project 100,000). The purpose of this program was not to benefit the army, which was required to expend extra effort, funds and training time on these men, but to improve these "substandard" men's chances for success in outside society after completion of their army training—make better, more productive citizens of them "the army way."

In Project Transition the army is charged with preparing men who are getting ready to leave the service for a productive life on the outside. Complaints have also been made to the effect that the army ought to have training programs to expunge the "killer instincts" generated in war—in order to prepare men to enter into the civilian sector again. The army supports the Boy Scout program in numerous ways.[21] The civil role of the Corps of Engineers is universally known. Implicit in involvement in large domestic building projects is the allocation of funds which involves priorities—an essentially political matter. Command in-

[18] *Ibid.*, p. 79.
[19] *Ibid.*, p. 67.
[20] *Army*, October 1966, p. 3.
[21] For example, in Europe the Boy Scout chain of command parallels the military chain of command with senior generals in overall charge, subdivisions run by lesser generals and lower ranking officers running the troops.

formation programs require the officer to teach classes on subjects which are by nature social, cultural and political: race relations, the Vietnam war, the Soviet Threat, counterinsurgency, civil disturbances. All of these programs inhere in the army's numerous missions. Proper accomplishment of them requires expertise. In a growing number of cases this expertise is in the field of American society and culture.

Perhaps one of the army's missions which has involved it most deeply in the civil sector in recent years is the civil disturbance role. When federal troops were first employed in Detroit, there was almost no planning for the operation. No maps were on hand, no organizational intelligence was available and equipment, particularly radios which could communicate with the police, was not available. The army was unprepared. To prevent these insufficiencies from reoccurring, the Directorate of Civil Disturbance Planning and Operations (DCDPO) was formed. This organization, which is responsible for operations, plans, policy and programs and communications in preparing the military "to improve readiness to assist state and local authorities, as may be required in restoring civil order,"[22] institutionalizes the traditional role in the modern era. Lists and locations of facilities such as reservoirs, gas, electricity and telephone offices and plants are kept, in case they need protection. Units are maintained on alert status and, as is now well known, intelligence was collected.

Originally the army was not supposed to get into the intelligence gathering operation, but the imperatives of mission and the need to develop expertise make it obvious that best performance can be achieved with intelligence which is responsive only to the needs of the service. The normal emphasis on most efficacious mission accomplishment destined that the intelligence gathering operation would grow and grow. ". . . Any agency assuming police responsibility must have the information essential to the performance of its task."[23] Where this mission can lead in terms of intelligence-gathering techniques is discussed by another officer in *Army:*

[22]Donald W. Coble, "DoD Establishes a 'Watch' (Directorate of Civil Disturbance Planning and Operations [DCDPO] on the 'Battle at Home,' " *Armed Forces Management,* September 1969, p. 51.
[23]Lane, "The Right to Intelligence."

Urban warfare requires extraordinary countermeasures:

1. Infiltration, political and intelligence.
2. Identification of hideouts, transport and escape routes.
3. The writing of manuals and doctrine.

In sum the application of military intelligence techniques to the urban situation.[24]

It would seem that all dysfunctions in American society, so far as they have within them a potential for violence, are part of the army's mission. The link between the idea that "the soldier's function is the ordered application of force in the resolution of social problems,"[25] and the connection with "the army is the only damn thing holding this country together"[26] becomes increasingly clear.

At this point partial answers have been given to some of the questions posed earlier. The process of role-expansion in the military has occurred because of society's need to have new functions performed. The army has had the manpower and resources on hand to accomplish these missions in reasonably expedient manner. More important than the mere availability of resources, however, is the officer's sense of duty and the organizational imperatives and reward structures aimed at accomplishing missions. The army is an organization in being which is designed to get things done—to accomplish missions. This vital sense of mission, combined with the perceptions of the Soviet threat and domestic and foreign revolutionary warfare, has resulted in an inexorable drawing of the army into more political and social roles. The federal government has had a major hand in this process. It has often looked to the army to accomplish services which are within the army's capabilities but outside its primary function of national defense.

Given this fluid situation, no limited definition of military function or expertise can be formulated. Lieutenant Colonel Zeb B. Bradford and Major James R. Murphy gave what must now stand as the most accurate definition: "Military expertise will vary ac-

[24]Col. Robert F. Rigg, " 'Made in USA,' Urban Guerilla Warfare," *Army*, January 1968, p. 24.
[25]MG Joh H. Hay (USA), "Military Art and Science: A Profession Comes of Age," *Army*, April 1969, p. 45.
[26]Just, "Soldiers."

cording to whatever is required of the profession to support the policies of the state."[27] This definition, of course, puts no limits at all on military expertise or function. The need for expertise comes from missions given or anticipated. Missions are given because of the factors mentioned in the last paragraph but also because of expertise gained in similar or complementary missions. Thus the process of role-expansion and widening definition of expertise are interdependent and, barring outside forces, will continue.

Does the army officer have the right to object to these new roles and unlimited definition of military expertise? Yes, but he is bound to accept them unless he feels that in some way they are repugnant to the Constitution. If he believes this to be so, he is forced into a situation wherein his resignation is required. If he believes the army's actions to be patently unconstitutional, he is bound by oath to oppose such actions and by duty to do so from outside the service.

The discussion to this point has painted a picture not of a plot to involve the army more and more in foreign and domestic political affairs but of a process derived from values, attitudes, goals and recent historical experiences which have had that same effect. The myriad of constraints on the military, tangible and psychological, make a *Seven Days in May* infinitely unlikely. The first of these constraints is the tradition of civilian control. The Constitution is not a Hué "which must be destroyed in order to save it." The Constitution, the focus of an officer's oath, demands subordination to the properly constituted civil authority.

It is important that in the lower officer and enlisted grades, the army contains a fair cross-section of largely civilian attitudes. In Huntington's terms the army at least has a subjective constraint placed upon it. Subjective constraint in this case consists of the assurance that values and perspectives held by the larger civil society will have a marked impact within the service. This impact will tend to overpower more militarily oriented values and perspectives. For example, a sizeable percentage of enlisted men in the army have been draftees or men who enlisted to avoid the vagaries of the draft, not men who felt called to the military

[27]Lt. Colonel Zeb B. Bradford and Maj. James R. Murphy, "A New Look at the Military Profession," *Army*, February 1968, p. 60.

profession. The same reasoning applies to many junior officers. Thus, the army, albeit a "professional" service, is heavily leavened with men who are temporary soldiers. These temporary soldiers have their roots in American civil society, not in the service. The example of French conscripts in the 1961 putsch attempt in Algeria cannot be ignored. Those conscripts failed to respond to orders to implement the putsch because they were basically Frenchmen who were satisfied on the whole with the de Gaulle regime. They were not at root army men dissatisfied with his Algeria policy and the threat it posed to the French army's interests. "Most conscripts chose to respond to the putsch as outraged citizens, rather than as blindly obedient soldiers."[28]

Even the regular officer cannot escape the impact and pressures of the American civil life style. He is returned periodically to a civilian environment where his perceptions of the basic American antimilitary ethic will be reinforced. Better than 75 percent of all West Point graduates who stay on active duty receive advanced degrees at civilian universities. The lack of sufficient military housing requires that an officer often reside in a civilian community. These factors will become increasingly important in the event of an all-volunteer army, but at the present the requirement to deal in uniform on a day-to-day, professional basis with civilians reinforces societal attitudes, perspectives and goals for the military officer. Thus any coup scenario qualifies as science fiction.

A smaller, all-volunteer army, of course, would lack many of these subjective constraints, and civil-military strains could develop. Higher pay, better on-post housing, improved facilities, choice of unit assignment, reduction of distasteful housekeeping chores (e.g., KP, police call), building of more army recreation areas[29] will have the effect of separating the army from society. The army may become more of a trade and less of a service. A smaller army will lead to greater homogeneity in officer recruitment. The percentage of West Point graduates in the total officer corps will increase.

Even so, the hope is that these decreases in subjective con-

[28]Ambler, *Soldiers against the State,* p. 370.
[29]"More Posts Test VOLAR (Volunteer Army)," *Army Times,* 3 February 1971, p. 20.

straints should be offset by increases in the "objective controls" of the sort mentioned earlier which inhere in a professional military force. Objective constraints, however, may well be less efficacious where the army has a number of varied political roles and seems to be gaining more. What can be done then about potential civil-military strains? Little can be done by the army officer except to maintain his sense of perspective. He is part but still a servant of his society. However, he is primarily a member of a military culture which has goals, values and perspectives derived from its misson which, by definition, are different from those held by society at large. It is therefore primarily incumbent upon society to assure that it gets the army it wants. The army should allow by regulation that its officers be permitted to resign for cause when they feel duty requires actions which violate their oath to the Constitution. Society should assure that the composition of the army represents that society in proper proportions. An all-volunteer army which excludes from its ranks the white middle class does not meet this standard and should, in my opinion, be viewed askance. More important than regulating the composition of the army, however, is the need for continuous review of the army's missions with a view toward reducing, wherever possible, their social and political impact. If this is not accomplished, the army will be drawn inevitably into wider spheres of social and political impact. A weeding and cutting process is necessary on a continuing basis by civil authority to reverse this trend. If men need training to be better citizens, let them get their training outside the service. The army can do it, but the citizen taught by the army may not be quite the one desired by society as a whole. Society may not want the army to define good citizenship. The mission of making good citizens assures that the army will formulate such a definition. Advisors to military officers who control the governments of less-developed nations need to be political experts who understand the military, not military men with an understanding of politics.[30] Civil disturbance units

[30] At present the reverse is often true. See a comment by Alfred Stepan speaking before a House of Representatives Subcommittee on National Security Policy and Scientic Developments, *Military Assistance Training, Hearings before the Subcommittee on National Security Policy and Scientitic Developments of the Committee on Foreign Affairs,* 91st Congress, 2d session, October 6, 7, 8, December 8, 15, 1970, (Washington, D. C.: Government Printing Office, 1970).

should be primarily paramilitary rather than military. Politically charged projects such as harbors, rivers and dams need to be handled by an appropriate, politically oriented civilian agency. Army control or involvement in these projects is an anachronism.

The above list is, of course, not exhaustive, and expense and political problems of implemention militate against these roles ever changing; nevertheless the idea behind each suggestion is everywhere the same. Roles need to be checked against a criterion of appropriateness as well as cost and ease before they are given to the army, since after the mission is given, changing it becomes difficult. By then the model of *role receipt-gain expertise-institutionalization of role process* is too far developed to reallocate the role without enormous effort and expense. In some cases, however, the process has already apparently slowed or reversed itself, notably the removal of civil disturbance intelligence functions (due to congresssional and public pressure) and the apparent reduced emphasis on civil disturbance operations alerts (due to increased police and National Guard readiness). But the army's overt action in reducing these spheres was not highly self-generated.

This article has not been a call for relieving the army entirely of roles with a political context. Making or preparing for war is a political act. The world has become too complex for the army officer to allow himself to be politically unaware. There is, however, a difference between political awareness and operational political social roles which affect the greater society. Each of these roles must be individually scrutinized for its social and political effects. If these effects are deemed desirable, let the roles remain; if not, excise them—but always investigate them.

The New Military Professionalism

Clarence L. Abercrombie, III, and Major Raoul H. Alcalá,
U. S. Army

Introduction

With their image badly tarnished by the tragic events of the Vietnam war, our armed forces have entered the 1970s amid a public debate of unprecedented magnitude. Much of the clamor, no doubt, has been raised by the continuous journalistic din of dramatic headlines. But even after the sensationalism has been removed there remain at all levels of our society serious doubts about the nature and purposes of many military activities. A claim often heard in this debate is that many of the new missions— community development, counterinsurgency and psychological warfare, for example—have important political components and are thus inappropriately drawing the military into politics. Within the military profession the reaction to this claim is ambivalent. Some professional soldiers, such as Zeb Bradford and James Murphy, explicitly reject the notion of limiting the armed forces to the traditional "military" tasks:

Indeed, a military created or existing solely for the purpose of war may be dangerous to the values and goals of a democracy. . . . The military exists only for the service of the state, regardless of the skills required or functions performed. . . . It will develop whatever expertise is required to fulfill its unlimited contract for public service.[1]

NOTE: The views of the authors are their own and do not purport to reflect the position of the Department of the Army or of the Department of Defense.

[1]Lieutenant Colonel Zeb B. Bradford, Jr., U. S. Army and Major James R. Murphy, U. S. Air Force, "A New Look at the Military Profession," *Army*, 19 (February, 1969): 60, 62.

Thus Bradford and Murphy express their hope that the military will not be excluded from performing "socially productive" tasks. Other officers, as evidenced by James Dickey's essay in this book, point out that in order to accomplish political missions the military must incorporate political expertise into their norms of professionalism. This, they feel, is dangerous to both the profession and our society.[2] The seriousness and relevance of this debate is revealed by an examination of the military's position within the American political process. Traditionally our armed forces have been described as apolitical. In fact it has been the proud boast of many officers that "the army is above politics." And indeed, if "politics" is taken as the partisan contest for office, this claim must be granted true. But the political dimension of American life extends far beyond the party convention and the ballot box to encompass the whole process by which societal values and resources are allocated. The military participate in this process as advisors to the political decisionmakers, as advocates of particular policies and as executors of final political decisions. It is well known, for example, that Congress seeks military advice when choices arise between military and nonmilitary programs. The political significance of this advisory function becomes especially clear when we take into account Jong Lee's findings elsewhere in this book that defense allocations are often made at the expense of needed social programs. The military also become primary political actors to the extent that the tasks they are called upon to execute have political components, as has often been the case from reconstruction in the American South to pacification in Vietnam.

Thus we see that the army has long been concerned with politics and that the expertise required by the professional soldier to accomplish his assigned missions must necessarily have a concomitant political component. Numerous authors have been concerned with politics and military professionalism, but the bulk of their essays has been either normative, time-bound or unsystematic. Even Samuel Huntington's monumental *The Soldier and*

---

[2] Colonel Robert N. Ginsburgh, U. S. Air Force, "The Challenge to Military Professionalism," *Foreign Affairs*, 42 (January, 1964): 255–268, also argues for a more restricted, less political, military professionalism.

the State, which includes both normative and empirical analyses, does not measure systematically the components of military professionalism.[3] The purpose of this article is to examine some indicators of the political component of military professionalism and to trace their trends over the past fifty years. We hope that this initial effort will be substantively useful and will also encourage further, more sophisticated studies.

Procedures

Since we could not interview the officers themselves, we had to employ other techniques in measuring the political content of their professionalism. One obvious data source is the structured system of schools which provides for the officers' formal professional socialization. Since these schools impart to student officers the functional expertise required by the services, an analysis of their curricula can be expected to reveal the political content of military professionalism. But complete reliance on this source, we feel, would subject our study to a bias: institutions are often slow to change, and military schools may not always reflect the most current trends in the expertise required of professional soldiers. We therefore decided to supplement our analysis of curricula with an examination of the actual concerns of officers reflected in their professional journals. These journals serve two important functions in the U. S. armed forces. First, they constitute a medium for the internal communication of factual data of current interest to the services and a forum for debates on controversial issues. Second, the semiofficial journals of certain service schools, together with the unofficial publications of fraternal and special-interest military associations, provide a forum for authors who wish to articulate service interests and to advocate programs which require executive and congressional action.

[3]Samuel P. Huntington, *The Soldier and the State: The Theory and Politics of Civil-Military Relations* (New York: Vintage Books, 1957). For an interesting attempt to examine the influences of technology on military professionalism, see Maury Feld, who presents a limited content analysis (1936–1938, 1947–1949, 1957–1959) of two military journals: "The Military Self-Image in a Technological Environment," in Morris Janowitz, ed., *The New Military: Changing Patterns of Organization* (New York: Russell Sage, 1964), pp. 159–188.

We limited ourselves to one service, the army. The air force has existed as a separate service only since 1947 and its inclusion would not have permitted us to adopt the broad historical perspective which we deem essential to our analysis. The navy has historical continuity but has not been so deeply immersed in the new "political" missions in which we are most interested. Besides, we were more familiar with the army and had maintained certain attachments (legal and emotional) to it. Within the army we examined three courses for officers, each of which marks an important step in the process of professional socialization. First, we chose the Officer Candidate School (infantry) in which the transition is made from civilian and enlisted man to commissioned officer. Here the student is taught the minimum essential elements of professional expertise.[4] The second course we selected was the "advanced" or "career course" (again infantry). This course separates the short-term officer from the career professional. Finally there is the Army War College which provides entrance to the highest military strata. Its graduates become the decisionmakers who will largely define the future norms of professionalism.[5]

[4]The Officer Candidate Course was selected over the Military Academy course and the Reserve Officers' Training Course for several reasons. The West Point course is designed for two purposes: to provide cadets with a liberal education and to impart some minimum essential expertise required of military professionals; it is not possible to identify which curricular items are related to which goal. Besides, much of the required professional expertise is provided by military schools which West Pointers attend only after graduation and commissioning. The ROTC presents similar problems: students are supposed to receive some professional training in civilian-taught academic classes. More is imparted by the actual "Military Science" classes of the ROTC program itself (a program whose scope and nature has been subject to radical fluctuation, especially in its early years). Finally, the ROTC officer completes his basic military education in post-commissioning schools similar to those attended by Academy graduates. All these factors made the Officer Candidate Course a more profitable area of study. The Infantry School courses were selected over those of other branches because the infantry is the largest combat branch and could thus be expected to contribute a major portion of future military professionals.

[5]The Officer Candidate School and advanced course curricula were obtained from the official "Programs of Instruction" of the Infantry School at Fort Benning, Georgia. The Infantry School library has these documents on file for most of the post-1940 years. Academic researchers are permitted access to the bulk of this library's unclassified holdings, including theses of student officers. The Army War College curricula were obtained from official course outlines and transcriptions of lectures available in the military history research collection of the Army War College at Carlisle Barracks, Pennsylvania and the reference library of the

We chose specific journals to examine on the basis of three criteria. First, we desired continuity over a fifty-year time span. This was particularly important, for we did not find such continuity in the military schools, and we were aware that our analysis in certain time periods would depend entirely upon the military journals. Second, we wanted publications that would be representative of the entire army. Third, we concentrated on journals which were not explicitly limited to discussions of nuts-and-bolts techniques. Four periodicals were initially considered: *Army, Infantry, Military Review* and *Ordnance*. We eliminated *Military Review* (journal of the U. S. Army Command and General Staff College) because, in the early years, it consisted almost entirely of very brief digests of articles printed in other journals. *Infantry* (journal of the U. S. Army Infantry School) was also rejected since it is aimed chiefly at an audience of junior officers and devotes itself almost exclusively to low-level tactical problems. *Ordnance* (journal of the American Ordnance Association) fulfilled admirably our requirement for continuity, and it was examined over the entire period covered by our study. The results of this analysis, however, showed an over-emphasis on the problems of industrial mobilization, especially in the five or six years immediately preceding World War II. Its bias in favor of the supply and support services and its military-industrial linkages led us to reject *Ordnance* as a major indicator of general military concerns, though in our findings we do briefly evaluate its content. *Army* (published by the Association of the U. S. Army and devoted to advancing and representing the interests of the entire army) best fit our criteria of continuity, representativeness and policy analysis. Both *Army* and *Ordnance* have substantial staffs consisting of professional civilian journalists and retired military officers. They are financially supported by their parent associations without the use of official government funds. Although their readership is primarily active duty and retired professional soldiers, both journals maintain close ties with interested civilians, defense industries and sympathetic congressmen. The contributing authors

army's Office of the Chief of Military History, Washington, D. C. These two facilities also allow academic researchers access to their unclassified holdings. There were Army War College curricula available for the entire period of our analysis except the years 1940–1950, when Army War College classes were suspended.

include active duty and retired military personnel, government bureaucrats and decisionmakers and civilian scholars.

To use both the schools' curricula and the content of military journals as indicators of the political content of military professionalism, we had to develop definitional guidelines that would allow us to separate political from apolitical material. We coded as "political" those topics which concerned the formulation or justification of national policy or sought to define the functions of the military within that policy. Topics which included both national policies and the technical or tactical measures taken by the army in conjunction with such policies were also considered "political," as were discussions of international affairs. We coded as "apolitical" topics which included the strictly technical and tactical concerns of armed forces and any other items that did not clearly fall within the "political" category. Thus the categories were mutually exclusive and exhaustive. They were constructed after analyzing a sample of the journals and the schools' curricula for several time periods, and the following lists were drawn up as a guide for coding:

I. Apolitical Concerns
      Foreign tactics and material
      Human interest stories
      Logistics
      Military unit administration
      Principles of war
      Technical application of strategic principles
      Technical procedures of administering military justice
      Tactics
      Weapons: research, development or employment
      Writing arts and skills
II. Political Concerns
      A. National Policy
            Budgetary and appropriations processes
            Civil-military relations
            Civilian control of the military
            Ideology, loyalty and patriotism
            Position of armed forces in national policy processes
            Role of the armed forces in defining national strategy
            U. S. foreign policy

U. S. policies toward arms control and disarmament
B. Civil and Military (except purely technical application)
  Civic action
  Dissent versus discipline, civilian-military value dif-
    ferences and life styles
  Domestic intelligence
  Draft, universal military training, Citizens' Military
    Training Camps, Civilian Conservation Corps
  Propaganda and public information
  Psychological warfare
  Military assistance
  Population and riot control
  Race relations
  Reserve and National Guard policies
  Substantive (and critical) military justice matters
C. International Affairs
  Balance of power
  Customs and language of foreign nations (except
    purely human interest stories)
  Diplomacy
  General topics on arms control and disarmament
  Law of land warfare
  Law of outer space
  Law of the sea
  Treaties and alliances not involving U. S.
  The United Nations
  Wars not involving U. S. (except purely tactical or
    technical aspects)

It is possible, of course, to argue the propriety of certain categories within our coding scheme; they were developed not as a
formal definition of "military politics," but rather as a sort of
verbal plumb line to insure our internal consistency. Thus we
sought to make our coding system sensitive to changes in levels
of military concern with politics so that the *trends* which we shall
presently discuss would have a validity beyond that possessed by
the "political score" of a solitary year.

For Officer Candidate School and for the advanced course, an
hour of instruction was taken as the unit of analysis. Similarly, for

the Army War College we defined one period[6] of instruction as the unit of analysis. In the case of periodicals, one indexed, signed article (including pseudonyms) became the unit of analysis. The data were thus coded and aggregated by year according to the "political" and "apolitical" categories we have defined. We then defined the percentage of "political" units in the total number of units in each journal or course for each year as our index of the political content of that source. In the case of many advanced courses and officer candidate courses and in all the Army War College courses, the course extended over two calendar years. It was assumed that prearranged curricula of any given course reflected the thinking of the year in which they were approved (the earlier of the two years); thus, for example, we decided to list the advanced course of academic year 1965–1966 under the year 1965 and so forth.

Although we did not approach this project with any precise preconceptions of how the data would look, we did have certain general expectations. Given the current clamor over the "politicization" of army officers, we expected our indexes of political concerns to show increasing trends (especially in recent years), rising from very low levels prior to the Second World War. We also expected our indexes of political content to be much higher for the Army War College than for the Infantry School courses for it is clear that as an officer progresses up the ranks, his potential impact on military and national policy increases. In terms of political involvement this means that junior officers can be expected to be involved in actions with high political content only in the *execution* phase, while top-level officers will be likely to become involved in such actions as *advisors, advocates and executors.*

Findings

Figures 1 and 2 present the results of our analysis for the Officer Candidate School and the advanced course, respectively. As we expected in courses designed to train small unit combat leaders, the indexes of political content are quite low. Yet there are several

---

[6]"Periods" varied between years, some being, for example, a day or a half day of instruction. However, within the individual academic years over which we aggregated the data, a single measure was consistently used.

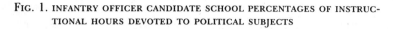

FIG. 1. INFANTRY OFFICER CANDIDATE SCHOOL PERCENTAGES OF INSTRUC-
TIONAL HOURS DEVOTED TO POLITICAL SUBJECTS

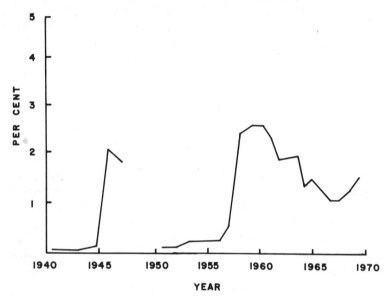

factors worthy of note. First are the low points for both World War
II and the Korean conflict. During these years the schools were
struggling to meet the war-time demands for infantry officers.
Curricula were pared to the bone, and apparently "political"
subjects were a luxury that the Infantry School could not afford.
One should also consider the high points immediately following
World War II. The army had been assigned the mission of governing occupied territory, and the curricula show that it was deemed
necessary that every officer become familiar with world affairs and
the principles of military government.

After the Korean War there was another rise in the political
content of both Infantry School courses as the army began to
emphasize the political dimensions of the cold war. After 1960
Officer Candidate School showed a general decline which
reached its nadir in the big years of the Vietnam buildup, 1966,
1967 and 1968. Here again the demand for infantry lieutenants
was apparently too high to permit the teaching of luxuries. Yet
even then the political content did not drop to World War II or
Korean War levels.

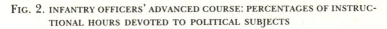

Fig. 2. INFANTRY OFFICERS' ADVANCED COURSE: PERCENTAGES OF INSTRUC-
TIONAL HOURS DEVOTED TO POLITICAL SUBJECTS

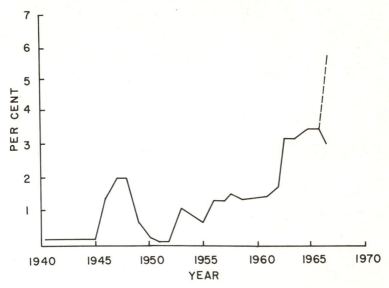

The advanced course presented a different picture. From the
Korean War to the present there was no real decline at all in our
index;[7] the Vietnam buildup, in fact, brought with it an increased
political content. The explanation for this departure from the
Officer Candidate School pattern appears to be that for the more
senior officers Vietnam turned out to be a very unusual kind of
war. In addition to combat commanders and staff officers, the
United States needed advisors for Vietnamese government officials. There was no "colonial office" from which such men could
be drawn, and our government decided that it was easier to
assign the advisory mission to the action-oriented military than
to recruit and train foreign service officers on such short notice

[7]The *apparent* 1967 decrease in the index of political content shown by the
graph's solid line was due to a rearrangement of curriculum hours to allow the
broad expansion of a program of academic electives introduced the previous year.
Of 1976 elective hours from which the students could choose, 378 (about 24
percent) were devoted to political matters. Each student was required to take 200
hours of electives, and there is subjective evidence that the political subjects were
the most popular. But even if the students had selected their electives in a random
fashion, the political-content index for 1967 would have risen by about 2.5 percent, as indicated by the broken line.

for this difficult and dangerous mission. The path of least political and practical resistance, then, led straight to the army, and the Infantry School began to teach its students how to advise Vietnamese district chiefs as well as battalion commanders.

Despite these changes, the political content of the Infantry School's officer candidate and advanced courses has remained at a rather low level. It can be argued that this would not have been the case had we considered only classroom hours of instruction, thus eliminating physical training, bivouacs, etc. from our instructional totals to yield a "purer" measure of the political content of the formal curriculum. This coding approach was rejected for three reasons. First, the data necessary for such a conversion were not available for all years. Second, an analysis of years for which such data were available indicated that while our index scores would be increased, such increases would *not* be very great and would not affect the trends which were the more important part of our analysis. Third, only a small part of the professional skills needed by an infantry officer can be learned in a classroom, and it seemed that a coding scheme which counted only classroom hours would misrepresent the instructional intent of the Infantry School. Therefore, we included all hours of instruction in our totals, aware that we might slightly underestimate political content for these courses but confident that our index would still be a fair representation of Infantry School concerns—which, at least until recently, have had very little political content, with increases occurring largely in response to the assignment of new missions.

There were some similarities between the Infantry School curricula and that of the Army War College (Fig. 3). The army's wartime concern with the nuts and bolts of combat was reflected in the complete shutdown of the War College during World War II.[8] Also, an increase over pre-1940 levels in the index of political content was evident immediately following the Korean War. But here the similarities with the Infantry School curricula end. The

[8]The Army War College suspended classes after the 1939–1940 academic year. However, it did not reopen immediately after World War II. From 1946 until 1950 the army, in the interest of service unification, did not operate a war college of its own, and instead sent its eligible officers to the National War College (operated by the Joint Chiefs of Staff). See Colonel George S. Pappas, U. S. Army, *Prudens Futuri: The U. S. Army War College, 1901–1967* (Carlisle Barracks, Pa.: The Alumni Association of the U. S. Army War College, 1967), pp. 139–150.

FIG. 3 ARMY WAR COLLEGE PERCENTAGES OF INSTRUCTIONAL PERIODS DE-
VOTED TO POLITICAL SUBJECTS

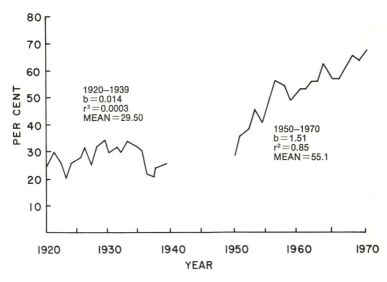

overall level of political content was much higher in this school
for colonels, even in the earlier years, than in the more junior
officers' schools. From 1920 to 1939 the political subjects covered by the Army War College included both domestic national
policy and strategic analyses of foreign countries. For these years,
on the average, 29.5 percent of the curriculum was devoted to
political matters. There are fluctuations throughout the period
but no discernable trend. A regression line fitted to the data had
a slope of only 0.014. If this line were extended back to 1900, it
would define a score of 29.1 percent. Carried forward to the year
2000, the score would still be only about 30.5 percent! This
certainly reinforces Pappas's finding that the Army War College
curriculum planned in 1919 "was retained almost unchanged
until 1940."[9]

[9] *Ibid.*, p. 91. It should also be noted that there are certain problems involved
in the application of a linear regression model to data which have been transformed into percentages. Obviously, trend analysis becomes virtually meaningless when carried below 0 percent or above 100 percent. Furthermore, the nature
of our data is such that scores would tend to behave asymptotically as they neared
the 0 percent or 100 percent mark. Therefore, we have applied regression analysis only to middle-range values and not, for example, to the extremely low scores
of the Infantry School.

The Army War College resumed operation in 1950, just after the beginning of the Korean conflict. The political subjects covered were very similar to those of the latest pre-1940 years, including domestic national policy and strategic intelligence. However, a clear increasing trend for the entire period since 1950 was evident. The index of political content rose above 50 percent in 1956 and, thereafter, never dropped below that figure. After 1957 (and the launching of *Sputnik*) cold war issues more strongly influenced the curriculum. In addition to international relations and U. S. foreign policy, the Soviet Union, now clearly defined as the enemy, came under close scrutiny. As American advisors were sent in ever-increasing numbers to Southeast Asia (1963–1964) followed by ground combat troops (1965 to mid-1972), the War College added counterinsurgency studies to its cold war curriculum. Following the outbreak of large-scale urban riots and student unrest, U. S. domestic issues and even the American social order became subjects of interest as the political content of the Army War College course continued to increase.

To summarize the trend of this recent period, another regression line was fitted to the War College time series, this time using the data from 1950 to 1970. The slope of this line was 1.51 (compared with 0.014 for the pre-World War II years); r^2 was 0.85 in the recent period, compared with the infinitesimal r^2 of 0.0003 before World War II. The average value of the index of political content for 1950–1970 was 55.1 percent, nearly twice that of 1920–1939 (29.5 percent). These data indicate, as we expected, a substantial increase in the political content of military professionalism since the Second World War. We were also able to examine a small sample of the curriculum of the National War College and although our data are incomplete, they indicate an even higher percentage of political content than we found for the Army War College.[10]

Turning to military journals, we found that the political content of *Ordnance*[11] from 1920 through 1970 disclosed some now-

[10]The National War College curricula were obtained at the National War College Library, Washington, D. C. As with the other military libraries we visited, the civilian academic researcher may easily get access to the unclassified holdings of the National War College Library.

[11]To test reliability, a coder was given the coding instructions included in this paper and asked to code a sample from *Ordnance*. The coefficient of intercoder reliability was 0.87.

familiar features (Fig. 4). There were wartime troughs for both
World War II and the Korean War. There was also a marked peak
for 1946–1950 and a general rise since the end of the Korean
War. However, the overall similarity to our data for the Army
War College was very low ($r^2 = 0.008$),[12] due mostly to the years
from 1934–1939. In 1934 and 1935 *Ordnance* (a periodical dedi-
cated to "scientific and industrial preparedness") reacted quite
strongly to the prevalent civilian sentiment for pacifism and
disarmament. In neither the Army War College nor, as we shall
see, *Army* magazine, was this reaction nearly so strong. In 1937
Ordnance began a loud outcry for mobilization and war-prepared-
ness, and again our other data sources failed to reflect so great
a change.

FIG. 4. POLITICAL ARTICLES IN *Ordnance* JULY, 1920–JUNE, 1970

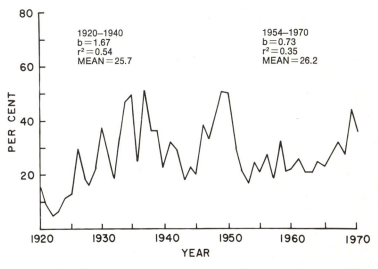

Army (Fig. 5) shows a much greater similarity to the Army War
College ($r^2 = 0.76$).[13] Political topics in the 1920s and 1930s
included universal military training, Citizens' Military Training
Camps, ROTC, pacifism and disarmament, communism and congressional appropriations. The average year saw 16.4 percent of
its articles devoted to political topics; this was considerably

[12]Correlation was calculated using the data for the years 1920–1939 and 1953–
1970.
[13]Again the correlation was calculated using the data for the years 1920–1939
and 1953–1970. Coefficient of intercoder reliability for *Army* was 0.84.

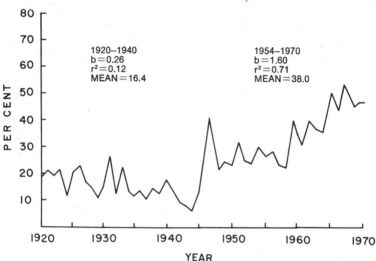

FIG. 5. POLITICAL ARTICLES IN *Army* 1920–1970

higher than we had expected. From 1920–1940 there was no noticeable increase in levels of political concern (the slope of a regression line, in fact, was –0.259 with $r^2 = 0.116$). The war years (1941–1945) were low, showing the concern with the technical-tactical business of achieving victory. There was also a definite post-World War II high point. Service unification and reorganization was then perhaps the topic of greatest concern to *Army* writers, but demobilization problems and questions of nuclear strategy also captured a great deal of space. The Soviet Union was being defined as the new enemy, and officers began to ask what political mistakes had led to the "loss" of Eastern Europe. As in the advanced course, the business of military government also received wide attention.

During the Korean War military writers worried about how much mobilization would be necessary to accomplish the U. N. mission in Asia without jeopardizing the security of Western Europe. Interservice rivalry revived questions of reorganization and unification. Nuclear strategy was discussed (especially regarding the possible use of atomic weapons in Korea), and MacArthur's relief caused extensive comment. In the post-Korean War years (1954–1970) we found a very marked upward trend in the index of political content. A regression line showed a slope of 1.60 (r^2 = 0.705, compared with a slope of −0.259 and r^2 = 0.116 for 1920–1940). The mean value of the index of political content was 38.0 percent (versus 16.4 percent before World War II). This increase was due to the addition of numerous political topics to the periodical. A few of the more common ones included:

Civic action,
Civil disturbances,
Counterinsurgency,
Effect of the Korean War on nuclear strategy,
Ideology,
Limited war and national policy,
Military and civilian life styles,
Molding public opinion,
Psychological warfare,
Role of the National Guard and reserves,
World-wide implications of French operations in Indochina and Algeria.[14]

Conclusions

There are three alternative models of military behavior in politics that we have found helpful in thinking about the growing "politicization" of the army which we discovered in our study. Although we are not presently able to determine which of these models best fits the contemporary reality, it seems useful to outline them briefly for their possible heuristic value to future research.

THE CAPABLE-SERVANT MODEL

In this model the army is politicized because it is required to undertake new missions with significant political components.

[14]It is unfortunate that *Military Review's* early format prohibited its use in our analysis—especially in view of the fact that we were unable to examine curricular changes at the Command and General Staff College. A partial analysis of *Military Review*, however, indicates that it follows those same trends which we discovered in the Army War College and *Army* magazine; between 1950 and 1970 the percentage of articles dealing with political concerns nearly doubles. The subject matter of those articles contributing to this change is strikingly similar to that listed above.

Civilian policymakers are sometimes faced with situations in which a large, responsive organization is needed to implement some preferred course of action. If the government's extant civilian agencies are seen as unable to execute the program and if the creation of a new organization involves long delays or high economic costs, then assigning the new mission to the military may become the path of least resistance for the civilian politicians. Most military leaders readily accept the legitimacy of all orders from the nation's political decision-makers, and they bring to any new task their positive attitude toward mission-accomplishment ("there is no substitute for victory"). Thus, if the military are required to undertake some political task, they will attempt to develop whatever talents and expertise are necessary to get the job done. In this model there is no real conflict between civilian and military leaders. Politicization of the army is attributable to externally imposed missions; depoliticization can be accomplished by the withdrawal of these same missions.

THE AMOEBA-IN-UNIFORM MODEL

This model assumes that there is an active desire on the part of the military to subsume new missions, including political missions, for any of several reasons. First, the military may think that the nation can be saved only if certain vital functions and activities are removed from the hands of inept, bumbling civilians and are taken over by the military. Second, professional soldiers may feel that they must have a greater range of political action in order to accomplish certain essentially traditional defense missions. Third, military officers may desire new political missions simply to enlarge their organization, to allow for more promotions and so forth. Whatever the rationale, the situation described by the amoeba-in-uniform model is essentially one of real civil-military conflict and is much more dangerous to democratic values than the capable-servant situation.

THE CHANGING-ENVIRONMENT MODEL

In this model politicization is attributed to neither the actions of the civil government nor the desires of the military establishment. Rather, a series of changes occur (either within the nation-state or within the international community as a whole) that radically increase the importance of military establishments, irrespective of the wishes of civilian decisionmakers or of military officers. In a supercharged situation such as the height of the cold war, more and more political decisions are perceived to have grave military implications. Thus politics (to turn a phrase) becomes too important to be left to politicians, and the military must actively participate. In this situation there is no real conflict between the military and the civil government; both recognize (perhaps with varying degrees of joy or despair) the necessity for military expansion into the political realm. This situation may be reversed only by another system change, particularly the lowering of international tensions as Wayne Moyer suggests elsewhere in this book and Harold Lasswell argues in his "Garrison State" essays.[15]

A fourth possible explanation of the military's increased interest in political matters would be a praetorian model suggesting that military politicization is only one aspect of the politicization of society as a whole. In the praetorian case the political sphere so loosens in form and so broadens in scope that it comes to color many sectors of life—including not only the military but also other professions normally held to be apolitical. While such a praetorian model once held great appeal for the authors of this paper, our more recent research has shown fairly conclusively that it does not obtain in America today; a content analysis of journals for three nonmilitary professions (medicine, education and the ministry) strongly indicates that the politicizing trends which we discovered in the military are *not* present in society at large.[16]

Admittedly the "models" as we have sketched them are simplistic, single-variable caricatures. Clearly a more comprehensive model should be synthesized from all three. Organizational pressures for the accretion of power should also be considered, as should the special interests of certain military groups (e.g., Green Berets, Strategic Air Command, nuclear attack submarines) in

[15]Harold D. Lasswell, "The Garrison State," *American Journal of Sociology,* 46 (Jan., 1941):455–468; "The Garrison State Hypothesis Today," in Samuel P. Huntington, ed., *Changing Patterns of Military Politics* (Glencoe, Ill: Free Press, 1962), pp. 51–70.

[16]Clarence L. Abercrombie, III, "Politicization: The Military and Other American Professions." Forthcoming.

specific types of missions (e.g., counterinsurgency, countervalue nuclear deterrence, counterforce nuclear deterrence). Nevertheless, even in a more sophisticated framework of analysis, a basic question will remain: were the military politicized by new assigned missions; did the military choose to politicize themselves; or did military politicization result from a system change in the broader socio-political environment? Although our data do not enable us to reply with any degree of certainty, we do hope that we have been able to formulate the question in terms of variables that will be of use to future researchers.

Besides our general models there are other conclusions that we can draw more directly from our data. As we had expected, levels of political content in the Army War College and in *Army* magazine were much higher after World War II than they had been before the war. Further, since the Korean conflict and the intensification of the cold war, our indexes of the political content for these two sources have demonstrated sharply increasing trends. Also in line with our expectations, we found the levels of political content much higher in upper-grade officer courses (the Army War College) than in more basic instruction (the Infantry School courses).

Three findings, on the other hand, were unexpected. First, the *Army* articles and the Infantry School courses showed low points during World War II and the Korean War and high points immediately following these wars. Second, the Vietnam war clearly breaks this pattern of wartime lows. From the standpoint of the general public, the political decisionmakers and the armed forces, this was a new sort of war. Public opinion was less supportive of the endeavor; the debate between the executive and legislative branches on war issues was more acrimonious; and the expertise demanded of the professional soldier was more political than in previous wars. Finally, for the 1920–1939 period the indexes of the political content of military professionalism for the highest strata in the military hierarchy (as evidenced by the Army War College curricula) were surprisingly high and surprisingly constant.

During the period between the world wars, the pattern of military participation in the political process varied but little. Similarly, as Huntington notes, "the military interpretations of international politics and their prescriptions for foreign policy remained remarkably static."[17] This constancy contrasts sharply with the increasing trend shown by our indexes of political content following World War II. These findings are more surprising when we consider that there are few military activities of the sixties that did not have parallels in the twenties. Why, we might ask, do missions that apparently had so little impact forty-five years ago seem to have such important effects today? We must again step beyond the clear implications of our data in order to explain this unexpectedly high but steady political content of military professionalism between the world wars. Here we shall suggest that certain parameters of civil-military relations existing within the United States during the interwar years defined a "floor" below which military politicization could not drop. World War II and the Korean War, moreover, caused changes in some of these parameters that have resulted in increasing politicization in recent years.

The legal pattern of military-political involvement had been established by the National Defense Acts of 1916 and 1920; it remained unchanged until the outbreak of World War II. Huntington, as we have said, noted a similar constancy in military perceptions of external threats. Until the late 1930s the assimilation of technological advances by the armed forces was extremely slow. All these factors argued for stability in the military's level of political concern. Yet while this level was stable, there were factors that kept it fairly high. The military perception of external threats to national security was consistently higher than civilian evaluations of the same threats. In their legally defined function of national security advisors, the military brought discussions of security threats and weapons procurement into the arena of political debate, and thus politicization was kept above a certain level by the constraints of the American political system. Turning to the post-Korean War and especially the post-1964 period, we note that the momentum of technology and the size of the defense budget have greatly increased. Similarly, civilian and military perceptions of the Soviet threat converged, only diverging again in the most recent years. The creation of the Defense Department, together with mounting public and political pressure for social welfare programs, has greatly increased the competi-

[17]Huntington, *Changing Patterns*, p. 305.

tion for scarce federal funds, both among the services and between military and nonmilitary programs. That is, the political system's parameters have changed in a way that appears to have raised the ante, as it were, so that every military activity today may have a greater impact than it would have had in the twenties and thirties. It may be, then, that an analysis of the military's new political missions is less useful than an examination of the broader technological, social and political context in which they are to be carried out. Such an analysis would obviously suggest the application of our third model above.

We have already noted that the cold war and Vietnam war years witnessed steady increases in the political content of military professionalism, increases strong enough to affect even the lower strata of the professional socialization process, the Infantry School courses. Perhaps this trend is most readily observed in the fields of counterinsurgency and riot control. Military men have learned at least some tentative lessons from the tragic experience of Vietnam. First, the concept of a military advisor as one who teaches only the use of military equipment has changed. The Military Assistance Officer Command and Staff Course given at the U. S. Army Institute for Military Assistance at Fort Bragg, North Carolina, is designed to prepare army officers "for assignments in the field of international security assistance" (advisory duties abroad). It is at least worth noting that the current curriculum contains not a single hour of instruction that could be classified as apolitical, as the following excerpt indicates:[18]

Academic Subjects	Hours
Introduction	13
Survey of the social sciences	63
Comparative social institutions	100
U. S. and international government organization, policy and operations	157
Considerations of national planning	99
Civil-military planning and operations	76
Guest speaker program	102
Field trip and symposium	52

The objectives of these specific academic subjects include en-

[18]United States Army Institute for Military Assistance, *Program of Instruction for 7B–F3, Military Assistance Officer Command and Staff Course* (Fort Bragg, N. C.: June 1971), Approved: Commanding General, Continental Army Command, 26 July 1971, p. 201.

hancing "the student's ability to analyze and evaluate causes of internal social and political conflict . . . [and to formulate] a viable national strategy for defining development objectives," all for the foreign country to be assisted, of course.[19] This is a far cry from the technical tasks of teaching foreign armies to use our material and tactics, the original mission of the military assistance program.

The difficulties of defeating an established revolution are also recognized, and some military counterinsurgency experts insist that the army enter the next war much earlier, before the guerrillas can win over appreciable segments of the population. In *Military Men* Ward Just quotes an officer of the Institute for Military Assistance:

Look. Get in there early, get in there very early and really analyze the situation. Analyze the revolution. Find out all about it, the people, the methods, the particulars. Get in there early and form it, shape it.[20]

Similarly, in *Army*, George Fielding Eliot presents an argument for early intervention in counterinsurgency situations:

Get in there fast has been our tactical name of the game in Vietnam. Get in there faster will be the strategical name of the game the next time the whistle blows. Or else.

and,

In short, the next time the commander in chief (sic) in the White House finds himself compelled to use force to defeat "revolutionary war" he will also find himself compelled to rely on competent military advice so as to make sure he uses enough force and the right kind of force to insure early success and deny the enemy their cherished strategy of protraction.[21]

It is only fair to say that these statements probably do not represent the views of all or even most American military professionals, but they do indicate how strategies of containment lead to the necessity of counterrevolution, which acts in turn to insure that military professionalism will have a high (and perhaps a growing) political content.

In its role of suppressing civil disorders, the army has again

[19] *Ibid.*, pp. 4D01, 4E01.
[20] Ward Just, *Military Men* (New York: Alfred A. Knopf, 1970), p. 210.
[21] George Fielding Eliot, "Next Time We'll Have to Get There Faster," *Army*, 20 (April, 1970): 33, 34.

shown how new missions can lead to increased political activity. As plans were made targeting specific units to specific cities, questions of priority arose. The operations personnel found that they could not make good decisions with inadequate information, and the army entered the field of domestic intelligence:

> . . . while the application of pure military firepower [to an urban insurrection] would be a poor solution, political efforts might prove not much better. There are measures that offer a better solution if we are to keep our cities from becoming battlegrounds: penetration by police intelligence, application of military intelligence, and reliance on traditional FBI methods. . . .
>
> To prevent and to curb urban violence of any order we must establish an effective system of intelligence in the ghettos of urban America.[22]

As the Ervin Committee showed, the military's domestic intelligence network eventually extended beyond the ghettos to include surveillance of government officials and even members of Congress.

In every empirical work there comes a point when the authors must stand back from their data and ask, "So what?" In this study we found that today's professional soldier is becoming increasingly more involved in political matters. That is interesting, but is it of any importance to the society or the political system? We believe that it is. Elsewhere in this volume, James Dickey asserts that the political component of an officer's newly required expertise is creating certain tensions within the army itself and is making it more difficult for the officer to reconcile his duty to serve the nation with his (and society's) ethical standards. If Dickey's observations are valid and if the trends we found in our data continue, then we might expect the internal tensions and ethical dilemmas among army professionals to increase, perhaps to the point of downgrading military efficiency. More important, the post-World War II trends in military politicization show such steady increases that we might wonder if the process can be reversed—if there is some "ratchet" effect at work in which increasing degrees of political involvement will fall irreversibly upon our armed forces. The dangerous potential of such a situation is obvious.

None of this should be taken as an indictment of the American

[22]Colonel Robert B. Rigg, U. S. Army, "Made in USA," *Army*, 18 (January, 1968): 24.

professional soldier. We certainly do not foresee the U.S. Army of the seventies resembling the mutinous French Army of the late fifties and early sixties. What we do suggest is that our armed forces are becoming increasingly politicized and that the social and political effects of this politicization must be carefully evaluated by the civilian decisionmakers.

Percentages of Curricula and Articles Devoted to Political Concerns

Year	Off. Candidate School	Off. Advanced Course	Army War College	Ordnance Magazine	Army Magazine
1920			26.1%	15.4%	19.2%
1921			31.6	9.4	20.8
1922			27.6	4.9	9.9
1923			21.0	6.5	21.2
1924			26.8	11.8	16.6
1925			28.6	13.1	20.7
1926			33.4	30.3	22.8
1927			27.5	18.9	16.9
1928			33.5	15.6	14.8
1929			35.1	22.8	10.8
1930			30.9	37.5	15.1
1931			34.6	29.8	26.5
1932			32.6	18.3	12.5
1933			36.7	33.3	22.5
1934			34.1	47.4	13.0
1935			31.3	50.0	11.5
1936			23.0	25.0	13.6
1937			22.8	51.4	10.2
1938			25.3	37.8	14.5
1939			27.4	37.8	12.7
1940				22.2	18.1
1941	0%	0%		32.0	12.5
1942	0	0		28.8	9.8
1943	0	0		18.1	8.6
1944	0	0		22.9	6.1
1945	0.13	0		20.3	13.3
1946	2.15	1.42		38.8	41.7
1947	1.98	2.12		32.7	36.9
1948		2.10		38.8	22.0
1949		0.77		51.0	24.7
1950		0.31	30.3	50.0	23.9
1951	0	0	39.5	29.3	32.4
1952	0	0	41.7	21.3	25.6
1953	0.21	1.18	49.0	16.4	24.7
1954	0.21	0.94	41.3	24.4	30.2
1955	0.21	0.78	49.5	21.1	27.4
1956	0.20	1.39	57.3	25.7	28.0
1957	0.49	1.35	55.8	18.8	24.0
1958	2.54	1.61	54.4	32.1	23.3
1959	2.65	1.47	51.9	20.8	41.0
1960	2.65	1.49	57.3	21.4	35.5
1961	2.47	1.62	57.9	25.3	30.8
1962	1.93	1.80	60.9	20.6	41.6
1963	2.02	3.30	61.0	20.6	37.9
1964	1.37	3.30	64.2	24.7	36.7
1965	1.55	3.56	58.4	22.9	51.7
1966	1.21	3.56	59.5	27.1	44.6
1967	1.21	3.21	63.6	32.2	54.7
1968	1.31		68.8	27.6	45.8
1969	1.68		66.7	44.3	46.7
1970			68.4	35.5	46.7

Part 2
MILITARIZATION OF THE POLITY

Changing National Priorities of The United States

BUDGETS, PERCEIVED NEEDS AND POLITICAL ENVIRONMENTS, 1945–1971

Jong Ryool Lee

Introduction

The military establishment of this nation is under severe interrogation from many segments of society. There is a growing conviction among informed people that it has gained an undue influence in setting national priorities, determining thus the course of the nation. One of the common indicators of such influence is the enormous size of the defense budget, its persistent claim on the nation's resources which are not unlimited. Over $1 trillion have been consumed during the past two decades in the name of national security.

The core of the problem is thus economic as well as political. What political risks does the United States take by acquiescing to such power of the military? And what additional economic and social price does this nation really pay for the maintenance of high levels of defense expenditure? Many aspects of these two questions have been subjected to academic analyses. But there is still considerable controversy over a wide spectrum of issues involved in defense spending.

NOTE: Research for this chapter was supported in part by grant No. GS–614 from the National Science Foundation. No individual or agency, however, is responsible for opinions or errors found here.

This paper investigates the implications of military priorities in their interaction with the political environment. This is an attempt to put one of the most important problems of civil-military relations into a broader perspective. Not only the causes but also the consequences of high defense spending are considered. We will examine the interrelationship of various types of public spending, their relation to priorities expressed in presidential statements and to events in the American economy and the world at large. A theoretical task is to test widely shared beliefs that high defense spending is essential for national security, and that even if it is higher than necessary, it comes free because it is an essential component of American economic prosperity.

Some results of these analyses seem to have grave implications. The empirical data indicate that a high defense priority is likely to lead to increased foreign commitments and to hurt sound economic growth as well. In addition, it is domestic welfare spending that suffers most when defense expenditures rise. At the heart of these phenomena lies bureaucratic inertia.

This is a quantitative analysis based on empirical data. But, in order to avoid burdening the reader, methodological details will be kept to a minimum in the text, hopefully without loss of information and continuity.

1. THEORIES OF NATIONAL PRIORITIES IN ACTION

From the Korean War on, the postwar growth of the military establishment is unique in American experience. It offers many challenging and thought-provoking problems that have no parallel in history. Before we can speculate intelligently about the political or economic implications of the growing burden of defense we must understand the context in which it operates.

If national priorities can be viewed as the adaptive strategy a nation chooses in its struggle for survival or progress in a changing world, then it is hardly surprising that national defense has dominated the political arena in the United States since World War II. It has probably been a sense of threat and partly a sense of responsibility on the part of the American people with their vast resources and potential that have thrust the U. S. into a lonely role of world leadership.[1] Within two decades of conflict

[1]The foreign policy mood and the psychological impact of the cold war was well discussed by Gabriel Almond, *The American People and Foreign Policy* (New York:

with Soviet Russia, the United States has projected its military as well as its economic power into every sphere of world affairs, with the result that international developments now no longer are independent of U. S. intentions and actions.[2] The nation has gained this new status under the formidable threat of nuclear war and the "tyranny of technology,"[3] when choices of policy or strategy have involved unprecedented risks and costs.

It is not only the military establishment that has undergone a significant change since World War II, however. The role of government has also rapidly expanded.[4] Just as the level of defense expenditures is one indicator of the military role, so the high level of federal spending, it can be said, indicates the expanded role of government. Federal activities, which were managed with merely $4 million at the start of the nation, now absorb more than one-fifth of the total national income, over $200 billion every year, and the various programs of the government now touch upon almost every pressing national need and concern. The federal government has also assumed to intervene through a variety of means, including federal spending and taxation, in order to maintain a specific responsibility (economic stability and prosperity) when the free market is not likely to do so properly.[5] There are also rising expectations about a new role of government from segments of society which live in the shadow of an affluence they do not share.

This is the context in which national priorities have been molded for a quarter of a century. The concern of this paper is to find how the priority system has worked *within* the above context. Assigning a specific period, the time since World War II,

---

Praeger, 1960), pp. 11–28. And as to permissive popular attitudes toward military priority until late 1960s, see Bruce Russett, "The Revolt of the Masses: Public Opinion on Military Expenditures," In Bruce Russett, ed. *Peace, War, and Numbers* (Beverly Hills, Calif.: Sage, 1972).

[2]Adam Yarmolinsky, *The Military Establishment* (New York: Harper & Row, 1971), p. 94. He rightly points out that foreign development or environment is itself to some degree determined by American policy choice.

[3]Ralph Lapp, *Arms beyond Doubt: The Tyranny of Weapons Technology* (New York: Cowles, 1970). He uses this phrase in a little different vein, with an emphasis on the grave danger stemming from the race for weapons development.

[4]As to the expanded role of the federal government in the economy, See Murray Weidenbaum, *The Modern Public Sector* (New York: Basic Books, 1969).

[5]The Unemployment Act in 1946 provided a legal basis for such a commitment of the federal government in the performance of the national economy.

has the effect of controlling other variables which would compli-
cate the study if it reached back further in time. National security
has been constantly near the top of the list of priorities during
this period. Yet there were fluctuations in the relative importance
of the military priority as well as in the role of the federal government in the economy, as is indicated by the varying levels of
spending in times of war and peace on items composing the
budget. What interests a researcher is how this variation is
related to the economy and to politics.

Two levels of national priorities are usually distinguishable.[6]
The first is the allocation of resources between public and private
sectors; the second is the allocation of resources among the various programs wthin the public sector.[7] What complicates budgetary decisionmaking is that it involves these two kinds of decision
on priorities at the same time.

The objective of budgetary allocation is to divide the national
resources so that each additonal billion dollars spent will have
the same social utility.[8] But often the total amount of money the
federal government uses depends on the purposes to which it is
put. For instance, when an urgent need for national defense is
seen, as in the case of the Korean War and the war in Vietnam,
total federal outlays go up.

Theories and views about national priorities naturally become
ideological beliefs and calls to action for certain political and
social forces. Public discussion, including that of scholars and
policymakers, can be classified by what each eventually publicly
supports, regardless of the underlying logic or justification for
the position taken. Two broad spectra of opinion can be separated and analyzed.

First, there is a controversy between views which, for convenience, we will call "militarist" and "pacifist." The "militarist"
goes on the assumption that more defense expenditure assures
greater national security, whereas the "pacifist" sees danger in a

[6]This distinction includes the state or local share of national resources in the
category of the public sector. In this paper, however, only the federal share is
considered.

[7]Charles Schultze, "Budget Alternatives after Vietnam," in *Agenda for the Nation*
(New York: Doubleday, 1968), p. 14; and Weidenbaum, *Modern Public Sector.*

[8]James Tobin, *National Economic Policy* (New Haven, Conn.: Yale University
Press, 1966), p. 45. M. Weidenbaum, *Modern Public Sector*, p. 157.

reckless arms race and military overpreparedness. The focus of the controversy is: how much is enough? A wide spectrum of opinions on this issue can be put simply as a "hawk vs dove" continuum. It is a typical argument of a hawk that this country is too rich to risk its survival by maintaining only a slim margin of security.[9] A dove will argue that the marginal return of additional military preparedness is close to zero.[10]

The second spectrum of opinions causing controversy is about the proper role of government in society and in the economy in particular. Keynesian theory stands on one side of the continuum. It states that high and deficit government spending is often essential if the recession-bound capitalistic economy is to work. Deficit financing is employed not infrequently as a deliberate fiscal policy intended to promote production by increasing aggregate demand at a time when the economy is in a slump. The idea is "balancing the economy," rather than balancing the budget.[11] This line of reasoning, emphasizing the discretionary power of government, can be designated as "fiscal activism."

Opposing this line of thought, however, there is a more deep-rooted belief that federal spending should be kept to a minimum because government is, by its nature, less efficient than the private sector in providing services. Private firms, the theory contends, are relatively free of bureaucratic red tape and political maneuvering.[12] It is argued that private production is carried on at closer to minimum cost than public production. A balanced budget is preferred to a deficit. And there is an underlying tradi-

[9]J. Tobin, *National Economic Policy*, p. 60. "We are too rich a country to keep our defenses at the margin of taking very serious risks to our very survival. A nation on the edge of starvation might of necessity be on the edge of insecurity. The U. S. has no private uses of resources so compelling that they justify keeping the Western World in such a precarious position that any reduction in the budget will gravely threaten the security."

[10]Sidney Lens, *The Military Industrial-Complex* (Kansas City, Mo.: Pilgrim Press and National Catholic Reporter, 1970), pp. 143–144. "If a nation is ready to accept the simple theorems on which militarism is predicated—whether real or made to look real—each "crisis" will evoke the demand for "more" . . . and its spokesmen and theoreticians will soon be scurrying for new "crises" on which to peg their argument for more preparedness. Seymour Melman challenges the basic assumptions of defense spending in his book, *Pentagon Capitalism* (New York: McGraw Hill, 1970), pp. 163–169.

[11]J. Tobin *National Economic Policy*, pp. 35, 49–55.

[12]David Ott and Attiat Ott, *The Federal Budget Policy* (Washington, D.C.: Brookings Institution, 1966), pp. 54–57.

tional belief that a minimum of government is still the best government. In a sense this feeling is more widespread among the public than the Keynesian theory is.[13]

These two dimensions of controversy can be illustrated in a four-cell diagram in which the defense budget over the years is plotted on the vertical axis to represent the choice made in national priorities between hawks and doves, and the nondefense budget is plotted on the horizontal axis to represent the choice made between fiscal activism and fiscal conservatism or between monetary and fiscal economic policy. The resulting diagram shows how over the years the national resources have been divided among various public programs according to decisions made on national priorities. Any theory or argument can be put in one of the four cells made by the cross combination of these two dimensions of controversy.

Thus each of the four types of theories has had an opportunity to become the basis of national policy decisions at one time or another with the changing foreign or domestic environment.

If each of these dimensions is independent of the other, the conclusion is evident. For instance, a hawk and fiscal conservative would agree with a defense increase, but he would suggest cuts in other civilian spending instead. Conversely, a dove-activist would suggest defense cuts but increases in other civilian spending.

The reality is more complex than this model can present. Because of the unprecedented high level of defense spending throughout the postwar era, the two dimensions often either combined or conflicted with each other with a balanced budget never having been achieved. Thus the focus of debate was how and to what extent to minimize the federal deficit.

Since each of the four types of theory is not only a theory but also an operating policy, each has its proponents and practitioners who try to put their theory or persuasion into action in the political arena. The course that this nation finally took each year is indicated by the curved line in Fig. 1. Each decade has its own character.

[13]The controversies between the two positions in terms of purely economic theories, that is, "fiscal vs. monetary policies," is well summarized in the discussion between Milton Friedman and Walter Heller, *Monetary vs. Fiscal Policy: A Dialogue* (New York: W. W. Norton, 1969).

FIG. 1. THEORIES OF PUBLIC ACTIVITY

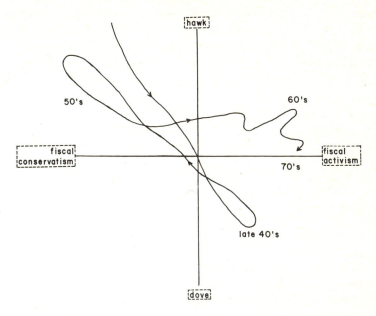

The relevant data are presented in Figure 3. The curved line with arrows indicates the course year by year taken by the nation in the allocation of resources.

Further, the political process is assumed to be the bargaining and compromise among diverse and legitimate interests comprising the pluralistic political system. Sometimes, as Wayne Moyer's findings suggest, it is competition and conciliation among different theories and political ideologies held by decisionmakers, rather than their material interests.

Since there is a broad consensus on the method by which the conflict of diverse interests and views is resolved, the final policy advocated at different levels of the political process reflects the distribution of influence held by those groups and individuals.

The annual budget is a package of the most important and comprehensive decisions on priorities which the society makes in the course of a year.[14] The annual preparation of the budget may require the review of major programs and goals before limited

[14]Charles Schultze, as quoted in Robert Benson and Harold Wolman, ed. *Counter Budget* (New York: Praeger, 1971), p. 4.

resources can be allocated in order to meet the most pressing national problems as perceived by the relevant political actors in a changing environment. As McNamara often maintained, the federal budget is "a quantitative expression of policy preferences in that year."[15] It, therefore, will also provide a clue as to whose policy preferences prevailed in the choice of alternative uses of resources. If each group can be assumed to try to maximize its influence in dividing up the national pie, the final decision arrived at may not necessarily be a rational choice for the whole nation.

2. NATIONAL PRIORITIES AS EXPRESSED IN THE BUDGET

The focus on the military priority naturally points to the question of what defense spending means in terms of dividing up the national resources. Russett has stated that "defense spending has to come at the expense of something else."[16] He showed that it came partly at the expense of private consumption and partly at the expense of social welfare programs such as education and health.

[15]Kenneth Clark et al, ed. *The President and the Management of National Security* (New York: Praeger, 1969), p. 19, and the same line of expression appears in Aaron Wildavsky, *The Politics of the Budgetary Process* (Boston: Little Brown, 1964), p. 4.

[16]Bruce Russett, *What Price Vigilance?* (New Haven, Conn.: Yale University Press, 1970), p. 26, pp. 137–156. A criticism of such findings was raised on methodological grounds. Jerry Hollenhorst and Gary Ault, "An Alternative Answer to: Who Pays for Defense," *American Political Science Review* (Sept. 1971), pp. 760–763. By a replication analysis using dummy variables, they claim that they had found a significant change in subperiods among "tradeoff" relationships between defense spending and the other GNP expenditure categories. Their criticism is misleading, however, on methodological grounds. First, their model hypothesizes that the slope coefficient changed during war times while the intercept did not. It is more plausible to hypothesize that the intercept rather than the slope is changed. Secondly, use of a dummy variable is equivalent to breaking down samples into subsamples, and in view of small number of data points in the subperiods, it would be equally meaningless as in the case of separate regressions. And finally, the most crucial flaw is that they gave undue interpretation to the separate significance test of each parameter, even though they were aware that "the effects of the Korean War and the Vietnam War are given by the sums $b_1 + b_2$, and $b_1 + b_4$, respectively." These coefficients should have been meaningfully interpreted by joint-significance tests. J. Johnston, *Econometrics* (New York: McGraw Hill, 1960), pp. 221–228, and Arthur Goldberger, *Econometric Theory* (New York: John Wiley, 1964), pp. 224–227.

The impact of defense expenditure increases on the federal share of the national output is apparent in a crossplot of the two indices in Fig. 2. With the exception of 1951 each increase in defense expenditure resulted also in an increase in the total outlay of the government, thus limiting the private uses of resources (r = 0.97).

FIG. 2. CHANGES IN THE TWO LEVELS OF NATIONAL PRIORITIES
(defense vs. total federal)

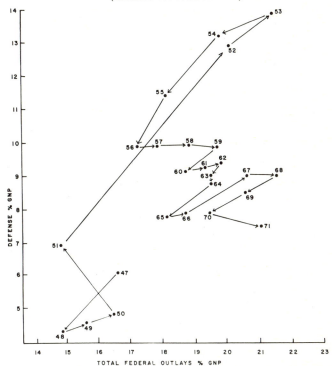

Note for Figure 2:   Each year expressed as a point in the plot is connected by arrow lines in a sequential order to show the trajectory of year-to-year changes on the two dimensions. The horizontal scale represents total federal outlays as a percentage of GNP, whereas the vertical scale denotes defense expenditure as a percentage of GNP.

One notable trend is that defense spending goes up more sharply than it comes down. Though the overall trend toward a greater federal role in the economy is visible, it is to be noted that military expenditures since 1956 have sustained their position in claims on the national income with only minor fluctuations somewhere between the levels of the late forties and the Korean War peak. Considering that the national economy has grown considerably during this period, this has meant a growing defense budget, and it is not too unreasonable to infer that the military establishment has a stabilized voice in national politics. President Eisenhower's warning against "the acquisition of unwarranted influence by the military-industrial complex" is to be read against the background of his experience in office, as indicated by the line in the diagram linking 1956 to 1959.

If defense expenditures are, as discussed above, an indicator of the prominence of military influence in the political system, whether due to foreign threats or not, and if nondefense spending is an indicator of fiscal activism, the relative emphasis during each decade in the postwar era can be clearly seen in the course taken by this nation. The two dimensions vary somewhat independently of each other, since various functional breakdowns of nondefense spending cancel each other out.

The course of this nation and the relative influence of political forces is visible in Fig. 3. Each decade has its distinct characteristics in the pattern of dividing up the national resources. The relative importance of defense expenditure in the national priority list was at its lowest in the late forties. Right after World War II the national mood emphasized peace and caring for social needs which had been left unmet during the war. Then the ideological confrontation with Soviet Russia culminating in the Korean War went hand in hand with a national policy of maintaining high levels of defense expenditure. At the same time conservatism forced decisionmakers to cut down civilian spending in an attempt to offset the menace to economic instability caused by high defense spending.

The data make it clear that the relative importance of defense spending was decreasing and domestic needs such as education, health and housing were gaining political footholds until curbed by the war in Vietnam.

Given the total amount of resources that the government can afford to spend, determining priorities each year takes the form of allocating limited resources to meet the most urgent national

FIG. 3. TWO LEVELS OF NATIONAL PRIORITIES (defense vs. non-defense)

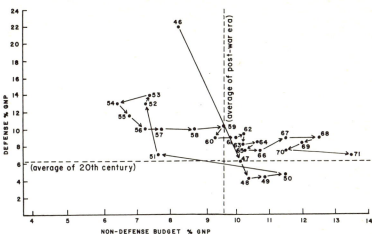

Note for Figure 3:   Each year is expressed as a point in the plot and the trajectory of year-to-year change is shown by the arrow lines linking each year in sequence. The horizontal scale represents non-defense federal outlays as a percentage GNP, and its average for the period since 1946 is indicated by the dotted line. On the other hand, the vertical scale denotes annual defense expenditures as a percentage of GNP, and the average for the 20th century is marked by the dotted line. Compare this figure with Figure 1 given before.

needs. Which government programs then suffered most when security needs pushed up the defense budget?[17]

The data collected consist of a breakdown by functions of the federal budget as percentages of the total federal outlays of that

[17]Since the budget of fiscal year 1969, a unified budget concept has been adopted by the recommendation of the President's Commission on Budget Concepts submitted on October 10, 1967. In the past, three sets of budget totals had been highlighted: the administrative budget, the consolidated cash budget and the national income accounts budget. Minor inconsistencies of budget figures among sources result from the intermingling of the three concepts as well as from the change of criteria stemming from the new budget concept. The data used for 1958–1972 were given by the Bureau of the Budget based on this new concept. For earlier periods the administrative budget figures were used. Two functional categories, "space research and technology" and "income security" were removed from the data set because of some missing data points. For an explanation of the different budget concepts, see David Ott and Attiat Ott, *Federal Budget Policy* (Washington, D.C.: Brookngs Institution, 1967), pp. 14–15, and also Bureau of the Budget, *Budget in Brief* (Washington, D.C.: U.S. Government Printing Office, 1969), pp. 63–64.

TABLE 1

Claims on National Resources in Dimensions of Competing Budgetary Allocation (1947–1972)

	Factors		
Functions of Government	F_1 Defense vs. Social Welfare	F_2 Government Infrastructure	F_3 Urban vs. Rural
Defense	.74		
Commerce & transportation	−.91		
Health	−.77		
Education	−.58	.58	
Veterans		.97	
International affairs & finance		.95	
Interest		.92	
General gov't		.91	
Natural Resources		.82	
Housing			.89
Agriculture			−.83
% Total Variance	45.4	22.6	18.3 86.3%

Factors with latent roots greater than or equal to 1.0 were varimax-rotated. Signs were adjusted. Principal component factor technique was applied, putting 1.00 in the main diagonals of the correlation matrix.

year. They were analyzed by several related, but yet different techniques, in order to be sure that the results were not distorted by any one method.

A factor analysis of the federal budget classified by the function it is called upon to perform outlines the basic dimensions of the necessary choices that underlie the process of dividing up resources for competing national needs. This is a way of describing succinctly the interrelationship among various categories of functions performed by the government. Three independent dimensions of competing claims on national resources were discovered in this analysis of the data. The factor loadings given in the table can be understood as equivalent to correlation coefficients, i.e. they measure the degree of association, between the categories of government functions in the rows and the three underlying dimensions of competing claims on resources, the factors, in the columns.

The first factor is best described as a bipolar dimension, defense versus social welfare. This result is in line with Russett's finding: Defense expenditures tend to come largely at the expense of social welfare.

The second factor is interpreted as government infrastructure, since these variables include government functions that require some minimum level of spending if the government is to be operative. It seems logical that "international affairs and finance" loads here because performance of that function requires trained personnel and a reasonable degree of continuity.

The third factor is interpreted as urban versus rural. Though relative importance in the budget composition (5 percent) is almost negligible, this factor indicates that emphasis on urban spending has been accompanied by neglect of agriculture and land. There is a natural trend toward more urbanization.

Next, another factor analysis (not reported in detail here) was applied to the elasticity[18] of categories of government functions, their proportional increase or decrease in relation to the total budget. The basic relationships among the categories of government functions remained the same, revealing even more strikingly the conflict between defense and social welfare in dividing up the budgetary pie. The only important difference between the two different analyses was that in the elasticity analysis the "urban-rural" dimension merged with the "defense-welfare" dimension, and "veterans" constituted a distinct pattern. Except for "housing," which showed association with defense, this analysis revealed that the choice between defense and social welfare was the primary concern that decisionmakers have had to face during the period, even when, in dividing up the pie, they considered only the marginal increase or decrease of each function of government.

An alternative technique used for uncovering the underlying relationships among variables is to present in a diagram a two-dimensional configuration of variables with their dissimilarities indicated by the distance between points. In multidimensional scaling, the closer two points are in the plot, the closer relationship those variables have.

[18]Elasticity is defined as the ratio of the proportional increase in Y to the proportional increase in X. That is

$$\text{Elasticity} = \frac{\triangle Y}{\triangle X} \cdot \frac{X}{Y}$$

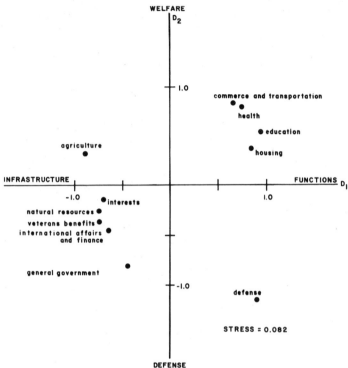

Fig. 4. multidimensional scaling, budget percent (1947–1972)

The two dimensions revealed by this analysis can also be interpreted in the same way as those of the factor analysis described above, "government infrastructure" and "social welfare versus defense," respectively. This is a striking result, considering that the two methods are based on quite different mathematical assumptions.[19]

[19]This scaling method does not assume a linear relationship among entities. Instead, multidimensional scaling is a technique of representing N objects or variables geometrically by N points, so that the interpoint distances correspond in some sense to dissimilarities between objects. Instead of dissimilarities, the actual measurements may be similarities, interaction rates between groups, correlation coefficients as in the case of this paper, or other measures of proximity or association of diverse kind. The basic notion is the "psychological nearness" between a pair of entities, and the technique is designed to reveal the spatial structure contained only latently in the original data. The procedure uses only the rank order of the measurements. The first of the two fundamental conditions imposed on the solution is "monotonicity," which requires that the rank order of N(N–1)/2 distances between the N points should be monotonically related with the rank order implied in measuring the degree of association of the variables.

The meaning of these results of the analyses is obvious. Policy choices or decisions as to priorities tend to take the form of alternatives between high defense spending and social development.

It is not difficult to see why social welfare has significantly suffered from the defense program. Since defense makes the government budget large and taxes unpleasantly high, political considerations and pressures inherent in the bargaining process force policy-makers to look for "controllable programs" to maintain the ceiling of total expenditure. Social welfare has indeed been considered fair game in the search for such "controllable programs," since many items of infrastructure spending are committed by law leaving little discretionary power to decisionmakers to alter them.

In some eyes social welfare has been a residual function of government, contingent upon relaxation of defense needs. In the fiscal years of 1964 and 1965, it is evident that the declining defense budget was a new catalyst in producing Johnson's magic compound of great new social programs, tax cuts and tight control on the total of the federal budget. But the war in Vietnam reversed this trend.[20]

An additional requirement is that the final configuration should be of the smallest possible dimension. A criterion to judge goodness of fit of the configuration to the data is "stress," which measures to what degree the monotonicity is violated in a given configuration. This can be understood as the "residual sum of the squares" in other linear statistical models.

Stress = S

where, d = a rank order number in the data
d = fitted rank order number in the configuration
It is positive, and the smaller, the better fit. Kruskal suggests a criterion of verbal evaluation in terms of a percentage of "stress."

Stress	Goodness of Fit
20 %	poor
10	fair
5	good
2.5	excellent
0	perfect

By perfect, it is meant here that there is a perfect monotonic relationship between dissimilarities and the distances. J. B. Kruskal, "Multidimensional Scaling by Optimizing Goodness of Fit to a Non-metric Hypothesis," R. Shepard, *Psychometrika*, vol. 29, no. 1 (March, 1964), pp. 1–27. "The Analysis of Proximities: Multidimensional Scaling with an Unknown Distance Function I," *Psychometrika*, vol. 27, no. 2 (June 1962), pp. 125–140.

[20]Arthur Okun, *The Political Economy of Prosperity* (New York: W. W. Norton, 1970), p. 125.

It is no coincidence that civil rights leaders and supporters of the welfare state were among the earliest critics of the war effort in Vietnam. It seems fair to conclude that high defense expenditure comes at the cost of schools, hospitals and public transportation.

3. NATIONAL NEEDS AS PERCEIVED BY PRESIDENTS

The second question raised in examining the establishment of national priorities is how the president perceives pressing national problems each year. For most Americans the president is an important focus of political attention. In an opinion poll, when asked who was "in the best position to see what the country needs," 61 percent of Americans indicated the president, and only 17 percent chose Congress. On the other hand only 10 percent thought the president had the "most to say in the way our government is run," while 52 percent indicated Congress had.

It is generally observed that the president is at the heart of the budgetary decisionmaking process. In fact budgetmaking is a continuous process of interchange among the president, the executive agencies and the Congress. If the president is responsible for recommending the order of national priorities to Congress, Congress is, at least in theory, responsible for legislatively determining with independence and authoritativeness, the nature and rank of the nation's priorities.[21] It is frequently pointed out, however, that the role of Congress is in reality quite marginal.[22]

Though the Bureau of the Budget is at the center of the budgetary process for aggregating and adjusting national demands and aspirations, its chief role is to help the president carry out his policy goals. Therefore, the orientation of the Bureau depends upon that of the president. The president here should be under-

[21]Kenneth Boulding, ed. *National Priorities* (Washington, D. C.: Public Affairs Press, 1969), Introduction and p. 48. The poll data by Survey Research Center were quoted by Roberta Sigel, "Image of the American Presidency," *Midwest Journal of Politics*, vol. 10, no. 1 (February 1966), p. 128.

[22]Benson and Wolman, ed., *Counter-Budget*, pp. 339–342, Alain Enthoven and K. Wayne Smith, *How Much Is Enough?* (New York: Harper & Row, 1971), p. 311. He speaks of the "need for more balanced debate on basic defense issues outside the Defense Department." And also A. Yarmolinsky, *Military Establishment*, pp. 38–53. The point here is that "the role of the Congress is limited primarily by the complexity of the budgetary process, as well as by the fear of being charged with neglect of the nation's defenses, and by the concern of individual Congressmen and Senators with the welfare of their states and districts."

stood to mean not only a single person, but also the top decision-making institution known as the Office of the President and including his influential advisors and staff. Presidential policy preferences are expressed in the annual State of the Union Message to the Congress.

The president's State of the Union Message is an institutionalized review of national problems and policy preferences presented by the top decisionmaker before the whole nation. Though it is invariably overlaid with rhetoric and justifications for his policy choices, it is certainly the most comprehensive single document with which to trace his values and further specifies how those goals are to be attained. Furthermore, the president's position expressed in the message provides a guideline for members of the administration during the course of that year.

The style or content of each message is far from uniform. In the process of preparing the message, however, the most pressing problems facing the nation come to be included in one way or another. Preparation of the message is a part of the decision-making process.[23] We will next examine the kind of themes the president has particularly emphasized in these messages and how the emphasis has changed since World War II.

The data consist of content analyses of presidential State of the Union Messages from 1946 to 1972. Twelve major themes appear in every message. The first subset of data was obtained by assigning rank-order scores from twelve to one to each theme, according to the order in which each appeared in the message. The minimum amount of text given a rank score was a paragraph, or alternatively three sentences that stressed that theme; if the theme did not meet these criteria, the rank score was considered to be zero. A second independent subset of data was obtained by considering the number of sentences a president used to emphasize a particular theme as a proportion or a percentage of the total number of sentences devoted to substantive problems in the whole message. We will call the first subset of data "message

[23]K. Clark, *President and the Management of National Security*, p. 232. Usually the annual State of the Union Message is viewed as a product of reconciliation and interaction among diverse demands and opinions in the administration. The decision process involved in speech writing is dramatically depicted in Eric Goldman, *The Tragedy of Lyndon Johnson* (New York: Dell, 1968), pp. 40–43, 47–48, 53–54, 579–580. A general account is given by Seymour Fersh, *The View from the White House* (Washington, D. C.: Public Affairs Press, 1961).

rank," the second, "message length."[24] A chart showing "message length" over the years, major themes as a percentage of the total contents, is presented below.

The diagram shows that presidential perception is more sensitive and flexible than is the budgetary process, as will be seen later. In an attempt to delineate patterns of needs perceived by the presidents, each of the two subsets of data was factor-analyzed. As there is a high degree of congruence between the two data sets, only the results based on the rank-order score are reported.

In the first place the emphasis on national security was not the only dominant theme in each speech; the president spent much time in talking about the economy and social welfare as well. (The mean of the defense content was 18.4 percent, whereas the mean of the economic content was 15.4 percent.)

Secondly, unlike the composition of the budget in its current value or as a percent of the total, the variables of presidential perception of needs do not show high correlation with similar data for preceding years. In the case of the message rank data, only five variables show auto-correlation significant at the level of 0.05, and in the case of the message length data, only four. This is contrasted with the high degree of auto-correlation of budget data to be discussed later.

Here again, the first rotated factor is interpreted as "foreign concern" versus "social welfare," just as in the case of budgetary allocation. The second factor is called "economic stability," the third factor is "equality." The fourth factor is "budgetary conservatism" of government and the fifth factor is "peace." These results illustrate how a president perceives national problems.

What is striking is that a president perceives defense needs as conflicting with those of social welfare, such as health and unemployment. Social welfare is, the data indicate, something to be seriously considered primarily when the foreign threat is al-

[24]In 1953 both Truman and Eisenhower and in 1961 both Eisenhower and Kennedy gave separate State of Union Messages. Those of the new incoming presidents were taken in such cases. However, in 1969 Johnson, not Nixon, gave the message. And in 1971 Nixon's separate address on foreign policy was assumed to be a continuation of his State of Union Message. There is a high degree of congruence between the two data sets. The average correlation between corresponding themes from the two sets of data was .61. The overall fit by canonical correlations shows that 45 percent of each can be reproduced by the knowledge of the other set.

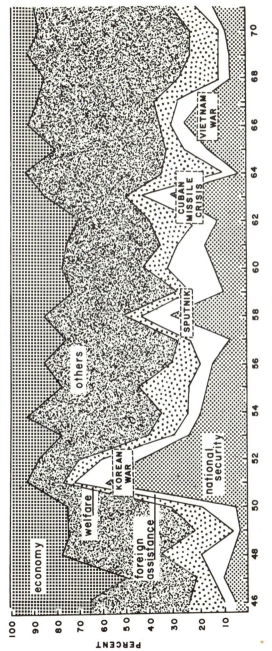

FIG. 5. NEEDS AS PERCEIVED BY THE PRESIDENT

Note for Figure 5:   Scores for the five categories in each State of the Union message add up to 100%. The five categories are: ▓ *= percentage of themes on national economic problems;* ▒ *= percentage of all other themes;* ░ *= percentage of social welfare;* ▫ *= percentage of foreign assistance;* □ *= percentage of themes for national security in the annual State of the Union messages. In this figure, the four peaks for national security are marked by four historic events: the Korean War, the launching of Sputnik, the Cuban missile crisis, and the War in Vietnam.*

TABLE 2
Dimensions of Competing Perceived Needs (Message-Rank Data, 1946–1971)

Themes	F_1 Foreign vs. Social Welfare	F_2 Econo. Stability	F_3 Equality	F_4 Fiscal Conservatism	F_5 Peace
Foreign aid	.79				
National defense	.77				
Space & tech.	.55				
Unemployment & poverty	−.86				
Health	−.82				
Farm & farmers		.85			
Economy & inflation		.82			
Civil rights			.86		
Education			.85		
Balanced budget				.79	
Urban problems				−.65	
Peace & negotiation					.88
% Total Variance	27.2	14.7	15.8	11.2	11.2 80.0%

leviated. The president's concern with education constitutes a different dimension of needs perceived, along with civil rights. Education is approached from the viewpoint of the egalitarian principle, such as "equality of opportunity."

The analysis also indicates that a president tends to view national security, foreign assistance and the space program as a set of needs that should be handled together. The reader will recall that in the factor analysis of the budget described above, "national defense" varied independently of "international affairs." What does this imply? A speculation is that over the entire period military policies and strategies did not go hand in hand with a framework of foreign policy. This relationship changed in the sixties, however. In a factor analysis for the budget data of 1959–1971, "international affairs and finance" correlates 0.97 with the "defense vs. welfare" factor.

It is possible to conjecture that at the turn of the decade, either the Defense or the State Department was gaining in importance over the other if the budget is viewed as a quantitative indicator of departmental activities. The possibility of the Defense Department having gained more control than the State Department seems more plausible for explaining what happened.[25]

In order to explore how the relative emphasis given to each theme varies from year to year during different administrations, factor analysis was applied, treating each year as a variable. The analysis indicates that there were five distinct clusters of years, grouped around common characteristics.

The first cluster of years may be called the "cold war era." Many of the Eisenhower years are grouped here. In this period there was considerable stress on national security and foreign assistance, on the buildup of military strength and on national survival in the cold war.

The Korean War in particular changed the national environment perceived by decisionmakers. The shift of Truman's verbal behavior from 1950 to 1951 is striking.

In 1950 he stood firm toward "challenges of communism," which, "in its ruthless struggle for power, seizes upon our imperfections and takes advantage of the delays and setbacks" of democratic nations. But he used only 4.8 percent of his speech for national security. This makes a striking contrast with 61 percent in 1951, his first message after the outbreak of the Korean War. In that message he devoted only 3.0 percent to the needs of the economy in contrast with 20.0 percent in the previous year. He stressed that "many of the things we would normally do must be curtailed or postponed," because "the threat of world war is real." In 1952 he made it clear again that "we have no choice but to build up the defense." The cold war era was opened with the acceptance or even encouragement of the American public as indicated in public opinion polls favoring an active role in world politics.

The second group of years is characterized by postwar adjustment to peace. There is a relatively high emphasis on conversion to a peacetime economy, peace and negotiation, and above all, return to a balanced budget. The whole nation is urged to be prepared for demobilization and release of this tension. This pattern is consistently revealed in the postwar years of three administrations.

[25] According to one observer, "the State Department is scarcely equipped to have the last word on allocation of the defense budget, even though its views on the issue should obviously be given some weight." K. Clark, *President and the Management of National Security*, p. 19.

TABLE 3
Grouping of Years by Needs as Perceived by Presidents

Incumbent President	Year	F_1 Years of Cold War	F_2 Years of Con- version	F_3 Years of Guns & Butter	F_4 Years of Equal- ity	F_5 Years of Decis- ion	Mean Rank Order
Truman	1951	.50					1) Defense
"	1952	.75					2) Foreign Aid
Eisenhower	1953	.88					3) Budget
"	1957	.62					4) Economy
"	1958	.74					5) Science &
"	1959	.91					Technology
"	1960	.65					
Truman	1946		.88				1) Economy
"	1947		.86				2) Budget
Eisenhower	1954		.73				3) Poor
"	1955	.50	.55				4) Health
"	1956		.78				5) Peace &
Nixon	1970		.77				Negotiation
"	1971		.55				
Kennedy	1961			.70			1) Poor
Johnson	1964	−.59		.69			2) Defense
"	1966			.61			3) Education
"	1967			.86		.56	4) Health
"	1969			.69			5) Urban Problems
Truman	1943				.91		1) Economy
"	1949				.92		2) Health
Kennedy	1962	−.54			.58		3) Civil Rights
"	1963			.53	.53		4) Agriculture
							5) Education
Truman	1950					.81	1) Peace & Negot.
Johnson	1965					.90	2) Defense
"	1968					.87	3) Foreign Aid
							4) Economy
							5) Poor
Percent Variance		20.0	17.3	15.4	12.1	15.1	80.9 percent

The third group of years are those in which the messages express as much concern about domestic problems, such as unemployment, the economy, education, civil rights and so on, as about national defense. Themes of international peace or foreign economic assistance except for the sake of national security are relatively less apparent. In the four Johnson years that cluster here, high priority was given to both defense and social problems.

There was an explicit effort in these messages to justify the war in Vietnam in terms of national security. In 1966 Johnson showed his firm determination on Vietnam, "but we will give our fighting men what they must have, every gun and every decision, whatever the cost or whatever the challenge."

There was more concern in these years for urban problems than for rural ones. It is not surprising that two Kennedy years are clustered on this dimension. In 1961 his accentuated theme was the economy and how to "get the country moving again." However, he gave attention to space research and security as well in his pronounced effort to build a credible deterrent. Keynesian economics became a theoretical tool of expansionistic policies while a "balanced budget" also appeared tenaciously in each message. Economic problems such as labor-management disputes began to be included specifically as part of the national agenda. Those years grouped here are years of "guns and butter," those in which the messages stressed an effort to balance foreign and domestic needs.

The fourth cluster of years may be called "the years of equality." There was a particular emphasis in the messages of these years on equality or civil rights and on economic growth. The first weight was given to economic prosperity. Yet "investment in youth," "safeguarding its health" and "protecting the basic human rights of its citizens" were particularly emphasized as a means "to strengthen the nation," as in 1963, or because the "basic sources of our strength are spiritual" as in 1948.

The fifth group of years, which includes Johnson's program for the "Great Society" in 1965, is characterized by a heavy emphasis on international peace, economic cooperation with foreign countries and national security, though high priority is also given to domestic problems. It seems ironic that peace is particularly emphasized in the messages immediately preceeding a major war both in 1950 and 1965. There was a grave choice for the nation between war and peace.

Compare Table 3 with the plot of the budgetary course taken by the nation in Figures 1 and 3. On the whole the "years of the cold war" correspond to the decade of "hawk-conservative"; the years of "guns and butter" are mostly in the sixties, which fits the theory of "hawk-activism." One important difference, however, in the presidential perception of national needs is that the years of the sixties divide into three clusters, reflecting a notable shift in a brief period. In short the data indicate that the sixties was the most turbulent era.

It seems fair to say that within the period since World War II, there have been notable shifts of patterns in presidential perception of national needs, as well as in the allocation of resources, thus reflecting the changing priorities of the nation. From a longer historical perspective these changes may seem merely a matter of degree. But in these times a difference of degree counts.

What then did these variations mean to the nation, and how can they be explained in terms of the nation's struggle with the changing environment, foreign or domestic? The focus will be narrowed down to the two spectra of controversy on national priorities discussed above, "hawk" versus "dove" and "activism" versus "conservatism." Did this nation really buy national security? If so, what price did the nation pay for it?

4. FOREIGN CRISIS AND ECONOMIC GROWTH

Almost no American would argue that the United States has no need of a defense posture. There is a general consensus that it takes great cost and sacrifice for this nation to survive in the nuclear age. The real issue is, how much defense is enough to protect this nation and its vital interests at home and abroad from existing and potential threats posed by hostile forces?

A hawk argues that the high priority given to national security, and thus high defense spending, has been necessitated by the foreign situation. The high cost has been, it is claimed, simply a response to foreign developments which is necessary for national survival. What is implied in such an argument is the evident assumption that any additional defense buildup will contribute to national security.[26]

[26] Though it is a difficult task to estimate the society's benefits and costs from additional units of many types of federal expenditures, the problem of priorities arises when even national security is assumed to be a matter of degree. If additional defense expenditures do not add to the national security, such spending

A dove follows a different logic. He emphasizes that an arms race is a mutual provocation. Therefore, to ward off a nuclear war that, if it ever happened, would leave no victor, a race for peace is suggested. High defense preparedness, it is often argued, contributes not to security, but to the "likelihood of resort to a military solution."[27]

History offers no experiment as to the correctness of one or the other of these theories in precipitating or averting a nuclear war. But in an attempt to test how these alternative theories fit into the world situation, the defense budget can be studied in its relationship to foreign crisis. The difficulty, however, is that there is no agreed upon yardstick to measure a foreign crisis.

---

would be useless. Military decisionmakers always tend to emphasize that defense posture is essential under a mounting foreign threat. In his first "posture statement," Defense Secretary Melvin Laird declared, "Never have the challenges to our national security exceeded in number and gravity those which we found on taking office."

Laird later said again, "Any further cut of the defense budget would be a very dangerous course." To press his point he pointed to a new Russian threat, that is, "the Soviet Navy has more ships deployed away from the Soviet Union than ever before," *New York Times,* (August 22, 1969).

[27] R. Barnet puts this point bluntly: "The policy of seeking national security through permanent war preparation and intermittent wars directly contributes to the crisis of planetary survival, . . . it generates an atmosphere of conflict and competition in which the minimal measures of cooperation necessary to insure planetary survival become impossible." Richard J. Barnet, "The Illusion of Security," *Foreign Policy,* no. 3 (Summer 1971), p. 84.

Walter Reuther takes a similar stand: "It has been apparent that the massing of armies and armament leads to war, not to peace." Walter Reuther, "Goals for America," Kenneth Boulding, ed., *National Priorities,* p., 66.

The Cuban missile crisis, which is generally believed to have been a success of nuclear U. S. superiority, is subject to an alternative interpretation. Ralph Lapp, *Arms beyond Doubt,* pp. 7–10. He puts it this way: "I believe that Khrushchev's decision to invest missiles in Cuba was not an insane gesture, but rather an act of political desperation designed to offset the U. S. missile advantage in the early 60s. Thus Kennedy may have induced the Cuban crisis by his missile decision." There is a view that the "missile gap" was a myth. Lapp states again: "We had built more missiles than we needed, and we had most likely forced the Soviets to do the same." Sidney Lens, *Military Industrial Complex,* pp. 81–92. "With strategies worked out in such detail and with the forces at hand to implement them, it is virtually inevitable that there will be a few occasions when the American government, whatever the rhetoric of its leaders, will be carried across the brink to actual combat." C. Wright Mills may have been simplistic when he prophesied in 1958 that "the immediate cause of World War III is the preparation for it," but there is a large element of truth to what he said. "The mere availability of plans and weapons is a temptation to use them. It may be a temptation which is acceded to in a minority of instances, but it is enough to make the preparation for war an independent factor in creating it." C. Wright Mills, *The Causes of World War III* (New York: Ballantine Books, 1960), p. 86.

Foreign crisis is basically a matter of perceived environment rather than an objective external state of affairs. Therefore it involves a cognitive process. One way to measure an unmeasurable environment is, as in the common practice of psychology,[28] by observing the response of the subject to the environment to be measured. When there is an international crisis judged to threaten vital interests, the nation will deploy more troops to foreign bases ready to fight a war or for any other contingency. Thus the changing level of troops abroad in relation to the total military force will indicate the degree of overseas involvement. The index used was the annual change in the percentage of U. S. troops abroad as a proportion of total U. S. military forces.

Presidential perception of security needs, as expressed in his speeches, is another indicator used to measure foreign crisis.

If a hawk's position is indeed determined by his observation of external events, then the correlation between the defense budget and preceding foreign crisis will turn out to be high, since high defense expenditure is presumably only a response to the foreign environment. Conversely, if a dove's argument holds, foreign crisis or overseas military involvement will follow, rather than precede, high military expenditures. One necessary assumption is that future events cannot *cause* precedent events.

The result of correlational analysis appears to support both hawks' and doves' positions with some qualifications. First, there is some indication that defense expenditure varies at least somewhat with the president's perception of the need for security. The size of the defense budget in relation to the total federal budget is to some extent explained (30.3 percent) by fluctuations in the proportion of the State of the Union message which is devoted to discussing security. But defense expenditures do not show significant correlation with the president's view of security needs until

[28] For instance, a widely used method of attitude measurement is to let the subject report his response to some experimental stimuli. This is actually equivalent to "measuring attitude from behavior, since the report is a kind of overt behavior." See Charles Kiesler et al. *Attitude Change* (New York: John Wiley, 1969) pp. 23–38. Harold and Margaret Sprout, "An Ecological Paradigm for the Study of International Politics" Princeton Center of International Studies, Research Monograph, no. 30 (Princeton: Princeton University Press, 1968). They discuss the "psychological interaction" of an actor with his environment, as the actor perceives it. In analyzing the bearing of conditions and events of the environment on behavior, what matters is how the milieu appears to the decisionmakers, not how the milieu actually is or how it might appear to a hypothetical, sane, omniscient observer.

the time-serial effect, the effect of the previous budget upon the present one, is removed. The extent to which the defense budget is only marginally related to the president's perception of security needs is more evident when the defense budget as a percentage of the GNP, rather than as a percentage of the total federal budget, is used as an indicator of the priority given defense.

Dependent Variable = Defense Budget, percent of GNP_{t_1}

Independent Variable	Regression Coefficient	Standard Error	Cumulative Percent Variance Explained
Defense, Percent GNP at t_0	.44	.057	63 percent
Security needs (Message length)	.106	.026	76 percent
Constant = 2.89	(Significant at 0.001 percent level)		

Thus it seems fair to give partial credit to the hawk's argument that high defense priority has been merely a response to the changing foreign environment and the security needs it has generated.

More important, however, is the persistent evidence that foreign crisis or overseas involvement, as indicated by an increase in the proportion of U. S. troops stationed abroad, is a consequence of high defense priority rather than its cause. After time-serial effects are removed from the variables, the following relationship persists between military priority and foreign involvement:

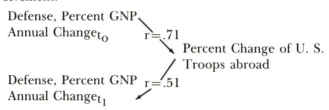

Note that the U. S. troop level abroad is "as of June 30" of each year, when the fiscal year ends. Awareness of the exact location of the variable in time is essential for possible causal inference. This empirical relationship tends to reinforce the dove's position that intentions and actions of this country are largely responsible for foreign crises. In exploring contingencies which might affect the vital interests of the U. S. under conditions of nuclear stale-

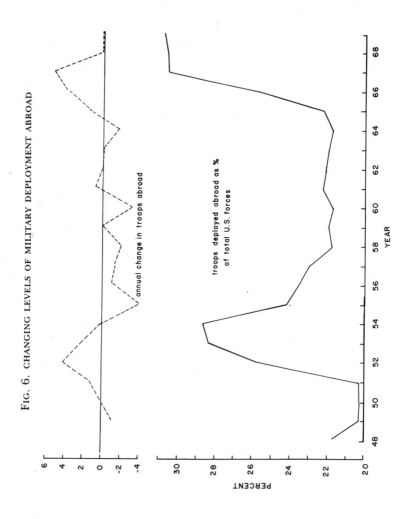

FIG. 6. CHANGING LEVELS OF MILITARY DEPLOYMENT ABROAD

mate, the judgment of the policy choices of the decisionmakers may well lead to a spiral of interaction between higher defense priorities and military solutions.[29]

A possible explanation for the phenomenon of military spending seeming to cause foreign crises is psychological. High defense expenditure will provide more plans and readiness: "Maybe the greatest risk from possessing a needlessly big military force is the temptation to use it too readily."[30]

Next, what is the relationship of defense spending to economic growth? One focus of the controversy between fiscal activism and conservatism is whether defense spending preempts national resources or whether it increases economic prosperity. Keynesian theory states that government spending can play a role in the economy when the economy is sluggish. But because government spending is limited by domestic politics, some economists believe that the economy can receive the stimulus it needs from defense expenditure.[31]

The argument is that resources will remain idle if their use is not prompted by effective creation of aggregate demand. Yet some Keynesian economists argue that not all public spending is beneficial. Tobin points out, "demand can be expanded in ways that do not accelerate, indeed may even retard, the growth in capacity itself."[32] It is a common belief, however, that if defense spending goes down abruptly, it will create difficulties for a few sectors of the economy and certain cities and regions that are deeply dependent on military contracts.

The data show that, with a six month lag, the unemployment rate is negatively associated with defense expenditure as percentage of GNP statistically significant at the 0.05 level. However, if the effect of the trend which unemployment statistics have shown over a long period of time is removed, this relationship almost

[29]C. Schultze discusses "the propensity of military planners to prepare against almost every conceivable contingency or risk." Charles Schultze, "Balancing Military and Civilian Programs" Kenneth Boulding, *National Priorities*, p. 41. Note that the general purpose forces were built to fight simultaneously nuclear, conventional and limited war. A definition of "threat" posed by a happening in a foreign land is likely to give weight to the judgment of professional military men.

[30]Bruce Russett, *What Price Vigilance?* p. 183.

[31]Kennedy and Johnson were supposedly the two presidents who took Keynsian economics to heart. Charles L. Cole, *The Economic Fabric of Society* (New York: Harcourt Brace Jovanovich, Inc., 1969), pp. 225–226.

[32]James Tobin, *National Economic Policy*, p. 94.

disappears. Thus it is hard to credit defense expenditure with a positive effect on unemployment.

There is, however, considerable indication that defense expenditure is detrimental to the real GNP growth rate. For the period 1946–1969, 61 percent of the variation in the real GNP growth rate can be related inversely to defense expenditure as a percentage of GNP.

Linear Regression
Independent Variable — Defense Expenditure as a percentage of GNP
(1946–1969, one year lag)

Dependent Variable	Regression Coefficients	Percent Explained
Real GNP Growth Rate	–.49**	61 percent**
Consumer Price Index	.24*	22 percent*

**significant at 0.01 level
*significant at 0.05 level

The negative impact of defense spending on economic growth is thus clearly visible. Explanations are many. First of all, it would be misleading to say that a high priority on defense expenditure was the product of a deliberate fiscal policy. The high level of defense spending has been primarily brought about by sudden foreign crises, war and commitments abroad. This has complicated fiscal-monetary policy.

An official view has been that American prosperity does not depend on the defense buildup and would not need high military spending to support it in peace time: "The cost of war has been a load for the economy to carry—not a supporting 'prop.' "[33]

It may be true that a sharp cut in defense spending would cause transitional unemployment in areas with a high proportion of defense industry. It is recognized that military contracts go to a highly concentrated market with a relatively small group of companies doing most of the business. For this reason most of the increases, if any, in domestic employment caused by defense spending tend to be centered in industrialized areas where the labor force and the industrial base are likely to be mobile and which would therefore be able to adapt fairly quickly to change. This is perhaps the reason why the decrease in the relative importance of the defense budget is not high-

[33]"Report to the President, from the Cabinet Coordinating Committee on Economic Planning for the End of Vietnam Hostilities" (1968), p. 187.

ly correlated with unemployment as a national aggregate.

Next, it is conceivable that the diversion of productive investment in human resources such as manpower training, education and health to investment in defense as shown above, is responsible particularly for the subsequent low GNP growth rate. The loss in productivity during the war years is demonstrated by statistics;[34] during the late fifties and early sixties, the rate of growth of output per man-hour was 3.2 percent on the average; but in some of the major Vietnam war years the rate fell to 0.8 percent in 1969 and 2.0 percent in 1967, though the year 1968 showed a good performance of 3.3 percent.

When high defense expenditure has resulted from sudden war or other such foreign commitments, it has eventually involved a problem of conversion to peacetime, which has complicated the task of fiscal and monetary policy. A war usually necessitates mobilization of resources and their diversion from a consumer-oriented economy to use in effectively prosecuting the war. When the war ends, the economy naturally faces the basic problem of detaching itself from government control or direction.

These arguments tend to be proven valid because the data demonstrate the strong negative correlation between the level of defense spending and the real GNP growth rate.

The belief that high defense spending is essential for economic prosperity often stems from the widely shared observation that World War II solved the Great Depression; it is said that the need for war production and mobilization enabled the government "to spend itself out of the Depression."[35] However, this lesson, which is derived from only one historical fact, is at variance with the relationship described above between defense spending and real economic growth in the postwar era.

A comparison with other economies will illuminate this point further. If war production or a high defense budget were essential for the economic viability of a mature capitalist state, then the countries with the most heavy military spending would show high rates of economic growth.

This does not hold true in most of the European countries, which demonstrated far better economic growth rates than the U. S. with much less defense spending than the U. S. because they

[34] *The Review of Radical Political Economics, Special Issue* (August, 1970), p. 2.
[35] Charles Cole, *Economic Fabric of Society*, p. 224.

relied on the U. S. military shield. The average growth rate of twenty-two Western capitalist political systems including Japan for 1950–1960 was 4.61 percent with an average of only 3.3 percent of national output used for defense purpose. The correlation between defense expenditure and economic growth rate in Western political systems turns out to be negative although statistically insignificant. For example, West Germany, which in one year allocated 4.1 percent of total national output to defense, showed a 5.3 percent growth rate in output per employee, almost double that of the U. S., and Japan, with defense spending only 1.0 percent of total output, achieved a 7.7 percent growth rate in the same year.[36]

The impact of a high military priority on the American economy is notable in the postwar years, 1946, 1954, 1967 and 1969. Because the magic of compound interest makes a small difference in the GNP growth rate much bigger and more meaningful in the future, the burden of heavy defense expenditure

[36]For twenty-two western countries, including Japan, Pearsonian correlation coefficients were calculated. Countries included in this analysis are Australia, Austria, Belgium, Canada, Denmark, Finland, France, W. Germany, Iceland, Ireland, Italy, Japan, Luxemburg, New Zealand, Netherlands, Norway, Portugal, Spain, Sweden, Switzerland, the U.K. and the U.S.A. The data are from Charles L. Taylor and Michael C. Hudson, *World Handbook of Political and Social Indicators*, 2d ed. (New Haven, Conn.: Yale University Press, 1972).

Correlation Coefficients

Indices of Defense Expenditure	Indices of GNP Growth rate		
	Average 1960–1965	Average 1950–1965	Per capita 1950–1965
Per capita 1965	−.31	−.14	−.15
Percent of GNP* 1965	−.29	−.17	−.13
Percent of GNP** 1965	−.35	−.13 ⸍	−.13

(No coefficient is statistically significant.)

*U.S. Arms Control and Disarmament Agency Figures.
**Institute of Strategic Studies Figures.

A caveat is in order in interpreting this table, since the data for GNP growth rate precede the data for defense spending from the point of view of time. GNP growth rate is an annual average for the period ending in 1965, whereas defense expenditure is for 1965 alone. Thus the point argued in the text is relevant to this table when the defense expenditure in 1965 is interpreted as not different considerably from the overall level of defense spending through the period.

falls on both present and future generations by retarding economic growth. Here seems to lie a grave "offense of defense."

Then what is the picture of defense expenditure when it is considered as a dependent variable, since decisionmakers are presumably responding to the changing environment? What are the primary causes of defense spending? In the data there is no evidence that defense spending is increased to solve the unemployment problem. The unemployment rate correlated −0.45 with the next year's defense budget as a percentage of GNP. On the contrary the data indicate that since World War II the defense buildup has happened when the economy was in full gear. It is possible to reason that a decisionmaker can afford to be more sensitive to foreign developments when the economy has no serious problems. The Vietnam buildup provides a good example. It happened when the economy had shown its longest and most balanced growth in history. Because of the defense buildup, it is pointed out in one official view, fiscal-monetary policy has been handicapped.

It is evident that defense expenditure depends only partially on foreign crisis, and that it seems to generate more foreign involvement with a severe negative impact on economic prosperity. Then what explains the high level of defense expenditure? Much of the explanation seems to lie in the phenomenon of bureaucratic inertia called "gradualism."

There is a well-taken argument that the budgetary process is incremental, not a "zero-base budgeting."[37] It is argued that the largest determining factor of the size and content of this year's budget is last year's, with special attention given to a narrow range of increase or decrease. In the case of defense budgeting, Benson deplores such a situation:

The Defense Department budgeting process virtually concedes last year's amount and focuses on whatever incremental changes have been requested. The result, of course, is higher budgets, with past year's errors compounded year after year.[38]

This is not peculiar to the defense budget. All items of the budget show significantly systematic auto-correlation. On the

[37]Aaron Wildavsky, *The Politics of the Budgetary Process* (Boston: Little Brown, 1964), p. 13.
[38]As quoted by William Proxmire in Kenneth Boulding, *National Priorities*, p. 129.

average 70 percent of the variation of each expenditure can be predicted by its previous value. It is hard to believe that this is merely a coincidence.

Once a commitment to a defense program is made, the momentum is often too great for it to be subjected to complete reevaluation or control. Actually the Bureau of the Budget applies different rules to military budget recommendations from those it uses to control civilian programs.[39]

The data show that 63 percent of the variation in the defense budget as raw amount can be predicted by a simple equation for the 1947–1971 data. (The statistical significance of a coefficient is indicated by the standard error in parenthesis, since the coefficient divided by the standard error gives the t-test score; e denotes random error.)

$$\text{Def}_{t_1} = 0.72\ \text{Def}_{t_0} + 2.8 + e$$
$$(\text{S.E.} = 0.12)$$

(in billion dollars)

What is more, if one knows how much the last budget was and how much it increased last year over the year before, 86 percent of the variation in the new defense budget can be predicted by using the following equation:

$$D_{t_1} = 0.46\ D_{t_0} + 0.42 \triangle D_{t_0} + 0.42 + e$$
$$(\text{S.E.} = .04) \qquad (0.06)$$

(in billion dollars)

In this equation, both regression coefficients are statistically significant at the 0.01 level.

The problem of gradualism leads into theories regarding organization, but what is important is that high levels of military spending reflect the distribution of power in the bureaucracy, since, as Halperin puts it, "Organizations are concerned not only about their absolute share of the budget, but also their relative share of a relevant larger budget."[40]

[39]Adam Yarmolinsky, *The Military Establishment*, p. 87. President Nixon has officially ruled that the defense budget must be subjected to reevaluation by the Bureau of the Budget.

[40]Morton Halperin, "Why Bureaucrats Play Games," *Foreign Policy*, vol. 2 (Spring 1971). "When American government officials consider a proposed change in foreign policy: they often see and emphasize quite different things and

Frequently, after a crisis, the Defense Department, whose functions were expanded during the crisis, tries to argue that "it has now established a new precedent and should continue to perform the new function." This seems to explain the "ratchet effect" of the defense expenditure. This explains why the defense budget seldom goes down as rapidly as it went up.

If it is true that the military establishment, with its sense of mission and its professional outlook, prefers a larger to a smaller budget and supports policy changes which are likely to lead to a larger budget, it is understandable why foreign crisis has a positive correlation with last year's budget.

Based on these results, a simple model of defense priorities was constructed; 89 percent of the variation in the defense budget can be explained by the following equation:

$$D_{t_1} = 0.55 \ D_{t_0} + 0.09 \ S_{t_0} + 0.35 \ G_1 + 0.97 + e$$
$$\quad (0.05) \qquad (0.02) \qquad (0.07)$$

> where,
> D = defense budget as a percentage of GNP
> S = percent of security contents in Presidential
>   State of the Union Message
> G = GNP growth rate

This equation can be put in verbal terms: the relative size of defense expenditure is determined by the previous year's budget's share of the gross national product, security needs as perceived by the president and the rate of economic growth, with previous defense expenditure being by far the most important item.

In the final analysis of the extent to which the defense budget is determined by previous budgets, incrementalism may be entrenched in the ideals or values of this democratic system as it is justified both by complex institutional arrangements and partially by the need for continuity of policy. But in face of the mounting evidence that national choices of policy have an impact which results in significant feedback to the environment, a call for reordering national priorities is not irrelevant in the light of the way the system of assigning priorities—with both its costs and its

---

reach different conclusions. A proposal to withdraw American troops from Europe, for example, is to the Army a threat to its budget and size. . . ."

benefits—has worked during the last almost three decades. Richard Barnet raises, if in somewhat harsh words, an important choice before the nation:

Can we change America's present destructive definition of national security without dismantling the bureaucratic structures which promote a military definition of the national interests? Can we still have a military establishment anything like the present one without continuing to have an interventionist policy?[41]

Conclusion

What conclusion can be drawn from these analyses? Within the context of the postwar era, the high level of defense spending has been the price this nation felt it should pay. This nation has attempted to buy national security in the sense that additional defense spending was a response of the nation to a changing foreign environment. But there is reason to believe that the United States at the same time has also bought some foreign crises.

The price has been real. The burden of defense has meant for the nation not only less butter, less schools and less hospitals but also less prosperity than it was capable of achieving. There is a clear danger of a possible spiral of "crisis-begets-defense, defense-begets-crisis." That would mean a much heavier economic burden for present and future generations.

When the economy has appeared to be growing rapidly, there has been less grumbling about the way the pie is divided. But when it grows more slowly than expected, there will be greater displeasure.

One sign is in the "revolt of the masses" that have turned against the high priority given the military. Whatever the trigger event may have been, the people may have been wiser than their leaders in learning the lesson. The analysis in this study on the whole tends to justify grave concern that the grand choice before this nation is taking the form of welfare state or warfare state. The strength of the political system, at least to a foreign eye, seems to lie in the extent to which the political process is receptive to the new national mood.

[41]Richard Barnet, *Illusion of Security*, pp. 84–85.

Appendix: Further Results

It seems appropriate to present further results of this analysis for the interested reader, since this research has been based on a broader conceptual scheme than has been reported in the text. Even if a nation is broadly viewed as adapting to or coping with changing environments, foreign or domestic, like a biotic organism, it is basically the human agent that determines what will be the final policy output in the form of national priorities.

The primary goal of this analysis has been to demonstrate a theoretical linkage between two conceptual areas, national priorities as perceived by the president and the political environment.

This analysis is not intended as a conclusive finding, but rather an invitation to further investigation with emphasis on the context in which national priorities are set or operate. Factor analysis, canonical analysis and multiple regression analysis have been the basic methods used in this attempt to uncover the underlying dynamics.[42]

---

[42]To understand the process a large number of variables must be reduced to a small number. The usefulness of factor analysis is in the reduction of many variables into a smaller, more manageable set. If a small number of original variables can be found which account for most of the variance, then considerable time and effort is saved. However, an exploratory factor analysis is only a preliminary phase of analysis. Once the investigator has decided what the important variables are, he will want to know the interrelations among them and the mechanism of their formation. (Rudolph Rummel, *Applied Factor Analysis*. 1970).

A further advantage of factor analysis is that an individual unit of analysis (a year in the case of this paper) can be given a composite score in the factor space by weighting each variable in proportion to its contribution to the factor that represents the underlying construct. Such use of factor analysis is a combination of psychometric and scaling theory.

The goal of canonical analysis is to find the number of ways in which two sets of variables are related, the strengths of the relationships and the nature of the relationships so defined. The procedure makes it possible to determine the maximum correlation between a set of predictor variables and a set of (rather than a single) criterion variables. The advantage is that the researcher is no longer required either to pick and choose among criteria in order to select that one which seems best to reflect the behavior being studied or to assign arbitrary weight to the criterion variables. The logic is to define canonical variates and a linear transformation of each set of variables so that the new composite variable from one set correlates maximally with that of the other set. (M. G. Kendall, *A Course in Multi-Variate Analysis*. 1957).

There are commonly two statistical criteria used to judge how good the fit is. The overall fit between two sets of variables is usually represented by trace correlation, a mean variance explained. This measures how much variance of the criterion set of variables can be reproduced by the predictor set of variables. The

A working hypothesis is that there must be a dynamic relationship between national priorities and the political environment. National priorities may be determined in part in such a way as to meet changing situations, and once the priorities are determined, they will affect the situation, whether or not the effect was desired. For instance, the emphasis given domestic programs at the beginning of the sixties is credited to the sagging economy, which in turn can be traced back to the high defense expenditure which followed the Korean War. In general, federal fiscal policy is expected to have not only a stabilizing influence on the economy but also a stimulating effect on economic growth.

The research concern here centers around the extent to which domestic or foreign environment influences the determination of national priorities. Eighteen socioeconomic variables were factor-analyzed. Unlike the two sets of data analyzed in the text of this study, this needs clarification. Each of the two sets of data—budgets and presidential messages—can be characterized by a coherent and synchronic interrelationship, while the group of socioeconomic variables is a collection of different kinds of variables.

A criterion in selecting the socioeconomic variables was the relevance of the variable to the themes that appear in the State of the Union Message, as well as theoretical ground. As possible indicators of foreign crisis perceived by decisionmakers, as reported in the text, this selection included the level of the U. S. troops deployed abroad and the U. N. vote on the China problem as indicators of a changing international climate. Because the budgetary process represents stabilized planning on an annual rather than a day-by-day calculation, annual aggregates rather than particular events were chosen as the primary form of the data. Note that in this analysis every variable is transformed into the yearly difference or change rate except that the number of war dead and that of civil disturbance have been subjected to logarithmic transformation. Whatever functional simultaneous or lagged relationships they may have assumed, it is environmental conditions as they exist in each year that force decisionmakers to make choices.

---

second measure is canonical correlation between corresponding canonical variates from each set, indicating the strength of the particular relationship.

Seven dimensions of the changing environment were revealed by factor analysis. Based on this analysis, seven indexes were selected as representing the seven environmental variables.

Diagram A

Environmental Variables	Index Selected
Foreign crisis	Annual change in percentage of U.S. troops abroad
Economic growth	Real GNP growth rate
Economic stability	Annual change in consumer price index
Social instability	Logarithmic value of civil disturbance
Social frustration	Divorce rate change
International climate	U.N. vote rate change in suSport Gf Mainland China
Imbalance of trade	Import/export rate

First, based on each factor analysis on each data set, canonical analysis was conducted to reveal any environment-perception-budget cycle, with appropriate time lag. Overall fit between hypothesized dyads of the different factor score sets is indicated in Diagram A. What is striking is the staying power of the budgets. Sixty-nine percent of the variance in budget composition can be reproduced by knowledge of the budget last year.

On the other hand it is indicated that a president's perceived needs have *much less* effect on the shape of final budget output. The trace canonical correlation between budget composition (1941–1972) and message length (1946–1971) turned out to be .690. In other words, 47.3 percent of national priorities as expressed in the budget composition can be explained by presidential perception. On the whole, the incrementalism model holds better. Only the table of canonical analysis for environment-budget interaction is reported here. Some results of the canonical analysis deserve mentioning when the focus is on meaningful coefficients:

$$.50 \text{ (Defense)} + .90 \text{ (Infrastructure)} \blacktriangleright\!\!\longrightarrow$$
$$.61 \text{ (Economic Recession)} + .88 \text{ (Social Frustration)}$$
$$+ .52 \text{ (Social Instability)}$$
$$(r^2 = .723)$$

The analysis indicates that a weighted sum of defense expenditure and infrastructure tend to *increase* a weighted sum of social frustration, economic recession and social instability. This does not support, at least as far as the United States is concerned, the theory that rational decisionmakers are likely to engage in aggressive foreign behavior or building armaments in an attempt to divert domestic instability or frustration. On the contrary, this analysis tends to indicate that domestic instability or social frustration is likely to be followed by a decrease in the priority given military spending, which implies that a political system is to a certain degree receptive to social demands. On the whole, however, it can be said that this receptiveness is rather marginal in the light of the large proportion of variance in defense spending which is explained by the shape of last year's priorities.

The bivariate relationships among selected original variables is partly revealed in the correlation coefficients presented in Fig. B. The focus was to highlight bivariate relationships between defense expenditure as percentage of total federal outlays and major environmental variables. Bivariate linkages between the priority given defense and a multiplicity of hypothesized determinants of the environment, and the effect of these relationships are apparent in the diagram. First, presidential perception of the need for national security explains about 30 percent of defense expenditure. On the other hand, social instability tends to cause a decrease in the relative importance of defense expenditure and an increase in the relative importance of urban spending. Government infrastructure expenditure seems to be influenced by presidential emphasis on foreign assistance. It is to be recalled that in the factor analysis decribed above, international affairs and finance loaded on the factor of "infrastructure." Though not reported here, the analyses indicate recession or economic instability tend to be associated with the relative importance of infrastructure spending. When the economic situation suggests the need for government action in fiscal policy or other measures, general government expenditure is likely to be increased.

As an alternative method to investigate further, the relationships between defense, presidential perception of security needs, foreign crisis and the environment, multiple regression was applied to a reduced number of variables from each of original data sets. Results relevant to defense spending are reported in Table B.

FIG. A. INTERACTION OF NATIONAL PRIORITIES WITH ENVIRONMENT

COMPOSITION

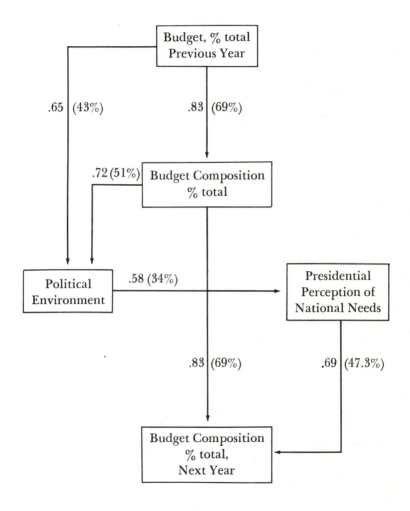

Coefficients given are trace *correlations fom canonical analysis based on the factor scores of each data set. This criterion measures the overall goodness of fit between the two batteries of variables linked by arrows. The average percent of variance explained is given in each set of brackets.*

FIG. B. INTERACTION OF DEFENSE PRIORITY WITH ENVIRONMENT

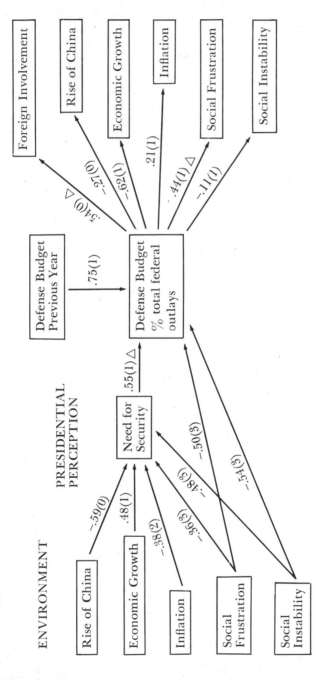

Correlation coefficients between two indicators linked by arrows are given with number of years lag in parentheses. Original variables were used as specified above. A small triangle (△) means that the bivariate correlation is based on annual difference of the defense budget as a percent of the total federal outlays.

TABLE A

Interaction of National Priorities and National Environment
—Canonical Analysis—

I. Impact of Budget Composition on Environment (one year lag)

Budget Composition				Environment							
Defense	Infra-structure	Urban	Econ. Stability	Econ. Recession	Social frustration	China	Foreign crisis	Social instability	Trade Imbalance	R	% Var. Explained
.50*	.90*	-.05	-.09	.61*	.88*	-.02	-.12	.52*	-.26	.85	72.3%
-.53*	.19	.87*	.36	-.81*	-.67*	-.26	.69*	.73*	.04	.59	34.8%
-.70*	.40	-.51*	.22	-1.19*	-.57*	.65*	-.20	.33	.29	.46	21.2%

II. Influence of Environment on Budget Composition

Budget Composition				Environment							
Defense	Infra-structure	Urban	Econ. Stability	Econ. Recession	Social frustration	China	Foreign crisis	Social instability	Trade Imbalance	R	% Var. Explained
.10	.92*	-.33	-.69*	.41	.00	-.05	-.24	-.53*	.13	.93	86.5%
-.67*	.32	.68*	-.40	.30	.33	.08	-.05	.79*	.06	.69	47.6%
.74*	.65*	.22	-.10	-.29	.29	-.15	.45	-.08	.77*	.50	25.0%

Coefficients given are canonical coefficients.
Coefficients greater than .50 were asterisked for attention.
Signs were adjusted.

TABLE B
Regressions

Dependent Variable	Independent Variable	Years Lagged	Regression Coefficient	Standard Error	Standardized Coefficient	Probability	Cumulative Variance
Def. % total	Security need (message length) Constant = 39.76	1	.46	.14	.55	.004	30.2%
Def. % total	Def. % total Security need % Constant = 14.2	1 1	.57 .31	.13 .11	.60 .37	.000 .01	50.4% 63.0%
Def. % total	Security need (Message rank) Constant = 29.59	1	2.13	.67	.55	.004	29.9%
Def. % total	Def. % total GNP Growth R Economy need % Troops abroad Constant = −13.16	1 1 1 1	.95 1.93 .86 1.03	.07 .21 .31 .42	.99 .70 .20 .17	.000 .001 .01 .02	50.4% 84.8% 87.5% 90.3%
Def. % total	Civil disturbance GNP Growth R Constant = 55.97	3 2	−7.65 1.15	2.04 .42	−.57 .42	.001 .011	29.5% 47.2%
Security need (Message length)	UN China vote GNP Growth R Troops abroad Civil dist. Constant = 22.54	1 1 1 1	−.98 1.0 2.19 −4.07	.26 .48 1.11 2.37	−.59 .32 .31 −.25	.001 .040 .065 .100	34.4% 44.6% 50.9% 56.9%
GNP Growth R	Def. % total Constant = 12.97	1	−.19	.05	−.61	.001	37.8%
U. S. Troops abroad %	Mil. Procurement % GNP, Change Constant = .257	1	.55	.17	.60	.004	36.4%
Troops abroad % change	Def. % GNP change Constant = .79	0	.29	.07	.70	.000	48.9%

All the results reported here are significant at 0.001 level by Joint–F test

Bibliography

1. Budget Composition:
    U.S. Bureau of the Budget. *The U.S. Budget*, and supplementary documents, *The Budget in Brief, 1944 through 1972*. Washington, D.C.: Government Printing Office.
2. State of Union Messages:
    Fred Israel, ed. *The State of the Union Messages of the Presidents 1905–1966* vol. III. Washington, D.C.: Harold Steinberg & Robert Hector, 1966.
3. Socioeconomic Data:
    GNP growth rate is based on "Flow Fund Accounts, 1945-1968." *Federal Reserve Bulletin* (August 1970), pp. A70 ff.

    Balance of Payments and Gold Stock data come from International Monetary Fund. *International Financial Statistics.* Washington, D.C.: IMF, 1950, 1956, 1964, 1970.Civil Disturbance data are compiled and weighted by population from Adam Yarmolinsky, *The Military Establishment.* New York: Harper & Row, 1971, pp. 165–182.Most of other data are based on *Historical Statistics of the United States, from Colonial Times through 1957,* and its supplementary edition, *Continuation to 1962 and Revisions.* Washington, D.C.: Government Printing Office, 1965, and for later period, *Statistical Abstract of the U.S.*, Washington, D.C.: Government Printing Office, 1964–1970.U.S. troops deployed abroad, U.S. Department of Defense *U.S. Military Logistics* Washington, D.C.: Government Printing Office, 1970.
4. The data compiled and analyzed for this paper will be available at the World Data Analysis Program, Yale University at the request of interested readers.

House Voting on Defense: An Ideological Explanation

Wayne Moyer

I. Why the Correct Explanation of Congressional Voting on Defense Is Important

How do congressmen view defense issues? Is their voting determined by constituency or idiosyncratic factors, or does it reflect other more generalized ideological perspectives on the U. S. role in the world, the "international communist conspiracy," government regulation of society and social welfare programs? Much of the recent debate on the role of the "military-industrial complex" presupposes the former view: that defense preparedness is not really an ideological question, that the driving force behind congressional behavior on such questions as the Anti-Ballistic Missile system is a defense lobby so powerful it can sustain or inflate military expenditures. Yet attempts to link voting behavior with the "military-industrial complex" heretofore have proven inconclusive.[1]

This chapter will attempt to support the hypothesis that, indeed, ideological factors determine House voting on defense questions, and that constituency and idiosyncratic factors

---

[1]See Bruce M. Russett, *What Price Vigilance?* (New Haven, Conn.: Yale University Press, 1970), pp. 56–86; Charles H. Gray and Glen W. Gregory, "Military Spending and Senate Voting: A Correlational Study," *Journal of Peace Research*, vol. 5, no. 1 (1968), pp. 44–54; and Stephen A Cobb, "Defense Spending and Foreign Policy in the House of Representatives," *Journal of Conflict Resolution*, vol. 13, no. 3 (September 1969), pp. 358–369.

(related or not related to the "military-industrial complex") are of only secondary importance.[2] I first shall examine roll call voting patterns to show that voting behavior on defense is close enough to voting patterns on other issues to make an ideological explanation more than plausible. Then, to strengthen the case, multiple regression analysis will show that an ideological model provides better explanatory power for defense voting than do models representing the influence of the "military-industrial complex," constituency or idiosyncratic factors.

Prior to proceeding with the analysis, it is important to deal with two questions. First, why is an analysis of voting patterns more than an academic exercise, since the principal defense budget decision-making locus largely excludes Congress? Second, what difference does it make for the future whether congressional behavior is determined by ideological considerations, constituency considerations or whatever? In answering the first question, one can say that the past half dozen years have seen a great resurgence of congressional interest on defense questions, obviating many of the earlier findings of Huntington and others that the legislature tends to rubber stamp the decisions of the executive.[3] It has become acceptable and even fashionable for congressmen to exercise their prerogatives and attempt to limit the military establishment. Various investigating committees compete with each other in uncovering waste, inefficiency and corruption within the military, while the number of defense roll calls in both House and Senate has increased dramatically.[4] The antiadministration vote has grown steadily with each passing year until now a shift of only forty or so representatives would be sufficient to defeat the ABM deployment or to pass a measure similiar to the Nedzi-Whalan amendment to expedite the U. S. withdrawal from Vietnam.[5] It has become apparent, as Huntington notes, that we are standing on the threshold of an era—where

---

[2]By constituency factors we are referring to variables applicable to the congressional district (i.e. region, party, urbanization, defense expenditures, competitiveness, etc.).

[3]See Samuel P. Huntington, *The Common Defense* (New York: Columbia University Press, 1961), pp. 123–146.

[4]A dramatic increase in the number of roll calls on an issue is considered indicative of increasing salience and growing controversiality. Thus, when the national consensus existed over defense expenditures in the 1950s and early 1960s, there were few defense roll calls in the House. Now that the consensus has broken down there are many roll calls.

[5]The ABM vote in 1969 was 223 in favor, 141 opposed; Nedzi-Whalen was rejected in 1971 by a vote of 255 to 158.

instead of the military and Congress pushing weapons on the executive, now the military and the executive will have to try to persuade an ever more recalcitrant Congress.[6]

Increasing recalcitrance is not necessarily equivalent to an increasing role for Congress, but it is probably a precondition. The budget is still *sent* to Congress, and cuts or additions at best can still have only *marginal* impact in the short run. However, cutting research and development on certain strategic programs (ABM, SABMIS, ULMS, etc.) can have policy implications. Congress' new interest, if focused on *key* issues with strategic implications, can help mold basic U. S. defense policies. Continued concern may also encourage congressional expertise and reform of the structural machinery, which may allow Congress to insert itself into the budget-making process. Roll call analysis allows us to gain insights into the current congressional interest, opposition and activity in the policy making process, and for activists it facilitates identification of desirable qualities for future congressmen.

This still begs the second question—why it makes much difference whether ideological or constituency pressures best explain voting behavior. The answer here is clear: the ability of Congress to exercise a judgment on defense questions independent of the "military-industrial complex" depends largely on which situation obtains. A Congress which votes on the basis of ideological convictions is less likely to be swayed or controlled by a large defense establishment than a Congress particularly sensitive to constituency considerations.

II. The Dimensions of Defense Voting

Is there consistency to a congressman's defense voting? If so, is his pattern of defense voting similar to patterns of voting on other issues? Use of the Guttman scale is intended to answer questions such as these. If congressmen vote consistently, we would expect similar voting alignments on similiar questions; those alignments would change in a consistent way (i.e., the same congressmen would swing over to the other side) as the questions became more extreme one way or the other, provided that the

[6]Samuel P. Huntington, "The Defense Establishment: Vested Interests and the Public Interest," In Omer L. Carey, ed., *The Military Industrial Complex and U. S. Foreign Policy* (Pullman, Wash.: Washington State University Press, 1969).

questions all concerned the same attitudinal dimension. That dimension—the continuum along which individual congressmen range—is the basis of a Guttman scale.[7]

I isolated the dimensions of congressional voting for two Congresses—the 90th and 91st—using a computer program developed by Professor John L. McCarthy of the Yale History Department.[8] This technique looks only at the alignments. It may find no scale, or it may find several, each representing a dimension of voting. But, it makes no predetermination of the character or content of the issues within the scale. *We* must examine those issues and *infer* from them the nature of the dimension. Each congressman is given a score for each scale, and the score allows us to predict with better than 90 percent probability how he voted on any question (also ranked) included in the scale.

The major findings of this section are that congressional voting on defense is consistent, not random: better than *85 percent* of the defense questions voted upon for each Congress scaled quite well (whereas only about 40 percent of all the nonunanimous roll calls turned up on any scale). Moreover, congressional voting on defense falls within a more general pattern of liberal-conservative voting on many other issues, indicating that congressmen see defense issues along an ideological dimension. (We might also have found a defense scale that bore little similarity to scales of other issues.) Finally, a comparison of the two Congresses reveals that interesting and important changes are occurring in the nature of the relationship between defense voting patterns and patterns on other issues.

For this analysis I submitted *all* nonunanimous roll call votes in the 90th and 91st Congresses to the scaling program. The

---

[7] The basic procedure is named for its developer, Louis Guttman. This technique was first applied to legislative roll call analysis by Duncan MacRae in his *Dimensions of Congressional Voting* (Berkeley and Los Angeles; University of California Press, 1958), and George Belknap, "A Method for Analyzing Legislative Behavior," *Midwest Journal of Political Science,* 2 (November 1958): 377–402. A good introduction and bibliography on legislative voting analysis and scaling is Lee F. Anderson, Meredith W. Watts Jr. and Allen R. Wilcox, *Legislative Roll Call Analysis* (Evanston, Ill.: Northwestern University Press, 1966).

[8] McCarthy's technique utilizes Yule's Q as the measure of similarity between roll calls. Its use was developed by MacRae in "A Method for Identifying Issues and Factions from Legislative Votes," *American Political Science Review,* 59 (December 1965): 909–926 and in his *Parliament, Parties and Society in France, 1946–1959* (New York: St. Martins Press, 1967). The analysis reported here was performed on the Yale University 7090–94 computer with McCarthy's SCALE and SCORE programs. I owe McCarthy a great debt of gratitude for his assistance in deriving the scales reported in this paper.

procedure produced four scales for the 90th Congress and six scales for the 91st Congress. These scales, and the names that seemed best to describe them, are listed in Table 1. Defense-related roll calls did not initially form a separate dimension but largely clustered in the domestic liberal-conservative and civil

TABLE 1
House of Representatives Roll Call Voting Scales[a]

	No. of Items	Coefficient of Reproducibility[b]
90th House Voting Dimensions		
Scale 1–Domestic Liberal-Conservative Scale (Housing, urban development, internal security, welfare, food stamps, education and labor)	47	.95
Scale 2–Foreign Assistance Scale (Foreign economic, military and technical assistance)	15	.95
Scale 3–Government Spending Scale (Debt ceiling, public works, created civil service jobs and DoD appropriations)	30	.97
Scale 4–Civil Liberties Scale (Penalties for court interference, no funds for student disrupters and school desegregation)	19	.95
90th House Defense Scales		
Scale A–Cold War Scale (Defense appropriations, HUAC, Subversive Activities Control Board and arms control)	30	.96
Scale B–Preparedness Scale (Defense appropriations, selective service and arms control)	24	.96

[a]All scales were arranged such that those congressmen at the more liberal end were placed at the top and assigned a score of zero (antidefense, proforeign aid, procivil liberties, prodomestic welfare programs). With each shift in alignment in a conservative direction represented by a roll call descending the scale, an additional value of one was added, until at the bottom of the scales, the most conservative congressmen were assigned the highest scores, corresponding to the number of items in the scales. (see note a, Table 2 for the scoring particulars of the defense scales.)

[b]The coefficient of reproducibility represents the probability that a congressman's vote on any given issue on the scale can be predicted by knowing his score. More precisely, the coefficient of reproducibility $= 1.0 -$ (errors in voting/total possible errors).

91st House Voting Dimensions

Scale 1–Domestic Liberal-Conservative Scale (Housing, urban development, civil liberties, internal security, welfare, food stamps, education and labor)	63	.93
Scale 2–Foreign Assistance Scale (Peace Corps, foreign aid and the United Nations)	17	.94
Scale 3–Government Spending Scale (Public works and AEC appropriations, minimum wage for hospital employees and federal employee pay comparability)	42	.92
Scale 4–Race-Urban Scale (School desegregation, voting rights, stop funds to campus rioters, Economic Opportunity Act and welfare reform)	40	.94
Scale 5–Foreign Trade Scale (Bills relating to foreign trade)	5	.96
Scale 6–Agriculture Scale (Farm subsidies, etc)	7	.94

91st House Defense Scales

Scale A–Cold War Scale (Defense appropriations, Vietnam, military procurement, internal security, military aid, Cooper-Church, Peace Corps and arms control)	52	.95
Scale B–Preparedness Scale (Military appropriations, military procurement, Vietnam, military construction, ABM, arms control and Cooper-Church resolution	39	.95

liberties dimensions for the 90th Congress and in the domestic liberal-conservative and race-urban dimensions for the 91st Congress.[9] This phenomenon supports the hypothesis of an ideological explanation for House voting in that it shows that attitudes on defense are strongly associated with those on such domestic issues as civil rights, civil liberties and the urban crisis.

The analysis was refined by separating from the full roll call sets (including the roll calls not located in any of the initial voting dimensions) those issues possibly representing each of the two

---

[9]The domestic liberal-conservative scale was given its name because it—unlike the other scales which are liberal-conservative—contained issues which ranged too widely for me to peg it any other way.

strongest themes of recent defense voting: perception of the cold war and defense preparedness.[10] These new subsets were then submitted to the scaling procedure, yielding for each Congress the cold war scale and the preparedness scale (see Appendix).

Congressional attitudes on defense questions are closely tied to cold war assumptions and anticommunism. Observe the issue-clustering pattern in the cold war scale for both Congresses (see Appendix): voting alignment patterns for such "military" issues as military construction, defense appropriations, funds to conduct the war in Vietnam and the loan of military vessels to foreign countries scale together with such issues as funds for the House Un-American Activities Committee (HUAC, now House Internal Security Committee), funds for the Subversive Activities Control Board and appropriations for the Arms Control and Disarmament Agency (ACDA). In addition we see evidence from the 91st Congress cold war scale that issues relating to foreign assistance, particularly military assistance and the Peace Corps, are viewed in the same light as defense. For each Congress a single set of scale scores describes the voting record of every congressman on this wide spectrum of issues. It is not likely that such a situation could obtain unless attitudes on these questions were strongly associated, reflecting common underlying assumptions and values.

Further evidence that congressional attitudes toward defense are not formulated in isolation from attitudes toward other questions is provided by gamma rank order correlations between the congressmen's scores for the cold war scales and for the other issue dimensions.[11] These coefficients are listed in Table 2. For the 90th Congress voting on cold war issues shows a strong association with voting on foreign assistance, the civil liberties dimension, the domestic liberal-conservative dimension and the preparedness scale. For the 91st Congress the cold war scale

[10]The first of these subsets was chosen to represent the broader, more ideological aspect of defense; the second subset represented the narrower, more economic aspect.

[11]The gamma coefficient is Kruskal and Goodman's coefficient of ordinal association. It is the ratio of predominance of agreement (+) or inversion (−) between two sets of rankings to the maximum possible agreement or inversion. A gamma of .6 indicates that there is 60 percent greater agreement than disagreement between two sets of rankings. See L. C. Freeman, *Elementary Applied Statistics* (New York, London and Sydney: John Wiley and Sons, Inc., 1965), p. 8.

appears strongly associated with the preparedness scale and the urban-race scale, less strongly associated with the domestic liberal-conservative dimension, foreign assistance and government spending and weakly related to voting on agriculture and foreign trade questions.

TABLE 2
Congressional Score Correlations Between the Cold War Scale and Other Dimensions

90th Congress *Cold War Scale*[a] *correlated with:*	*Gamma*[b] *Correlation*
Foreign Assistance Scale (Scale 2)	.82
Civil Liberties Dimension (Scale 4)	.82
Domestic Liberal-Conservative Scale (Scale 1)	.77
Preparedness Scale (Scale B)	.45
Government Spending Scale (Scale 3)	.45
91st Congress *Cold War Scale* *correlated with:*	
Preparedness Scale (Scale B)	.87
Urban-Race Scale (Scale 4)	.80
Government Spending Scale (Scale 3)	.72
Domestic Liberal-Conservative Scale (Scale 1)	.63
Foreign Trade Scale (Scale 5)	.45
Agriculture Scale (Scale 6)	.44
Foreign Assistance Scale (Scale 2)	.64

[a] Scoring for the 90th House cold war scale was as follows: The congressman (George Brown of California) who voted dovishly on all issues in the scale (i.e. even voted against authorizing $70 billion for DoD, against construction at military installations and against a 4.5 percent pay increase for military personnel—the top three items in the scale) was assigned a score of zero. Congressmen who voted to authorize $70 billion for DoD, but who voted dovishly on all other issues were assigned a score of one. Those who voted to authorize the $70 billion to authorize construction at military installations but dovishly on all other items (even opposing the 2.5 percent military pay increase) were assigned a score of two. Thus, as the number of items voted on hawkishly increased, larger scores were assigned until at the bottom of the scale are found congressmen who voted in favor of all defense appropriations and authorization items, who supported HUAC and the Subversive Activities Control Board but who opposed arms control and disarmament apropriations. These most hawkish of representatives were assigned a score of thirty. All the other defense scales were scored in a similar manner. The scale scores thus provide an index of hawkishness. (See Appendix.)

[b] See note 9.

These correlations suggest that basic liberal-conservative attitudes in large measure may explain congressional voting along
the spectrum of issues covered in our scales. However, the liberal
has changed his substantive position considerably in recent
years. In the 1950s and early 1960s he could be characterized as
favoring a strong U. S. role in international affairs; hence he
supported high levels of foreign economic and military assistance.[12] He backed high levels of domestic spending—including
defense spending. Finally, he took strong stands for civil liberties
and civil rights. By the 91st Congress the liberal still supported
high levels of foreign economic assistance (though not foreign
military assistance). He continued to favor domestic expenditures for urban problems and had not changed his stance on civil
liberties and civil rights. But he now tended to oppose defense
expenditures and no longer indiscriminately favored large federal expenditures. The low correlations between the 91st Congress preparedness scale and the agriculture and foreign trade
alignments indicate that agriculture and foreign trade questions
are not encompassed by the basic liberal-conservative dimension
and that voting on these issues is determined by other factors.

The low correlation between the 90th Congress cold war scale
and 90th Congress preparedness scale at first blush seems most
surprising, particularly since some of the same roll calls are contained in both dimensions and since the equivalent two scales for
the 91st Congress exhibit a strong intercorrelation. This suggests that the 90th Congress represents the transition period
when the liberal attitude was changing from a prodefense posture to a defense-limiting posture; thus liberalism and preparedness temporarily appeared unrelated.[13] Normally, it would not be
possible to detect evidence of such a trend in the analysis of two
adjacent Congresses, because congressional attitudes evolve
only gradually. Yet, we have strong grounds to believe, just as
1930 was a "critical election" in that it witnessed a major new
realignment of political forces, we might view the 91st Congress

[12]See Huntington, *Common Defense*, pp. 251–259.

[13]We would hypothesize that, had the analysis been extended back into the
1950s, the correlation between Cold War and preparedness scales—high in the
91st Congress—would again be high, only the liberals would be pushing the
administration for higher defense spending.

TABLE 3
Gamma Rank Order Correlations between 90th and 91st Congress Scales

90th House Scales	90th House Preparedness Scale (Gamma)	91st House Cold War Scale (Gamma)	91st House Preparedness Scale (Gamma)
Cold War Scale (Scale A)	.45	.83	.84
Civil Liberties Scale (Scale 4)	.31	.81	.80
Foreign Assistance Scale (Scale 2)	.38	.79	.74
Domestic Liberal-Conservative Scale (Scale 1)	.42	.69	.68
Preparedness Scale (Scale B)	——	.31	.30

as a "critical Congress" for defense issues in that very significant changes occurred in voting alignments—probably as a direct result of the Vietnam war and the 1968 presidential campaign. For instance, the number of votes against the defense appropriations bill grew from three in 1967 to forty-six in 1970. Again, during 1968, only forty congressmen voted against the ABM program, while by 1969 this number had grown to 141.

The differences which showed up in the two Congresses led me to compare them directly. For each congressman who sat in both Congresses, scores on scales in the 90th were compared with those in the 91st by means of rank order correlation to confirm the hypothesis that defense voting has become more closely related with general liberal-conservative attitudes since the 90th Congress. We can see from Table 3 that foreign assistance, civil liberties and domestic scales were mere closely associated with the 91st House preparedness scale than they were with the 90th House preparedness scale. In effect, then, knowlege of a congressman's voting record on these 90th Congress nondefense dimensions gives better predictive power for his 91st Congress defense voting record than his 90th Congress defense record.

Surprisingly, the civil liberties dimension for the 90th Congress appeared nearly as strongly associated with defense voting behavior in the 91st House as the 90th House cold war dimension. This indicates that attitudes on the importance of maintaining domestic order, perhaps held partially in response to a perceived danger from communism, have become strongly associated with attitudes on defense. Those congressmen who still consistently support the military took a hard line on civil liberties issues in the past. Those who on at least some occasions vote to limit the military have strong civil libertarian records. That defense attitudes have shifted so that they closely parallel civil liberties attitudes implies that the dovish voting shift is about complete for the present (only the civil libertarians have shifted and now they have nearly all switched). Further increases in the defense limiting coalition may await an increase in the number of congressmen opposed to repressive legislation to preserve domestic order. This state of affairs may occur, if, as seems likely in the absence of U. S.–Soviet and U. S.–Chinese confrontations, the perceived threat of communism decreases. However, the inevitablity of the trend may be determined far more by future levels of domestic violence in the nation's cities and college campuses. While the growing association of defense voting alignments with ideological attitudes does not tell us that those congressmen who would limit defense expenditures will prevail in the future, still it indicates that congressmen tend to vote according to their beliefs rather than to the dictates of the defense establishment.

We should note here that the observed dimensions of House roll-call voting show some similarities with the dimensions of budgetary allocations and presidential State of the Union messages described in Jong Lee's article. Lee found that presidents have tended to perceive national defense as associated with foreign aid, unemployment and health, which we have inferred is also the case for congressmen. Yet he also found that the economy and inflation, civil rights, education, balanced budget and urban problems were perceived by the president as issue areas not directly related to defense. Our findings would indicate that congressmen do see these issues directly related to defense. The suggestion here is that the president is able to more easily perceive independent issue areas than can congressmen. The vast quantity of information and staff time available to the president may facilitate his suppression of ideological biases tending to lead to a perceived unidimensionality of issues. In other words, the chief executive may have less need than congresmen to rely on ideology for cues. The differences between the congressional voting dimensions and the presidential State of the Union speech dimensions also tend to indicate that Congress does not necessarily buy presidential arguments as to what issues are interrelated, though a strong influence may be exerted. Lee's finding (relevant to the dimensions of budgetary allocation) that defense expenditures are negatively associated with expenditures for health and education shows that the budget closely reflects the congressionally perceived association between issues, at least as this can be inferred from roll-call analysis.

III. Explanatory Models

Any hypothesis that congressmen vote on defense-related issues according to ideology remains speculative unless one can show that this provides a better explanation for roll-call behavior than do constituency pressures, the "military-industrial complex" (MIC) or idiosyncratic factors. Substantive models were formed representing each of these possible explanations (see Table 4). Included in each of the models were variables which I thought indicative of the forces operating on each congressman inherent in the underlying explanation (see Table 5). To test the relative importance of each of the possible explanations for defense voting, I intended to regress the variables of each model on the cold war and preparedness scales.

The MIC model included variables directly indicative of linkages between the MIC and Congress. I formed two such variables by aggregating for congressional districts, defense-related payrolls and defense prime contract awards.[14] The third variable in this model represented the military affiliation of congressmen, whether they had served previously in the armed forces and had retained reserve commissions.

The constituency model contained variables representing congressional district influences on defense voting. Defense payrolls and prime contracts were included, of course, along with other

[14]This information is not available in tabulated form in any publication at this time (See Russett, *What Price Vigilance?* pp. 30, 238). I calculated it from city and county figures in OEO's *Federal Outlays*. See note.

TABLE 4
The Explanatory Models and Their Included Variables

The "Military-Industrial Complex" Model

  Defense payrolls
  Defense prime contract awards
  Military affiliation

The Reinforced "Military-Industrial Complex" Model

  Defense payrolls
  Defense prime contract awards
  Military affiliation
  Born after 1920
  Federal outlays (per capita)
  Low self-esteem
  High efficacy
  Competitive district
  Elected 1947–1953
  Esteem-competitive (Interaction term between low esteem and competitive)
  Efficacy-competitive (Interaction term between high efficacy and competitive)

The Constituency Model

  Party
  Region (All region variables compared to South)
    West
    Mountain
    Plains
    Midwest
    Northeast
    Border
  Urbanization (All urbanization variables compared to rural and small town)
    Large city
    Suburb
    Medium city
  Federal outlays (per capita)
  Competitive district

The Idiosyncratic Model

  Low esteem
  High efficacy
  Born after 1920
  Elected 1947–1953
  Minority
  Military affiliation

The Ideological Model

  Democratic Study Group membership
  Born after 1920
  Elected 1947–1953
  Labor support

variables indicating region, party, urbanization, electoral competitiveness and total federal outlays (also aggregated by this author for congressional districts from city and county figures).

The idiosyncratic model was designed to include variables pertaining to a congressman's background and personality which could reflect biases on defense questions. Military affiliation and minority group status (defined as women and blacks) provided two such variables. Another represented a congressman's age. My hypothesis here was that legislators born before 1920 would more consistently support military preparedness than would their younger colleagues; they had matured during the period of U. S. isolationism with military deemphasis and had seen the failure of these policies in the late 1930s.[15] Another experience of possibly great significance was exposure to the rampant anticommunism of the McCarthy era. My expectation was that congressman first elected between 1947 and 1954 would have been the most influenced and that thus they would have a consistent promilitary bias. First election to Congress during the McCarthy era was therefore entered into this model. Finally, following the work of Conrad Morrow, it was suspected that congressmen exhibiting lower self-esteem (defined as the difference between ideal self-image and actual self-image) and a higher generalized sense of efficacy (the capability of the individual to influence society) would tend to take the more alarmist view of the communist threat and advocate higher levels of military preparedness.[16] Therefore, variables indicative of self-esteem and generalized efficacy were entered into the idiosyncratic model.[17]

[15]This hypothesis stems from the discussion of the alternating trends, in U. S. history between introversion and extroversion in Frank L. Klingberg, "The Historical Alternation of Moods in American Foreign Policy," *World Politics,* 4 (January 1952): 239–273.

[16] Morrow has hypothesized that low self-esteem and a high generalized sense of efficacy are associated with aggressiveness expressed as degree of support for a strong, anticommunist defense policy. (i.e., seeing the crisis we are facing in America, the high efficacy individual must blame it on the external menace—the communists—because of his implicit faith in the "rightness" of the U. S. government). This tendency is reinforced in the low self-esteem individual who tends to attribute to the communist menace his failure to achieve ideal status. See Conrad Morrow, "Aggression toward Whom: A Psychological Model of Aggressive Political Behavior," Ph. D. dissertation, Yale University, 1972.

[17] Evaluating self-esteem and efficacy could not be done as we might have desired by administering a questionnaire. Instead Morrow and I content-analyzed the biographical sketches on each congressman found in the *Congressional Direc-*

TABLE 5

The Explanatory Variables for the Various House Voting Models

Variable	Abbreviated Title	Definition	How Coded	Hypothesized Relationship
Employment-related defense expenditures	Defense pay	The aggregate of civilian[a] DoD payrolls, military payrolls, reserve, National Guard and retired payrolls, plus prime civil functions contracts	1968—Values for each cong. district divided by personal income then $\log_{10}$	Increasing defense payrolls should be associated with Hawkish voting (beta coeff. = +)
Defense prime contract awards	Defense contracts	The aggregate of prime supply contracts,[b] prime RDTE contracts, prime service contracts and prime contracts less than $10,000	1968—Values for each cong. district divided by personal income then $\log_{10}$	Increasing contract awards should be associated with hawkish voting (beta coeff. = +)
Military affiliation	Mil. affl.	No military service, past military service but no current reserve commission, current reserve commission	No military service coded 0, past military service coded −1, current reserve commission coded +1	Congressmen with past military service should vote more dovishly than those with no military service, congressmen with reserve commissions should vote more hawkishly (beta coeff. = +)
Born after 1920	Youth	Congressmen dichotomized into those born before 1920 and those born in 1920 and after	Born in or after 1920 coded 1, born before 1920 coded 0.	Younger congressmen should vote more dovishly (beta coeff. = −)
Per capita federal outlays	Fed. exp.	The aggregate of federal outlays by cong. dist. divided by population	1968 values for each cong. district divided by pop. then $\log_{10}$	The greater per capita expenditures the more dovish the voting (beta coeff. = −)

Low self-esteem	Esteem	Whether congressman made excessive mention of past accomplishments, awards, etc. in *Cong. Directory* biog. sketch	Excessive awards, accomplishments, etc. coded 1, others coded 0	Low self-esteem associated with hawkish voting (beta coeff. = +)
High generalized sense of efficacy	Efficacy	Mention of membership in organizations with high efficacy credos such as Chamber of Commerce, Masons, K. of C. considered high efficacy	Membership in high efficacy organization coded 1, others coded 0	High efficacy associated with hawkish voting (beta coeff. = +)
Competitive district	Competitive	District considered competitive if no candidate received more than 60 percent of vote each of last three elections	Competitive coded 1, others coded 0	Competitive district associated with dovish voting (beta coeff. = −)
Elected 1947–1953	Elected 1947–1953	Congressmen elected during McCarthy era	Congressmen elected McCarthy era coded 1, others coded 0	Elected 1947–1953 associated with hawkish voting (beta coeff. = +)
Party	Party	Whether Democrat or Republican	Democrat coded 1, Republicans coded 0	Democrat associated with dovish voting (beta coeff. = −)
Northeast	Northeast	District in following states: Connecticut, Maine, Massachusetts, Rhode Island, Vermont, New Hampshire, New York, New Jersey and Pennsylvania	Northeast coded 1, others 0	Northeast congressmen should be more dovish than southerners (beta coeff. = −)

(Continued)

TABLE 5 (continued)

Variable	Abbreviated Title	Definition	How Coded	Hypothesized Relationship
Midwest	Midwest	Illinois, Indiana, Iowa, Michigan, Minnesota, Ohio and Wisconsin	Midwest coded 1, others coded 0	Midwest congressmen should vote more dovishly than southerners (beta coeff. =−)
Plains	Plains	Kansas, Nebraska, North Dakota and South Dakota	Plains coded 1, others coded 0	Plains congressmen should vote more dovishly than southerners (beta coeff. =−)
Border	Border	Delaware, Kentucky, Maryland, Missouri, Okla. and West Virginia	Border coded 1, others coded 0	Border congressmen should vote more dovishly than southerners (beta coeff. =−)
Mountain	Mountain	Arizona, Colorado, Idaho, Montana, Nevada, New Mexico, Utah and Wyoming	Mountain coded 1, others coded 0	Mountain congressmen should vote more dovishly than southerners (beta coeff. =−)
West	West	California, Oregon, Washington, Alaska and Hawaii	West coded 1, others coded 0	Western congressmen should vote more dovishly than southerners (beta coeff. =−)
Large City	Lrg. City	District largely contained within city of 500,000 or more population	Large City coded 1, others coded 0	Large city congressmen should vote more dovishly than their small town and rural colleagues (beta coeff. = −)
Suburb	Suburb	District largely contained within metropolitan statistical area of large city	Suburb coded 1, others coded 0	Suburban congressmen should vote more dovishly than their small town and rural colleagues (beta coeff. = −)

Small City	Sm. City	District contains at least one city of between 100,000 and 500,000 population	Small City coded 1, others coded 0	Small city congressmen should vote more dovishly than their small town and rural colleagues (beta coeff. = −)
Minority Group	Minority	Congressmen who are women or black	Minority group coded 1, others coded 0	Minority group congressmen should vote more dovishly than their colleagues (beta coeff. = −)
Democratic Study Group	DSG	Congressmen who are members of the Democratic Study Group	DSG members coded 1, others coded 0	DSG members should vote more dovishly than their colleagues (beta coeff. = −)
Labor Support	Labor Sup.	Congressmen who received support from AFL-CIO, COPE	Congressmen who received labor support coded 1, others coded 0	Congressmen who received labor support should vote more dovishly than their colleagues (beta coeff. = −)

[a] The author compiled defense expenditures and per capita federal outlays by congressional district by aggregating city and county figures in each category listed in OEO's *Federal Outlays for 1968*. Personal income by congressional district was calculated in an analogous way from the Department of Commerce, *County and City Data Book* (1967). The aggregated defense expenditures, personal income and per capita federal outlays were $\log_{10}$ to reduce the influence of outliers in the regressions.

[b] See note a.

The reinforced MIC model included the direct linkage variables of defense payrolls, prime contract awards and military affiliation. In addition I entered other "reinforcement" variables from both constituency and idiosyncratic models which, it was hypothesized, would act as cóntrol variables to increase the significance of the defense expenditures variables. Included in this category were: total federal outlays by congressional district, born after 1920, first election to Congress during the McCarthy era and electoral competitiveness.

Finally, the ideological model contained variables most probably associated with basic liberalism and conservatism. Membership in the Democratic Study Group, first election during the McCarthy era and age were three variables which obviously fit into this category. To these we added election support by the AFL-CIO Committee on Political Education (COPE). This latter variable had the advantage of identifying Republican liberals.

My hypotheses were first that the ideological model would provide the best explanation for defense voting; second, it would increase in power between the 90th and 91st Congress because of the increased correspondence between defense voting and ideological stance in the 91st Congress; and third, it would provide the best explanation for changes in voting behavior of individual congressmen.

We decided to test the first hypothesis by regressing the explanatory variables of each model on the cold war scale for the 90th Congress and both cold war and preparedness scales for the 91st Congress, where the scale scores were standardized in such a way that the most dovish position on all three scales was assigned a score of zero and the most hawkish position was assigned a score of 52 (the number of roll calls in the longest scale) —so that the beta coefficients (slopes) associated with each of the

---

tory. These contain roughly the same information for each congressman, and presumably each representative writes or at least approves his own biographical sketch. It was judged as evidence of low self-esteem when excessive mention was made (compared to the mean) of awards and accomplishments (i.e., listing all combat awards and ribbons, referencing of high school accomplishments, detailing of meteoric rises in business and politics, etc.). We utilized as a measure of high generalized sense of efficacy, whether mention was made of membership in organizations which have been characterized by the American Dream individual high efficacy credo, such as the Chamber of Commerce, Lions, Rotary Club. See Morrow, "Aggression toward Whom."

explanatory variables would be comparable between scales. In order to test the third hypothesis—change in voting—we created two new composite scales to measure the change in voting behavior between the 90th and 91st Congresses. In the first of these the standardized 90th Congress cold war scale scores were subtracted from the 91st Congress standardized cold war scale scores. In the second case 90th Congress standardized cold war scale scores were subtracted from the 91st Congress standardized preparedness scale scores (i.e., a negative score on either of these two scales indicates that the congressman in question became more dovish).

TABLE 6
Percentage of Variance Accounted for in Defense Voting Scales
through Bivariate Correlations

	90th House Cold War Scale	91st House Cold War Scale	91st House Preparedness Scale	91st House Cold War— 90th House Cold War Scale	91st House Preparedness— 90th House Cold War Scale
Democratic Study Group	41%	55%	48%	37%	28%
Labor support	29%	43%	34%	32%	20%
West-Democrat	14%	11%	—	—	—
Large city	16%	14%	14%	—	—
Party	11%	14%	12%	10%	—
Northeast	—	12%	12%	12%	10%

Omitted figures indicate less than 10 percent of variance accounted for.

Before discussing the regression results for each of the respective models, it is worthwhile noting the bivariate correlations between the various explanatory variables and the defense scales. The strongest relationships are reported in Table 6. We can see here that by far the most strongly associated variables were labor support and membership in the Democratic Study Group—two variables most closely related to a liberal ideological perspective. As expected, the explanatory importance of these two variables increased dramatically between the 90th and 91st Congresses and accounted for a considerable proportion of the shift in voting patterns which took place between the two Congresses. One should note that though these two variables individually account for one-fourth to one-half of the total variance, as compared to less than one-fifth for the next most highly associated variables;

the variance explained is to a considerable degree the same variance since the two ideological variables are significantly intercorrelated with a Pearson's r of .71.

A. THE "MILITARY-INDUSTRIAL COMPLEX" MODELS

Table 7 lists the percent of variance in each of the defense scales which can be accounted for by each of our models utilizing regression analysis.

TABLE 7
The Explanatory Models and
Variance Accounted for in Defense Voting Scales

	90th House Cold War Scale	91st House Cold War Scale	91st House Preparedness Scale	91st House Cold War Scale—90th House Cold War Scale	91st House Preparedness— 90th House Cold War Scale
Military-industrial complex model	4%	5%	4%	3%	2%
Reinforced MIC model	21%	23%	21%	13%	12%
Constituency model	45%	55%	46%	38%	27%
Idiosyncratic model	17%	17%	16%	19%	7%
Ideological model	42%	62%	53%	43%	40%

We can note that the MIC model, where only military affiliation and our aggregated figures for employment-related defense expenditures were employed as explanatory variables, explains little of the variance for any of the scales.

When the defense "reinforcement" variables were entered into the equation, a very significantly increased percentage of the variance was accounted for in each of the defense scales (see Table 7). As anticipated, the T-ratios and beta coefficients for employment-related defense payrolls increased significantly (as can be noted from Tables 8a and 8b) indicating that high defense payrolls are more important when per capita total federal outlays are low, the congressman was born before 1920, the district is competitive and the representative was first elected during the McCarthy era. There was no such reinforcement effect for military affiliation. Because the total variance explained by this model never exceeded 23 percent and because much of this is explained by the "reinforcement" variables in their own right, further doubt is cast on the MIC theory and hence on the ability of the military establishment to control congressional behavior through spending or military affiliation.

It is important to note how the absolute and relative importance of the various explanatory variables changes between scales. This can be measured by the magnitude of the various beta coefficients. (A positive coefficient indicates a conservative-hawkish association, while a negative coefficient tends to show that a given variable is associated with liberal-dovish tendencies.)[18]

Two variables which were not appreciably associated with defense voting in the 90th Congress became significant in the 91st Congress and were significantly associated with changes in voting

[18]Beta coefficients are the slopes of the lines of least squares where the respective explanatory variables are regressed on the defense scales. A negative coefficient means that the presence or increase of a given factor is associated with lower scale scores of voting to limit the defense establishment. A positive coefficient means the variable is associated with higher scale scores of voting to support the defense establishment. The substantive interpretation of the beta coefficients is as follows:

Defense Pay.   The number of scale positions shifted in a hawkish direction (increased number of prodefense votes) associated with an increase of 1 percent of defense pay as a proportion of total personal income.

Fed. Exp.   The number of scale positions shifted in a dovish direction (decreased number of prodefense votes) associated with an increase of $100 of per capita total federal outlays by congressional district.

All Other Variables.   The number of scale positions shifted (changed number of prodefense or antidefense votes) associated with the presence of a given variable as compared to nonpresence. (For the regional variables, the coefficient represents the scale differences for other regions as compared to the South; for the urbanization variables, the coefficient represents the scale differences for large city, small city and suburban constituency as compared to small town and rural constituency.

The beta coefficients are reported if they are significant at the .01 level (2-tailed test) which means, in effect, that there is a 99 percent probability that the reported beta coefficient does not represent chance association between the explanatory variables and the defense scales.

There is one school of thought which would have us report all coefficients as significant since our scales include all congressmen and most of the defense roll calls in the 90th and 91st Congresses. However, statistical significance does provide an indicator for the importance of an observed relationship between variables even when the sampling universe is complete. Hence, it has been employed as a reporting criterion.

The 90th House preparedness scale was not employed in the regressions because it provides insufficient information on gradations in voting behavior, particularly in the ranges of moderate hawkishness and moderate dovishness, to allow testing of the importance of the various hypothesized explanatory variables.

TABLE 8

Significant Beta Coefficients for the Defense Voting Models

Table 8a: The "Military-Industrial Complex" Scale

	90th House Cold War Scale		91st House Cold War Scale		91st House Preparedness Scale		91st House Cold War (-) 90th House Cold War		91st House Preparedness(-) 90th House Cold War	
	Mil. affl.	1.77	Mil. affl.	3.06	Mil. affl.	2.59	Mil. affl.	1.28		
	Defense pay	.06	Defense pay	.17	Defense pay	.15	Defense pay	.10	Defense pay	.08
	Intercept	47.8	Intercept	44.0	Intercept	48.9	Intercept	-3.91	Intercept	1.01

Table 8b: The Reinforced "Military-Industrial Complex" Model

90th House Cold War Scale		91st House Cold War Scale		91st House Preparedness Scale		91st House Cold War (-) 90th House Cold War		91st House Preparedness(-) 90th House Cold War	
Efficacy	4.44	Efficacy	7.57	Competitive	-7.44	Competitive	-5.05	Competitive	-5.61
Youth	-2.78	Competitive	-6.87	Efficacy	6.26	Efficacy	3.12	Elect. '47–53	2.96
		Elect '47–53	4.37	Elect '47–53	5.12				
		Youth	-3.32	Youth	-3.67				
		Mil. affl.	3.06						
Fed. exp.	-.33	Fed. exp.	.54	Fed. exp.	-.49	Fed. exp.	-.21	Fed. exp.	-.16
Defense pay	.11	Defense pay	.22	Defense pay	.19	Defense pay	.11	Defense pay	.09
Intercept	81.2	Intercept	99.7	Intercept	101.1	Intercept	18.5	Intercept	20.0

Table 8c: The Constituency Model

90th House Cold War Scale		91st House Cold War Scale		91st House Preparedness Scale		91st House Cold War (-) 90th House Cold War		91st House Preparedness(-) 90th House Cold War	
West-Dem.	-11.1	Northeast	-19.5	Northeast	-16.6	Northeast	-11.3	Northeast	-8.51
Northeast	-8.15	West-Dem.	-14.4	West-Dem.	-15.2	Midwest	-8.09	Party	-4.81
Lrg. City	-6.39	Midwest	-13.9	City	-10.3	Party	-6.75	Midwest	-4.53
Midwest	-5.81	Party	-11.5	Midwest	-10.3	Mountain	-6.21	City	-3.98
Plains	-5.71	Lrg. City	-9.79	Party	-9.50	West	-5.27	Compet.	-3.17
Party	-4.61	Mountain	-9.37	Suburb	-4.06	City	-3.40	Suburb	-2.96

Border	-2.97	Plains	-9.37	Competitive	-3.61	Suburb	-3.43	Intercept	15.9	
		West	-8.12			Sm. Cities	-2.65			
		Border	-6.00			Competitive	-2.02			
		Suburbs	-4.53							
		Sm. Cities	-3.70							
		Competitive	-2.46							
Fed. Exp.	-.17	Fed. Exp.	-.25	Fed. Exp.	-.24					
Defense Pay	.03									
Intercept	71.6	Intercept	85.4	Intercept	87.4	Intercept	13.9			

Table 8d: The Idiosyncratic Model

Minority	-7.83	Minority	-12.55	Minority	-11.46	Minority	-4.73	Elect '47-53	3.54	
Efficacy	5.18	Efficacy	9.35	Efficacy	8.57	Efficacy	-4.16	Efficacy	3.39	
Youth	-3.13	Elect '47-53	4.89	Elect '47-53	5.72	Elect '47-53	2.72	Esteem	1.97	
Mil. affil.	1.44	Youth	-4.37	Youth	4.82	Esteem	1.84			
		Esteem	3.31	Esteem	3.44					
		Mil. affil.	2.50	Mil. affil.	1.98					
Intercept	42.2	Intercept	32.0	Intercept	37.1	Intercept	-10.3	Intercept	-5.16	

Table 8e: The Ideological Model

DSG	-9.57	DSG	-18.7	DSG	-18.69	DSG	-9.12	DSG	-7.01	
Labor sup.	-3.91	Labor sup.	-9.45	Labor sup.	-7.14	Labor sup.	-5.41	Labor sup.	-2.72	
Youth	-1.72			Elect '47-53	2.63			Elect '47-53	2.00	
				Youth	-2.25					
Intercept	49.04	Intercept	45.9	Intercept	49.8	Intercept	-3.09	Intererept	.79	

behavior. On the one hand, competitiveness of the congressional district becomes an important factor. This was not unexpected; we would have anticipated that those congressmen likely to face strong opposition would have had to respond to the antimilitary attitudes engendered by Vietnam more than would their colleagues from noncompetitive districts. Also we can observe that first election to Congress during the McCarthy era appears as an important factor making for hawkish voting behavior and against change in attitude. This may be an example of Mannheim's political generation effect—common experiences shared by a group during one period can create a common world view or frame of reference through which members view their subsequent political experience.[19] Congressmen first elected during the early years of the cold war probably are most engrained with anticommunist attitudes and thus are more resistant to changing their prodefense voting habits than are their colleagues elected before or after.

The "reinforced" MIC model shows the growing importance of ideology. The important explanatory variable—election between 1947 and 1954—has strong ideological connotations. To be sure, variables more closely related to constituency, such as competitiveness and total federal outlays do exhibit strong associations with defense voting, but significantly, we have no evidence that defense expenditures by congressional district exercise any such strong influence.

B. THE CONSTITUENCY MODEL

Table 8 shows that the constituency model explains more of the variance in defense voting behavior than does the "reinforced" MIC model. In fact it has nearly as much explanatory power as the ideological model. However, this does not detract from the importance of the ideological model when one considers that the constituency model includes most of the factors usually thought important for explaining congressional voting, such as party, region and urbanization. What appears notable is that the constituency model does no better in explaining the variance in

---

[19]For a discussion on political generations in another context see Maurice Zeitkin, *Revolutionary Politics and the Cuban Working Class* (Princeton, N. J.: Princeton University Press, 1967), pp. 211–212.

defense voting than membership in the Democratic Study Group (see Table 6). The various beta coefficients of this model as listed in Table 8d again confirm the growing importance in the 91st Congress of competitive districts in explaining defense voting behavior. Congressmen from the Northeast, Midwest, the Mountain states and Western Democrats are more dovish than are their colleagues from the South and have been more likely to change their voting patterns. By 1969 party became more important, with Democrats showing more of a tendency to vote dovishly, probably because the need no longer exists to support a Democratic president. Congressmen from the big cities voted more dovishly than did those from either rural or suburban areas in the 90th Congress. By the 91st Congress suburban congressmen appeared less prodefense and were more likely to change their voting patterns (in a dovish direction), probably because of the Vietnam war. The total number of large city and suburban congressmen will probably increase during the coming decade. On the basis of this finding we would expect greater congressional pressure to limit the expansion of the military establishment.

C. THE IDIOSYNCRATIC MODEL

We can observe from Table 7 that the explanatory power of the idiosyncratic model is poor. The beta coefficients associated with this model (listed in Table 8d) indicate that minority group status is the most important of this set of variables not only for defense voting but also for the liberal shift. There is also some evidence to confirm the hypothesis that a high sense of efficacy and low self-esteem is associated with hawkish voting behavior and reluctance to change in a dovish direction. Again we see negative association between first election to Congress during the McCarthy era and the tendency to shift defense voting behavior in a dovish direction. It must be emphasized that all the variables in this model put together account for less of the variance in voting behavior than either Democratic Study Group membership or labor support.

D. THE IDEOLOGICAL MODEL

Table 7 shows that the ideological model explains considerably more of the variance in defense voting than any of the other models. The beta coefficients associated with this model (see

Table 8c) demonstrate the increased association of labor support with dovish voting between the 90th and 91st Congresses and the very great importance of this variable in explaining the dovish voting shift which occurred. Thus, in spite of George Meany's consistent support of administration foreign policies and the so-called "hard hat" mentality, the congressmen most closely affiliated with labor were the most likely to turn against the Vietnam war and the defense establishment. It would, therefore, seem that AFL-CIO's COPE is most concerned with how a congressman votes on domestic labor issues and gives him a relatively free hand to choose his own position in other areas. Most defense bills are too broad in scope for them to be considered primarily as domestic labor issues. Democratic Study Group membership also showed greater association with dovish voting in the 91st Congress than in the 90th Congress. It appeared even more strongly associated with changes in voting than did labor support.[20] We again see evidence of positive association between first election during the McCarthy era and "hawkish" voting on defense as well as the great resistence of representatives elected during this era to modify their prodefense posture. In the 90th Congress few congressmen were willing to challenge defense expenditures. By the 91st Congress this number had increased greatly. Who changed his position? Who remained steadfast? The analysis of this section indicates that the conservative continued to support the defense establishment, while the liberal saw the need for defense reduction. Other factors appear to be less important.

IV. The Implications of an Ideological Explanation

Evidence has been presented that House roll call voting on defense can best be understood in an ideological framework of generalized liberal-conservative attitudes, especially in the past few years with the disintegration of the cold war-inspired prode-

[20]One might suggest that there is some sort of group dynamic effect in the DSG —i.e., with so much to read, a congressman on many issues will get his information and cues from a reference group. This process is still ideological since the congressman chooses that group for ideological reasons (unlike any other of the explanatory variables—even party). The mediating effect of group interaction may explain why the explanatory power of DSG membership is clearly greater than that of any of the other variables—even labor support.

fense consensus. We have seen through Guttman scale analysis that defense voting patterns fall into highly regular alignments, and that these are strongly associated with ideologically oriented voting across a wide spectrum of other questions including civil liberties, civil rights and the urban crisis. We noted that this association increased significantly between the 90th and 91st Congresses when the principal liberal shift from support to opposition of defense expenditures occurred. The voting shift was almost exclusively in a defense-limiting direction; those congressmen who switched almost without exception had strong civil rights and strong civil libertarian records. Indeed, we found that voting behavior on general ideological issues in the 90th Congress was an excellent predictor for defense voting in the 91st Congress.

Regression analysis provided further support for an ideological explanation of congressional voting on defense. Here, it was found that the ideological model had the best explanatory power for roll-call voting behavior; that its importance increased between the 90th and 91st Congresses; and that it best explained individual changes in voting. We saw that variables indicative of liberalism—membership in the Democratic Study Group and support by AFL-CIO's COPE—were strongly associated with voting to limit the defense establishment, particularly in the 91st Congress and largely explained the large voting switch which occurred. On the other hand, a variable linked to conservatism —first election to Congress during the McCarthy era—was significantly associated with hawkish voting in both Congresses and with resistance to shifting voting behavior to limit defense expenditures.

None of the other models provided as good an explanation; in fact only the constituency model explained as much of the variance in voting as did either membership in the Democratic Study Group (DSG) or labor support. We did gain some interesting findings from these models, however. For instance, there was some support for the hypotheses that competitiveness of district tends to make congressmen more responsive to the prevalent public opinion (i.e., increasing opposition to defense expenditures);[21] that low self-esteem and a high generalized sense of

[21]See Bruce M. Russett, "The Revolt of the Masses: Public Opinion on Military Expenditures," in Russett, ed., *Peace, War & Numbers* (Beverly Hills, Calif.: Sage, 1972.)

efficacy (linked to aggressiveness by Morrow) are associated with a strong promilitary stance and resistance to dovish voting shifts; and that suburban and Northeastern congressmen were more likely than their colleagues to turn against the prodefense consensus still evident in the 90th Congress.

The weakest of the models was the MIC model. In no instance did it explain more than 5 percent of the total variance (as compared with as much as 62 percent for the ideological model). Prime contract awards never showed any significant association with defense voting; defense payrolls and military affiliation exhibited only moderate association. Adding "reinforcement" variables to the MIC model did increase somewhat the variance accounted for, but very little of this could be attributed to the MIC variables. These findings lend no support whatsoever to the hypotheses that the "military-industrial complex" has gained control over Congress and that it has now grown strong enough to be able to sustain itself.

What then are the implications of the ideological explanation? We can say first that there is no apparent reason why Congress could not assert itself to *control* future military spending—at least the MIC link does not appear strong enough to provide a real obstacle to congressional power. Some would say that such a role is undesirable, since Congress can be counted upon to favor higher levels of defense expenditures than would the president. We have presented evidence that this assertion is of very doubtful validity, at least for the present and probably also for the future.

The ideological voting alignment patterns for defense in the House do not necessarily mean that Congress is ready to exert a real influence in the formulation of defense policy, even though some administration-backed bills will undoubtedly go down to defeat. All we can say now is that a large voting bloc exists to limit defense expenditures and that the members of this bloc are mostly liberals. If they vote against defense merely because it is the liberal thing to do, Congress is not yet capable of taking a direct hand in the formulation of defense policy. Such a capability requires the capacity to evaluate defense issues critically on their merits.

Now that the congressional forces willing to challenge military expenditures have achieved formidable strength, the president is going to have to work much harder to make his policies acceptable to the liberals, without, of course, losing the support of the conservatives. He may have to cut defense expenditures. On the other hand, he may employ such strategems as shifting more defense funds to metropolitan areas, the coupling of defense contracts with urban programs and shifting the composition of the military budget further away from the maintenance of troops toward "job-creating" strategic systems development.

What can we say about long-term trends? Now that the cold war prodefense consensus has been broken, we can look forward to the liberals continuing to oppose defense expenditures as incompatible with desired domestic programs. Whether the conservatives will remain consistent in their support of defense expenditures is a moot question; one might speculate that a further relaxation of cold war tensions would cause at least some of them to extend fiscal conservatism to defense. Preliminary analysis of 92d Congress roll calls shows some evidence that the conservative bloc is indeed beginning to break down.

There are two apparent trends which would indicate that the number of congressmen willing to question defense may increase in the future. First, those legislators elected during the McCarthy era will gradually be eliminated from Congress through age, death or defeat. We have seen that these men are among the most consistent supporters of the military establishment. Second, the number of congressmen born after 1920 will inevitably increase. These representatives have shown themselves significantly more likely than their older colleagues to support limitations on the military.

But, more can be done to assure that future Congresses will question hawkish defense policies than wait for the attrition of the McCarthy-era congressmen and their colleagues born before 1920. We have seen that those representatives who share the liberal ideology can now be counted on to force the military establishment to justify its proposed budget. Therefore, one might suggest that the best strategy for ensuring that future defense expenditures will be kept under close scrutiny would include electing more liberal congressmen—be they Republican or Democrat—and efforts to convert incumbent congressmen to the ideology of liberalism. This effort would have a good chance to succeed since the evidence is very slim indeed that the MIC exerts enough influence in Congress to force liberals to vote hawkishly on defense. Since congressmen from competitive districts are most likely to switch from hawkish to dovish positions, greater electoral activities by liberal voters may succeed in changing policies even where they do not throw out the incumbents.

To sum up we have shown that if present trends continue, the outlook is favorable for strong sentiment in future congresses to limit the defense establishment. The House of Representatives, at least, should be able to exercise influence on defense policy by effectively reacting to the executive position and by forcing the president to take Congress into account. One might also suggest that an attempt be made to convince the conservatives that true conservatism does not demand unswerving support for the military establishment. Perhaps this can best be accomplished by emphasizing that national honor, national prestige and national security—values which are important to the conservative—are not necessarily associated in any direct way with high and increasing defense expenditures.

APPENDIX

Date of Roll Call	Subject of Roll Call	Whether Yea or Nay in Majority
	90th House Cold War Scale[a]	
6/13/67	Authorize $70 Billion for Department of Defense (DoD)	Yea
	Pass construction as military installations	Yea
10/26/67	Pass 4.5 percent pay increase for military personnel	Yea
5/09/67	Pass $21 billion for defense in fiscal 1968	Yea
8/12/67	Conference rpt. on DoD appropriations	Yea
10/11/68	Adopt conference report on DoD appropriations	Yea
9/12/68	Pass defense appropriations for fiscal 1969	Yea
7/29/68	Recommit Military Construction Appropriations Act 1968	Nay
3/16/67	Pass $12 billion for Vietnam	Yea
3/08/67	Amend military funds bill to support Geneva Conf.	Yea
10/24/67	Authorize $2.2 million DoD military construction	Yea
7/10/68	Pass defense procurement authorization	Yea
3/02/67	Recommit—more military funds—none for Vietnam	Nay
5/14/68	Amend agriculture bill—no commodity sales to North Vietnam	Yea
4/25/68	Authorize construction at military installations	Yea
2/20/67	Pass reserve forces bill of rights	Yea
9/10/68	Agree conference rpt. S3293 defense procurement authorization	Yea
4/05/67	Pass funds for HUAC	Yea
3/13/68	Pass funds for HUAC	Yea
12/02/67	Authorize extension of naval vessel loan to foreign countries	Yea
12/04/67	Pass H.R. 996 ammendment to Subversive Activities Control Act	Yea
3/13/67	Recommit authorization for HUAC funds without open hearing	Nay
11/17/67	Pass consideration H.R. 8 interfere with military in U.S.	Yea

[a]See note a, Table 2.

Date of Roll Call	Subject of Roll Call	Whether Yea or Nay in Majority
4/05/67	Recommit open hearings on HUAC funds	Nay
4/05/67	Authorize $350,000 for HUAC	Yea
12/13/67	Pass conference report and House amendment to Subversive Activities Control Act	Yea
11/28/67	Amend Internal Security Act to provide more curbs on communists	Yea
5/08/68	Adopt Conference report amending Arms Control and Disarmament Act	Yea
9/12/68	Amend defense approp., no foreign aircraft parts purchase	Nay
3/06/68	Pass ammendment to Arms Control and Disarmament Act	Yea
	90th House Preparedness Scale	
6/13/67	Authorize $70 billion for DoD	Yea
5/09/67	Pass $21 billion for defense in fiscal 1968	Yea
	Pass Construction at military installations	Yea
10/26/67	Pass 4.5 percent increase in pay for military personnel	Yea
8/12/67	Conference rpt. of DoD appropriations	Yea
9/12/68	Pass defense appropriations for 1969	Yea
10/11/68	Adopt conf. rpt. for DoD appropriations	Yea
5/25/67	Pass draft law extnd induction authority of govt.	Yea
3/16/67	Pass $12 billion for Vietnam	Yea
3/08/67	Amend military funds bill—support Geneva conference	Yea
4/25/68	Authorize construction at military installations	Yea
7/10/68	Pass defense procurement authorization	Yea
9/10/68	Agree conf. rpt. S3293 defense procurement auth.	Nay
3/02/67	Recommit more military funds—none for Vietnam	Yea
10/24/67	Auth $2.2 million DoD military construction	Yea
6/20/67	Conference rpt. on Selective Service Act of 1967	Yea
7/29/68	Recommit Military Construction Approp. Act 1968	Nay
10/06/67	Conference rpt. of military construction auth.	Yea
11/17/67	Pass consideration H.R. 8 interfere with military in U.S.	Yea
9/10/68	Pass Foreign Military Sales Act	Nay
8/12/67	Byrnes amendment Deleted in defense appropriation	Nay
3/06/68	Recommit Arms Control and Disarmament Act	Yea
5/08/68	Adopt conf. rpt. Amendment to Arms Control and Disarmament Act	Nay
3/06/68	Pass amended Arms Control and Disarmament Act	Nay

91st House Cold-War Scale

Date	Measure	Vote
8/05/69	Authorize certain construction at military installations	Yea
3/27/69	Pass authorization for planes for military 1969	Yea
11/13/69	Pass appropriation for military construction 1970	Yea
12/08/69	Pass DoD appropriation 1970	Yea
12/16/70	Adopt conf. rpt. H.R. 19590 defense approp.	Yea
12/02/69	Pass peace with justice in Vietnam	Yea
6/11/69	Pass D.C. limit on demonstrators' use of federal property	Yea
10/03/69	Pass military procurement authorization for 1970	Yea
5/21/69	Adopt amd. colleges show antiriot measures	Yea
10/01/69	Adopt rule to consider military procurement authorization bill	Yea
5/06/70	Pass military procurement authorization $20 billion r & d new weapons	Yea
3/35/70	Provide $450,000 for expenses House Internal Security Committee	Yea
4/01/69	Authorize funds for internal security committee	Yea
12/14/70	Table H. Rs. 1306 print rpt. Internal Security	Nay
12/14/70	Adopt H. Res. 1306 Print committee internal security report	Yea
10/08/70	Pass H. R. 19590 defense approp. 1971	Yea
8/05/69	Recommit military construction bill with instructions to remove section on Pentagon picketing	Nay
2/18/69	Adopt HUAC name change	Yea
10/08/70	Recommit H.R. 19590 defense appropriation 1971	Nay
7/31/69	Adopt amendment stopping funds to campus rioters	Yea
3/23/70	Authorize loans of subs, etc. to some Asian countries	Yea
4/01/69	Recommit funds for Committee on internal security	Nay
12/21/70	Pass H.R. 14233 modify ammunition record requirement	Yea
1/29/70	Authorize security procedures for defense industry employees	Nay
10/03/69	Recommit military procurement authorization bill—no ABM funds	Yea
6/08/70	H. Res. 976 authorize committee to study Southeast Asia first-hand	Yea
12/01/69	Adopt rule for consideration of a Vietnam resolution	Yea
2/18/69	Order HUAC name change	Yea
10/30/69	Rule for considering modification of Selective Service System	Yea
5/20/70	Recommit fiscal 1971 military construction auth.	Yea

Date of Roll Call	Subject of Roll Call	Whether Yea or Nay in Majority
12/09/69	Amend foreign aid approp. $50 million assist. Korea	Yea
7/09/70	H.R. 15628 Amendment to Foreign Military Sales Act	Yea
5/06/70	Recommit military authorization—Stop Leggett Amendment	Yea
12/01/69	Order rule for consideration of a Vietnam resolution	Yea
5/07/70	Stop vote on Cambodia—consider 1970 supplemental appropriation	Yea
12/20/69	Recommit foreign aid appropriations—no $54.5 million—China planes	Nay
12/10/69	Adopt conf. rpt. cont. auth. to regulate exports	Nay
7/09/69	Table motion instruct conferees Cooper-Church	Yea
10/03/69	Recommit military procurement autho—no ABM funds	Yea
10/08/69	Recommit public works and AEC approp.	Yea
11/20/69	Recommit foreign aid auth. bill—redevelopment loan $50 million	Yea
11/20/69	Adopt Sykes amendment for $54.5 million more to China	Yea
12/19/69	Agree conf. rpt. on foreign aid approp.	Yea
9/08/69	Reduce Peace Corps funds $11.1 million	Nay
3/12/69	Recommit H.R. 33 increase U. S. involvement in AID	Nay
3/12/69	Pass H.R. 33 increase U. S. involvement AID	Yea
7/07/70	Recommit H.R. 16327 amending Peace Corps Act	Nay
4/28/70	Recommit and reduce ACDA auth. for 1971	Nay
6/27/69	Agree conf. rpt.—no duty chicory roots	Yea
9/08/69	Amend further the Peace Corps Act	Yea
7/07/70	Pass H.R. 16327—amending Peace Corps Act	Yea

91st House Preparedness Scale

Date of Roll Call	Subject of Roll Call	Whether Yea or Nay in Majority
8/05/69	Authorize certain construction at military installations	Yea
3/27/69	Pass authorization for planes for military 1969	Yea
11/13/69	Pass appropriation for military construction 1970	Yea
12/16/70	Adopt Conf. Rpt. H.R. 19590 defense approp.	Yea
12/08/69	Pass defense approp. 1970	Yea
10/13/70	Adopt conf. rpt. H.R. 17604 military const.	Yea
5/20/70	Pass auth $2 billion for 1971 military construction	Yea
11/18/69	Waive pts. of order against approp. for military construction	Yea
12/02/69	Pass peace with justice in Vietnam	Yea
10/03/69	Pass military procurement auth. for 1970	Yea

Date	Description	Vote
10/01/69	Adopt rule to consider military procurement authorization bill	Yea
5/06/70	Pass military procurement $20 billion r & d new weapons	Yea
6/11/70	Pass H.R. 17970 1971 defense appropriations	Yea
11/16/70	Pass H.es. 1355 war pwrs., President and Congress	Yea
10/08/70	Pass H.R. 19590 defense approp. 1971	Yea
8/05/69	Recommit military construction bill with instructions to remove sections on Pentagon picketing	Nay
3/16/70	Increase rank of Natl. Guard Chief to three stars	Yea
10/08/70	Recommit H.R. 19590 1971 defense approp.	Nay
3/23/70	Auth. loans of subs., etc. to some Asian countries	Yea
12/21/70	Pass H.R. 14233 modify ammunition record requirement	Yea
1/29/70	Authorize security procedures for defense industry employees	Yea
6/03/69	Order previous quest. H.R. 1051 increase public debt	Nay
10/03/69	Recommit military procurement authorization	Yea
6/08/70	H.R. 976 authorize committee to study Southeast Asia first-hand	Yea
12/01/69	Adopt rule for consideration of a Vietnam resolution	Yea
10/30/69	Rule for considering modification of Selective Service System	Yea
6/08/70	Amend H.R. 976, Strike preamble—committee to study Southeast Asia	Yea
5/20/70	Recommit military construction authorization	Yea
12/09/69	Amend foreign aid approp. $50 million to assist Korea	Yea
7/09/70	H.R. 15628 Amend For. Mil. Sales Act	Yea
5/06/70	Recommit military authorization—stop Leggett amendment	Yea
12/01/69	Rule for consideration Vietnam Resolution	Yea
5/07/70	Stop note on Cambodia—consider 1970 supplemental appropriation	Yea
12/20/69	Recommit foreign aid appropriations—no $54.5 million for China planes	Nay
7/09/70	Table motion instruct conferees Cooper-Church	Yea
10/03/69	Recommit military procurement auth. bill—no ABM funds	Yea
10/08/69	Recommit public works and AEC appropriations	Yea
4/28/70	Recommit and reduce ACDA authorization for 1971	Nay

Arms and the American Way: The Ideological Dimension of Military Growth

Douglas H. Rosenberg

The effect of a parade of sonorous phrases upon human conduct has never been adequately studied.

Thurman Arnold

I. Introduction

The impression one gets from the current debate on national security is that the U. S. has created a Frankenstein monster, running amuck, out of all control. Precious resources are gobbled up by an ever-expanding defense budget, while urgent domestic needs go unmet. Absurdly destructive weapons systems of questionable strategic value are developed and deployed with chilling inevitability. Secret wars and intrigues are carried on without the knowledge, and occasionally with the deliberate deception, of the American people and their representatives. Propaganda and "pacification" programs are directed at both foreign and domestic populations. U. S. citizens are kept under military surveillance; other groups are clandestinely funded through CIA "pipelines." And the nation is mired in a war which nobody seems to want, for reasons nobody seems to understand, with consequences which are ripping national legitimacy to shreds.

Americans in many areas are reacting with indignation to these abuses. Congress has launched investigations into military procurement, propaganda and snooping. It has seriously challenged (and nearly stopped) a major new weapons system. It has attempted to assert its authority over arms aid policy and even over the president's war plans. Until recently an expired draft law sat awaiting renewal. The military can no longer anticipate easy congressional passage of its every request; on the contrary, national security policies are being more closely scrutinized and more hotly challenged than at any time in the past thirty years.

Other groups have joined the attack. Radicals and pacifists have long opposed America's security policies. But their ranks have grown immensely in the recent past. Moreover, one now sees antiwar demonstrations attended by such unlikely critics as businessmen in their three-piece suits and veterans in their battle fatigues. College faculties and students throw ROTC units off campus. Former government officials turn out antiwar and antimilitary memoirs. Exweapons scientists write articles against ABM. One former RAND analyst has even risked prison to "expose" the American war machine.

And while critics read out their indictment, the attempt is made —by polemicists, by participants and lately by scholars—to analyze and explain what went wrong. How did we allow control of the military and military policy to slip beyond our grasp? Why has national security machinery expanded so—and why does it now seem so out of phase with American needs and values? What variables best "explain" our national security policies over time?

Political science is just beginning to seek explanations for military expansion. Indeed, the authors in this volume have all had to grapple with explanatory theories of bureaucratic momentum or military-industrial-political symbiosis or Soviet aggression or American imperialism. While it is essential that we ask what lies behind military policy, it is curious that we raise these questions just now. A decade ago, the justification, and hence the explanation, for America's foreign and military policies appeared self-evident to most of us: the U. S. needed a large and effective military to counter communist "aggression" around the world. Yet neither the policies nor their official justification has really changed much in the last ten years. The military's role in our national life, its claim on our resources, its enormous bureaucracy, its destructive weapons, its world-wide activities—all have remained relatively constant. Why then has the military only recently become a major political problem? Why does it only now require explanation?

Like the Europeans when they first "discovered" that their universe was not geocentric, Americans are now discovering their militarism through a shift in consciousness, a radical redefinition of their world. It is not the military, but our perception of it that has changed. Certain assumptions were once accepted without question: America's goals were noble and just; the country was threatened by a powerful and ruthless and wicked foe; the choice was between survival and annihilation. It did not occur to us, therefore, that the basic outline of defense policy required explanation. The visible reality was the threat; the military was merely the instrument to deal with that threat. Waste, concentration of power, reduced domestic programs and extended commitments were all unfortunate burdens of an effective military policy. Whether that policy was necessary in the first place was a question few people thought to ask.

In time of political upheaval, our most deeply held assumptions can lose their self-evident quality.[1] Questions we never thought to raise can suddenly become impossible to ignore. Like the camouflaged image in some optical illusion, a previously invisible problem can at once become so obvious that we believe the world has changed before our eyes. And we cannot again see things as we once did. The phenomenon which now stands so conspicuously before us (in this case, militarism) *demands* explanation. How did it get there? How does it work? What are its effects? Its very presence generates theories which, in a prior frame of mind, would have had little meaning. It is this shift in consciousness, and the set of questions which a new vision forces upon us, that makes a volume such as this possible.

The change in our perception of the military is as interesting a question for social science as is military policy itself. But beyond

[1]The "upheaval" to which I refer goes beyond the Vietnam war, though the war is certainly central to some change in American politics. While this essay is framed by a discussion of contemporary crisis, I have not undertaken to analyze the real dynamics of *shifting* consciousness, either at the beginning of the cold war or today. The prior task seems to be that of understanding the effects of relatively stable assumptions.

its intrinsic interest, this change suggests a possible explanation
for the phenomenal growth of military functions since World
War II. If new assumptions can hinder Pentagon expansion, consider the effects of previous assumptions in promoting expansion. The cold war beliefs which caused most scholars to ignore
the military as a political problem may well have been central in
allowing military power to grow. The current wave of antimilitary
feeling is dramatic only in contrast to prior feeling, which was
overwhelmingly promilitary.

While many factors share responsibility for security policy,
there is an important sense in which military power grew as
America's aims required it to grow. As Dickey's article in this
book indicates, the kind of job given to the military can place
heavy strains on an officer's politically "neutral" professionalism.[2] He may find it difficult to accomplish the job without expanding his organization or involving himself in politics. And yet
the demand for expanded missions and budgets has come from
many quarters *outside* of the armed forces. A promilitary stance
by politicians has traditionally won votes, not lost them. Congressmen have more frequently lobbied to increase defense
spending than to cut it. Even civil disturbance missions were
usually initiated by civilian leaders. Since World War II, military
expansion has been encouraged by most sectors of the society
and opposed by very few.

Control has never really left civilian hands. Of course there is
considerable "inertia" in the system, and the military often accept new missions eagerly or lobby for narrow organizational
interests. But most of the important military expansions—e.g.,
the 1950 rearmament (planned *before* the Korean war) and the
Kennedy-McNamara buildup of 1961—were conceived and
planned by civilians with popular acquiescence and usually popular support. As Sidney Lens observes,

It is inconceivable . . . that men as conversant with the mechanism of
power as our politicians would have yielded such power to the military
goliath if they hadn't felt it carried out their own goals.[3]

[2]See also William Appleman Williams, "Officers and Gentlemen," *The New York
Review of Books*, vol. 16, no. 8 (May 6, 1971), pp. 3–8.
[3]Sidney Lens, *The Military-Industrial Complex* (Philadelphia: Pilgrim Press and
Catholic Reporter, 1970), p. 12.

Whether genuine or induced, the goals of the American people with respect to foreign and military policy have resembled those of their politicians. Thus broadly shared goals have placed heavy demands on military structures—demands which often seemed to require the expansion of those structures. As popular goals change (and those of the "monster" remain the same), we come to perceive the defense establishment as out of control. But until recently such perceptions have been rare.

There is more behind security policy than the goals and beliefs of the American people and their leaders. Analysts have pointed to greed and ambition, power elite and bureaucratic management, economic interest and political maneuver. The goals and beliefs themselves may have arisen out of personality or socialization or economic advantage or political propaganda. They may be in conflict or consensus, reflecting the interests of elites or masses. And they may relate to actual decisions in various ways: as genuine motivations, as legitimizing rationalizations or as manipulated instruments of social control and convenient substitutes for force. But whatever their source and function, goals and beliefs are important in understanding our foreign and military policies.

The remainder of this essay will consider the place of goals and beliefs in the growth and development of national security institutions. Since national security is not usually discussed in this way and since my conclusions must still be rather speculative, I shall devote some space to laying a theoretical basis for the substantive hypotheses which follow. Thus Section II will deal generally with the concepts of myth and ideology and with how these relate to political and cultural processes in a society. Section III will describe more specifically the mechanisms by which symbols—particularly those of the cold war and national security—convey their meanings and hence produce mythic and ideological assumptions of great power. Readers interested primarily in the practical application of these ideas may prefer to skip Sections II and III. Section IV will build on the sociological and semantic discussions of the two previous sections and will examine American ideology more systematically, offering several hypotheses about its relationship to military growth. Finally, Section V will suggest some ideas about the apparent change in beliefs and goals noted above and about the prospects for any resulting change in policy.

II. The Mythic Setting of Politics

The whole body of beliefs existing in any given age may generally be traced to certain fundamental assumptions which at the time, whether they be actually true or false, are believed by the mass of the world to be true with such confidence that they hardly appear to bear the character of assumptions.

A.V. Dicey

THE POWER OF CONTEXT

The study of civil-military relations is most often the study of institutions: the army, the Congress, the presidency, the Department of Defense, the weapons manufacturer. Usually our attention is focused on structures, on activities and particularly on decisions—how they are made, what they accomplish. Institutions are thus abstracted from the rest of society. Research seeks to illuminate perspectives distinctive to the organization and to examine power wielded through organizational roles. Moreover, when a decision is analyzed at close range, the conflicts within the institution appear more intense, the differences more significant. Detailed analysis of conflict and choice in civil-military relations will therefore make us highly aware of the subtleties which separate Republican from Democrat, army from navy or General Dynamics from Lockheed.

The drawback of such an approach is that "decisions" tend to involve marginal changes, incremental compromises rather than choices which strike at the heart of the institution. To explain a decision is thus not to explain policy or to understand on-going practices. The "meaning" of an institution is more than the sum of its decisions; it can only be comprehended in light of real alternative meanings. And few decisions derive from real alternatives.

In Moyer's preceding study of the House, for example, we are drawn into the struggle over congressional voting. We are challenged to explain why one representative would support the Cooper-Church amendment or trim a few dollars from the defense budget while another would oppose such actions. We are reminded that the outcome of the fight made no great difference —at least not until recently—in the functioning of the military.

Even "antidefense" congressmen envisioned a rather substantial military establishment. The analysis can therefore not explain (and its author does not intend it to explain) our high defense expenditures. In light of the alternatives which were even *considered*, the Congress seems filled with sparrow hawks and chicken hawks: the latter are often mistaken for doves.

Jong Lee's article is another example of decision analysis: in this case, the focus is on the budget. We are led to look at incremental changes—hence obscuring any qualitative differences between a $12 billion and an $80 billion defense budget—because the actual size of the budget is best "explained" by the size of the previous year's budget. Thus $80 billions of Pentagon muscle—some potentially useful in influencing next year's budget decisions—are hidden in that concept of "inertia." And the essential character of a troubled society—one which could quadruple military spending in three years but cannot even consider a comparable reduction—remains unrevealed by those marginal changes in socioeconomic indicators.

These articles are valuable contributions to the literature on decision processes. Yet the ideological *context* in which alternatives are proposed or even thought about may be more important in the long run than the decision itself. How important is the personality or the party of the president when, as Nixon is fond of reminding us, the Vietnam involvement is now in its fifth administration? How important is the Cooper-Church amendment when it is interpreted simultaneously to criticize and to support presidential policy? What meaning can we give to the all-volunteer army if it still amounts to 3 million men and still polices the world? If most decisions only alter the margins of policy, then it is time we began systematically to examine the context—the assumptions—which gives policy its fundamental meaning.

Studying the context of a decision or an institution can be analytically useful. Context limits debate by defining acceptable or even possible solutions. It draws our attention to factors which affect politics in similar ways, in ways more compelling than the usual "influence" attributed to groups and institutions. Instead of decisions we begin to notice the "nondecisions"—activities and processes that go their way under assumptions that nobody wants to change or nobody thinks to change or nobody feels able to change. While these assumptions are not traditionally thought of as part of anybody's "power," the concept is just as useful in understanding why things are as they are or in predicting how they will be.[4]

We need not presuppose that assumptions are uniform across the whole of society. There are likely to be important differences within a population, and it is particularly useful to know what these differences are. We would especially want to compare members of governmental and national security institutions to the rest of the population. Still, while admitting differences, we must also ask ourselves if there are not significant areas of consensus. Is there some limited *range* within which beliefs may differ but which, as a whole, sets the population apart from other populations and from its severest critics? I believe that there is such a range and that the consensus within it is crucial to any understanding of national security policy since World War II.

MYTH, IDEOLOGY AND CULTURE

The beliefs, values and styles which make up this notion of "context" have been studied under various names: political culture, ideology and myth are perhaps most common. Though the literature on these concepts is broad and venerable, it has rarely been applied to the study of American security institutions. Before turning to the American case, it will be fruitful to draw out some of the insights of this more general literature. An understanding of myth and ideology in the broadest terms will make us less resistant to analysis of specific applications, i.e. analysis of *American* myth and ideology. We may never feel comfortable in subjecting deeply held beliefs to dispassionate scrutiny, but our conclusions will be more acceptable if firmly rooted in theory.

In this essay "myth" shall be taken in the broadest sense, encompassing both "ideology" and "political culture." Unlike the purely religious myth which focuses on stories, political myth consists of *all* of a society's fundamental beliefs, values, predispositions and symbols which have some relevance to politics. But the function of the political myth is much the same as that of the

---

[4]For a discussion of power and nondecision, see Peter Bachrach and Morton S. Baratz, "Two Faces of Power," *American Political Science Review* 56 (December 1962): 947–952, and Bachrach and Baratz, "Decisions and Nondecisions: An Analytical Framework," *American Political Science Review* 57 (1963): 632–642.

religious: it orients and binds a group both cognitively and affec-
tively, providing a *basis* for discussion and action. Also like religion, myth ranges in form from explicit elaboration of doctrine
to implicit attitudes and styles deeply imbedded in culture:

> Thus there develops a set of shared meanings, conscious and uncon-
> scious symbols, common themes of imagination and explicit doctrines
> of philosophy and religion which constitute the myth of society.
> The official pronouncements of our society show but the top and most
> rationalized layer of our social myth. . . . Often the myth of an age can
> be found in the issues, it takes for granted—in the questions it never
> asks, in the assumptions so universally shared they remain tacit.[5]

This "top and most rationalized layer of our social myth" is
what we usually mean by "ideology." It includes the beliefs,
values and action programs which are conscious, explicit and
systematic. Ideology is a *system* of beliefs. That is, its symbols have
a certain integrated, unified quality. They "hang together" with
a consistency which, while it may be artificial or illogical, is at least
recognized as a general standard for imposing constraints on
belief-elements. Beliefs which have this type of consistency will
normally be consciously recognized by the ideologue. Indeed, he
is usually able to identify his ideology by a specific *name* (though
he may not call it an ideology). And once we recognize the
ideology, the belief constraints allow us to predict his attitudes
across a wide range of issues.[6]

Those elements of ideology (i.e., particular symbols, beliefs,
values and action-ideas) which are held *less* consciously or systematically, yet are generally diffused throughout particular mass
publics, are often considered traits of "political culture."[7] They

[5]Kenneth Keniston, *The Uncommitted* (New York: Dell Publishing Co., 1965), p.
316. See also Harold D. Lasswell and Abraham Kaplan, *Power and Society* (New
Haven, Conn.: Yale University Press, 1950), pp. 116 ff.

[6]Karl Mannheim, *Ideology and Utopia* (New York: Harcourt, Brace and World,
1936) is still the classic and seminal work on ideology and the sociology of
knowledge. It includes an extensive bibliography. A useful collection of more
recent articles, with supplemental bibliography, is David E. Apter, ed., *Ideology and
Discontent* (New York: Macmillan, 1964).

[7]See Lucian Pye and Sidney Verba, eds., *Political Culture and Political Development*
(Princeton, N.J.: Princeton University Press, 1965), Introduction and Conclusion.
See also Alex Inkeles and Daniel Levinson, "National Character in the Perspectives of the Social Sciences," *Handbook of Social Psychology*, 2d ed., vol. 4, chap. 34,
for an extended bibliographic essay.

make up the "deeper layers" of the social myth. Also part of political culture is a group's attitudes, predispositions and "styles," or at least those with some relation to politics. Such attitudes might include a generalized deference toward technology, which supports weapons development. Another example might be a widespread predisposition always to pursue a course once it is set—which affects the implementation of contingency plans to the point where the plan is followed even when the contingency fails to arise. Finally, political culture would include particular personality traits—e.g., fear of failure, aggression, megalomania—which are found to reflect true modal characteristics of a society. ·

The concepts of myth, ideology and culture are intended to be used in a nonevaluative sense. That is, it is an open question whether the beliefs are accurate, the values worthy or the programs realistic. *We* may make these judgments, but the concepts themselves cannot do it for us. Moreover, it is misleading to evaluate ideological symbols according to their literal meaning. We must attempt to understand how the symbols function *qua* symbol, within their own political and cultural—not to mention semantic—milieu. Only then can their true "meaning" be discerned. Maintaining the nonevaluative character of these concepts is difficult but essential. It involves being able to say, for example, that policy X results from the *belief* of a Russian threat and the *goal* to counteract it, rather than that policy X results from a Russian threat. It involves being able to call those beliefs and goals "ideological" or "mythic" without implying that they are therefore imagined or fanatical. It is the only way, however, that we might agree on the cause of policy X while we disagree on its morality or wisdom.

FUNCTIONS OF MYTH

It is a principal argument of this essay that American myth—about strength and weakness, about communism and the Free World, about the world order and our place in it—provides a better explanation of the size and scope of U. S. military activities than any other factor. Unless one's view is particularly conspiratorial, however, it is hard to believe that increasing defense expenditure is the sole purpose behind social myth. As theorists have pointed out, myth performs numerous tasks, many quite fundamental to the smooth operation of society. In light of these more general functions, it is not surprising that myth appears to be both deep and ubiquitous, and that its influence on security policy is correspondingly great.

Myth is not limited to particular cultures or stages of development. According to Keniston, every person has a psychological *need* for myth to provide categories and purposes—the indespensible "map" which guides our understanding, our feelings and our action. Moreover, communication and socialization patterns promote widespread overlapping of personal myth and the development of collective myth. The passage of time reinforces these myths, strengthens their integrity and allows them to become deeply established in the performance of societal functions:

. . . all men have and need conscious and unconscious premises that shape their experience, their interpretations of life and their behavior; and in every individual or society these premises are organized into a more or less coherent mythic whole. . . .

To the extent that they interpret the world through prisms of a common myth, men and women will respond to reality in similar ways, will act in harmony, will support and help one another.

. . . Leaders have always known that if their followers believe they are engaged in an active struggle for a noble cause, they will make enormous sacrifices to achieve this cause.[8]

While it is commonplace to speak of anticommunism as a semireligious "cause" which inflates U. S. military commitments, it is sobering to think of this cause as fulfilling basic psychological needs, a part of the very process of social intercourse.

The political functions of myth and religion were recognized in the earliest societies. Moses handed down the law; Pharaoh embodied the cosmic order on earth. Political thinkers have not been above manipulating myth when they felt society's assumptions needed changing: Plato advocated cleaning up the activities which poets attributed to the gods, since the state should offer only worthy examples for young school children to follow. Plato also gave us the paradigm of political myth in his "convenient fiction" of the metals. Not only did his division of the population into gold, silver, brass and iron justify a ruling elite and a stratified social order, but a common, "earth-born" origin for all

[8]Kenneth Keniston, *The Uncommitted*, pp. 314–317.

citizens fostered social cohesion and attachment to the land. Similarly, Nixon's recent emphasis on the "work ethic" and the "competitive spirit" is more than mere political rhetoric to win support for a particular program: it is intended to supply the very roots of the economic order with a renewed wellspring of political legitimacy.

Even philosophers who doubted religious doctrines and opposed the organized church have recognized that myth fulfills indispensible political needs. Rousseau, for example, felt that Christianity had been a political disaster. Yet he did not question the need for religion itself:

. . . no State has ever been established without having religion for its basis; . . . [The "religion of the citizen"] is good in that it unites the divine cult with love of the laws, and, by making their country an object of the citizens' adoration, it teaches them to serve the State and to serve its tutelary God. . . . To die for one's country is martyrdom; to violate the laws is impiety;[9]

Or, more to the point of this essay, Machiavelli condemned the church, yet he saw the imperial potential of religion:

And whoever reads Roman history attentively will see in how great a degree religion served in the command of armies; . . . for where religion exists, it is easy to introduce armies and discipline. . . .[10]

It is essential that we do not necessarily interpret the myth as a lie, noble or otherwise. A mistake of many radical critics is that they see government statements about "preserving freedom" or "honoring our commitments" as simply so much callous hypocrisy. Such statements may be false. Buy while myth may be invented or manipulated by a ruling class, it serves that class best when it is believed by all. Social cohesion would be difficult to maintain if major parts of the elite were to deny—even silently —the beliefs upon which that society was based. The moral-legal justification which allows a regime to govern without the constant use of force would break down in the face of widespread challenges to its basic assumptions. Rulers would lose the confidence to meet those challenges if they did not feel they were right in

---

[9] Rousseau, *The Social Contract* (New York: Hafner, 1947), p. 119.
[10] Machiavelli, *The Discourses* (New York: Modern Library, 1950), p. 147.

what they did. The essential staying power of myth is that even when it *does* support an exploitative social order, it performs functions which inhibit both masses and elites from questioning it.

Hence Plato suggested that in a few generations the rulers of his republic would begin to believe the myths they had invented. And why not? They would have every incentive. No one likes to think himself a hypocrite, a tyrant, an exploiter. Even among the masses, there are powerful psychological pressures toward acceptance of myth: no one likes to see himself constantly fooled, bullied and robbed either. When the masses reject the myth, they become a potential revolutionary class. And as Brinton points out, when those who *govern* begin to doubt the moral superiority of their principles, the consequences can be just as momentous:

When numerous and influential members of such a class begin to believe that they hold power unjustly, or that all men are brothers, equal in the eyes of eternal justice, or that the beliefs they were brought up on are silly, or that "after us the deluge," they are not likely to resist successfully any serious attacks on their social, economic, and political position.[11]

The recent "shift in consciousness," discussed earlier, should be seen in light of these more basic social functions, for its implications reach beyond a mere change in our perception of the military.

Myth then fulfills deep psychological needs, unifies society and supports its political, social and economic arrangements. It is also accepted by persons of vastly differing status and role, and hence it must function differently for different groups within the society. Anticommunism, for example, might serve the economic interests of an overseas investor, the career interests of a military officer and the very survival of a soldier in the field.

Many writers have commented on how this differential functioning of myth helps governing elites establish legitimacy and social control. The most powerful ruler cannot rely on force alone ("Even the tyrant must sleep," says Hobbes), and so mythically supported legitimacy greatly increases what Easton de-

[11]Crane Brinton, *The Anatomy of Revolution* (New York: Random House, 1965), pp. 51–52.

scribes as the efficiency of the system. Myth, in other words, attaches right to might.[12] Or, as Marx more forcibly states:

Law, morality, religion are . . . so many bourgeois prejudices, behind which lurk in ambush just as many bourgeois interests.[13]

But if myth is one of the weapons of the elite, it is also one of their comforts. It integrates class interests into a more generalized pattern of ethical beliefs and social norms. This function explains why it is so hard to pin down the motivation behind the so-called military-industrial complex. If a dominant social myth (e.g., "world freedom") favors high defense spending, on what basis can we separate out the narrow interest of, say, the weapons contractor, military officer, international businessman or anyone else who stands to gain simply by subscribing to that myth? Again, the point is not hypocrisy, for it is a central *function* of myth to represent sincerely the group interest as the general interest. These people really do believe that bigger and better weapons are for the public good. Their narrow interests may reinforce the dominant myth, but there is virtually no way to prove that their self-seeking directly inflates defense budgets.

How does myth function for nonelite groups? Clearly, it could also favor *their* interests. It is sometimes said, for example, that myth supports an American empire, and if the American masses benefit economically from this empire, then the myth is no less rational for them than for their employers. It is also possible that freedom really *is* at stake in the cold war, in which case anticommunism would again serve popular interests. And finally, part of the American myth is "democracy," an idea portrayed by classical theorists as favoring the poor at the expense of the rich. We cannot analyze these myths, however, apart from the systems which they underlie. Democracy may favor the poor, but the word "democracy" is merely a symbol. It represents many different phenomena. And like many symbols (e.g., euphemisms), it may be used to obscure the reality it purports to represent.

---

[12]David Easton, *A Systems Analysis of Political Life* (New York: Wiley, 1965), p. 286.

[13]Karl Marx and Friedrich Engels, *Manifesto of the Communist Party* in Lewis S. Feuer, ed., *Marx & Engels: Basic Writings on Politics and Society* (New York: Doubleday, 1959), p. 18.

Another function of myth among the masses is commonly held to involve psychological "interests." That is, myth makes people more satisfied—or less discontent—with a bad lot. Not just religion, but law, morality and political doctrine itself can be opiates of the people. They can justify hardships and inequalities in the name of history or nature or general moral principle—and they can render evil more palatable to those who must suffer it. The reverse appears also to be true: the more people suffer, the more they are likely to support and believe the myth which justifies their suffering.[14] Some critics cite this function to explain the "hard-hat phenomenon," the working class superpatriotism which fits so poorly into a purely economic interpretation of military expansion. These functions of myth and their relation to military expansion, will be discussed in greater detail in Section IV.

SOURCES OF MYTH

The differing functions of myth suggest several ideas about its sources. Clifford Geertz divides these into "interest" and "strain" theories.[15] Interest theory, deriving from Marx, sees myth as "a mask and a weapon" arising out of, and supporting, class interests. Thus capitalist democracy, and American efforts to make the world safe for it, emanate from the owning class— or at least from

---

[14]This result would be predicted by cognitive dissonance theory. Negative feelings about U.S. policies are dissonant with the cognition that one fought to defend them. The pain of war is too severe to deny, and so the dissonance is reduced by denying one's feelings about the policies. A draft-deferred college student might have less "investment" in those policies. See Leon A. Festinger, *A Theory of Cognitive Dissonance* (Evanston: Row, Peterson, 1957). For an example of one of the "initiation" experiments, see Elliot Aronson and Judson Mills, "The Effect of Severity of Initiation on Liking for a Group," *Journal of Abnormal Social Psychology*, LIX (1959): 177–181. It should be noted that if both the negative feelings and the pain of war are too severe to deny, hostility would likely be directed at the agency which caused both, i.e. the U.S. government.

[15]Clifford Geertz, "Ideology as a Cultural System," in David E. Apter, ed., *Ideology and Discontent* (I would include here a somewhat more extended bibliographic discussion of the concept of ideology, if that were thought to be useful), p. 52 ff. Geertz's use of "ideology" is broad, and corresponds to my use of the term "myth." Both this and the next section of my essay owe a considerable debt to Geertz's incisive analysis.

the thinkers of the class (its active, conceptive ideologists, who make the perfecting of the illusion of the class about itself their chief source of livelihood)[16]

More specifically, military doctrines like preparedness would be seen to come from those sectors of the economy involved in defense production. While the beginnings of these ideas cannot, obviously, be precisely determined, it is worth noting that much of the strategic doctrine since World War II has originated not with the military but with academic national security analysts. "The *active* members of this class," explains Marx, "have less time to make up illusions and ideas about themselves."[17]

Geertz acknowledges the power of interest theory, but he finds its psychology either underdeveloped or implausible. Viewed broadly, there is indeed a striking correspondence between a society's myths and its dominant interests. Yet this does not explain the *origin* of these myths. Rational calculation of personal advantage is hardly a believable motivational model for the birth of ideas or for the sociology of knowledge. If nothing else, it breaks down upon examination of individual cases. Few people plan their thoughts as carefully as Plato, and many mistake their "interests" altogether.

Strain theory begins with interest theory and adds:

> . . . a developed conception of personality systems (basically Freudian), on the one hand, and of social systems (basically Durkheimian) on the other, and of their modes of interpenetration—the Parsonian addition.[18]

Similar to Nietzsche's theory of "resentments," myth arises out of personal and social malintegration, role conflict and other patterned or systemic psycho-social tensions.[19] The myth becomes both "a symptom and a remedy." People of a common cultural environment, facing similar patterns of social disequilibrium, express and hence assuage the tension through common symbolic

[16]Karl Marx and Friedrich Engels, *The German Ideology*, ed. R. Pascal (New York: International Publishers, 1947), p. 40.

[17]*Ibid.* My emphasis. Marx even allows that hostility might develop between the ruling class and its professional academic ideologists. This clash, of course, "automatically comes to nothing" if the class itself is endangered.

[18]Geertz, "Ideology as a Cultural System," in Apter, ed., *Ideology and Discontent*, p. 54.

[19]Friedrich Nietzsche, *Beyond Good and Evil*, tr. Walter Kaufmann (New York: Random House, 1966), chap. 4.

modes. Strain theory complements interest theory, since strain reduction makes possible the day-to-day performance of social roles and thus tends to support existing institutional arrangements.

Other factors may be adduced to explain the origin of ideas and ideologies. Moyer has included in his study variables intended to tap personality type, particular life experiences and even Mannheim's concept of "political generation."[20] These factors can be easily integrated into strain theory, since the latter only requires that we seek explanation in the interrelationship of social and psychological systems. They may be made effectively compatible with interest theory through Weber's notion of "elective affinity." According to Weber, individual ideologues and religious innovators do not necessarily share the same interests, class or even culture with the group which eventually adopts their myth. But as that group consolidates its power and status, its members choose and adopt those features of the idea which best support their needs.[21]

These modifications lend considerable flexibility to the interpretation of American national security myths. Ideas may arise out of all sorts of historical and idiosyncratic, as well as more predictable interest-based sources. Ideas will generally gain support when they correspond to the interests of society's dominant classes, but due to the wide variety of psychological and social strains, many anomalous individual cases are to be expected. And finally, the relationship between ideas and interests is likely to be a dynamic one. A myth may *lead* the society in the sense that it gains acceptance before the new social order is well established. Or the myth may linger long after it has ceased to be functional. This flexibility makes ideological analysis more plausible, but it adds considerable difficulty to predicting changes in myth.

I began this section with the general problem of understanding the context in which decisions are made—of illuminating the basis of unquestioned assumptions which guide policy—in the hope of finding an explanation for the growth of America's mili-

[20]Karl Mannheim, *Ideology and Utopia*, p. 270 *passim*.
[21]Max Weber, "The Social Psychology of the World Religions," in H. H. Gerth and C. Wright Mills, eds., *From Max Weber: Essays in Sociology* (New York: Oxford, 1958), pp. 284–285. See also Introduction, pp. 62–63.

tary sector since World War II. To this point I have discussed the sources and functions of myth in providing any society with its assumptions. In the following section I shall turn to the content and workings of America's mythic and ideological symbols.

III. Political Semantics

"When I use a word," Humpty Dumpty said in a rather scornful tone, "it means just what I choose it to mean—neither more nor less."

"The question is," said Alice, "whether you can make words mean so many different things."

"The question is," said Humpty Dumpty, "which is to be master—that's all."

Lewis Carroll

In Moyer's article "ideological orientations" (in this case, liberal-conservative) are hypothesized as the primary motivation for a congressman's vote on defense issues. Abercrombie and Alcalá note a rise in the political content of military writings and curricula—political ideas that are read and taught. Dickey discusses the crisis in an officer's "political formula" for carrying out his missions. And Lee measures how political ideals change in the president's verbal messages to the nation. Clearly, political ideals and beliefs, and the symbols through which they are communicated, are a central concern of this volume.

The discussion of the previous section will, I hope, expand the theoretical implications of these articles. That myth varies with personality type, cultural pattern, economic system and political practice; that it does *not* reflect a one-to-one correspondence to any of these; that it is subject to interpretation and manipulation; and that it is usually accepted even by its inventors, all leads to a conclusion implicit throughout this essay: myth is composed largely of symbols, visible in the public domain, with an independent capacity to influence behavior. This conclusion is not to imply the existence of some mystical Idea marching through history. Symbols are firmly grounded in the cultural milieu which gives them meaning, and they are at least potentially predictable from concrete causes. They may well reflect the mode of production, "the language of real life," as Marx supposes. Yet even if economic relationships were the ultimate "cause" of America's world role, we would want to investigate the function of symbols in mediating and modifying and perhaps obscuring the meaning of policy.[22]

It is essential, therefore, that we begin to focus on the particular elements of a nation's myth which find symbolic expression in the political arena—and especially in the field of national security. Whereas the previous section dealt with the sociology of myth, this section concerns its semantics. The discussion will focus not on what myth does, but on what it means, or more accurately, *how* it means: i.e., the particular ways in which the mythic symbol conveys its message.

Like any symbol, ideology and myth can be "read" or learned. And like any language, they condition the individual to accept categories of thought which are common to the society and which reflect society's norms. Reinhard Bendix, in a paraphrase of Durkheim, gives the following analysis:

Language, like moral rules, religious beliefs and practices, myth, . . . and other aspects of culture, is *external* to the individual and exercises a *moral constraint* upon him. That is, these collective "representations" exist when the individual comes into the world. He acquires them unwittingly.[23]

If these symbols can be learned, they can also be taught, manipulated or undermined. As mentioned above, myths and ideologies can be political weapons. The question is, how to do it.

One theory holds that symbols work by rewarding correct responses and punishing incorrect ones. Richard Merelman has developed some interesting hypotheses about the psychological mechanisms involved in the successful manipulation of legitimacy symbols.[24] Basing his argument on traditional learn-

[22]I should perhaps make clear that I have not developed and will not develop the notion of "interest" which recurs throughout this essay. I happen to agree that economic relationships are an ultimate cause of America's world role, but I have neither the space nor the evidence necessary to demonstrate the proposition at this time. I have intentionally limited my argument to the very important intermediate step in the translation of interest into action, a step which does not, I believe, depend on an economic interpretation. Such an interpretation is repeatedly referred to, however, first to indicate that it is compatible with my analysis, and second, because I believe it should be taken seriously.

[23]Reinhard Bendix, "The Age of Ideology: Persistent and Changing," in Apter, ed., *Ideology and Discontent*, p. 316. Paraphrase is from Durkheim's *The Rules of Sociological Method.*

[24]Richard M. Merelman, "Learning and Legitimacy," *American Political Science Review*, 60 (September 1966): 548–561.

ing theory and on cognitive dissonance theory, he sees political legitimacy as a stage in the learning process when symbols alone —i.e., without any other government output—can produce popular gratification, can become the "secondary reinforcement" for a population learning to comply with government policies. To reduce cognitive dissonance when no material gratification is forthcoming, the population begins to value the symbols themselves (like Pavlov's dog doing tricks merely in order to *hear* the dinner bell). This becomes rationalized into a general sense of legitimacy which enormously increases the government's "efficiency." Compliance is assured through the manipulation of symbols alone; the government does not have to prove the validity of its actions each time.

Concrete examples may be found in the manipulation of cold war symbols. After World War II the demand for demobilization was so great that, to reverse the trend, Senator Vandenberg is quoted as saying it was necessary to "scare the hell out of the country." Governmental legitimacy at the time was high, and scare symbols were not far removed from the real "reinforcement" of the war. Moreover, scare tactics themselves added strain to an already tense society. Vigilance against an enemy could therefore be "taught" to the population by rewarding (as positive reinforcement) with the *symbols* of freedom and survival and by punishing (as negative reinforcement) with the *symbols* of betrayal and destruction.

The weakness of this theory is that secondary reinforcements derive their power only from their association with some primary reinforcement. This ignores a major factor in a symbol's effectiveness because it ignores content. Symbols are more than simply powerful reinforcements for learning. They "teach" primarily because they have meaning. Nixon's use of the label "Pink Lady" in the campaign of 1950, for example, conveyed a message to the voters which was potentially devastating to his opponent. A spreading, blood-red blob on the map of Asia, depicted in military public information films, induced us to support the containment policy because of the "information" it contained. A scare symbol could reinforce official anticommunism because it had something to say about communism:

Newspapers are not content with saying that communism is a menace; they supply political cartoons depicting communists as criminally insane people placing sticks of dynamite under magnificent buildings labeled "American way of life."[25]

There are many ways to pack meaning into these symbol-weapons. Marcuse has described with great vigor the art of "political linguistics." "Bad words" are reserved for the establishment's enemies in order to isolate and condemn them. Definitions are changed to correspond with symbolic intent rather than historical connotation. "Law and order" is used to mean anything the establishment does, no matter how violent, while "violence" is defined by opposition to the system, no matter how peaceful.

[O]ne of the most effective rights of the Sovereign is the right to establish enforceable definitions of words. . . . The language of the prevailing Law and Order, validated by the courts and by the police, is not only the voice but also the deed of suppression. This language not only defines and condemns the Enemy, it also *creates* him; and this creation is not the Enemy as he really is, but rather as he must be in order to perform his function for the Establishment.[26]

Symbol-weapons are not limited to the establishment. Marcuse also describes the widespread "linguistic rebellion" by which radicals are expressing their opposition to the politico-symbolic order.[27] The cultivated use of obscenities, for example, develops a vocabulary which the establishment cannot co-opt. One need only adopt a few disgusting habits and such slogans as "Today's Army Wants to Join You" become absurd. Incongruity and inversion of meaning, as in "flower-power," attempt to confound establishment rationality. Adoption and earthy reinterpretation of lofty concepts—e.g., the term "soul"—provide what Marcuse calls a "de-sublimation" of language. Maligning or irreverence toward sacred symbols is one of few weapons with which the weak can harm the strong.

The drawback of a symbol-weapon theory, of a "military" interpretation of meaning, is that the symbols, the myths, the ideologies must inevitably be seen as pathological—a kind of linguistic germ warfare, where weapons are only as powerful as they are malignant. Myth is seen as distortion, whether in-

[25]S. I. Hayakawa, *Language in Thought and Action*, 2d ed. (New York: Harcourt, Brace and World, 1964), p. 103.
[26]Herbert Marcuse, *An Essay on Liberation* (Boston: Beacon, 1969), p. 74.
[27]*Ibid.*, pp. 32 ff.

tentional or not, as thinking which violates truth, as a some-
times-necessary evil whose eradication is a legitimate goal of
social progress. No one really *wants* to use symbols in this
way, and few would admit to holding an ideology which fits
this description. It would be hard to claim that such a concept
is nonevaluative.

We run into this problem because we expect the symbol to do
something it is not always intended to do: to convey accurate
information about the world:

Whether a statement is true or false, validly or invalidly deduced from
others, and so on, are questions important only with regard to those
statements whose successful functioning requires these characteristics.
There is a considerable tendency to misunderstand semantics as requir-
ing of all symbols the properties essential to scientific discourse. The
mistake is made of supposing that symbols lacking these properties are
to be rejected as "nonsense" rather than analyzed in terms of functions
other that that of conveying knowledge.[28]

To expect factual accuracy of poetry or prayer would be absurd.
Neither, then, should political analysis be forced to use such a
restricted notion of meaning.

Following the literary analogy a step further, the meaning of
a political symbol cannot really be separated from its "performance of itself." Like a poem, the symbol has meaning which a
paraphrase or an analysis cannot expect to reproduce. We can,
however, illuminate its meaning by increasing our sensitivity to
the semantic devices it employs.

There are different *kinds* of meaning. Ideology is defined above
(p. 151) to include beliefs, values and action programs, and we
would expect ideological symbols to be able to express at least
these elements. Thus the kinds of meaning most relevant to
ideology can be divided into cognitive, affective and hortatory
meanings. Returning to our map of Asia, for example, we would
say the symbol teaches the belief that communism tends to
spread, expresses the value that communism is bad and urges
support for the program of containment. Only the cognitive
meaning can be judged according to its factual accuracy, and
even here poetic license permits a rhetorical treatment of facts.

[28]Laswell and Kaplan, *Power and Society*, p. 12.

What does it matter that the red blob of communism spills over into unthreatened or uninhabited areas of the map—if our point gets across?

Such analysis cannot capture the symbol's full meaning, however. If it could, we might simply substitute the analysis for the symbol, and perhaps gain some clarity in the process. Obviously such a substitution would lose more in *effectiveness* than it would gain in clarity. The affective and hortatory power of the symbol would be all but lost. We would be closer to understanding what the symbol is trying to do but further from actually doing it.

One reason the map symbol is effective is that it has a certain elegance, a certain richness and economy of form. With a single expression it can convey its cognitive, affective and hortatory meanings. Moreover, each of these is strengthened by a variety of related ideas and images. The horror of the blob, the taint of its color, the threat of its macabre movement and growth—and standing opposite, wearing the familiar uniform (order, strength), holding the pointer (knowledge, solutions) is handsome and kindly Col. Containment, U.S.A.

Mythic symbols are especially economical and effective because they cultivate the historical and cultural roots which more neutral or "scientific" symbols, seeking universality, attempt to sever. How damning would it be in some European country, for example, to be called The-Sixth-President-to-Lose-a-War? Or, in this society, which has been described as straining between the anal-retentive and the phallic-aggressive, where virility is prized and sensuality shunned, consider for a moment the import of the following slogans: containment; soft on communism; effete snobs; intellectual eunuchs; missile gap; rocket rattling; number one; third world neutralism. Of course, any language operates through some kind of "cultural allusion" process. But in myth this process is particularly direct.

Economy and effectiveness are also achieved through the same wide variety of rhetorical practices which we find operating in other literary efforts. This is why we should not demand literal accuracy from even the cognitive import of myth. It is commonplace now to ridicule the phrase "the Free World" on the grounds that it includes Spain, Greece and other countries which are manifestly not free. Yet such grounds ignore the powerful metaphor that has carried our self-conception over two decades.

z points out, metaphor is effective precisely because it
.[29] The collection of noncommunist countries is neither
free a world, yet using the phrase influences our beliefs and
values—as outright lying could not.

Thus "the Free World" treats its opposite, "communism,"
as something both unfree and alien—darker, more mysterious
and hence more evil even than the dictatorships we reluctantly
support. Among those who share the same world, there is at
least unity and familiarity, if not unexceptionable virtue. "Free
World," the synecdoche of substituting the whole world for a
mere part of it, testifies to the universality of "our side" and
hints that there is really no room for "their side." The figure
is strengthened by what Americans see as their particular historical claim on the idea of freedom—as opposed to the
"slave labor camps" they associate with the Soviet Union. And
finally, the planetary image conjured up by a Free World is
sharpened by the cultural setting of the last twenty-five years:
an age of UFO's and science-fiction movies, where invading
aliens insidiously take over the world by assuming the identity
of your friends, and creatures and blobs grow and multiply on
a diet of human flesh.

The meaning of a symbol is fluid rather than fixed, and it is
often made more complex by allusion to other, interrelated symbols. Myth takes advantage of this richness by providing a
vocabulary of symbols which interact easily. Thus the policy of
the Free World is called containment, plugging off any leaks
which would allow contamination from the alien world. Communism must be kept from "spreading" (this image does not permit
us to identify the organism precisely, but then alien life forms are,
perhaps, part of that which man was not meant to know). During
the Korean War the Chinese were almost universally described
as "swarming" over the border. And yet they cannot penetrate
the Iron Curtain (an oxymoron which reflects the paradox of an
organism that spreads, yet remains isolated.) Here at home, we
must beware of "creeping socialism." Full infection turns one
zombie-like and rather discolored; clearly one is "better dead
than red" (a rhyming slogan which suggests the all-or-nothing
character of the struggle and tells us what we have to lose). Above

[29]Geertz, "Ideology as a Cultural System," p. 58.

all there must be no attempt to "appease" communism's insatiable appetite (an allusion to another complex of symbols dating back to an earlier war.)

Not all myth which affects security policy is centered on communism. Some grows out of the nation's conception of self: democracy, free enterprise, American way of life, world leader, anticolonial heritage. Some reflects more specifically military meanings: preparedness, first-rate power, control of the seas, intervention. All, however, includes complex, interrelated and not-easily separable beliefs, values and programs expressed with symbolic tools designed to encourage enthusiastic acceptance. The tools themselves have a long history of respectable use. We should not judge them when we mean to judge the motive or the effect of the myth they convey. Personification need not be arrogant; loaded words need not lead to demagogy; ambiguity, irony, overstatement or understatement need not imply deceit.

And mythic symbols do not consist solely of slogans. The cognitive beliefs of U. S. history and the "action program" of the U. S. Constitution both express American myth. Moreover, symbols need not be verbal: war toys, the ABM display which tours local shopping centers, the converted jet used as a jungle gym at the playground—all begin to construct a pattern of mythic symbols. Other examples could be drawn from the media, from schools, from music. Rituals like parades or patriotic days or flag saluting are important parts of myth and subject to their own special rhetorical devices—rhythm, repetition, color—to heighten some aspect of their meaning. Even where this meaning has lost its emotional intensity, the mere act of making noises at one another, as Hayakawa points out, can be socially cohesive. Thus it is not true, despite the apparent decline of old fashioned patriotism, that the symbols of the American myth no longer have meaning. For even where the national anthem has become merely a ritualist grunt before the ball game, it is a symbol whose proper interpretation can tell us something about our society.

A politician might quite consciously manipulate mythic symbols, yet remain sincere in the beliefs he wishes to convey. There is a real sense in which the film narrator *does* see a red blob overwhelming his map of Asia. It is at least theoretically possible to extract the cognitive meaning from myth and to state it in a straightforward, unembellished manner. Moreover, many ideological statements are *already* intended in just this way—as quite candid assertions of factual belief, value or program (e.g., history). We have a right to interpret these statements literally and to judge them directly for what they say. We may agree with their cognitive assertions even while we disagree with the affective connotation intended (e.g., "the U. S. is the world's 'number one' military power"). To call such statements mythic is not to deny their accuracy.

Extracting precise ideological ideas, however, is often impossible in practice. We know symbols are manipulated for effect, but we do not know how much of their meaning is believed by those who manipulate them. In a private memorandum of a 1954 Eisenhower-Dulles meeting (collected in the Pentagon Papers), the effect sought appears to overshadow the precise belief:

> The President went over the draft of the speech which Dulles is going to make tonight, making quite a few suggestions and changes in the text. He thought additionally the speech should include some easy to understand slogans, such as "The U. S. will never start a war," "The U. S. will not go to war without Congressional authority," "The U. S., as always, is trying to organize cooperative efforts to sustain the peace."

This manipulation of peace symbols is followed directly by a statement of opposition to the French ceasefire proposal on the grounds that, among other things, it would "destroy the will to fight of French forces," and by a proposal that the U. S. "go to Congress for authority to intervene with combat forces." These latter statements, of course, were not intended for public view.[30]

Perhaps more common is the symbol which is manipulated for near-literal interpretation by the masses and at the same time used to stand for a complex of more sophisticated or realistic beliefs on the part of elites. Dominoes, for example, represent to most people a theory whereby governments are quite literally toppled by spreading communism. The version of this theory held in official government is more elaborate—some countries are directly taken over, some are forced to make "accommodation" to China or to their own domestic revolutionary groups, some are made to feel uncomfortable and some are less responsive to U. S. influence—but there is little doubt that the metaphor

---

[30] *New York Times, The Pentagon Papers* (New York: Bantam, 1971), p. 41. Memorandum by Robert Cutler, special assistant to President Eisenhower, May 7, 1954.

was used meaningfully (and accepted) as a rationale by policy-makers. According to a memo from McGeorge Bundy to Lyndon Johnson,

> The fact that South Vietnam has not been lost and is not going to be lost is a fact of truly massive importance in the history of Asia, the Pacific, and the U. S. An articulate minority of "Eastern intellectuals" (like Bill Fulbright) may not believe in what they call the domino theory, but most Americans (along with nearly all Asians) know better.[31]

Even when myth *is* hypocritically manipulated, however, the user cannot help being affected by it. While he is busy controlling some of its symbols, he is unconsciously a slave to others. Or he is forced to act *as if* he accepted them because he thinks his constituency demands it. Or the symbols take on meanings he never intended, creating pressures he never wanted. Or he exploits the symbols but never questions the myth as a whole, and thus he limits his alternatives and screens out information that does not fit.

All this is to say that the symbols are objective social facts with an independent capacity to influence behavior. Often they are interpreted literally. Often ideologies become reified and symbolic interconnections rigidified. The symbols can be confused with what they symbolize; an attack on one becomes an attack on all (this is, after all, the logic of falling dominoes); and defense of the myth becomes indistinguishable from defense of the self. In such an instance, "our symbols" become the first line of defense, "their symbols," the invading enemy. Men die to raise the flag at Iwo Jima, and the City Council of Cambridge, Massachusetts, unanimously passes a resolution (in 1939) making it illegal

> to possess, harbor, sequester, introduce or transport within the city limits, any book, map, magazine, newspaper, pamphlet, handbill or circular containing the words Lenin or Leningrad.[32]

Humpty Dumpty's question—which is to be master, the man or the word?—is not an easy one. The symbol can be manipulated but not entirely dominated. We can make it do our work, but we must pay it extra wages. It can be a weapon of our class interest,

---

[31] *Ibid.*, p. 572.
[32] Cited in Hayakawa, *Language in Thought and Action*, p. 33.

but it can also begin to define that interest. As Marcuse observes,

the class interest employs the mass media for the advertising of violence and stupidity, for the creation of captive audiences. In doing so, the masters only obey the demand of the public, of the masses; . . . the masters have created the public which asks for their wares.[33]

This paradox is also the basis of Reich's observation that the American corporate state is autonomous. The great revelation about the "executive suite" is that it is empty—*no one* is in charge.

What looks like a man is only a representation of a man who does what the organization requires. He (or it) does not run the machine; he *tends* it.[34]

And in large part, prevailing myth—the symbols that have become the masters—is responsible for this autonomy.

This lack of understanding is not merely a phenomenon of the masses, for it extends to the powerful, the well educated, and the elite. . . . Indeed, the central fact about America in 1970 is the discrepancy between the realities of our society and our beliefs about them. . . . Unreality is the true source of powerlessness.[35]

Whatever the accuracy of these observations, they are nowhere more commonly applied than in the areas of national security and military growth. To these areas I now turn.

IV. The Ideological Dimension of Military Growth

The greatest contribution Vietnam is making—right or wrong is beside the point—is that it is developing an ability in the United States to fight a limited war, to go to war without the necessity of arousing the public ire. In that sense, Vietnam is almost a necessity in our history, because this is the kind of war we'll likely be facing for the next fifty years.

Robert S. McNamara

---

[33]Marcuse, *An Essay on Liberation,* p. 12.
[34]Charles A. Reich, *The Greening of America* (New York: Bantam, 1971), p. 115.
[35]*Ibid.,* pp. 12–13.

There ain't no time to wonder why,
Whoopie, we're all gonna die.

Country Joe McDonald

Two schools of thought hold that military expansion has been a
necessary development in our history. The first blames the threat
of communism abroad and of radically fomented insurrection at
home. The second cites the need of force in first expanding, then
protecting, a world empire and an exploitative social and economic system. Both schools would agree that America's dominant ideology—her fundamental beliefs, values and intentions—
prescribe a mission which the American polity is sorely taxed to
accomplish.[36]

Both schools would also reject the notion that military expansion is an inadvertant mistake, that the American people at some
point dropped their guard and the generals or the politicians or
the armsmakers added a few divisions and invaded a few countries. Or that a mindless and unresponsive bureaucracy grew
large because, well, that's just what bureaucracies do. Or that it
is simply a case of popular or governmental hysteria. The radical
school holds that our mission derives from the demands and
interests of capitalism and the American ruling class. The conservative school ties it to the demands and interests of freedom,
democracy and the American people. The major hypothesis of
this section is that, in a sense, both are right.

The interesting dilemma of cold war history is that both the
traditionalists and the revisionists present good documentary
evidence to make their point. The revisionists have cited dozens
of statements by high officials linking the central goal of postwar
foreign policy to markets, raw materials and "running the world
the way it ought to be run," in Harry Truman's revealing
phrase.[37] Traditionalists rely on a great preponderance of pro-
fessed concern with Soviet and then Chinese military expansion

[36] *Cf.*, for example, William Appleman Williams, *The Tragedy of American Diplomacy* (New York: Dell, 1959), and George Liska, *Imperial America: The International Politics of Primacy* (Baltimore, Md.: Johns Hopkins Press, 1967).

[37] Quoted in Williams, *ibid.*, p. 240. See also Sidney Lens, *The Military-Industrial
Complex*, pp. 22 ff.

and subversion. What should be evident is that these motives may be *ideologically* interrelated, such that each supports the other and both underlie policy. The ideology may shape perceived reality to the extent that a leader will prepare for Soviet aggression even when he has *said* that the Russians neither can nor will intervene; his preparations may "incidentally" bring the protected country under U. S. economic control. Or he will send troops to a war which the *economic* gains and repercussions could not possibly have warranted, where the stock market rallies with each hint of peace. Neither example disproves the motive, for the leader may at all times act *as if both* economic and security interests were at stake. The cohesiveness of the ideology makes it impossible to prove that one interest is merely a function of the other. The leader feels both.

An ideology was defined earlier to be a *system* of beliefs, values and programs. This leader's ideology, therefore, has a kind of consistency, its elements bound together into a more or less coherent whole. Try to pin him down to the reason for his intervention, and he slides back and forth from "Vital to American security and the balance of power" to "We want to see that these brave people don't have an unwanted (communist) government imposed upon them" to "The U. S. is not going to be pushed out of a crucial part of the world" to "Other countries fighting the same battle are depending on us to show resolve in this test case." He has no *single* reason: first, because all his motives are part of an integrated pattern, all defining the same response (i.e., some form of intervention); and second, because these assumptions are so deeply held that the response becomes a kind of reflex, the reasons for his actions evolving almost after the fact.

This is not to say his reasoning is faulty: the left-wing takeover of a country might well appear at the same time to harm the people, threaten U. S. interests in the area, encourage other insurrections and upset the world balance of power. Moreover, the leader might know this so well that he need not ponder the details of each case before he decides to act. Within the government he debates, of course, over what exactly to do: intervene directly in Vietnam; offer only arms or money or covert operations somewhere else. But the debate is merely about tactics. There is never any question that he should do *something* to oppose communism.

This assumption is not limited to a few government leaders. It has been widely held: articles and editorials analyzed from major newspapers during 1963, for example, indicate that while there were differences over *how* we should fight communism in Vietnam, there was no questioning of our basic mission to do so.[38] Alternatives that did not fit this mission were simply screened out. Few people outside the radical left suggested we had an obligation to remain neutral, much less to help the rebels. On at least eight occasions in 1945–1946, Ho Chi Minh requested aid from the U. S. to deny France's attempt to reconquer her former colony. These messages were apparently ignored.[39]

These observations suggest several related hypotheses about the process of military expansion. Drawing from the languages of economics and inflation spirals, I call this collection of hypotheses a theory of "ideology-pull." Briefly, the following propositions are offered:

1. There is an American ideology.
2. This ideology prescribes a mission which not only justifies, but also *demands* an immense and active military establishment.
3. Because of a combination of circumstances, the "rhetoric" of the ideology has been extremely effective in mobilizing support and evaporating opposition among the population. Even where the ideology is not understood in its entirety, the underlying myth is deep and pervasive.
4. The result has been what we might call the "hyperlegitimacy" of security symbols—where almost anything could be done (and often had to be done) in the name of defense, including especially the expansion of military functions and capabilities.
5. Generated by this expansion is a whole set of narrower interests (e.g., of defense contractors), which, however, are sub-

[38]This conclusion is based on a systematic content analysis of over 2,000 articles, editorials, and columns in the *New York Times* and two other newspapers. Categories were established for several dozen different kinds of statements or implications. While there was criticism of our Vietnam policy, not once during 1963 do the authors (including such doves as Walter Lippman and Tom Wicker) suggest that the U.S. had no right to be in Vietnam. James H. Burnley, "The Influence of the Press on U.S. Foreign Policy Toward Cuba in 1957–58 and Vietnam in 1963," Unpublished Honors Thesis (Yale University, Political Science Department, 1970), pp. 116–117.

[39] *The Pentagon Papers, Times* edition, p. 4.

sumed by, and integrated with, the dominant ideological interest. These narrower interests become legitimized as part of the "public interest" while they simultaneously reinforce the dominant ideology.

The evidence for these hypotheses is at this point only impressionistic. Systematic data are yet to be collected. On the other hand, the evidence is all around us. I will be satisfied that the theory has utility if it begins to make sense of the statements and actions of our political leaders and if it illuminates the analyses of those statements and actions offered in this volume. What follows, then, is intended as a clarification of the theory, not as a proof.

AMERICAN IDEOLOGY

What is the ideology which is so central to this discussion? Where does it come from? The American system does not have the same kind of "scriptures" as Marxist-Leninist systems: i.e., it has no set of authoritative writings one could point to as the fount of all legitimate ideas and upon which all other ideological discussion is commentary. We must, therefore, look a little harder—to those statements which form a consistent pattern of belief and value throughout the last several decades of our history or to those ideas which are used again and again to justify policy. We must synthesize a picture not only from the kinds of symbols described in the previous section but also from the pronouncements in official documents and from descriptions by independent analysts.

It is less important to be exhaustive than to uncover the central core of belief upon which there is wide agreement. I shall be concerned only with that which is particularly relevant to national security. As I hope to make clear, much of this ideology was decisively formulated in the immediate World War II period and afterward. But much also can be traced from the founding of the American nation and before.

For convenience I shall arrange my description into five categories.

1. *The American Identity.* A few years ago, I was asked by a seventh-grade student if the communists hated and feared

democracy as much as we hate and fear communism. I patiently explained the difference between political and economic systems, pointing out that communism and democracy are not necessarily opposites. I have since come to believe that my student's picture of the world was far more accurate than mine, that in the most important meaning of the words, "communism" and "democracy" are semantically at war. Official pronouncement and popular understanding have made the two systems not only polar opposites but mirror images: each is practically *defined* as the negation of the other.

The existence of a divided world, both physically and spiritually, has been the fundamental fact of American ideology for at least twenty-five years. In that sense our very identity is tied up with opposition to an alien and virulently hostile "they." The threat of communism was of course perceived much earlier. Winston Churchill, at the time of the Bolshevik Revolution, foresaw the titanic struggle to come and warned that "the baby must be strangled in its crib."[40] Secretary of State Lansing urged Woodrow Wilson to intervene against the new regime because its revolutionary ideas posed "a direct threat at existing social order in all countries."[41] But it was not until after the break-up of the World War II alliance that Truman declared the world divided into communists and anticommunists; the American identity was cast as the protagonist in a bipolar struggle, and "every nation was now faced with a choice between alternative ways of life."[42]

As I described in the last section, the symbols of the cold war represent not simply two competing "expansionist powers," in Huntington's phrase, but rather two different orders of being, as unlike as they are antagonistic. Thus *we* protect world freedom, while *they* are bent on world enslavement; *we* seek democracy and fair play, *they* spread conspiracy, treachery, destruction, dictatorship and godlessness. George Frost Kennan, one of the most distinguished and enlightened of the early cold war ideologues,

[40]Lewis Broad, *Winston Churchill: A Biography* (New York: Hawthorn, 1958), p. 186.

[41]Quoted in William Appleman Williams, "American Intervention in Russia: 1917–20," in David Horowitz, ed., *Containment and Revolution* (Boston: Beacon, 1967), p. 43.

[42]Quoted in David Horowitz, *The Free World Colossus* (New York: Hill and Wang, 1965), p. 103.

saw the opposition as almost total. In a telegraphic message he stated:

> [W]e have here a political force committed fanatically to the belief that with US there can be no permanent modus vivendi, that it is desirable and necessary that the internal harmony of our society be disrupted, our traditional way of life be destroyed, the international authority of our state be broken, if Soviet power is to be secure. This political force has complete power of disposition over energies of one of the world's greatest people and resources of the world's richest national territory . . . an elaborate far-flung apparatus for exertion of its influence in other countries . . . [and] is seemingly inaccessible to considerations of reality in its basic reactions.[43]

Kennan saw the Kremlin as the center of a monolithic conspiracy, promulgating its policies through many agencies, from labor and women's groups to the Eastern Orthodox Church. He also felt that no person or country could be exempt from the struggle, since the Russian leaders are "by their own choices, the enemies of all that part of the world they do not control."[44] In time, the belief in a monolithic structure became less tenable. But a monolithic spirit remained, and the struggle became a battle for men's minds.

There still could be no real middle ground. The communists had to be opposed at every point. ("Do not be afraid to use heavy weapons for what seem to us to be minor matters.")[45] Containment is meaningless unless it is total. Thus what was not "theirs" became "ours" (a proposition that made it possible for us to "lose" countries which we did not own). And with technology bringing a choice between survival and annihilation, there could be no losing, no compromise. It was an all-or-nothing, life-and-death struggle between good and evil. Everyone had to choose sides, and America's very identity hung on the outcome.

Not everyone holds America's anticommunist myth in its pure form. Those who do are not extremists: the myth's most elequent spokesmen have been "good liberals." And feelings have changed some over the years. But it should not be thought that the myth was merely a passing manifestation of early cold war

---

[43]George F. Kennan, *Memoirs: 1925–1950* (Boston: Little, Brown, 1967), p. 557.

[44]*Ibid.*, pp. 554–555, 560.

[45]*Ibid.*, p. 563.

hysteria. The ostensible reason we have troops almost anywhere in the world today may still be traced to communism. And how many congressional "doves" do *not* consider communism still our most threatening foreign opponent? How many still see Our Way and Their Way as the two alternative development patterns facing the Third World? How would the doves react if large areas of the world began choosing Their Way? The majority of those who oppose the Vietnam war, I believe, do so for "tactical" reasons. Were a similar rebellion to break out in Thailand or the Philippines or Brazil, they might not favor direct intervention with troops, but it is doubtful that they would be neutral in behavior, much less in spirit.

2. *Economics.* There are many reasons why the American identity is so tied to anticommunism, but surely a central factor is economic. The roots of the communism-democracy antagonism run very deep. The intellectual origins of liberal democracy, reflected in Locke, tie human fulfillment and the foundations of the nation-state itself to the institution of private property. In America's own "bourgeois" revolution the desire for security of property influenced the structure of government and the Bill of Rights. President Wilson held that "if America is not to have free enterprise, then she can have freedom of no sort whatever."[46] And Truman expanded these capitalist fears into a global struggle between "free enterprise" and the "regimented economies":

. . . the whole world should adopt the American system . . . [because that system] could survive in America only if it became a world system.[47]

Without question these sentiments reflect Marxism's own opposition to capitalist economies; anticommunism includes a wellfounded belief that its opponent seeks the eventual destruction of the free enterprise system. But America's economic program goes beyond "protective reaction." Cold war revisionists have claimed that defense of Our Way of Life involves defense of an imperialist world order, that the motivating force behind our foreign policy is not an attempt by Russia to bury us, but an attempt by us to expand markets, protect investments and con-

[46]Quoted in Williams, "American Intervention in Russia: 1917–20," p. 28.
[47]Quoted in D. F. Flemming, *The Cold War and Its Origins* (New York: Doubleday, 1961), p. 436.

trol sources of raw materials. "It is a problem of markets," Dean Acheson said in 1944; we had to develop foreign markets for our tremendous productive capacity, and if we did not, it would have "the most far-reaching consequences upon our economic and social system."[48]

Though revisionists have assembled many similar statements, it is unlikely that economics is the only direct motivating force in foreign policy decisions (though economics may, in some ultimate sense, underlie those decisions). Rather, politics and economics are tightly intertwined. Cutting the U. S. off from raw materials or isolating it from trade may not only hurt American businessmen but also weaken the country in its "global power struggle." Overthrowing a leftist government in Latin America may not only secure U. S. investments but also re-establish American influence in a strategically important area. We should recognize an important economic component in the American ideology. But we cannot always isolate that component in individual cases, especially when the decisionmakers themselves often fail to do so.

3. World Politics.   The American ideology consists in part of a set of beliefs acquired before and during World War II on how the international system works. The American picture contains a balance of power, but one unlike the classical British concept, where the hegemony of any one country was prevented by skillfully shifting Britain's weight from one side of the balance to the other. The American concept, on the other hand, sees two superpowers, each immutably fixed on its own side of the balance, each trying to increase its relative weight by adding to its side and subtracting from its opponent's. The balance is precarious. Indeed, while "our power" has always been superior to "their power," our leaders have almost always thought of the superiority as only temporary.[49] When the delicacy of this balance is regarded along with the horror of its tipping the wrong way, many of our policies become more understandable.

It is often said that the U. S. overlearned the lessons of World War II. Surely our ideological symbols equate that event meta-

[48]Quoted in Lens, *The Military-Industrial Complex,* p. 22.
[49]See Samuel P. Huntington, *The Common Defense* (New York: Columbia University Press, 1961), p. 59ff.

phorically with our present danger. The words "Munich" and "appeasement" are as common as they are derogatory, and the comparison by American officials of Hitler and Stalin has been frequently drawn.[50] A cardinal rule of the World War II balance is that the enemy who commits aggression in small steps will sooner or later be at your door anyway, and his power will be greater than when he started his aggressions. The current demand to "stop them now or they'll be in Hawaii" has historical precedent. It reflects more than simply impatience; it expresses the belief that they will be harder to defeat in Hawaii if they have won all of Asia's resources to fight with. Appeasement leads to the same result as weakness. Firmness is the only way to preserve both peace and security against such a foe.

The logic of deterrence is also based on balance-of-power thinking. A totally wicked enemy will exploit any weakness, attack whenever he can do so at an acceptable cost to himself (and this enemy does not "value human life" as we do). Modern technology—i.e., rapid delivery of decisively destructive weapons—has given him this chance. Mobilization strategies, no matter what our *potential* power, could never be effected in time to offset the advantage of a first strike, i.e. of a "nuclear Pearl Harbor." This also means that the psychological effect of power is itself power and must be reckoned in the balance. Even a fictitious missile gap can tip that balance; the gap must be closed for the *credibility* of the deterrent is as vital as the deterrent itself.

A belief in monolithic communism means that a victory for any communist group anywhere will add to the enemy's power, and hence may tip the balance. The domino metaphor is a more specific way of describing the same phenomenon. Indeed, the ultimate conclusion of this theory of world politics is that *anything* that strengthens them or weakens us is to be opposed as potentially deadly; anything that weakens them or strengthens us is to our advantage and may be pursued. Thus foreign aggression or communist subversion need not occur for there to be a threat to our security; our intervention can be justified on security grounds if a revolution brings a *possible* increase in communist influence

[50]Bruce M. Russett has collected a good number of quotations to this effect. *No Clear and Present Danger: A Skeptical View of the United States' Entry into World War II* (New York: Harper & Row, 1972), pp. 83–85.

in a country or a possible decrease in our influence. In a zero-sum game there are no neutral moves.

4. Great Power Prerogatives.   It is not true that every U. S. action follows the extreme implications of our world-political beliefs. That would verge on paranoia. But the potential and justification for such action are always there. It is also not true that anticommunism is the only official justification for our military policies. Goals symbolized by such words as freedom, peace, prosperity, stability, order and free trade are deemed good for our country and for the world, whether or not they are threatened by communism. (It should be noted, however, that, characteristic of the coherence of ideological ideas, these goals *are* seen to be threatened by communism. Indeed, communism is said to depend on their absence, "like a malignant parasite which feeds only on diseased tissue," in Kennan's words.)[51] But whether acting in pursuit of a noble goal or in protection of a vital interest, American policymakers are impressed by an important realization: the U. S. is now a great power, perhaps *the* great power, and there are certain obligations and prerogatives which that status entails. This realization has become a part of the American ideology.

Great power status carries with it a higher morality of its own. This is more than the "reasons-of-state" which are said to define standards for any sovereign. Most countries are at least constrained by other countries' sanctions, which make them operate within certain norms. For the great power these sanctions are simply less; there is no one to withdraw aid, tighten credit or land marines on its shores. The great power thus has the power and the right to wage covert war, disregard sovereignty, overrun borders and abrogate treaties. As Daniel Ellsberg said of Vietnam:

I had accepted the official answer . . . that there was a civil war going on, that we had a right to intervene and pick one side or the other if our interests were involved, and our interests were involved. That if the wrong side should win this war, it would be worse for the Vietnamese people, worse for the United States and for world peace.[52]

[51]Kennan, *Memoirs: 1925–1950,* p. 559.
[52]"Ellsberg Talks," *Look,* vol. 35, no. 20 (October 5, 1971), p. 34. See also Richard J. Barnet, *Intervention and Revolution* (New York: New American Library, 1968).

These rights do not come free; there are obligations as well. Other countries may be violently opposed to communism and may believe their survival hangs in the balance. But the U. S. is Leader of the Free World. American ideology includes a certain sense of responsibility for settling disputes, uplifting the poor, spreading democracy. American ideology also feels responsible for giving the world a particular kind of order and stability, keeping it on an even keel, having things under control. In short the ideological plan calls for the spreading of American civilization in this, the American century.

Many instruments are available to fulfill these obligations. Some are military: conventional, counterguerilla and covert warfare; military training, advice and aid; military threats or military alliances. But in a sense military means constitute only the tip of the bayonet. We must also include economic aid, technical assistance, monetary and World Bank controls, credits, trade, investments, cultural contacts, Peace Corps, propaganda—in addition to more traditional diplomatic means of exerting pressure. A great power has a vast bag of tricks. It also has the right—indeed the responsibility—to use them in pursuit of great aims.[53]

5.Preparedness and Power.   Much of America's ideological belief about preparedness and power follows from tenets already described. Pearl Harbor taught us the importance of being always ready, and for a time, a proportion of our strategic bomber force was kept continuously aloft, nuclear-armed. We learned that the only language an aggressor understands is force, and so we took care to maintain nuclear superiority, and began planning strategies to make "surgical" nuclear strikes relevant to political bargaining.[54] World War II also showed us the importance of overwhelmingly superior productive power. But since a mobilization stragegy was not feasible in the nuclear age, we developed Charles (G. E.) Wilson's suggestion for a "permanent war economy."[55]

[53]See Harry Magdoff, *The Age of Imperialism* (New York: Monthly Review Press, 1969).

[54]The best discussion of these strategic gymnastics is Marcus G. Raskin, "The Kennedy Hawks Assume Power from the Eisenhower Vultures," in Leonard S. Rodberg and Derek Shearer, eds., *The Pentagon Watchers* (New York: Doubleday, 1970), pp. 65–98.

[55]Quoted in Lens, *The Military-Industrial Complex*, p. 18.

The myths of preparedness and power extend beyond their application to major war. The U. S. must be ready to apply force instantly and appropriately, anywhere in the world. This requires not only an extensive floating (and underwater) strike force but also military bases, airlift-sealift capabilities and trained commando groups ever in readiness. Productive power also applies to problem-solving in general and is at the core of what has been called America's "engineering approach." Whether in sophisticated weaponry or pacification programs, the engineering myth expresses, as Hoopes says,

that troublesome American belief that the application of enough resources can solve any problem; if no solution is forthcoming, it means the resources were inadequate and the answer is to apply more.[56]

Myths of preparedness and power have a most direct influence on military expansion. But they have little meaning except in the context of the larger goals of American ideology.

The possibility that America's ideology causes militarism tempts one to assert that the problem is all "in our heads," that military expansion can be reversed simply by changing our assumptions about the world. This conclusion is not justified. Real, entrenched interests—whether power or wealth or the standard of living of the American people—*may* be served by the ideology. Indeed, some will think the ideology I have described is too transparant a mask for selfish motives. (Recall that one function of myth is to rationalize interests in terms of universal values.) To change ideology substantially *may* thus require that we change fundamental political and economic relationships in this country and the world.

But this begs the question of what are the "real" causes of military expansion. The answer depends in part upon our interpretation of the real sources and functions of myth. I outlined the beginnings of one such interpretation in Section II, and since these theories depend in part upon my own ideology, I shall not pursue the point further here. Rather, I shall take ideology as a given—whatever the truth of its beliefs and whatever its relation-

[56]Townsend Hoopes, *The Limits of Intervention* (New York: McKay, 1969), p. 70.

ship to "underlying" causes—and I shall simply discuss the way it appears to work in influencing military growth.

MISSIONS

It is often said that the U. S. has more military might than it needs. But an examination of American ideology reveals that there can really never be enough power: a task without limits has been defined. Thus it is not the military or the armsmakers or bureaucratic inertia which establishes the basic outline of U. S. defense posture, though these factors may be responsible for minor adjustments within that outline. Rather it is what our leaders conceive to be America's mission in the world (and their success in carrying it out) which justifies ever-expanding military activities and capabilities.

That the ideology makes insatiable demands is simply a result of trying to keep every event in the world under control, especially where two-thirds of the world's people are impoverished and conflict abounds. These demands grow out of the ideas: not only opposition to communism anywhere and any time but opposition to any "aggression" or revolution or movement which might upset the balance of power or the world order; not only deterrence of nuclear attack but intervention against any threat to U. S. interests, whether political, economic or even symbolic. Such a program requires omnipotence and ubiquity; what is amazing is that the U. S. has come so close to carrying it out.

The U. S. has not always tried to meet these demands fully. But the pressure is always there. Where the means exist, the temptation to use them is great, since the goals could always stand to be more completely fulfilled.

More often, the means have been seen by the national security planners as insufficient to carry out the prescribed mission. When this occurs, the national interest seems to *require* that the executive or the military or even the Congress mobilize support for expansion. The tools for this mobilization (and some have recently come under fire) include a massive bureaucratic machine, a huge defense budget, a wide range of interest groups and a set of powerful symbols. Since ideological goals are generally accepted anyway, this pressure, for the few who oppose it, is virtually irresistible.

The cycle repeats itself, however. For once the means are expanded, the ideology has a new list of goals—and a never-ending one—which beckon to be pursued. Our leaders outwardly admit that American might is limited, but they often act as though a great power, with all these new instruments at its disposal, should be able to bend any problem to its will. It is simply a matter of applying enough resources.

The power of the mission may be seen in the three major military expansions since World War II. When we concentrate on the continuity of incremental changes or on the pressures for this or that weapons system, we may fail to see the infrequent "quantum leap" which sets the parameters for further military change in the next several years. Such major jumps occurred with the rearmament of the early 1950s and the Kennedy-McNamara build-up of the early 1960s; if the historical pattern repeats itself, the Vietnam expansion following 1965 will be another such jump.[57]

While Truman's rearmament coincided with the Korean War, it was, according to Huntington, largely unrelated to the actual military needs of that war. The Truman Doctrine of March 1947 (actually conceived as early as 1945) pledged to "support free people who are resisting attempted subjugation by armed minorities or by outside pressures." Diplomats, on the other hand, were complaining that the U. S. lacked the necessary force to back up their assertions of America's interests. The result was that the State Department's Policy Planning Staff began to map out a program for major rearmament which they expected would raise the defense budget by $35 billion (it was $12 billion in mid-1950).[58] The military apparently had less enthusiasm for the plan than did the State Department. Moreover, the Secretary of Defense was partially circumvented in the process of getting it accepted. But in April 1950 the National Security Council recommended the rearmament in its paper NSC–68. Two months later the U. S. entered the Korean conflict, and with patriotic feeling high, NSC–68 became a reality. For the remainder of the decade,

[57]See Bruce M. Russett, *What Price Vigilance?* (New Haven, Conn.: Yale University Press, 1970), chap. 1.

[58]Huntington *The Common Defense*, p. 51. The following discussion is based on Huntington and on Paul Y. Hammond, "NSC–68: Prologue to Rearmament," in Warner Schilling, Paul Hammond and Glenn T. Snyder, *Strategy, Politics and Defense Budgets* (New York: Columbia University Press, 1962).

the incremental changes departed only moderately from a military budget of $50 billion. There was no return to the prewar level, not because of "inertia" but because the mission remained impossible.

The Kennedy-McNamara buildup is not as visible in budgetary changes as it is (due to McNamara's celebrated efficiency) in military might. After two years in office, they could report:

A 100-percent increase in the number of nuclear weapons available in the strategic alert forces.

A 45-percent increase in the number of combat-ready Army divisions.

A one-third increase in the number of tactical fighter squadrons.

A 60-percent increase in the tactical nuclear forces deployed in Western Europe.

A 75-percent increase in airlift capability.

A 100-percent increase in general ship construction and conversion.

A sixfold increase in counterinsurgency forces.[59]

Pre-World War II strategy for fulfilling the American mission had relied on distance from potential enemies and the ability to mobilize vast resources in the event of a real threat. In the postwar period there was a change in technology and a change in mission. (Truman declared that "wherever aggression, either direct or indirect, threatened the peace, the security of the United States was involved.")[60] The Eisenhower strategy for preserving this security was, first, deterrence by threat of massive nuclear retaliation (what Herman Kahn called "wargasm"), and, second, control of events on a day-to-day basis through intervention by the CIA, foreign aid and other measures short of actual war.

During the 1950s there was a growing belief that the Eisenhower strategy was insufficient to carry out the American mission.[61] On the one hand, there was much doubt that massive retaliation would be used against minor aggressions. Hadn't Eisenhower said nuclear war was unthinkable? On the other hand

[59] *Hearings on Military Posture and H.R. 9637 to Authorize Appropriations during Fiscal Year 1965 for Procurement . . . before the Committee on Armed Services of the House of Representatives,* 88th Congress, 2d session (Washington, D.C.: USGPO, 1964), p. 6899. Testimony of Robert S. McNamara.

[60] Quoted in Robert Borosage, "The Making of the National Security State," in Rodberg and Shearer, *The Pentagon Watchers,* p. 9.

[61] Much of this discussion is based on Raskin, "The Kennedy Hawks Assume Power from the Eisenhower Vultures."

the CIA and foreign aid were not able to hold the line in every instance. "Leftist" governments were successfully ousted in Guatemala and Iran, but the CIA could not have turned back Dien Bien Phu, and the Bay of Pigs was a failure.

Kennedy was elected on the cry of a missile gap and with the pledge to "get the country moving again." In Vienna he faced Khruschchev, and in Washington he faced a map full of trouble spots: Berlin, Laos, Vietnam, Cuba and a host of those still in the "potential" stage. American ideology obviously needed a new strategy.

In the area of strategic weapons, planners developed the concept of "greater-than-expected threats," which anticipated decisions the Soviets were not thought to be entertaining but which they *could possibly* make. The Russians were not trusted even to be rational. And when planning merges with fantasy, the demand for resources knows no limits. To this worst-case planning was added the strategy of *counterforce.* Counterforce was designed to give policymakers flexibility and options which simple deterrence lacked and which would thus restore credibility to the nuclear threat. It involved knocking out the enemy's missiles (with cities held as "hostages") and hence making it possible still to bargain with him to stop his aggressions. The city-defending ABM and the fallout shelter have essentially the same effect: they act as "will-stiffeners" to help us hold firm in pursuit of our mission. With such a notion of security, it is hard to imagine buying more than we need.

But it is in fighting "brush-fire" wars—wars of national liberation—that the new strategies had their greatest impact on military expansion. Nuclear weapons would not deter this kind of war; the CIA *could not* win it. The U. S. thus developed the strategy and capacity for fighting limited wars and for doing so at various levels of escalation.

This "flexible response" capability was to increase the options open to policymakers. It also, of necessity, increased the size and functions of the army, the airlift and sealift forces and the special forces for psychological warfare, counterinsurgency, pacification and all types of political activities. Ultimately, since there were trouble spots all over the globe, the American mission required that we develop the ability to fight many wars simultaneously: general wars, limited wars, wars of counterinsurgency. We were to remain at all times prepared to fight "two-and-one-half" wars —a general war in Europe, a major war in Asia and a more limited "police action," for example in Latin America. Is it any wonder that the military had to grow?

The other half of the cycle dictates that, once the forces are there, it is foolish to let them sit idle when there are things to be done. The third major buildup —Vietnam—grew out of an ideological mission undertaken in 1950. At that time Truman began aiding the French in Indochina, and the reason given was to stop the spread of communism by keeping them out of power in Vietnam. A policy of aid, advice and CIA activity during the Eisenhower period grew with the new srategy to a major counterinsurgency operation under Kennedy. In 1965 it grew again to a limited war. At first it was a matter simply of using the tools Kennedy had built. Then it began to show as another major jump in the defense budget. Each phase reflected a new effort to accomplish a mission which has not changed in twenty years.

Adventures in the Congo, Santo Domingo or Cambodia suggest the likelihood that forces-in-being will be used to achieve ideological goals. The increased use of the military in domestic disturbances reflects the same kind of thinking. We have a large army trained in counterinsurgency, and the U. S. has a mission to keep order. With the increase in the number and severity of riots lately, it is foolish not to use our best resources when they are available. As in Vietnam, it is merely a matter of using enough power. And also as in Vietnam, the army cannot be effective without helicopters, spying, pacification and all the other tools of counterinsurgency.

To some the Nixon Doctrine suggests a new mission. I think it is rather a change in strategy. Like the other strategies, limited war does not work. The costs are too great, both in the field and at home. It does not work principally because of the unlimited nature of the mission it tries to accomplish. The Nixon Doctrine will use other means. But the mission has not become any easier.

HYPERLEGITMACY

The theory behind "ideology-pull" is that the internal logic of ideas can motivate action—in this case by prescribing an unlimited mission. By proposing a pull, I do not deny the "push" of pressure, money, interest or propaganda. But a push implies that there is resistance—as if pressure groups pushed weapons upon an unwilling Congress, and Congress, in turn, pushed them onto an unwilling public. This description is inaccurate. While not all people hold every ideological tenet described, the body of myth in which the ideology finds itself is extremely pervasive, powerful and without substantial opposition. Instead of an "end of ideology" in post war America, there has been an end of ideological conflict, a consensus of myth.

National security myths have been not only widespread but also highly effective. In the twenty or so years after World War II, large majorities consistently favored higher defense budgets, or at least opposed any cuts.[62] Few other government programs enjoyed as much support. And few people dared oppose the myths of security. There were those, of course, who opposed increases in defense spending (more often the president than the Congress). But the polls rarely asked whether people accepted the symbols of the American mission—whether, for example, they would vote for someone who was "soft on communism." The answer was a foregone assumption.

The reasons for this "hyperlegitimacy" of security symbols are complex. Much has to do with World War II. Patriotic feeling had been aroused, fear for the safety of the American continent had been genuine, and the allied victory brought confidence that America had intervened in a noble cause. Following the war, the symbols of Nazi domination were transferred to the communists, who had never enjoyed very good public relations in this country. Within a short time our former ally was our enemy, and our former enemy was our ally. Despite the sincerity of this switch, it necessitated a vigorous "public information" campaign. Kennan telegraphed:

We must see that our public is educated to realities of Russian situation. I cannot overemphasize the importance of this. Press cannot do this alone. It must be done mainly by government, which is necessarily more experienced and better informed on practical problems involved. In this we need not be deterred by ugliness of the picture.[63]

[62]See Bruce M. Russett, "Revolt of the Masses: Public Opinion on Military Expenditures," in Russett, ed., *Peace, War, and Numbers* (Beverly Hills, Calif.: Sage, 1972).

[63]*Kennan, Memoirs: 1925–1950*, p. 558.

The government's propaganda effort emphasized the evil of Soviet communism and the imminent threat of war. The military began producing films and radio broadcasts, while politicians used their considerable rhetorical talents to out-anticommunist one another. Acheson advocated going beyond the "realities of the situation," as Kennan had recommended. He described his technique of symbol manipulation as follows:

Qualification must give way to simplicity of statement, variety and nuance to bluntness, almost brutality in carrying home a point. . . . [P]oints to be understandable had to be clear. If we made our points *clearer than the truth,* we . . . could hardly do otherwise.[64]

A war-scare no doubt put a strain on the American people. The Soviet A-bomb explosion and the "loss" of China simply emphasized the validity of the country's fears of destruction and Russian expansion. The Korean War then increased the burden by bringing home bloodshed, inflation and more tension.

Strain theory provides some insight into why these tensions might have strengthened the anticommunist myth, by showing how the myth might have reduced tension. Geertz divides the mechanisms into four kinds: cathartic, morale, solidarity and advocatory.[65] Cathartic is the familiar process of "scapegoating," where responsibility for the strain is transferred by the myth to the enemy, and thus the pain is eased. The morale mechanism legitimizes the strain in terms of a higher value: it is easier to bear the burdens of a thankless cold war when the myth declares the goals to be peace and freedom. Solidarity (fostered by myth) reduces strain by binding a group to a common cause. And the advocatory mechanism brings strain reduction by offering the possibility of success: if the myth helps us stop communism, we will finally be free from fear.

Whatever the causes of this hyperlegitimacy of security symbols, its effects were momentous. We need not review the history of the McCarthy era and the loyalty program to note that the question of security weighed heavily on the minds of the American people and their leaders. The symbols of defense, security, loyalty, Americanism—as well as their opposites—became

[64]Dean Acheson, *Present at the Creation* (New York: Norton, 1969), p 375.
[65]Geertz, "Ideology as a Cultural System," p. 55.

charged with great emotional power. And those who dealt in power could not ignore the new currency.

"Pinkness" became, like corruption, an issue which was both highly political and noncontroversial: politicians fought over it but always on the same side. "Defense" became the same kind of issue. And this was perhaps the most forcible kind of "push" in the expansion of the military. Throughout the Eisenhower period, the Democratic Congress pressured the executive for higher military expenditures—first with a bomber gap, then a missile gap. Rarely did they play the traditional "watchdog" role over the president and the military. Candidates for office were usually true believers. But even if they were not, none risked political suicide by rejecting the myths and slogans about military means and missions.

The symbols of security were so powerful that they were often transferred to other purposes. Politicians campaigned on their military records. Weapons manufacturers advertised themselves and their wares in picture magazines. Domestic programs like interstate highways and aid to education were linked to the phrase "national defense." And when Eisenhower tried to cut military spending during the post-Korean War "New Look," he felt he had to justify even a balanced budget, tax cuts and policies for economic growth *in terms of* their future contribution to national security.[66]

Clearly, in such an atmosphere, few people were worried about *over*-emphasizing security. Likewise, few people saw any threat in the expansion of activities which were undertaken in the name of defense. Much of what today is criticized as military propaganda was produced in the 1950s with wholehearted public approval or at least with no hint of impropriety. Indeed, some of the same newscasters who now criticize the propaganda films were themselves the narrators of those films. Military lobbying, which today is deplored as self-seeking, was a decade ago regarded as a patriotic effort to safeguard the nation's security. Can we be surprised at the willingness of the military to expand into social welfare, education, riot control, and social science research? A large and wealthy organization, with competence in many fields and high

---

[66]See Glenn H. Snyder, "The New Look," in Schilling, Hammond and Snyder, *Strategy, Politics and Defense Budgets.*

public esteem, can only see itself as expanding its efforts to do good. And for many years, few people argued with this interpretation.

Even less publicized efforts—like CIA funding of student groups, Defense Department support of CBW research in universities, government aid to the AFL-CIO's international activities or military surveillance of civilians—to cite just a few—are assumed to have widespread public support. If they are secret, it is only because the nature of the activity demands that it be kept from the enemy. But the purpose of the activity is to protect the security of the United States. With security as the goal, security institutions as the actors and security symbols to light the way, it is unthinkable that any *loyal* opposition would be heard.

The other major "push" to military expansion is said to come from the great and varied impact of defense spending. This is the so-called symbiotic relationship of the military-industrial complex: the military officer seeking a promotion, the contractor seeking profits, the labor union seeking jobs, the congressman seeking satisfied constituents, the academician seeking a research grant and so on. If this is a symbiotic relationship, it is that of the birds who pick the teeth of the shark. For it is the dominant myth which makes these interests legitimate in the first place. And while narrower interests no doubt reinforce the myths, and occasionally influence this or that decision, they do not establish the overall perception of defense needs.

In individual instances there is certainly a push on military growth from special interests. The army has defense contractors lobby their senators to win support for weapons systems. International corporations consult with the government to urge protection of their overseas interests. Labor groups rally to protest the closing of defense plants. But when the decisions are finally made, it is often done at a higher level, where the pressure serves only to remind the decisionmaker of his overriding ideological commitment. That ideology may, of course, rationalize and integrate the narrow interest—but in the end, the narrow interest is subsumed by the broader purpose.

Thus Moyer finds no strong relationship between a congressman's ideological position and the defense spending in his district. Defense contractors justify their business optimism by pointing to the weapons developments of the Russians. Air force generals display an anticommunism which goes far beyond enthusiasm for carrying out their professional duties. And when the president tells a local audience how many jobs a new defense installation will create, the unspoken (or spoken) assumption is that the work will be very patriotic.

One more point should be made about the economic effects of defense spending. There is much debate about whether a capitalist system *needs* military spending to prevent depression. Lee has given evidence that such spending actually retards growth. But many observers feel *some* kind of heavy government spending is needed to take up slack in the economy, and that domestic nondefense spending is the alternative more conducive to growth. One might expect, then, some economic counterpressure against military expansion and in favor of conversion. Such an expectation, however, ignores the political realities. For here too, interest is subsumed by ideology. If the economy needs government spending, the pressure is toward the military. The alternative is "creeping socialism."

In this section I have attempted to relate ideology, foreign policy, military expansion and domestic environment in a way that would put some perspective on the more specialized studies in this volume. The central concept has been myth; I drew on my discussion of the previous two sections to integrate a particular myth's meaning with its social causes and effects, toward a theory of military change. The trend of that change over the last twenty-five years angers me. The thought of the next twenty-five years gives cause for both fear and hope. My concluding remarks are directed toward the present and the future.

V. Conclusions: The Dis-integration of an Ideology

To understand military expansion is not necessarily to arrest it. America's ideology could involve beliefs which are quite true and values which are quite genuine. And it may be based on interests which are very real. The spread of communism—whether that means Sino-Soviet power, social revolution or even simple self-determination for the rest of the world—is not entirely an illusion. Moreover, it may, in any or all of its manifestations, threaten the American way of life. If so, knowing our ideology will only mean knowing ourselves, and military growth will remain a part of American growth.

Whether the Marxists are right that the developed capitalist economies must control the underdeveloped areas of the world to survive, I do not know. But it does appear that we are now governed by an ideology of expansion. Prosperity in our domestic economy—our way of life, our standard of living—depends on our ability to grow, to solve our problems through increased productivity instead of redistribution or a change of life-style or a restructuring of social relationships. That growth includes a growth in power and an expansion of that power into the rest of the world. It seems to me likely that, to assure growth, American power will clash with the aspirations of people around the world. It is difficult to maintain order in a world which will not allow three billion people to live as Americans live or to grow as the American economy grows.

Thus it appears that American ideology is ultimately coincident with interest, and not just the interest of a ruling elite. If that interest does not change, there is a limit to how far ideology can change. The American mission for the foreseeable future will continue to oppose "communism" in all its forms. Even most of the doves have not abandoned that goal. The weapons of the future may be more automated, more sophisticated, less violent, even less expensive. But it is not likely that the American war machine will grow any weaker or that the American mission will be forgotten.

On the other hand, the change of the past few years is undeniable. For the first time in several decades, a set of countersymbols is beginning to emerge: words like "priorities" communicate a whole range of social issues. Can *this*, finally, be the end of ideology?

I believe the change reflects not the end—for many interests are still very much alive—but the "dis-integration" of ideology. That is, American ideology is beginning to lose its tightness, its cohesiveness. Concepts which once fit together easily (indeed, were almost inseparable), now exhibit a great tension. "Internationalism," which used to mean helping the rest of the world, naturally required a large military. Now it appears the American military is not the best way to help the rest of the world. Government expenditures, social and military, were once part of the same Keynesian package. Now it comes in two packages, and getting one keeps us from getting the other.

This dis-integration derives in part from contradictions within the ideology. Perhaps military spending *never* made much economic sense, but the economy was not taxed enough to know it. Or, for another example, the "we-they" dichotomy of the anticommunist myth presumed a near perfect "we," a presumption which could never be substantiated. Finally, the myth of power and problem-solving was based upon the belief that our resources really *were* infinite. It took the strain of our longest war to uncover the contradiction there.

The dis-integration also follows from a change in our perception of the world, perhaps because the world really has changed. The Soviet bloc is less monolithic, less hostile, even less different from us. The balance of power is hence less precarious—and imbalance less dangerous. If we know our security is not as threatened and yet if we still intervene around the world, the implication is that economic and great-power myths have grown more important at the expense of world-political and identity myths. But in any case the myths are no longer as integrated ideologically as they once were.

Along with dis-integration, the ideology and its component parts are no longer assumed true by all without question. Major assumptions are now openly challenged. The symbols do not have the same affective and hortatory meanings. They do not excite and they do not influence behavior as if by reflex in an ever-larger portion of the population. Symbols are now questioned and weighed against a new crop of countersymbols.

Most important, myth for many is no longer performing the same functions. The psychological power of the myth to reduce strain is diminished. For a few—sometimes called members of the counterculture—the myths no longer perform their interest functions either. These people see their very needs as different from the needs of most in the society. They claim to have made that Marcuse calls a "biological" transformation away from the human requirements which the American corporate state has cultivated in its people, requirements which are said to be ultimately enslaving and destructive, requirements like consumption and competition and domination.

If there is any truth to a counterculture, that culture, like any other, will have a language, symbols, myths and perhaps an ideology of its own. We need not adopt these symbols or emulate the culture to see the importance of what they are trying to say. For if a new ideology arises out of that which is now dis-integrating, our interests and our needs will have to change if a change in military mission is to follow. If interests and needs remain the same, it will be futile to point out that our myths are bad for us. They will only be replaced by a new ideology—stronger, more consistent, more realistic, more coherent—but still, in all, no less destructive.

The New Politics of National Security: A Selected and Annotated Research Bibliography

Douglas H. Rosenberg and Major Raoul H. Alcalá, U.S. Army

National security has long interested students of American politics. In the past few years, however, the focus of that interest has shifted radically. A major bibliography in 1954 asserted that "the Hitlers and Stalins" had forced the U. S. into permanent peacetime mobilization. That work held the central concerns of national defense to be directed "toward energizing our cumbersome defense machinery" through closer political-military-industrial cooperation.[1] Samuel Huntington summarized the outlook of many civil-military studies when, in 1957, he wrote:

Previously the primary question was: what pattern of civil-military relations is most compatible with American liberal-democratic values? Now this has been supplanted by the more important issue: what pattern of

NOTE: Preparation of this bibliography was assisted in part by contract no. N00014–67–A0097–0007 from ARPA, Behavioral Sciences, monitored by the Office of Naval Research. Of course no agency is responsible for errors of fact or the opinions expressed. We would like also to thank Mary Carrano for her tireless help with the manuscript and Andrew Kapi for his assistance in the research.

[1]Social Science Research Council, *Civil-Military Relations, An Annotated Bibliography, 1940–1952* (New York: Columbia University Press, 1954) [no. 2459], pp. vii, viii. (Numbers in brackets refer to identification numbers in the bibliography.)

civil-military relations will best maintain the security of the American nation?[2]

Huntington's statement appears curiously inverted today. Critics, scholars and policymakers have all begun to lose their preoccupation with external threats and to shift their attention to the effects of U. S. defense policy. Federal activities in the name of security overshadow everything else the government does. Analysts are now beginning to look more closely at the way these activities consume resources, permeate society and change the world.

The kinds of facts which now attract so much interest are those which show the size, scope and pervasiveness of the national security effort. For example:[3]

—Security is expensive. Defense functions in fiscal year 1970 (FY 70) consumed $80.3 billion—40.8 percent of the federal budget and 8.3 percent of GNP. Since the end of World War II, defense has taken well over $1 trillion, averaging about half the federal budget and one-tenth the GNP. To put these figures in perspective, the FY 70 defense budget nearly equals the combined before-tax profits that year of *all* U. S. corporations and exceeds the GNP of all but a handful of the world's countries.

—Security is the government's number one job. Defense accounts for about 72 percent of total federal employment, 80 percent of federal purchases of goods and services and 92 percent of federally held tangible assets. In FY 70 defense expendi-

---

[2]Samuel P. Huntington, *The Soldier and the State* (New York: Vintage Books, 1957) [no. 6], p. 3.

[3]These statistics are gathered primarily from the *Statistical Abstract of the United States* (U.S. Department of Commerce, Bureau of the Census, 1971 and various years). Data on contracts and congressional relations from *Congressional Quarterly*, "The Military-Industrial Complex, a Problem for the Secretary of Defense," *Congressional Quarterly Weekly Report*-Special Report (May 24, 1968) [no. 1120]. Data on Legislative Liaison and foreign bases also from Sen. William Proxmire, *Report from the Wasteland: America's Military-Industrial Complex* (New York: Praeger, 1970) [no. 1133], pp. 12 and 109. Information on military and State Department representatives overseas from Adam Yarmolinsky, *The Military Establishment: Its Impacts on American Society* (New York: Harper & Row, 1971) [no. 19], p. 115. Pentagon Public Affairs data from the *Congressional Record*, March 24, 1971, E2153. For public opinion data, see Bruce M. Russett, "The Revolt of the Masses: Public Opinion on Military Expenditures," in Russett, ed., *Peace, War, and Numbers* (Beverly Hills, Calif.: Sage, 1972) [no. 1628].

tures exceeded those for international affairs and finance by 2167 percent, health by 518 percent and income security (the second largest function) by 83 percent.

—Security involves many Americans. The Selective Service System keeps files on 22.7 million registrants and in 1970 conscripted 207,000 into the armed forces. Nearly 3 million men are on active duty today, and over 27 million others are veterans. Defense accounts directly for over 10 percent of all civilian and military jobs, much more in some areas of the country.

—The security effort touches political and economic institutions throughout the country. Military units and installations blanket the land with real estate holdings totaling an area the size of New York State. Defense agencies each year award about $40 billion in contracts to over 20,000 prime contractors and an estimated 100,000 subcontractors. Defense installations and industries can be found in all 50 states and in 363 of the 435 congressional districts. Contractors and service associations employ professional lobbyists, while the Pentagon services Congress with a $4-million, 339-man legislative liaison staff.

—The American security effort is both powerful and conspicuous around the world. Over 3,400 military installations operate in more than thirty countries. Military advisors to foreign armed forces are nearly twice as numerous as State Department representatives abroad. Intelligence operations, civic action projects and military and nonmilitary foreign aid are all intended to serve U. S. security interests. Forty percent of the world's military expenditures are American, providing a nuclear capacity equivalent to several tons of TNT for each person on the globe.

—Security functions extend beyond the purely military. The armed forces have been involved in social research, pacification and "nation-building" abroad, and in surveillance, riot control and social engineering at home. They are in intimate and daily contact as advisors to both the executive and legislative branches, and they dominate much of the data gathering and processing which is needed for political decisions. But civilians are nearly as involved in these functions as the military, whether as CIA operatives, think-tank or State Department strategists, government scientists or university researchers.

—Finally, national security pervades the public mind. In 1970 the Pentagon spent $37 million for public information, with a public affairs staff of 4,430. Millions of pages of documents are said to be locked up for security reasons; millions of persons are subject to loyalty or security checks. Even such programs as highways and student aid have been justified in terms of national defense. Public support has been high. Until recently few Americans felt the security effort was too great or too expensive.

These facts are not new. The military has had a major role in this society at least since the Korean War. What *is* new is the way we view these facts. Until recently, few people—certainly few scholars—looked at them as *political* issues. Few questioned the pervasive impact of national security policies. Few evaluated those policies on grounds other than that of efficiency. And few challenged the intentions or morality of America's aims and actions in the international arena. The study of national security has traditionally concerned power and survival; the threat of Soviet aggression and the corresponding need for a high level of mobilization were underlying assumptions, not questions.

Holding these issues "above politics" was a broad consensus about goals, threats and the legitimacy of government itself. Wide agreement on policy produced a bipartisanship from which there seemed no room for dissent. There was little point in examining the nonmilitary implications of policies which were thought to be the only alternatives to annihilation. But the consensus has now been shattered. Not only does the world appear less threatening, but the time-honored assumptions about national aims, interests and the allocation of resources are no longer above criticism. The benefits of America's security policy are thus increasingly open to question; it is only logical that the costs should be ever more critically evaluated.

If society's political consciousness has changed, so has the analysis of policy. These changes provide our principal motivation for a new bibliography. The last comprehensive bibliographies on American security were prepared some years ago and shared the cold war assumptions which many of our entries explicitly reject. Now, in 1972, we have not only numerous additional writings to include; we have a wholly different set of problems to consider.

A look at the "Outline of Categories" on pp. 204–207 should show that this bibliography does not follow a traditional format. Many of our entries reflect the declining popularity in recent years of military institutions and values, as well as the military's thinking in the face of these changes. Opposition to the military

—both from within and outside of the armed forces—is thus considered here to be an important part of the field of civil-military relations. Other writings discuss the far-reaching effects of our government's security activities upon American society and the world. Categories like "The Military-Industrial Complex," "Domestic Intelligence and Surveillance" or "Nation-Building" reflect growing concern about the proper role of the military and the government in this country and abroad.[4]

We have organized this literature to deal with security as a *political* problem—and with the military as a political institution. The practice is common in studies of foreign armies but has often been neglected when thinking about the U. S. Many works try to illuminate the causes of U. S. security policy through the fields of history, political culture, foreign relations or economics. Some of these should be viewed as primary data rather than secondary analysis, since they reveal the interests and assumptions of particular actors or observers. The point is that attempts to explain the underlying basis of security policy need no longer stop with the assertion of a foreign threat. We have listed a broad selection of writings which suggest that the explanation lies in politics or profits or empire.

In attempting to encompass these diverse new problems and concerns within an established field of political science, we were struck by the paucity of academic literature. It is common for the theoretically and methodologically rigorous studies simply to miss the security issues which are now so central to activists and participants. One would, of course, expect that those who openly attack or defend traditional assumptions would be more sensitive to issues which arise out of the confrontation than those who are not so engaged. But this is neither a narrow nor a trivial dispute. The issues bound up with national security appear to be causing deep and possibly lasting divisions in the American polity; some writers claim the country is undergoing fundamental change. It is disconcerting, then, that scholarly literature often fails even to *raise* the important questions, much less to take seriously some

---

[4]The reader will note that the names of our categories are often quite ideologically loaded (with both official and antiestablishment language). Science has not kept pace with politics, and we could think of no clearer way to identify these ideas. The reader should feel free to place quotation marks around those labels he finds offensive.

of the more penetrating critiques. It is our belief that the traditional field of civil-military relations will have to recognize a new politics of national security if it is to avoid becoming sterile and irrelevant.

By contrast, many of the more interesting arguments have been raised by critics and apologists. Although often weakened by a loose epistemology, a sloppy method or a lack of theoretical coherence, these polemical writings are heuristically valuable in positing relationships ignored elsewhere. They turn up information which surprises even those familiar with the field, or they present well-known facts in a completely different light, causing us to become aware of our ideological biases and assumptions. Critical or subjective writings may spread their sense of commitment to the reader, or they may provoke outrage, but they usually communicate the urgency and importance which the issue deserves. Often they provide insights from first-hand information or from the power of their ideological models. And frequently they contain much hard and useful data. Unfortunately, they are rarely read by academic researchers.

It is thus a second task of this bibliography to draw together writings from authors who are engaged—as participants or opponents—in the politics of national security. Many of the sources will be unfamiliar to students, but we felt this would be even greater reason to include them. We have paid particular attention to military journals and to the radical and underground press, since these can serve as primary sources in studies of the military establishment and opposition to it. We have, as a result, had to omit some of the more standard secondary works in the field— on the assumption that the student will likely have most of these sources already. To facilitate research in the traditional literature, Section IV includes a list of other bibliographies on national security topics.

The major function we intend for this bibliography is that of a research tool to lead scholars to sources they might ordinarily miss. The literature is quite voluminous, however, and it would be impossible to present anything approaching a complete listing of relevant articles and books. We have instead drawn only a selection to indicate to the reader the nature of the available material. Section IV includes more information on this literature and how to find it, including addresses and microfilm services. Even the very esoteric sources should be accessible in major libraries, or in a few cases, by writing directly to the publisher.

Accepting national security activity as a political question—rather than exclusively as a necessary response to foreign aggression—opens new and exciting work for social science research. We are faced with a set of phenomena of momentous impact at all levels of American and world politics. These phenomena cry out for explanation (among other things), and important proposed explanations need to be further developed and tested. Most of the analysis of these issues, however informative or insightful, has up to now come from polemicists, journalists or apologists. Scientific theory building and testing could add a new dimension to the debate.

One of the most difficult tasks facing any explanatory theory of national security politics is to integrate the many variables which seem to impinge on the problem. We became acutely aware of this difficulty because of the widely varied set of concerns we tried to deal with. Each topic seemed to present a different facet to a single question, and yet each claimed to be crucial to the solution. Many of the academic studies concentrate on a single aspect of security policy, and too frequently, they lack the perspective which an awareness of the scope of the literature could provide. The field is so broad, and the explanations so varied, that to take account of everything comprehensively is near-impossible. Yet to ignore plausible and powerful theory—even if it appears some distance from the problem at hand—can cause a study to be truncated and unconvincing. We thus see a third function of this bibliography in providing a rough guide to the many different kinds of ideas that are likely to bear on a given topic.

For example, several rigorous studies—including one in this volume—deal with congressional voting patterns on defense. Knowledge of these patterns is important for its own sake. But to develop general theoretical understanding of defense structures, we would have to place the congressional vote within the context of the entire military budgeting process and that process within the context of interests and expectations operating in the political system as a whole. Some analysts would find a discussion inadequate that did not deal with presidential leadership in a world of hostile international political aims. Others would want to learn what constraints might be imposed by international business investments or a military-industrial complex. The point is that, to develop a theory of national security, we would have to begin asking not only why a congressman votes as he does, but what that vote means to overall national policy—whether, in fact, it makes any difference at all. An awareness of the arguments in several different categories would force the researcher to consider these questions.

If there is anything upon which the two authors agree, it is that the military are only a part of the problem of national security. It is important to know (and sociologists have asked) what there is in a soldier's background or training or traditions that would cause him to involve himself in politics or otherwise expand his role in this country or abroad. Again, the question is interesting in itself. But the broader study of national security will ask, as Major Dickey asks, whether the political system gives that soldier a mission whose very success requires him to participate in politics. If so, why? Why must he lobby to get the necessary weapons from Congress? Why must he become a politician and prop up some inept government overseas? Possible answers suggest themselves from the categories and titles in the following pages: Is it because (due to industrial lobbying?) we had the weapons on hand in the first place? Or is it because (due to Pentagon propaganda?) the American people demanded we intervene? Or because a corporate elite wanted to protect its overseas interests? Or the world balance of power threatened to shift fatally if that country were to fall into communist hands? Again, the question cannot be answered if we confine ourselves to a single field of political analysis.

To study any one facet of national security politics, it is not necessary that we begin with a comprehensive model of all facets. We do not need to deal simultaneously with the fields of foreign policy, public administration, sociology, political culture and anything else that might affect our findings. But it is important that we be aware of how our research *might* fit into some broader framework. That is, we should have some idea of the importance of the questions we are *not* asking and of their relationship to those we are asking. We hope that this bibliography will in some way aid in the construction of such a framework.

A word about the organization of this bibliography and how to use it. While we hope readers will apprehend the structure and scope of the field as we see it, it is unrealistic to expect them to consider every entry when pursuing a topic. We have thus given first priority to utility in research projects. Each of the subcategories is relatively self-contained, so that the reader need not search too far to find the appropriate material. Writings that fall easily into several categories are listed more than once, though we tried to avoid excessive cross-listing by making use of "general" categories under major headings. Writings most closely related will usually be found in nearby categories, though it was occasionally necessary to refer the reader to a different section entirely. The organization of topics as a whole proceeds as logically as we thought possible to make it. The reader, however, will not always agree with our logic.

For convenience of reference, each entry is given an identification number. Writings listed more than once will have more than one number, with each subsequent listing referring the reader back to the first appearance of the entry where the annotation and complete bibliographic data will be found. Opposite each topic in the "Outline of Categories" is the identification number of the entry which begins that category so that the outline may serve as a table of contents for the bibliography as a whole. Entries are listed alphabetically within categories. Annotations are omitted on many short articles or in cases where the title and category are enough to describe the nature of the work.

Outline of Categories

Bibliography

I. The Military and Its Critics

1. Andreski, Stanislav. *Military Organization and Society.* 2d ed. Berkeley: University of California Press, 1968. Typologies, cross-national comparisons and general propositions about interdependence of armed forces and society. Bibliography.

2. Coates, Charles H., and Pellegrin, Roland J. *Military Sociology: A Study of American Military Institutions and Military Life.* College Park, Md.: Social Science Press, 1965. A text. Interesting and very comprehensive, proestablishment exposition of the sociology of military organizations and military life in the U. S.; includes military role definitions, values, future projections, excellent annotated bibliography in each chapter.

3. Donovan, Col. James A. (USMC, Ret.). *Militarism, U.S.A.* New York: Scribners, 1970. Wide-ranging expansion of Gen. David Shoup's article, "The New American Militarism," no. 14. Critical of U. S. policies and the MIC. An insider's view.

4. Enthoven, Alain C., and Smith, K. Wayne. *How Much Is Enough? Shaping the Defense Program, 1961–1969.* New York: Harper & Row, 1971. The inside view by McNamara's chief systems analysts.

5. Hanks, Capt. Robert J. (USN). "Against All Enemies." *U.S. Naval Institute Proceedings* vol. 96 (Mar. and June 1970): 22–29, 97–101. A controversial, harsh attack on critics of the military, defining them as "the enemy."

6. Huntington, Samuel P. *The Soldier and the State: The Theory and Politics of Civil-Military Relations.* New York: Vintage Books, 1957. A comprehensive, normative theory and a broad historical analysis; very influential, though controversial, among scholars and professional soldiers.

7. Janowitz, Morris, ed. *The New Military: Changing Patterns of Organization.* New York: Russell Sage Foundation, 1964. Some excellent empirical studies. See also his comprehensive and

authoritative earlier work, *The Professional Soldier: A Social and Political Portrait.* New York: Free Press, 1960.

8. _____, and Little, Lt. Col. Roger W. *Sociology and the Military Establishment.* rev. ed. New York: Russell Sage Foundation, 1965. Military values, socialization, organizational and group behavior. Bibliography.

9. Just, Ward. *Military Men.* New York: Knopf, 1970. Excellent portrait of the army's inner conflicts, attitudes, problems, rationales for action and ethical dilemmas.

10. Lens, Sidney. *The Military-Industrial Complex.* Philadelphia and Kansas City, Mo.: Pilgrim Press and the *National Catholic Reporter,* 1970. Wide-reaching critique: American society, foreign policy and military influence on academia, organized labor, etc.

11. Little, Roger W., ed. *Handbook of Military Institutions.* Beverly Hills, Calif.: Sage, 1971. A big book with much new and updated research. See also his (ed.) *A Survey of Military Institutions.* Chicago: Inter-University Seminar on Armed Forces and Society, 1969.

12. Oppenheimer, Martin, ed. *The American Military.* Trans-Action, 1971. Broad collection of articles.

13. Rodberg, Leonard S., and Shearer, Derek, eds. *The Pentagon Watchers: Students Report on the National Security State.* Garden City, N.Y.: Doubleday, 1970. Critical articles on the cold war, foreign policy and the MIC. Some new research. Includes highly useful appendix on how to research the military and bibliography of official and semiofficial publications.

14. Shoup, Gen. David M. (USMC, Ret.). "The New American Militarism." *Atlantic* vol. 223 (Apr. 1969). "America has become a militaristic and aggressive nation."

15. Smith, Maj. Mark E., III (USAF), and Johns, Maj. Claude J., Jr. (USAF). *American Defense Policy,* 2d ed. Baltimore: Johns Hopkins Press, 1968. Anthology of mostly civilian writings on defense strategy, civil-military relations and moral aspects of using force. Editors are political scientists at USAF Academy, and book is used in Academy courses.

16. United States, Department of Defense. *Department of Defense Annual Report.* Washington, D.C.: Department of Defense, annually by fiscal year. Includes reports of the Secretaries of Defense, Army, Navy and Air Force. Available from USGPO.

17. van Doorn, Jacques, ed. *Armed Forces and Society: Sociological Essays.* The Hague: Mouton, 1968. Papers from Sixth World Congress of Sociology covering the military, its ideology and its role

in social and political change; makes cross-national comparisons. See also later editions.

18. Weigley, Russell F., ed. *The American Military: Readings in the History of the Military in American Society.* Reading, Mass.: Addison-Wesley, 1969. Readings from the Virginia Constitutional Convention to the present: civilian control, militarism, professionalism, etc.

19. Yarmolinsky, Adam. *The Military Establishment: Its Impacts on American Society.* New York: Harper & Row, 1971. Provocative and most wide-ranging single study to date. Much hard data compiled from other sources. Lacking in coherence.

A. THE NATIONAL SECURITY ESTABLISHMENT
1. Organization, Decision Making, Civilian Control

20. Art, Robert J. *The TFX Decision: McNamara and the Military.* Boston: Little, Brown, 1968. A case study with broader implications for civil-military relations and the MIC.

21. Ballagh, Capt. Robert S., Jr. (USA). "The JCS Challenge." *Military Review* vol. 51 (Apr. 1971). Very critical of the "radical changes" in Joint Chiefs of Staff recommended by the Nixon-appointed Blue Ribbon (Fitzhugh) Defense Panel; evaluates previous similar studies.

22. Barrett, Raymond J. "Partners in Policymaking." *Military Review* vol. 45, no. 10 (Oct. 1965). Argues for civil-military partnership in policy making, instead of civilian supremacy *over* the military. Long article.

23. Bashore, Maj. Boyd T. "Organization for Frontless Wars." *Military Review* vol. 44, no. 5 (May 1964).

24. Beishline, Brig. Gen. John Robert. *Military Management for National Defense.* Englewood Cliffs, N.J.: Prentice-Hall, 1963. Revision of a 1950 book.

25. Benjamin, Roger W., and Edinger, Lewis J. "Conditions for Military Control over Foreign Policy Decisions in Major States." *Journal of Conflict Resolution* vol. 15 (Mar. 1971). Comparative analysis of 62 cases.

26. "Blue Ribbon Defense Panel Reports." *Defense Industry Bulletin* vol. 6 (Sept. 1970). Fitzhugh Panel report to the president and the defense secretary on the Defense Department reorganization.

27. Borosage, Robert. "The Making of the National Security State." In Leonard Rodberg and Derek Shearer, eds. *The Pentagon Watchers.* See no. 13. The creation of the postwar institu-

tions to rationalize military policy. Structural analysis with broad critical implications.

28. Brogan, D. W. "U.S.: Civil and Military." In Michael Howard, ed. *Soldiers and Governments: Nine Studies in Civil-Military Relations.* Bloomington, Ind.: Indiana University Press, 1962. Early article citing decline of Congress in direction of military affairs.

29. Brown, George W. *Generals and the Public: Recent Policy-Making in Civil-Military Relations.* Lawrence, Kan.: Governmental Research Center, University of Kansas, 1964. Covers the problem of the armed forces informing or "propagandizing" the public about the "enemy," etc.

30. Caraley, Demetrios. *The Politics of Military Unification: A Study of Conflict and the Policy Process.* New York: Columbia University Press, 1966. The best study of the post-1945 struggle for armed services unification.

31. Coles, Harry L., ed. *Total War and Cold War: Problems of Civilian Control of the Military.* Columbus, O.: Ohio State University Press, 1962. U. S., Nazi Germany, USSR, UK comparisons.

32. Davis, Vincent. "American Military Policy: Decision making in the Executive Branch." *Naval War College Review* vol. 22 (May 1970).

33. Dougall, I. "Green Berets: U. S. Army vs. CIA." *Peace News* vol. 17, no. 30 (22 Aug. 1969). A new organizational rivalry in the counterinsurgency infrastruture.

34. Edinger, Lewis J. "Military Leaders and Foreign Policy-Making." *American Political Science Review* vol. 57, no. 2 (June 1963). Presents a model for cross-national comparisons of civil-military relations by focusing on the foreign policy processes of modern industrial states.

35. Eliot, Maj. George Fielding (Australian Army, Ret.). "Blue Ribbon—Red Tape." *Ordnance* vol. 55 (Jan.-Feb. 1971). Critical of the Fitzhugh Blue Ribbon Defense Panel.

36. Enke, Stephen, ed. *Defense Management.* Englewood Cliffs, N. J.: Prentice-Hall, 1967. DoD's planning, programming, budgeting system, cost effectiveness, special defense problems such as R & D. By a former Deputy Assistant Secretary of Defense.

37. Finer, Samuel E. *The Man on Horseback: The Role of the Military in Politics.* New York: Praeger, 1962. Deals with U. S. only in passing; takes sharp issue with Huntington's *The Soldier and the State.* See no. 6.

38. "Fitzhugh (Blue Ribbon Defense) Panel Recommends Competitive Prototypes, Sweeping Organizational Changes." *Armed*

Forces Journal vol. 107 (3 Aug. 1970). A brief but complete précis of major recommendations. See no. 93.

39. Forrestal, James V. *The Forrestal Diaries.* Edited by Walter Millis. New York: Viking, 1951. An indispensible record of the early DoD by one of its most influential secretaries.

40. Fox, William T. R. "Representativeness and Efficiency: Dual Problem of Civil-Military Relations." *Political Science Quarterly* vol. 76, no. 3 (Sept. 1961). Problem of securing liberal values together with adequate defense.

41. Fulbright, J. William. "Public Policy and Military Responsibility." *Social Action* vol. 28 (Feb. 1962). Cites dilemma that the military "expert who knows what should be done finds himself at the mercy of the politician who knows what can be done."

42. Galbraith, John K. *How to Control the Military.* Garden City, N.Y.: Doubleday, 1969. A short critique of the MIC and the "bureaucratic truths" of the cold warriors.

43. _____. "The Plain Lessons of a Bad Decade." *Foreign Policy* (Winter 1970–1971). Organizational momentum in the Pentagon blamed for much of U. S. Vietnam policy.

44. Garvey, Capt. Gerald. "The Changing Management Role of the Military Departments Reconsidered." Part I: "Administrative Discretion vs. Constitutional Duty." *Air University Review* vol. 15 (Mar.-Apr. 1964). Examines power of DoD vis-à-vis the services, Congress and the President; notes early McNamara trends. Part II: "Civilian Control, the Preparedness Power and the Twilight of Congress" vol. 15 (May-June 1964). Analysis of presidential emergency powers; notes Congress has no practical competence to assume more active role.

45. Hammond, Paul Y. "A Functional Analysis of Defense Department Decision-Making in the McNamara Administration." *American Political Science Review* vol. 62, no. 1 (1968).

46. _____. *Organizing for Defense.* Princeton, N. J.: Princeton University Press, 1961. U. S. national security establishment, 1900–1960; effects of organization on policy.

47. Heiman, Grover. "Defense Reverses PPB Process." *Armed Forces Management* vol. 16 (Feb. 1970). Planning, programming, budgeting.

48. Heinl, Col. R. D., Jr. "Laird Dumps Fitzhugh Findings after Secret Meeting with JCS." *Armed Forces Journal* vol. 108 (7 Sept. 1970).

49. Hess, K. "Who Is Melvin Laird." *Ramparts* vol. 8, no. 2 (Aug. 1969).

50. Hitch, Charles J. *Decision-Making for Defense.* Berkeley, Calif.: University of California Press, 1965. DoD organization, management and broad strategy.

51. Hoopes, Townsend. *The Limits of Intervention: An Inside Account of How the Johnson Policy of Escalation in Vietnam Was Reversed.* New York: McKay, 1969. Chronicles disillusionment within LBJ administration. Clark Clifford emerges as the hero of deescalation.

52. Howard, Michael. "Civil-Military Relations in Great Britain and the United States, 1945–1958." *Political Science Quarterly* vol. 75, no. 1 (Mar. 1960). Military security is seen as the paramount priority to which all other national interests should defer.

53. _____. "Introduction: The Armed Forces as a Political Problem." In M. Howard, ed. *Soldiers and Governments: Nine Studies in Civil-Military Relations.* Bloomington, Ind.: Indiana University Press, 1962.

54. Huntington, Samuel P. "Civil-Military Relations." In *International Encyclopedia of the Social Sciences* vol. 2. New York: Macmillan, 1968. A précis of main points on "civilian control" and "the military mind" from his *The Soldier and the State.* See no. 6.

55. _____. "Civilian Control of the Military: A Theoretical Statement." In Heinz Eulau, Samuel J. Eldersveld and Morris Janowitz, eds. *Political Behavior: A Reader in Theory and Research.* Glencoe, Ill.: Free Press, 1956. Short précis of main theory in his *The Soldier and the State.* See no. 6.

56. _____. *The Common Defense: Strategic Programs in National Politics.* New York: Columbia University Press, 1961. Still the best description and analysis of (strategic) military policy making in the 1950s. Set in context of American politics.

57. _____. "Interservice Competition and the Political Roles of the Armed Services." *American Political Science Review* vol. 55 (1961). Rivalries bring military into politics, but criss-crossing conflicts diminish the probability of direct civil-military confrontations. Reprinted in Coles, ed. *Total War and Cold War* (see no. 2292) and incorporated into Huntington's *The Common Defense.* See no. 56.

58. Ingram, Capt. Samuel P. (USN). "Civilian Command or Civilian Control?" *U.S. Naval Institute Proceedings* vol. 94 (May 1968).

59. Kaufmann, William W. *The McNamara Strategy.* New York: Harper & Row, 1964. By one of McNamara's nuclear-war theoreticians. Bibliography.

60. Kissinger, Henry A. "Strategy and Organization." *Foreign Affairs* (Apr. 1957).

61. Kitner, William R.; Coffey, Joseph I.; and Albright, Raymond J. *Forging a New Sword: A Study of the Department of Defense.* New York: Harper & Row, 1958. On evolution of DoD and consequences for three services.

62. Kurth, Ronald J. "The Military and Power in the U. S." *U. S. Naval Institute Proceedings* vol. 91, no. 5 (May 1965).

63. Lang, Kurt. "Military Organizations." In J. G. March, ed. *Handbook of Organizations.* Chicago: Rand-McNally, 1965. See also his "Military." *International Encyclopedia of the Social Sciences* vol. 10. New York: Macmillan, 1968.

64. Lyons, Gene M. "The New Civil-Military Relations." *American Political Science Review* vol. 55, no. 1 (Mar. 1961). Holds traditional civilian control over military irrelevant, notes trends in "the 'militarization' of civilians and the 'civilianization' of the military."

65. MacCloskey, Monro. *The American Intelligence Community.* New York: Rosen Press, 1967.

66. McMahon, Maj. John F., Jr. (USAF). "Streamlining the Joint Chiefs of Staff." *Military Review* vol. 49 (Jan. 1969). Argues for greater role for the Joint Chiefs in formulating military strategy.

67. Mansfield, Harvey C. "Civil-Military Relations in the United States." *Current History* vol. 38, no. 224 (Apr. 1960). U. S. Constitution puts the military establishment directly into the executive and legislative policy processes.

68. Millis, Walter. *Arms and Men: A Study in American Military History.* New York: Putnam, 1956.

69. _____, ed. *The Forrestal Diaries.* See no. 39.

70. _____; Mansfield, Harvey C.; and Stein, Harold. *Arms and the State: Civil-Military Elements in National Policy.* New York: The Twentieth Century Fund, 1958. Historical perspective, twentieth century to early cold war.

71. Moorer, Adm. Thomas H. (USN). "Moorer: Viable Options, Purple Suit Questions and the Pendulum Theory." *Armed Forces Journal* vol. 108 (4 Jan. 1971). Interview with the Chairman of the Joint Chiefs of Staff.

72. Neblett, Col. William Hanaye. *No Peace with Regulars.* New York: Pageant, 1957. Critical opinion by former president of Reserve Officer's Association.

73. Norris, John G. "A Dangerous Proposal." *Navy* vol. 13 (July-Aug. 1970). Editorial critical of Fitzhugh Blue Ribbon Defense Panel recommendations.

74. Quade, E. S. *Analysis for Military Decisions.* Chicago: Rand-McNally, 1964.

75. _____, and Boucher, W. I., eds. *Systems Analysis and Policy Planning.* New York: Elsevier, 1968. A rather technical RAND study.

76. Raymond, Jack. *Power at the Pentagon.* New York: Harper & Row, 1964.

77. "Reorganization for DoD." *Ordnance* vol. 55 (Sept.-Oct. 1970).

78. Ridgway, Gen. Matthew B. (USA. Ret.). *The Korean War.* Garden City, N. Y.: Doubleday, 1967. "How We Met the Challenge. How All-Out Asian War Was Averted. Why MacArthur Was Dismissed. Why Today's War Objectives Must Be Limited."

79. Ries, John C. *The Management of Defense: Organization and Control of the U.S. Armed Services.* Baltimore: Johns Hopkins Press, 1964. Readings in Defense Planning, Programming and Budgeting Seminar. Includes bibliography.

80. Rovere, Richard H., and Schlesinger, Arthur M., Jr. *The General and the President, and the Future of American Foreign Policy.* New York: Farrar, Straus and Young, 1951. The Truman-MacArthur controversy.

81. Schilling, Warner R.; Hammond, Paul Y.; and Snyder, Glenn H. *Strategy, Politics, and Defense Budgets.* New York: Columbia University Press, 1962. Three case studies.

82. Schratz, Paul R. "A Look at Civilian Control." *U. S. Naval Institute Proceedings* vol. 88, no. 6 (June 1962). Brief outline of civilians control since 1776; applauds JFK-McNamara changes in Pentagon.

83. Scott, John F., and Cameron, John R. "Political Theory and Military Groups." *Military Review* vol. 45 (Nov. 1965). The military does and should act as interest groups in the national political arena.

84. Searls, Hank. *Pentagon.* New York: Geis, 1971. A novel by an insider (former Assistant Secretary of Defense) highlights the "self-centeredness" that permeates the Pentagon.

85. Smith, Louis. *American Democracy and Military Power: A Study of Civil Control of the Military Power in the United States.* Chicago: University of Chicago Press, 1951. Historical study, emphasis on role of military power in government..

86. Spanier, John W. *The Truman-MacArthur Controversy and the Korean War.* Cambridge, Mass.: Harvard University Press, 1959.

87. Stein, Harold, ed. *American Civil-Military Decisions: A Book of Case Studies.* Birmingham, Ala.: University of Alabama Press, 1963.

See especially Theodore Lowi's "Bases in Spain" in this volume.

88. Swomley, John M. *The Military Establishment.* Boston: Beacon Press, 1964. Critique of entire MIC and extreme right. Military influence on government policy due to "conscious planning for power."

89. Tansill, William R. *The Concept of Civil Supremacy over the Military in the United States.* Washington, D.C.: Legislative Reference Service, Library of Congress, Feb. 1951. Summary review; military role expansion due to lack of civilians to fill important jobs.

90. Tarr, David. "Military Technology and the Policy Process." *Western Political Quarterly* vol. 18, no. 1 (1965).

91. Tyrrell, C. Merton. *Pentagon Partners, The New Nobility.* New York: Grossman, 1970. Emphasis on weapons decisions, cost overruns, abuse of military political power. Describes the more notable "errors" in weapons systems and procurement.

92. U. S. Senate. Committee on Government Operations. Subcommittee on National Security and International Operations. *Planning-Programing-Budgeting—Rescuing Policy Analysis from PPBS.* Washington, D.C.: USGPO, 1969.

93. United States. Blue Ribbon Defense Panel. *Report to the President and the Secretary of Defense on the Department of Defense.* Washington, D.C.: USGPO, 1970. Report of the controversial Fitzhugh Panel on DoD reorganization and operations.

94. Vagts, Alfred. *Defense and Diplomacy: The Soldier and the Conduct of Foreign Relations.* New York: King's Crown Press, 1956. Far-ranging, comprehensive, traditional approach.

95. van Doorn, Jacques, ed. *Military Profession and Military Regimes: Commitments and Conflicts.* The Hague: Mouton, 1969. Very interesting cross-cultural comparisons; van Doorn essay, "Political Change and the Control of the Military; Some General Remarks," pp. 11–31, rebuts Finer, S.E. *The Man on Horseback* (see no. 37) and Huntington, S.P. *The Soldier and the State* (see no. 6) hypotheses on military behavior.

96. Weigley, Russell Frank. *History of the United States Army.* New York: Macmillan, 1967. Comprehensive and authoritative.

97. Weiss, George. "DoD Tightens Civilian Control over Intelligence, but No Reorganization." *Armed Forces Journal* vol. 108 (1 Mar. 1971). Results of Senator Ervin's subcommittee investigations of army domestic surveillance activities.

98. Wheeler, Gen. Earle G. (USA). "The JCS Decision Process." *Air*

Force Policy Letter for Commanders supplement no. 8 (Aug. 1968). Testimony at hearings of the Senate Armed Services Committee's Preparedness Investigating Subcommittee (23 Apr. 1968).

99. _____, and Parsons, J. Graham. "The Politico-Military Relationship." *Perspectives in Defense Management* (Mar. 1970). Address, National Security Seminar, Pensacola, Fla., Sept. 29–30, 1969.

100. Williams, William Appleman. "Officers and Gentlemen." *New York Review of Books* vol. 16, no. 8 (6 May 1971). Links civilian control and military political activity to mission prescribed by society. Cf. Dickey's article in this volume.

101. Yarmolinsky, Adam. "Bureaucratic Structures and Political Outcomes." *Journal of International Affairs* vol. 23 Argues that for structural/organizational reasons DoD is more influential than the State Department in foreign policy matters.

102. See also under specialized organizational units, e.g., CIA, public information, counterinsurgency, etc. See IIIC, "Foreign Policy Politics and Processes," for decision making in that field. See especially IIB, "Political Institutions," for civilian control.

2. Socialization, Education, Training, Indoctrination

103. Bourne, Dr. Peter G. "Some Observations on the Psychosocial Phenomena Seen in Basic Training." *Psychiatry: Journal for the Study of Interpersonal Processes* vol. 30, no. 2 (May 1967). Stress, dehumanization, powerlessness cause symptoms similar to those of concentration camp inmates.

104. Brown, Fred R. "Challenge to ICAF: More and More Highly Educated Students." *Perspectives in Defense Management* (Jan. 1971). Growth of the Industrial College of the Armed Forces.

105. "Chemical Warfare Training in U. S." *NACLA Newsletter* vol. 4, no. 1 (Mar. 1970).

106. Coble, Donald W. "Is DoD Becoming a Sociological Lion?" *Armed Forces Management* vol. 16 (Jan. 1970).

107. Engeman, Jack. *West Point: The Life of a Cadet.* New York: Lothrop, Lee, and Shepard, 1956.

108. "GAO Scores Military Graduate Education Programs." *Armed Forces Journal* vol. 108 (7 Sept. 1970). General Accounting Office study explained.

109. Gage, R. W. "Patriotism and Military Discipline as a Function of Degree of Military Training." *Journal of Social Psychology* vol. 64, no. 1 (1964).

110. "The Haines Board Report on Officer Training. Carlisle, Leavenworth, Knox." *Army* vol. 16 (May 1966).

111. Hays, Col. Samuel H. (USA). "Military Training in the U. S.

Today." *Current History* (July 1968). Ex-director of Military Psychology and Leadership at West Point.

112. Hessman, James D. "Military Men at the White House." *Armed Forces Journal* vol. 108 (1 Feb. 1971). Social aides, etc.

113. "The Industrial College and the A.O.A. Are Partners in Preparedness." *Ordnance* vol. 53 (Nov.-Dec. 1968). The Industrial College of the Armed Forces and American Ordnance Association.

114. "The Inter-American Defense College." *Military Review* vol. 50 (Apr. 1970).

115. "Join the Army—Learn a Trade." *Nola Express* vol. 1, no. 35 (14 Aug. 1969).

116. "Judge Discovers Military." *L. A. Free Press* vol. 6, no. 76 (31 Oct. 1969).

117. Just, Ward. *Military Men.* See no. 9.

118. Karsten, Peter, et al. "ROTC, MYLAI and the Volunteer Army." *Foreign Policy* no. 6 (Spring 1971). Supports ROTC on grounds that officer output is less authoritarian than from Service Academy and OCS.

119. Katzenbach, Edward L., Jr. "The Demotion of Professionalism at the War Colleges." *U.S. Naval Institute Proceedings* vol. 91, no. 3 (Mar. 1965). Argues for more specialization of military and political functions and less "political" war college curricula.

120. "Knowledge for Defense: The Role of the Armed Forces Industrial College Grows in Importance." *Ordnance* vol. 52 (Jan.-Feb. 1968).

121. Lovell, John P. "The Professional Socialization of the West Point Cadet." In M. Janowitz, ed. *The New Military.* See no. 7. Studies the "values" developed by West Point.

122. Lyons, Gene M., and Morton, Louis. *Schools for Strategy: Education and Research in National Security Affairs.* New York: Praeger, 1965. The intellectual community and the role of force in national policy.

123. Madsen, Maj. Gen. Frank M., Jr. "The Social Implications of Military Education and Training." *Air Force Policy Letter for Commanders* supplement no. 2 (Feb. 1971).

124. Masland, John W., and Radway, Lawrence I. *Soldiers and Scholars: Military Education and Military Policy.* Princeton, N.J.: Princeton University Press, 1967. A standard work in the field.

125. Palma, Capt. Henry. "Motivating the 'Now' Generation." *U. S. Air Force Instructors Journal* vol. 8 (Summer 1970).

126. "Psychologist Charges Brutality is 'Normal' in Marine Training." *New York Times* (1 April 1969), p. 28.

127. "Recruit Maltreatment Persisting in Marines Despite Official Ban." *New York Times* (13 Oct 1969), p. 1.

128. Scholossberg, Maj. Arnold, Jr. "Key Men for the Politico-Military Arena." *Army Digest* vol. 25 (Aug. 1970).

129. Steele, Maj. Gen. W. S. "How the Industrial College Meets the Management Challenge." *Armed Forces Management* vol. 11 (Jan. 1965).

130. Tamburello, Capt. Gaspare B. "Education: A Reciprocal Civic-Military Objective." *U. S. Naval Institute Proceedings* vol. 95 (Oct. 1969).

131. "U. S. Army School of the Americas." *Military Review* vol. 50 (Apr. 1970).

132. "USMA Board of Visitors Report to the President." *Armed Forces Journal* vol. 107 (6 Dec. 1969).

133. Wool, Harold. *The Military Specialist: Skilled Manpower for the Armed Forces.* Baltimore: Johns Hopkins Press, 1968. Includes bibliography.

134. ———. "The Armed Services as a Training Institution." In E. Ginzberg, ed. *The Nation's Children* vol. 2. New York: Columbia University Press, 1959.

135. See also IIC4. "ROTC and Other Military Education Programs, . . ." See the Index of Doctrinal, Training and Organizational Publications under no. 2476.

3. Professionalism: Old and New

136. Barber, Comdr. James A., Jr. (USN). "Is There a Generation Gap in the Naval Officer Corps?" *Naval War College Review* vol. 22 (May 1970).

137. Barrett, Raymond J. "Politico-Military Expertise: A Practical Program." *Military Review* vol. 46 (Nov. 1966). Claims foreign policy and military policy are interdependent, thus need more military-foreign service officer exchanges.

138. Bidwell, C. E. "The Young Professional in the Army: A Study of Occupational Identity." *American Sociological Review* vol. 26 (1961). Experiences of peacetime draftees.

139. Bletz, Col. Donald F. (USA). "Professionalism: A Conceptual Approach." *Military Review* vol. 51 (May 1971). Cites levels of "technical-military expertise" and "politico-military expertise" demanded of officers at various levels; asserts "politico-military

expertise" essential for "relevance" of military profession to society.

140. Blumenson, Martin. "Some Thoughts on Professionalism." *Military Review* vol. 44, no. 9 (Sept. 1964).

141. Boatner, Col. Mark M. III (USA, Ret.). "Seeing Ourselves as Others See Us . . . First." *Army* vol. 21 (Feb. 1971).

142. Bradford, Col. Zeb B., Jr., and Murphy, Maj. James R. "A New Look at the Military Profession." *Army* vol. 19, no. 2 (Feb. 1969).

143. Callahan, Col. L. G. "Do We Need a Science of War?" *Armed Forces Journal* vol. 106 (10 May 1969).

144. Cameron, Joseph M. *The Anatomy of Military Merit.* Philadelphia: Dorrance, 1960.

145. Clarke, Gen. Bruce C. "Attractiveness of a Service Career." *Armor* vol. 75 (Nov.-Dec. 1966).

146. Coates, Charles H. "America's New Officer Corps." *Trans-Action* vol. 3 (1965). Upward social mobility of officers.

147. Clatanoff, William B. "The Role of the Armed Services." *Current History* vol. 55 (July 1968).

148. Davis, Vincent. *The Admirals Lobby.* Chapel Hill, N. C.: University of North Carolina Press, 1967. Navy traditions and their effect on political activity.

149. Deininger, Lt. J. G. David G. (USN). "The Career Officer as Existential Hero." *U. S. Naval Institute Proceedings* vol. 96 (Nov. 1970).

150. Field, Maury D. "Military Self-Image in a Technological Environment." In Morris Janowitz, ed. *The New Military.* See no. 7. Details 20-year trend in military self-image by content analysis of service journals.

151. Flint, Lt. Col. Roy K. (USA). "Army Professionalism for the Future." *Military Review* vol. 51 (Apr. 1971). Professional soldiers must not succumb to "Stab-in-the-Back Complex" due to civilian criticism; must patiently accommodate social change.

152. Freed, Maj. DeBow. "The Compleat Officer." *Military Review* vol. 40, no. 9 (Dec. 1960).

153. Gard, Col. Robert G., Jr. (USA). "The Military and American Society." *Foreign Affairs* vol. 49 (July 1971). Argues for adapting military professionalism to new (political and technological) demands and missions.

154. Gellermann, Josef E. *Generals as Statesmen.* New York: Vantage, 1959. Includes bibliography.

155. Ginsburgh, Col. Robert N. (USAF). "The Challenge to Military

Professionalism." *Foreign Affairs* vol. 42 (Jan. 1964). Decries civilian intervention into purely military matters; fears military will lose distinctive expertise, and consequently the right to be heard.

156. _____, and Rocap, Capt. Pember W. (USAF). "Changing Role of the Military Profession." *Air University Review* vol. 22 (Mar.-Apr. 1971). There are many new, nonmilitary roles for the armed forces; civilian involvement in strategy and tactics has increased since 1964.

157. Guelzo, Lt. Col. Carl M. "As We Should See Ourselves." *Infantry* vol. 55 (Nov-Dec. 1965).

158. _____. "An Introduction to Professionalism." *Infantry* vol. 57 (Sept.-Oct. 1967).

159. Hackett, Lt. Gen., Sir John W. "The Profession of Arms." *Military Review* vol. 43, no. 10 (Oct. 1963).

160. Harris, Lt. Malcolm S. (USN). "Junior Officer Retention—A Lot of Little Things." *U.S. Naval Institute Proceedings* vol. 97 (Mar. 1971).

161. Hauser, Lt. Col. William L. (USA). "Professionalism and the Junior Officer Drain." *Army* vol. 20 (Sept. 1970).

162. Hay, Maj. Gen. John H. "Military Art and Science: A Profession Comes of Age." *Army* vol. 19 (Apr. 1969).

163. Holbrook, Capt. James R. (USA). "Volunteer Army: Military Caste." *Military Review* vol. 51 (Aug. 1971). Most of officer corps is already volunteer and professional but not a separate societal caste; all-volunteer lower ranks would not create a military caste.

164. Huntington, Samuel P. "Power, Expertise, and the Military Profession." In K. S. Lynn, ed. *The Professions in America.* Boston: Houghton Mifflin, 1965. Also in *Daedalus* vol. 92 (1963).

165. Katzenbach, Edward L., Jr. "The Demotion of Professionalism at the War Colleges." See no. 119.

166. Lehman, H. "The Age of Eminent Leaders: Then and Now." *American Journal of Sociology* vol. 52 (1967).

167. Lerche, Charles O., Jr. "The Professional Officer and Foreign Policy." *U. S. Naval Institute Proceedings* vol. 90, no. 7 (July 1964).

168. Lowe, George E. "The Importance of Being Professional." *Army* vol. 16, no. 1 (Jan. 1966). Due to cold war, there are no purely military (or political) matters; thus need broader base of professional military expertise to advise on but not to advocate policies.

169. Mahler, Maj. Michael D. "A Volunteer Army." *Army* vol. 21

(July 1971). Protest of civilian demands placed on military.

170. Metcalf, Lt. Col. Ramsey N. (USA). "The Continuing Requirement for the Professional Military Man in Diplomatic Roles." *Armor* vol. 74 (Jan-Feb. 1965). Cold war has blurred peace-war distinction; need more people with military background in diplomacy to prevent "diplomatic weakness and unnecessary compromise tantamount to appeasement."

171. Miles, Lt. Col. Jack L. (USMC). "The Fusion of Military and Political Considerations: Threat or Challenge to the Military." *Marine Corps Gazette* pt. 1, vol. 52 (Aug. 1968); pt. 2, vol. 52 (Sept. 1968).

172. Nelson, Lt. Comdr. Andrew G. (USN). "Politics and the Naval Officer." *U. S. Naval Institute Proceedings* vol. 87 (1961). Brief, superficial, but notes convergence and overlap of military and political issues, citing dangers for future.

173. Reese, Lt. Col. Thomas H. (USA). "The Oath of Allegiance." *U. S. Naval Institute Proceedings* vol. 91 (Sept. 1965). Analysis of divided loyalties inherent in officers' oath of office.

174. Reston, James, Jr. *To Defend, To Destroy.* New York: Norton, 1971. A novel; emphasizes ethical dilemmas between abstract duty and concerns of humanity; does "defending the country" necessitate risking its destruction?

175. Reynolds, Maj. Gen. Russell B. *The Officer's Guide,* 1966–1967 ed. (31st ed.). Harrisburg, Pa.: Stackpole, 1966. The "Emily Post" for professional officers.

176. Rovere, Richard H., and Schlesinger, Arthur M., *The General and the President, and the Future of American Foreign Policy.* See no. 80.

177. Segal, D. R. "Selective Promotion in Officer Cohorts." *Sociological Quarterly* vol. 8, no. 2 (1967).

178. Simons, William E. "Military Professionals as Policy Advisers." *Air University Review* vol. 20 (Mar.-Apr. 1969).

179. Spanier, John W. *The Truman-MacArthur Controversy and the Korean War.* See no. 86.

180. Strange, Lt. Col. Loren C. (USA). "Professionalism," *U. S. Army Aviation Digest* vol. 16 (Apr. 1970).

181. Tracy, William R. "Politico-Military Involvement—A Functional Imperative." *Military Review* vol. 49, no. 4 (Apr. 1969). Argues that senior military officers must participate in the political arena in advisory and executive roles and must represent the military's institutional needs.

182. U.S. Department of Defense. Office of Armed Forces Information and Education. *The Armed Forces Officer.* (Department of

Defense Pamphlet no. 1–20) Washington, D.C.: Department of
Defense, Dec. 1960. Includes bibliography.

183.   van Doorn, Jacques, ed. *Military Profession and Military Regimes:
        Commitments and Conflicts.* See no. 95.

184.   Vought, Lt. Col. Donald B. (USA). "Soldiers Must Be States-
        men." *Military Review* vol. 48 (Oct. 1968). Argues that profes-
        sional expertise must include political acumen.

185.   Wakin, Col. Malham M. (USA). "The American Military—
        Theirs to Reason Why." *Air Force Magazine* vol. 54 (Mar. 1971).

186.   Westmoreland, Gen. William C. (USA). "From Army of the 70s:
        'A Flawless Performance.'" *Army* vol. 20 (Oct. 1970).

187.   Williams, William A. "Officers and Gentlemen." See no. 100.

4. The Military Mind and Personality

188.   Barber, Comdr. James A., Jr. (USN). "Is There a Generation
        Gap in the Naval Officer Corps?" See no. 136.

189.   Campbell, D. T., and McCormack, T. H. "Military Experience
        and Attitudes toward Authority." *American Journal of Sociology,*
        vol. 62 (1957). Authoritarianism among officers.

190.   Chase, Capt. Jack S. (USA). "Military Ideals." *Armor* vol. 79
        (July-Aug. 1970).

191.   Eccles, Rear Adm. Henry E. *Military Concepts and Philosophy.* New
        Brunswick, N. J.: Rutgers University Press, 1965. Includes bibli-
        ography.

192.   Eisenhower, Dwight, D. *At Ease: Stories I Tell to Friends.* Garden
        City, N. Y.: Doubleday, 1967.

193.   Fredericks, Edgar. *MacArthur: His Mission and Meaning.* Philadel-
        phia: Whitmore, 1968.

194.   French, E. G., and Ernest, R. R. "The Relationship between
        Authoritarianism and the Acceptance of Military Ideology."
        Journal of Personality vol. 24 (1965).

195.   Gray, J. Glenn. *The Warriors: Reflections on Men in Battle.* New
        York: Harcourt, Brace, 1959. Treats military in context of
        larger society.

196.   Guttmann, Allen. *The Conservative Tradition in America.* New
        York: Oxford University Press, 1967. Rejects Huntington's de-
        scription of "The Military Mind." *The Soldier and the State.* See
        no 6.

197.   Huntington, Samuel P. "Civil-Military Relations." See no. 54.

198.   James, D. Clayton. *The Years of MacArthur* vol. 1: 1880–1941.
        Boston: Houghton Mifflin, 1970.

199.   Just, Ward. *Military Men.* See no. 9.

200.   King, Lt. Col. Edward L. (USA, Ret.). "The Death of the Army:

A Pre-Mortem." *Family* (17 Feb. 1971). (Semi-monthly magazine supplement to the *Army/Navy/Air Force/Times* weekly newspapers). Very critical and controversial on "what's wrong with the Army." See also subsequent rebuttals in the *Army Times*, espcially Col. Ray H. Smith, "King Piece 'Emotional' " (3 Mar. 1971).

201.   Knebel, Fletcher, and Bailey, Charles W. II. *Seven Days in May.* New York: Bantam, 1963. A novel about an attempted *coup d'état* in the U. S.

202.   Krulak, Lt. Gen. Victor H. (USMC, Ret.). "The Low Cost of Freedom." *U. S. Naval Institute Proceedings* vol. 96 (July 1970). A traditional exhortation to meet a great Soviet threat; cites lack of "guts" in "the vast bulk of our people."

203.   Lang, Kurt. "Technology and Career Management in the Military Establishment." In M. Janowitz, ed. *The New Military.* See no. 7.

204.   LeMay, Gen. Curtis E. (USAF). *America Is in Danger.* New York: Funk & Wagnalls, 1968. General LeMay's alternative to the McNamara strategy. Hair-raising.

205.   Lyons, Gene M. "The Military Mind." *Bulletin of the Atomic Scientists* vol. 19 (Nov. 1963). Brief but comprehensive review of the literature on the subject to 1963. Challenges Huntington. *The Soldier and the State.* See No. 6.

206.   MacArthur, Gen. Douglas. *Duty, Honor, Country.* New York: Rolton House, 1962.

207.   ———. *A Soldier Speaks: Public Papers and Speeches of General of the Army Douglas MacArthur.* Edited by Maj. Vorin E. Whan, Jr. New York: Praeger, 1965.

208.   Metcalf, Lt. Col. Ramsey N. (USA). "The Continuing Requirement for the Professional Military Man in Diplomatic Roles." See no. 170.

209.   Millis, Walter. *Arms and Men: A Study in American Military History.* See no. 68.

210.   Mills, C. Wright. *The Power Elite.* New York: Oxford University Press, 1956. The U. S. is ruled by an interlocking economic-political-military elite; the military predominates when reality is defined in military terms.

211.   Mitchell, V. F., and Porter, L. W. "Comparative Managerial Role Perceptions in Military and Business Hierarchies." *Journal of Applied Psychology* vol. 51 (1967).

212.   Neblett, William Hanaye. *No Peace with Regulars.* See no. 72.

213. Nelson, Lt. Comdr. Andrew G. (USN). "Politics and the Naval Officer." See no. 172.

214. Nelson, P. D., and Berry, N. H. "Change in Sociometric Status During Military Basic Training Related to Performance Two Years Later." *Journal of Psychology* vol. 61 (1965).

215. "Old Brass Never Die." *Fifth Estate* vol. 5 no. 5 (9 July 1970).

216. Partlow, Lt. Comdr. Robert G. (USN). "The Military Mind." *U.S. Naval Institute Proceedings* vol. 97 (Feb. 1971).

217. Power, Gen. Thomas S. (USAF). *Design for Survival.* New York: Coward-McCann, 1965.

218. Reese, Lt. Col. Thomas H. (USA). "The Oath of Allegiance." See no. 173.

219. Reston, James, Jr. *To Defend, To Destroy.* See no. 174.

220. Reynolds, Maj. Gen. Russell B. *The Officer's Guide.* See no. 175.

221. Ridgway, Gen. Matthew B. *Soldier: The Memoirs of Matthew B. Ridgway,* as told to Harold H. Martin. New York: Harper & Row, 1956. One of the most apolitical of the generals.

222. Rivkin, Robert S. "The Military Mind." Chap. 4 of *GI Rights and Army Justice.* See no. 260.

223. Roucek, J. S., and Lottich, K. V. "American Military Sociology: The American Military Mind." *Social Science Information* vol. 3, no. 1 (1964). Review Article.

224. Sloan, James P. *War Games.* Boston: Houghton Mifflin, 1971. A novel—central theme: "War is no longer waged merely to achieve ends; it is waged as proof of its own possibility."

225. Tauber, Peter. *The Sunshine Soldiers.* New York: Simon & Schuster, 1971.

226. Twining, Gen. Nathan F. (USAF). *Neither Liberty nor Safety: A Hard Look at U. S. Military Policy and Strategy.* New York: Holt, Rinehart and Winston, 1966. A discussion of NSC–68, the policy of containment and strategic deterrence and the general's fears about the policy.

227. U. S. Department of the Army. *Military Leadership. Department of the Army Field Manual no. 22–100.* Washington, D.C.: Headquarters, Department of the Army, Nov. 1965. Good reference for norms expected in interpersonal superior-subordinate relations.

228. van Riper, P. P., and Unwalla, D. B. "Voting Patterns among High-Ranking Military Officers." *Political Science Quarterly* vol. 80, no. 1 (1965). Electoral participation.

229. Vidich, Arthur J., and Stein, Maurice R. "The Dissolved Identity in Military Life." In M. R. Stein; A. J. Vidich; and D. M. White,

eds. *Identity and Anxiety: Survival of the Person in Mass Society.*
Glencoe, Ill.: Free Press, 1960.

230.   Walker, Lt. Col. Robert M. (Ret.). "In Defense of the Military
Mind." *Military Review* vol. 49 (Aug. 1969).

231.   Warner, William L. et al. *The American Federal Executive: A Study
of the Social and Personal Characteristics of the Civilian and Military
Leaders of the United States Federal Government.* New Haven, Conn.:
Yale University Press, 1963.

232.   "What Lifers Are Made of." *The Ally* no. 26 (May 1970).

233.   White, H. B. "Military Morality." *Social Research* vol. 13 (1946).

234.   Yeuell, Lt. Col. Donovan, Jr. "Soldiering Is a Way of Life." *The
Army Combat Forces Journal* vol. 5, (Sept. 1954).

5. Military Life and the New Military

235.   Aquarius, S. O. [pseud.]. "Military Discipline, the Public and
the Now Generation." *Army* vol. 20 (Jan. 1970).

236.   Ayres, B. Drummond, Jr. "Army Softens Rigors of Recruits'
Training." *New York Times* (29 Aug. 1971), p. 1.

237.   _____."Army Tightens Training; Jogging Is In, Beer Is Out."
New York Times (19 Jan. 1972), p. 1.

238.   "Barracks Life Now a Little Brighter, to Attract Volunteers."
Army vol. 21 (Jan. 1971).

239.   Chapman, Gen. Leonard R., Jr. (USMC). "Chapman: An Em-
phasis on Combat Readiness, Quality, Spirit, and Discipline."
Armed Forces Journal vol. 108 (4 Jan. 1971). Interview with the
Commandant.

240.   "For the Common Footsoldier." *Fifth Estate* vol. 5, no. 7 (6 Aug.
1970).

241.   Grajewski, Jr. "Love." *Liberation* vol. 15, no. 6 (Aug. 1970).

242.   "The Great Hair Conspiracy." *The Ally*, no. 28 (July 1970).

243.   Harris, Lt. Malcolm S. (USN). "Junior Officer Retention—A Lot
of Little Things." See no. 160.

244.   Heinl, Col. R. D., Jr. "Cheap and Unwise 'Reforms' Undermine
the Armed Forces." *Armed Forces Journal* vol. 108 (18 Jan. 1971).

245.   Howze, Gen. Hamilton H. (USA, Ret.). "Military Discipline and
National Security." *Army* vol. 21 (Jan. 1971).

246.   "Inside Club Ripoff." *The Ally* no. 25 (Apr. 1970).

247.   Jackson, K. "GI Wife Raps on Military Life." *Old Mole* vol. 1, no.
41 (12 June 1970).

248.   "Join the Army—Learn a Trade." See no. 115.

249.   Kelley, Roger T. "DoD Readies Proposals to Improve Service
Life." *Air Force Times* vol. 31 (6 Jan. 1971). Interview.

250.   Kerry, John, and the Vietnam Veterans against the War. *The*

New Soldier. Edited by David Thorne and George Butler. New York: Macmillan, 1971. Pictures, letters and text about the "new" army.

251. Kerwin, Lt. Gen. W. T., Jr. (USA). "Youth's 'Why?' Key Challenge to Today's Army." *Army* vol. 20 (Feb. 1970).

252. Kinney, William A. "Hair! Hair!" *Airman* vol. 15 (Feb. 1971).

253. Knebel, Fletcher, and Bailey, Charles W. II. *Seven Days in May*. See no. 201.

254. "Marine Corps Still Building Men." *Street Journal* vol. 2, no. 34 (6 Aug. 1970).

255. Moskos, Charles C., Jr. *The American Enlisted Man: The Rank and File in Today's Military*. New York: Russell Sage Foundation, 1970. Comprehensive sociological study of enlisted norms, attitudes, life styles; authoritative and current.

256. "Navy Heat Chafes Chaffee over Permissive Rulings." *Armed Forces Journal* vol. 108 (15 Mar. 1971).

257. Palma, Capt. Henry. "Motivating the 'Now' Generation." *U. S. Air Force Instructors Journal* vol. 8 (Summer 1970).

258. Palmer, Gen. Bruce, Jr. (USA). "Challenges Give Unique Chance to Better Army." *Army* vol. 20 (Oct. 1970).

259. Reynolds, Maj. Gen. Russell B. *The Officer's Guide*. See no. 175.

260. Rivkin, Robert S. *GI Rights and Army Justice: The Draftee's Guide to Military Life and Law*. New York: Grove Press, 1970. Practical and legal advice and caustic description of brutalizing and dehumanizing aspects of army life. Includes list of coffee houses, GI newspapers and counseling services.

261. Stivers, Capt. R. E. (USN). "ADM Zumwalt Relaxes Navy Policy on Hairstyles to Bolster Young Navymen's Morale." *Navy* vol. 13 (Oct. 1970).

262. Tarr, David W. "The Military Abroad." *Annals of the American Academy of Political Social Science* vol. 368 (1966).

263. U. S. Congress, Senate Committee on Government Operations, Subcommittee on National Security and International Operations. *The State-Defense Officer Exchange Program: Analysis and Assessment*. (91st Congress). Washington, D.C.: USGPO, 1969. Exchange of personnel since 1961.

264. U. S. Department of Defense, Office of Armed Forces Information and Education. *The Armed Forces Officer*. See no. 182.

265. Wakin, Col. Malham M. "The American Military—Theirs to Reason Why." See no. 185.

266. Waterman, Bernard S. "A Time to Be Flexible." *Army* vol. 20 (Mar. 1970).

267. Westmoreland, Gen. William C. (USA). "Westmoreland: Facing up to the External and Internal Challenges." *Armed Forces Journal* vol. 108 (4 Jan. 1971). Interview with the Army Chief of Staff.

268. "What Lifers Are Made of." See no. 232.

6. The National Guard

269. "Back to School." *The Ally* no. 29 (Aug. 1970).

270. Beaumont, Roger A. "Must the Guard Be a Police Force?" *Army* vol. 20 (Sept. 70).

271. Crowley, W. "On Strike." *Helix* vol. 2, no. 19 (7 May 1970).

272. Derthick, Martha. *The National Guard in Politics.* Cambridge, Mass.: Harvard University Press, 1965. Analysis of power of the NG and its lobby, NG Assn., as a pressure group since 1879.

273. Dupuy, Col. R. Ernest (USA, Ret.). *The National Guard: A Compact History.* New York: Hawthorn Books, 1971.

274. Furst, R. "Kent Guard-Shooting Unjustified." *The Militant* vol. 34, no. 25 (26 June 1970).

275. "The Guard on Campus." *National Guardsman* vol. 24 (Nov. 1970). Critique of the report of the President's Commission on Campus Unrest.

276. "The Guard vs. Disorder." *National Guardsman* vol. 24 (June 1970). Army and Air National Guard.

277. Kennedy, William V. "The Guard and the Reserve." *Ordnance* vol. 55 (Jan-Feb. 1971).

278. Liberation News Service. "Berkeley Life with the Guard." *Fifth Estate* vol. 4, no. 4 (9 July 1969).

279. ——."Soldiers for Peace." *Chinook* vol. 2, no. 32 (27 Aug. 1970).

280. National Guard Association of the U.S. "The Role of the National Guard in an Age of Unrest." *National Guardsman* vol. 24 (Sept. 1970). Report to the National Governors' Conference Committee on Law Enforcement, Justice and Public Safety (Aug. 10, 1970).

281. New Mexican National Guard. Series of articles in *El Grito Del Norte* vol. 3, nos. 6–10 (May-September 1970).

282. Oregon/Washington Guard. Series of articles in *Willamette Bridge* vol. 3, nos. 34–36 (Aug.-Sept. 1970).

283. Owen, W. "Kent State." *Chinook* vol. 2, no. 18 (14 May 1970).

284. Peers, Lt. Gen. William R. "Army Reserve and National Guard Meet the Test at Home and Abroad." *Army* vol. 19 (Oct. 1969).

285. Riker, William H. *Soldiers of the States: The Role of the National Guard in American Democracy.* Washington, D.C.: Public Affairs Press, 1957.

286. Stone, I. F. *The Killings at Kent State: How Murder Went Unpunished.* New York: Random House, 1971. Includes text of Justice Department secret summary of FBI findings.

287. United States. Department of the Army. *Civilian in Peace, Soldier in War: A Bibliographic Survey of the Army and Air National Guard.* See no. 2462.

288. Weixel, G. "A.S.U. Fights Back." *The Bond* vol. 4, no. 4 (22 Apr. 1970). American Servicemen's Union during postal strike.

289. York, M. "Report of Kent Massacre." *The Militant* vol. 34, no. 18 (15 May 1970).

290. See also IID, "Civil Disturbance Roles."

7. The Central Intelligence Agency and the Federal Bureau of Investigation

291. "Agents for Dollars—OSS and CIA." *NACLA Newsletter* vol. 2, no. 1 (Mar. 1968).

292. Arg. "Congo Puppet Here for Allowance." *Liberated Guardian* vol. 1, no. 8 (11 Aug. 1970). Mobutu.

293. Barnet, Richard J. "The CIA's New Cover." *New York Review of Books* vol. 17, no. 11 (30 Dec. 1971). The "new" CIA is not what it seems.

294. "Black Panther Press Statement." *Street Journal* vol. 2, no. 35 (7 Aug. 1970).

295. Burchett, Wilfred. "Sihanouk." *The Guardian* vol. 22, no. 39 (11 July 1970).

296. Chomsky, Noam. "Visit to Laos." *New York Review of Books* vol. 15, no. 2 (23 July 1970).

297. "CIA Agent Kidnapped in Africa." *The Guardian* vol. 22, no. 44 (29 Aug. 1970).

298. Countryman, Vernon. "The Russians Are Coming." *New York Reiview of Books* vol. 13, no. 2 (31 July 1969). About the FBI.

299. "Dope Dog Sniffs at Boston," *Old Mole* vol. 1, no. 41 (12 June 1970). New FBI Agent.

300. Dougall, I. "Green Berets—U.S. Army vs. CIA." See no. 33.

301. "Espionage in Latin America." *NACLA Newsletter* vol. 1 no. 10 (Feb. 1968).

302. Espye, E. "Big Brother Watches New Leftists." *Old Mole* vol. 1, no. 27 (4 Dec. 1969).

303. "Fascist Pigs—CIA Cause Brutality." *The Black Panther* vol. 5, no. 3 (26 July 1970).

304. "FBI Hunts Pun." *Fifth Estate* vol. 4, no. 23 (19 Mar. 1970).

305. "Finally Makes It." *Eyewitness* vol. 1, no. 6 (July 1969). FBI and its personalities.

306. Garrett, Banning. "Road to Phnom Penh." *Ramparts* vol. 9, no. 2 (Aug. 1970).

307. "Hoover Denounces Degeneracy." *Second City* vol. 2, no. 6 (May 1970).

308. Hoover, J. Edgar. "Battlefield." *Army Digest* vol. 23 (Oct. 1968). FBI cooperation with the armed forces.

309. ———. "Partners in Protecting America—The FBI and the Army." *Army Digest* vol. 25 (Dec. 1970).

310. Kim, Young Hum. *The Central Intelligence Agency: Problems of Secrecy in a Democracy.* Indiannapolis: Heath, 1968.

311. Kirby, B. "Free Press Phones Tapped." *L.A. Free Press* vol. 7, no. 18 (1 May 1970).

312. Lane, Mark. "CIA Killed JFK to Keep War Going." *L.A. Free Press* vol. 7, no. 32 (7 Aug. 1970).

313. Liberation News Service. "Big Brother is Watching." *Daily Planet* vol. 1, no. 18 (20 July 1970).

314. ———. "CIA Hand in Jordan Fighting." *Peoples World* vol. 33, no. 28 (11 July 1970).

315. ———. "Looks Like Lamb, Smells Like Pork." *WIN* vol. 6, no. 9 (15 May 1970).

316. ———. "The Master File." *Liberated Guardian* vol. 1, no. 7 (28 July 1970).

317. ———. "Pig Media Joins Police." *Fifth Estate* vol. 3, no. 21 (19 Feb. 1970). FBI.

318. MacCloskey, Monro. *The American Intelligence Community.* See no. 65.

319. Marchetti, Victor. *The Rope Dancer.* New York: Grosset & Dunlap, 1971. A novel by a former CIA official. Revealing of the organization's inner workings.

320. NACLA. "Belize." *Liberated Guardian* vol. 1, no. 6 (14 July 1970).

321. "The New Espionage." *Newsweek* (22 Nov. 1971).

322. *New York Times.* Series on CIA, April 25–29, 1966.

323. Nunez, C. "Bolivia—From Ambiguity to Crisis." *Direct from Cuba* no. 20 (15 July 1970).

324. Overstreet, Harry A., and Overstreet, Bonaro. *The FBI in Our Open Society.* New York: Norton, 1969.

325. Prouty, Fletcher. "Green Berets and the CIA." *New Republic* (30 Aug. 1969).

326. "Provocation á la FBI." *Dissent* vol. 17, no. 4 (18 Aug. 1970).

327. Ransom, Harry Howe. *The Intelligence Establishment.* Cambridge, Mass.: Harvard University Press, 1970. Its rationales, capabili-

ties and limitations; what can be expected of it; dangers to society.

328. Simonyan, Maj. Gen. R. (USSR). "CIA: The Black (sic) Stage-Manager." *Soviet Military Review* no. 8 (Aug. 1970).

329. Shields, A. "Silver Bullets of the CIA." *Peoples World* vol. 33, no. 36 (5 Sept. 1970). About the Congo.

330. Stone, I. F. "Military Spending, CIA—Search and Destroy." *I. F. Stone's Bi-Weekly* vol. 17, no. 19 (20 Oct. 1969).

331. Stork, J. "Send a Pig to Vietnam." *Liberated Guardian* vol. 1, no. 8 (11 Aug. 1970). CIA's police training program.

332. Suarez, A. "CIA and the Death of Yon Sosa." *Direct from Cuba* no. 22 (15 Aug. 1970).

333. _____. "Killing of Yon Sosa." *The Guardian* vol. 22, no. 47 (19 Sept. 1970).

334. Tully, Andrew. *The CIA: The Inside Story.* New York: Morrow, 1962.

335. _____. *The Super Spies: More Secret, More Powerful Than the CIA.* New York: Morrow, 1969. The National Security Agency.

336. Turner, W. "DePugh and the Minutemen." *Ramparts* vol. 8, no. 12 (June 1970).

337. Wall, Robert. "Special Agent for the FBI." *New York Review of Books* vol. 17, no. 12 (27 Jan. 1972). Confessions.

338. Weissman, G. "Hoover's FBI—Men and Myth." *Nola Express* no. 62 (21 Aug. 1970).

339. Wise, David, and Ross, Thomas B. *The Invisible Government.* New York: Random House, 1964.

340. _____. *The U-2 Affair.* New York: Random House, 1962.

341. _____. *The Espionage Establishment.* New York: Random House, 1967.

8. The Selective Service System

342. Aloyeto, O. "Draft Lottery—Russian Roulette." *WIN* vol. 6, no. 1 (1 Jan. 1970).

343. American Friends Service Committee, Peace Education Division. *The Draft?* New York: Hill and Wang, 1968.

344. Cadre. "The Draft Is in Trouble." *WIN* vol. 6, no. 5 (15 Mar. 1970).

345. Casper, B. "Selective Servitude." *Space City* vol. 1, no. 1 (5 June 1969, and following issues). A series on the draft running several months in this Houston underground paper.

346. Davis, James W., Jr., and Dolbeare, Kenneth M. *Little Groups of Neighbors: The Selective Service System.* Chicago: Markham Publishing Co., 1968. Military manpower policy; social effects.

347. Evans, Robert J. "The Military Draft as a Slave System: An Economic View." *Social Science Quarterly* vol. 50, no. 3 (1969). Serious comparison of draft with slavery systems and how they are ended.

348. Fisher, A. C. "The Cost of the Draft and the Cost of Ending the Draft." *American Economic Review* vol. 59, no. 3 (June 1969).

349. Friedman, Milton. "Why Not a Volunteer Army." *New Industrialist Review* vol. 4, no. 4 (Spring 1967).

350. Gerhardt, J. M. *The Draft and Public Policy: Issues in Military Manpower Procurement, 1945-1970.* Columbus, O.: Ohio State University Press, 1971. A history of the draft and related issues.

351. Gersh, F. "The Draft—Law vs. Reality." *Williamette Bridge* vol. 3, no. 32 (7 Aug. 1970).

352. Hoffmans, E. et al. "Draft Facts." *Prairie Primer* vol. 2, no. 7 (15 Dec. 1969, and later issues). Series.

353. Jacobs, Clyde E., and Gallagher, John F. *The Selective Service Act: A Case Study of the Governmental Process.* New York: Dodd, Mead, 1967.

354. Janowitz, Morris et al. "National Service Options." *Teachers College Record* vol. 73, no. 1 (Sept. 1971). Papers on the draft and alternatives from eight well-known contributors.

355. Johnson, Jerome, and Bachman, Jerald. *Young Men Look at Military Service: A Preliminary Report.* Ann Arbor, Mich.: Survey Research Center, 1970.

356. Kendall, David, and Ross, Leonard. *The Lottery and the Draft: Where Do I Stand?* New York: Harper & Row, 1970. Handbook; includes forecasting tables.

357. Lafferty, J. "Class and Race Bias in Draft System." *The Militant* vol. 34, no. 6 (20 Feb. 1970).

358. Lasley, John W., ed. *In Quest of Freedom: Abolish the Draft.* Chapel Hill, N.C.: Institute for International Studies, 1969. Pamphlet.

359. Liston, Robert. *Greeting: The Draft in America.* New York: McGraw-Hill, 1970.

360. Lynn, Conrad J. *How to Stay Out of the Army: A Guide to Your Rights under the Draft Law.* New York: Grove Press, 1967. Now somewhat outdated.

361. "Manipulation of the Draft." *WIN* vol. 6, no. 14 (1 Sept. 1970).

362. Margolin, B. "Inside the New Draft Laws." *L.A. Free Press* vol. 7, no. 28 (10 July 1970).

363. Marmion, Harry A. *Selective Service: Conflict and Compromise.* New York: Wiley, 1968. Finds draft unsuited for modern needs.

364. Miller, James C. III, ed. *Why the Draft? The Case for a Volunteer Army.* Baltimore: Penguin, 1968.

365. Oi, Walter Y. "The Economic Cost of the Draft." *American Economic Review* vol. 57, no. 2 (May 1967).

366. Reeves, Thomas, and Hess, Karl. *The End of the Draft.* New York: Random House, 1970. An attack on the draft and militarism. Contains the complete text of the original selective service channeling memo.

367. Ryder, E. Z. "Persecution of Draft Age Men." *Fifth Estate* vol. 5, no. 1 (14 May 1970).

368. Seven Mighty Anvils. "Shaft the Draft." *L.A. Free Press* vol. 6, no. 76 (31 Oct. 1969, and later issues). Series on the draft counseling running many months.

369. Shapiro, Andrew O., and Striker, John M. *Mastering the Draft.* New York: Avon, 1971. Comprehensive handbook.

370. "The Supreme Court and the Draft." *Peacemaker* vol. 23, no. 2 (7 Feb. 1970).

371. Tatum, Arlo, ed. *Handbook for Conscientious Objectors.* Philadelphia: Central Committee for Conscientious Objectors, revised periodically.

372. Tax, Sol, ed. *The Draft: A Handbook of Facts and Alternatives.* Chicago: University of Chicago Press, 1967.

373. U. S. Congress. House Committee on Armed Services. *Extension of the Universal Military Training and Service Act.* Hearings, 90th Congress, 1st session. Washington, D. C.: USGPO, 1967.

374. _____. *Review of the Administration and Operation of the Selective Service System.* Hearings, 89th Congress, 2d session. Washington, D. C.: USGPO, 1966.

375. U. S. National Advisory Commission on Selective Service. *In Pursuit of Equity: Who Serves When Not All Serve?* Washington, D.C.: USGPO, 1967. Burke Marshall Commission Report.

376. United States. Task Force on the Structure of the Selective Service System. *Report.* Washington, D.C.: USGPO, 1967.

377. "Visiting the Selective Service System." *WIN* vol. 6, no. 14 (1 Sept. 1970).

378. Young, B. "How to Stop the War by Ending the Draft." *Peacemaker* vol. 23, no. 9 (18 July 1970). See also ID3, "Draft Resistance." and IE6, "The Volunteer Army."

B. WEAPONS
1. General: The Pressure of Technology

379. "Absurd Military Appetite." *Progressive* vol. 34, no. 2 (Feb. 1970).

380. Barnet, Richard. *The Economy of Death.* See no. 1022.

381. Bobrow, Davis B., ed. *Weapons Systems Decisions: Political and Psychological Perspectives on Continental Defense.* New York: Praeger, 1969. Applied social science research.

382. Calder, Nigel, ed. *Unless Peace Comes: A Scientific Forecast of New Weapons.* New York: Viking, 1968. Essays on the possible effects of new weapons systems.

383. Davis, Vincent. *The Politics of Innovation: Patterns in Navy Cases.* Denver: Denver University Press, 1967. U. S. Navy, weapons systems, nuclear ships, and military politics.

384. Dawson, R. H. "Congressional Innovation and Intervention in Defense Policy: Legislative Authorization of Weapons Systems." *American Political Science Review* vol. 56, no. 1 (1962).

385. Deagle, Maj. Edwin A., Jr. (USA). "The Politics of Missilemaking: A Dynamic Model." *Public Policy* vol. 16 (1967). Mathematical model of arms races.

386. Erickson, John; Crowley, Edward L.; and Galay, Nikolai, eds. *The Military-Technical Revolution: Its Impact on Strategy and Foreign Policy.* New York: Praeger, 1966.

387. Feyereisen, Maj. Gen. Paul A. "Acquiring New Weapons." *Ordnance* vol. 54 (Mar.-Apr. 1970).

388. Foster, John S., Jr. "Science and Technology of the Future and Their Impact on Strategy." *Naval War College Review* vol. 23 (Sept. 1970). Lecture, Naval War College.

389. Greenberg, Daniel S. *The Politics of Pure Science.* New York: New American Library, 1968.

390. Hunt, Kenneth. *The Requirements of Military Technology in the 1970s.* London: Institute for Strategic Studies, 1967.

391. Institute for Strategic Studies. *The Military Balance.* London: Institute for Strategic Studies, annually. Estimate of military forces of the world.

392. ———. *Strategic Survey.* London: Institute for Strategic Studies, annually. Strategic policy, doctrine, and weapons of the world.

393. Knorr, Klaus, and Morgenstern, Oskar. *Science and Defense: Some Critical Thoughts on Military Research and Development.* Princeton, N. J.: Center of International Studies, 1965.

394. Kramer, Marc. "Buck Rogers Is Alive and Well—and Doing R & D for the Pentagon." In Rodberg and Shearer, *The Pentagon Watchers.* See no. 13.

395. Laird, Melvin R. *Statement of Secretary of Defense Melvin R. Laird before the House Armed Services Committee on the FY 1972–1976 Defense Program and the 1972 Defense Budget.* Washington, D.C.:

USGPO, 9 Mar. 1971. This is the annual posture statement on threats, strategies, and weapons.

396. Lang, Daniel. *An Inquiry into Enoughness: Of Bombs and Staying Alive.* New York: McGraw-Hill, 1965.

397. Lapp, Ralph E. *Arms beyond Doubt: The Tyranny of Weapons Technology.* New York: Cowles Book Co., 1970. The madness of the MIC.

398. ———. *Kill and Overkill: The Strategy of Annihilation.* New York: Basic Books, 1962.

399. ———. *The New Priesthood: The Scientific Elite and the Uses of Power.* New York: Harper & Row, 1965.

400. ———. *The Weapons Culture.* New York: Norton, 1968. The momentum of technological development.

401. Lewis, Richard; and Wilson, Jane with Rabinowitch, Eugene. *Alamogordo Plus Twenty-Five Years: The Impact of Atomic Energy on Science, Technology, and World Politics.* New York: Viking Press, 1971.

402. Melman, Seymour. "Who Decides Technology." *Columbia Forum* (Winter 1968).

403. Nelson, W. R., ed. *The Politics of Science.* New York: Oxford University Press, 1968.

404. Nieburg, H. L. *In the Name of Science.* Cleveland: Quadrangle, 1966.

405. ———. "Social Control of Innovation." *American Economic Review Supplement* vol. 58 (May 1968).

406. Packard, David. "R & D: Key to Our Nation's Strength." *Signal* vol. 25 (Mar. 1971).

407. "The Pentagon Wins Again." *Progressive* vol. 33, no. 12 (Dec. 1969).

408. Possony, Stefan T., and Pournelle, J. E. *The Strategy of Technology: Winning the Decisive War.* Cambridge, Mass.: Dunellen, 1970. A war is now in progress. It is "fought" by building better weapons and raising the level of technology.

409. Schilling, Warner. "The H-Bomb Decision: How to Decide without Actually Choosing." *Political Science Quarterly* vol. 86 (Mar. 1961). The U. S. acquired the H-Bomb not because it saw an existing need for it, but because it expected the Russians to get it.

410. Stockholm International Peace Research Institute. *Yearbook of World Armaments and Disarmament. 1970–1971.* New York: Humanities Press, 1971. Basic data and analysis. Annual Publication. See also earlier volumes.

411. Stone, I. F. "Heading for a Bigger Arms Race in the 70s." *I. F. Stone's Bi-Weekly* vol. 18, no. 1 (12 Jan. 1970).

412. ———. "The War Machine under Nixon." *Long Beach Free Press* vol. 1, no. 7 (11 July 1969).

413. Strausz-Hupe, Robert. "New Weapons and National Strategy." *Military Review* vol. 41, no. 5 (May 1961).

414. United States Arms Control and Disarmament Agency. *World Military Expenditures, 1970.* Washington, D. C.: USACDA, 1971. Basic data. Annual publication.

415. U. S. Congress. Committee on Armed Services (House and Senate). Military Procurement Authorization Hearings. Washington, D.C.: USGPO, annually.

416. U. S. Congress. Department of Defense Subcommittee, Committee on Appropriations (House and Senate). Defense Appropriations Hearings. Washington, D.C.: USGPO, annually.

417. Westmoreland, Gen. William C. (USA). "The Army of the Future." *NACLA Newsletter* vol. 3, no. 7. (Nov. 1969). A vision of painless imperialism.

418. York, Herbert. *Race to Oblivion: A Participant's View of the Arms Race.* New York: Simon and Schuster, 1970.

419. See also IICl, "R & D," and IIIH, ". . . Arms Race. . . ."

2. Advanced Strategic and Conventional Weaponry

420. Agan, Lt. Gen. Arthur A. "Aerospace Defense and National Security." *Air University Review* vol. 20 (Nov.-Dec. 1968).

421. American Security Council National Strategy Committee. *The ABM and the Changed Strategic Military Balance*, 2d ed. Washington, D.C.: Acropolis, 1969. Very pro-ABM.

422. Art, Robert J. *The TFX Decision.* See no. 20.

423. "Atomic Grenades." *Willamette Bridge* vol. 3, no. 30 (31 July 1970).

424. Baker, Sam, and Gruson, Kerry. "The Coming Arms Race under the Sea." In Rodberg and Shearer. *The Pentagon Watchers.* See no. 13.

425. Brennan, Donald G. "The Case for Missile Defense." *Foreign Affairs* vol. 47 (Apr. 1969). Pro-ABM.

426. Center for the Study of Democratic Institutions. *Anti-Ballistic Missile: Yes or No?* A Center Occasional Paper vol. 2, no. 2. New York: Hill and Wang, 1969. Pro and con discussions.

427. Chayes, Abram, and Wiesner, Jerome B., eds. *ABM: An Evaluation of the Decision to Deploy an Antiballistic Missile System.* New York: Harper & Row, 1969. Anti-ABM.

428. Dougall, I. "Safeguard System Is Suicide." *Peace News* vol. 17, no. 29 (15 Aug. 1969).

429. Dupuy, Trevor N. et al. *Almanac of World Military Power.* Harrisburg, Pa.: Stackpole Press, 1970.

430. Frisbee, John L. "The B-1—Blue Chip in the Deterrent Stack." *Air Force and Space Digest* vol. 53 (Apr. 1970). Claims B-1 needed for credible deterrent; need redundant strategic offensive weapons systems, ICBMs, bombers, and sub-launched missiles.

431. Gallagher, T. "Cancer as the Highest Stage of Imperialism." *Old Mole* vol. 1, no. 20 (28 Aug. 1969).

432. Gofman, John Jr. "Confronting the AEC." *The Center Magazine* vol. 3, no. 3 (May 1970).

433. Hersh, Seymour. "20,000 Guns under the Sea." *Ramparts* vol. 8, no. 3 (Sept. 1969).

434. Holst, John J., and Schneider, William, Jr., eds. *Why ABM? Policy Issues in the Missile Defense Controversy: A Collection of Papers by Staff and Fellow Members of the Hudson Institute.* New York: Pergamon, 1969. Pro-ABM

435. Jordan, P. "Twenty-five Years." *Catholic Worker* vol. 36, no. 6 (July 1970). Nuclear weapons.

436. Kintner, William R. *The Prudent Case for Safeguard.* New York: National Strategy Information Center, 1969.

437. ———, ed., *Safeguard: Why ABM Makes Sense.* New York: Hawthorne, 1969.

438. Klass, Philip J. *Secret Sentries in Space.* New York: Random House, 1971. Reconnaissance satellites.

439. Klein, Tom. "The Capacity to Intervene." In Rodberg and Shearer. *The Pentagon Watchers.* See no. 13. U. S. airlift-sealift capability. Many references to articles in military journals.

440. Kondrake, Morton. "Our First-Strike Capability." *Washington Monthly* (June 1969).

441. Lipton, Nancy, and Rodberg, Leonard. "The Missile Race—the Contest with Ourselves." In Rodberg and Shearer. *The Pentagon Watchers.* See no. 13.

442. McCarthy, Mary. "The Manned Bomber—A Mystique in Search of a Mission." In Rodberg and Shearer. *The Pentagon Watchers.* See no. 13.

443. "The Original Safeguard." *Progressive* vol. 33, no. 7 (July 1969).

444. Plate, Thomas G. *Understanding Doomsday: A Guide to the Arms Race for Hawks, Doves, and People.* New York: Simon and Schuster, 1971.

445. Rapoport, Roger. *The Great American Bomb Machine*. New York: Dutton, 1971. Nuclear weapons.

446. Raser, J. "ABM and the Mad Strategy." *Ramparts* vol. 8, no. 5 (Nov. 1969).

447. Rathjens, George W. *The Future of the Strategic Arms Race: Options for the 1970s*. New York: Carnegie Endowment for International Peace, 1969.

448. Russett, Bruce M. "The Complexities of Ballistic Missile Defense." *Yale Review* vol. 56 (Spring 1967).

449. Salkeld, Robert. *War and Space*. Englewood Cliffs, N.J.: Prentice-Hall, 1970. Space weapons as the answer to the strategic stalemate.

450. Schratz, Paul R. "The Caesars, the Sieges, and the Anti-Ballistic Missile." *U.S. Naval Institutute Proceedings* vol. 94 (Mar. 1968). A naval officer's analysis of the "Thin" ABM system and a proposal for a sea based ABM system.

451. Seamans, Robert C., Jr. "The Growing Soviet Threat and What to Do about It." *Air Force and Space Digest* vol. 53 (May 1970). USSR is increasing in all types of military power; thus U.S. must have ABM, and new manned bomber to keep up.

452. Smart, Ian. *Advanced Strategic Missiles: A Short Guide*. London: Institute for Strategic Studies, 1969.

453. Stone, I. F. "Nixon and the Arms Race: The Bomber Boondoggle." *New York Review of Books* (2 Jan. 1969).

454. Tompkins, John S. *The Weapons of World War III*. Garden City, N. Y.: Doubleday, 1966. Return to "conventional" weapons.

455. Tyrrell, C. Merton. *Pentagon Partners, the New Nobility*. See no. 91.

456. United States. Congress. Senate. Committee on Foreign Relations. Subcommittee on Arms Control, International Law and Organization. 91st Congress, 2d session. *ABM, MIRV, SALT, and the Nuclear Arms Race, Hearings*, Mar. 16-June 29, 1970. Washington, D.C.: USGPO, 1970.

457. Webb, L. "Liberals May Save Nixon's ABM." *Guardian* vol. 21, no. 41 (19 July 1969).

3. CBW: Chemical and Biological Warfare

458. Ansara, M. "Gas Is Cleaner and Cheaper." *Old Mole* vol. 1, no. 19 (14 Aug. 1969).

459. Brown, Maj. Frederic J. *Chemical Warfare: A Study in Restraints*. Princeton, N.J.: Princeton University Press, 1968. Examines history of restraints on toxic agents in order to apply similar restraints to new CBW weapons.

460. Burchett, Wilfred. "CBW Attacks in Korean War." *Guardian* vol. 21, no. 43 (2 Aug. 1969).

461. Celick, Lt. Col. Arnold J. "Humane Warfare for International Peace-keeping." *Air University Review* vol. 19 (Sept.-Oct. 1968).

462. "Chemical Warfare Training in U.S." *NACLA Newsletter* vol. 4, no. 1 (Mar. 1970).

463. Clarke, Robin. *The Silent Weapons.* New York: McKay, 1968. Bibliography.

464. Cookson, John, and Nottingham, Judith. *A Survey of Chemical and Biological Warfare.* New York: Monthly Review Press, 1969. Research, production, use, effects. Comprehensive.

465. Fiddick, T. "U. S. Extending Chemical Warfare to Cambodia." *The Militant* vol. 34, no. 31 (7 Aug. 1970).

466. Hennacy, A. "Moratorium Brings Protest in Salt Lake." *The Catholic Worker* vol. 35, no. 8 (Nov. 1969). About Dugway Proving Grounds.

467. ———. "No Taxes for War in Vietnam." *The Catholic Worker* vol. 35, no. 6 (Aug. 1969).

468. Hersh, Seymour M. *Chemical and Biological Warfare: America's Hidden Arsenal.* New York: Bobbs-Merrill, 1968. No longer "hidden."

469. ———. "Dare We Develop Biological Weapons?" *New York Times Magazine* (28 Sept. 1969).

470. ———. "Germ Warfare—For Alma Mater, God, and Country." *Ramparts* vol. 8, no. 6 (Dec. 1969).

471. ———. "On Uncovering Great Nerve Gas Cover." *Ramparts* vol. 7, no. 13 (June 1969).

472. Kanegis, Art. "U. S. CBW Policy." *Liberation* vol. 15, no. 9 (6 Nov. 1970). Analyzes Nixon's November 1969 CBW speech against realities of CBW policy. Useful references in notes.

473. Klare, Mike. "CBW—Arsenal For Mass Slaughter." *Guardian* vol. 22, no. 7 (15 Nov. 1969).

474. ———. "Timetable of CBW Exposures." *Guardian* vol. 22, no. 8 (22 Nov. 1969).

475. Larson, Carl A. "Ethnic Weapons." *Military Review* vol. 50 (Nov. 1970).

476. McCarthy, Richard D. *The Ultimate Folly: War by Pestilence, Asphyxiation, and Defoliation.* New York: Random House, 1969. Very critical of U. S. CBW policies.

477. Nixon, Richard M. "Biological Warfare Renounced: A Statement by the President of the U. S." *Ordnance* vol. 54 (Jan.-Feb. 1970). See no. 472 for analysis of this statement.

478.   "Pentagon Hides New Nerve Gas Plans." *Peacemaker* vol. 22, no. 11 (9 Aug. 1969).

479.   "Restraints on CBW." *Progressive* vol. 33, no. 9 (Sept. 1969).

480.   Robinson, C. "CBW Use and Development Exposed." *Guardian* vol. 21, no. 42 (26 July 1969).

481.   Rose, Steven, ed. *CBW: Chemical and Biological Warfare.* Boston: Beacon Press, 1969. London conference report.

482.   Shapiro, B. "On CBW, Nixon's a Gas." *Old Mole* vol. 1, no. 28 (16 Dec. 1969).

483.   Stockholm International Peace Research Institute. *The Problem of Chemical and Biological Warfare.* New York: Humanities Press, 1971 and 1972. A six-volume study of the historical, technical, military, legal and political aspects of CBW, and possible disarmament measures.

484.   Stone, I. F. "Nixon Disapproval of CBW." *I. F. Stone's Bi-Weekly* vol. 17, no. 15 (28 July 1969).

485.   Thomas, Ann V., and Thomas, Aaron J. *Legal Limits on the Use of Chemical and Biological Weapons.* Dallas: Southern Methodist University Press, 1970. SMU School of Law Study.

486.   United Nations. *Chemical and Bacteriological (Biological) Weapons and the Effects of Their Possible Use.* New York: United Nations Publication, 1969. Technical.

487.   U. S. Army. Field Manual FM 3–10, *Employment of Chemical and Biological Agents.* Washington, D. C.: USGPO, Mar. 1966.

488.   U. S. Army. Technical Manual TM 3–215, *Military Chemistry and Chemical Agents.* Washington, D. C.: USGPO, Dec. 1963.

489.   U. S. Army, Technical Manual TM 3–216, *Military Biology and Biological Agents.* Washington, D. C.: USGPO, Mar. 1964.

490.   United States. Congress. House. Committee on Foreign Affairs. Subcommittee on National Security Policy and Scientific Developments. *Chemical-Biological Warfare: U. S. Policies and International Effects, Hearings* 18 Nov.-19 Dec. 1969. Washington, D.C.: USGPO, 1970.

491.   U. S. Library of Congress. Legislative Reference Service, Science Policy Research Division. *Chemical and Biological Weapons: Some Possible Approaches for Lessening the Threat and Danger.* Washington, D. C.: USGPO, May 1969.

492.   Veterans Day Teach-in on CBW. *Freedom News* vol. 3, no. 11 (Nov. 1969).

493.   Wald, George. "Corporate Responsibility-War Crimes." *New York Review of Books* vol. 15, no. 1 (2 July 1970). Dow and Napalm.

494. Weisberg, Barry ed. *Ecocide in Indochina: The Ecology of War.* San Francisco: Canfield Press, 1970. Essays on all aspects of destruction. Excellent bibliography on CBW.

495. See also IE3, "War Crimes and Atrocities," and IIF2, "Ecology."

4. Weapons of Counterinsurgency, Urban and Rural

496. ABT Associates. *Counter-Insurgency Game Design Feasibility and Evaluation Study.* Washington, D.C., Nov. 1965.

497. Applegate, Rex. *Riot Control—Materiel and Techniques.* Harrisburg, Pa.: Stackpole, 1969.

498. "Army Rushes Riot Training and Gear." *National Guardsman* vol. 25 (Feb. 1971).

499. Council on Economic Priorities. *Efficiency in Death: The Manufacturers of Anti-Personnel Weapons.* New York: Harper & Row, 1970.

500. "Counter-revolutionary Software Keeps up with Hardware." *NACLA Newsletter* vol. 1, no. 4 (July-Aug. 1967).

501. Klare, Michael. "The Pentagon's Counterinsurgency Research Infrastructure." *NACLA Newsletter* vol. 4, no. 9 (Jan. 1971). Summary description of wide range of research institutions.

502. Kohn, H. "Pig Riot Manual Exposed." *Fifth Estate* vol. 4, no. 6 (6 Aug. 1969).

503. Kolko, Gabriel. "Chemical Warfare against Civilans." *Black Panther* vol. 3, no. 22 (20 Sept. 1969).

504. Larson, Carl A. "Ethnic Weapons." See no. 475.

505. Liberation News Service. "New Riot Weapon." *Liberated Guardian* vol. 1, no. 7 (28 July 1970).

506. Long, Col. William. "Urban Insurgency War Game." *The Naval War College Review* vol. 21 (May 1969).

507. Miksak, T. "Wooden Bullets." *Willamette Bridge* vol. 3, no. 30 (24 July 1970).

508. National Action/Research on the Military Industrial Complex (NARMIC). *Weapons for Counterinsurgency.* Philadelphia: American Friends Service Committee. Available directly: 160 N. Fifteenth St., Philadelphia, Pa., 19102.

509. Nemethy, Col. Frank J. "New Devices for Guerrilla Warfare." *Military Engineer* vol. 60 (May-June 1968).

510. Ney, Col. Virgil (USA, Ret.). "Tactics and Techniques of Riot Warfare." *Military Review* vol. 50 (May 1970).

511. "No More Tear Gas." *Old Mole* vol. 1, no. 44 (24 July 1970).

512. "Producers and Developers of the Incendiary Weapon." *Guardian* vol. 21, no. 41 (19 July 1969).

513. Pustay, Maj. John S. *Counterinsurgency Warfare.* Glencoe, Ill.: The Free Press, 1965.

514. Reston, J. "Can Nixon Trust the Army." *L.A. Free Press* vol. 7, no. 26 (26 June 1970).
515. Tompkins, John S. *The Weapons of World War III.* See no. 454.
516. U. S. Army Special Warfare School. *The Counterinsurgency Planning Guide.* Washington, D.C.: USGPO, 1963. Now called the John F. Kennedy School for Military Assistance, Ft. Bragg, N.C.
517. U. S. Department of the Army. "Employment of Riot Control Agents, Flame, Smoke, Antiplant Agents, and Personnel Detectors in Counter-Guerrilla Operations." *U. S. Army Training Circular No. TC 3–16* (1969).
518. "World War II Planes in Guerrilla Actions." *NACLA Newsletter* vol. 2, no. 4 (July-Aug. 1968). Article from the *Wall Street Journal.*
519. *See also IIIF "Counterinsurgency Warfare and Its Techniques."*

C. ASSAULT ON MILITARY INSTITUTIONS AND VALUES: INSIDE THE MILITARY
1. Organizing GIs

520. "Ally News Service." *The Ally* no. 28 (July 1970).
521. "Anti-Military HQ Searched." *L.A. Free Press* vol. 7, no. 23 (5 June 1970).
522. "Antiwar GIs Fight Transfers." *The Militant* vol. 34, no. 34 (18 Sept. 1970).
523. "ASU History-Part One." *The Bond* vol. 4, no. 8 (26 Aug. 1970). American Servicemen's Union (ASU).
524. Cortright, David. "Greening of the Green: The Movement in the Military." *Liberation* vol. 15, no. 11; vol. 16, nos. 1 and 2 (single issue, Spring 1971).
525. Ellis, G. "How to Polish the Brass." *Peoples World* vol. 33, no. 38 (19 Sept. 1970). About the American Servicemen's Union.
526. "Enlisted Men Have Rights." *WIN* vol. 5, no. 21 (1 Dec. 1969).
527. Frederick, B. "Fort Lewis 35." *WIN* vol. 5, no. 21 (1 Dec. 1969).
528. Gardner, F. "In the Army Now." *Hard Times* no. 50 (3 Nov. 1969).
529. Getler, Michael. "Trouble in the Ranks." *Armed Forces Management* vol. 16 (June 1970). Editorial.
530. "The GI Anti-War Movement: Little Action and Money—And Few GIs," *Armed Forces Journal* vol. 108 (7 Sept. 1970).
531. Marine. "GI Press." *WIN* vol. 5, no. 21 (1 Dec. 1969).
532. "The GI Revolution—Dig It." *Berkeley Tribe* vol. 3, no. 6 (14 Aug. 1970). About the Movement for a Democratic Military.
533. "GIs March in Augusta." *Southern Patriot* vol. 28, no. 7 (Sept. 1970).

534. "GIs Organize in Japan." *The Bond* vol. 4, no. 4 (22 Apr. 1970).

535. "Its Happening on Lotsa Bases." *Old Mole* vol. 1, no. 46 (11 Sept. 70).

536. Liberation News Service "GIs Form Alliance." *Fifth Estate* vol. 5, no. 4 (25 June 1970).

537. Marshall, S. "Military Affairs." *L.A. Free Press* vol. 7, no. 13 (27 Mar. 1970).

538. "MDM." *Berkeley Tribe* vol. 3, no. 11 (18 Sept. 1970). Movement for a Democratic Military.

539. "MDM-Camp Pendleton." *Black Panther* vol. 5, no. 10 (5 Sept. 1970).

540. "Movement for a Democratic Military—Anonymous Group Platform." *L.A. Free Press.* vol. 6, no. 81 (5 Dec. 1969).

541. "A National Struggle." *Fatigue Press* no. 23 (May 1970).

542. "Opposition within the Military." *The Peacemaker* vol. 23, no. 8 (20 June 1970).

543. "Our Goal—Protest or Power." *The Bond* vol. 4, no. 7 (22 July 1970).

544. Piloti, J. "Ft. Dix Radicals Plan Protest." *Village Voice* vol. 14, no. 51 (2 Oct. 1969).

545. Smith, B. "A Day at ASU Headquarters." *Fifth Estate* vol. 4, no. 25 (29 Apr. 1970).

546. Stapp, Andy. *Up against the Brass.* New York: Simon and Schuster, 1970. The origins of the American Servicemen's Union by one of its founders.

547. ———. "The Army Is Revolting." *The Movement* vol. 5, no. 7 (Aug. 1969).

548. "U. S. Servicemen's Fund." *WIN* vol. 5, no. 21 (1 Dec. 1969).

549. Wiener, J. "Dr. Levy on the GI Movement." *Old Mole* vol. 1, no. 24 (23 Oct. 1969).

550. This topic is treated regularly in *The Bond, The Ally, Fatigue Press,* and *Vets Stars & Stripes for Peace.* See also the list of GI newspapers and coffeehouses in the appendix of Rivkin. See no. 260.

2. *Protest, GI Rights, Harassment*

551. Adelsberger, D. "GI Gets Undesirable Discharge." *WIN* vol. 6, no. 9 (15 May 1970).

552. "Air Force Cops Raid Union Paper." *The Bond* vol. 4, no. 7 (22 July 1970).

553. Brown, Harold. "When Can a Military Man Disagree?" *Air Force Times* vol. 28 (12 June 1968). Speech.

554. Bourdow, Joseph A. "Dissent and the Code." *Army* vol. 20 (July 1970). The Uniform Code of Military Justice.

555. "Crackdown on GI Dissent." *Washington Post* (10 Nov. 1969) p. A–6.

556. Crume, M. Sgt. R. L. (USMC). "Combating Internal Strife." *Marine Corps Gazette* vol. 55 (Jan. 1971).

557. "Dix GIs Rebel." *Veterans Stars and Stripes for Peace* vol. 2, no. 3 (July 1969).

558. "Dix Rebellion." *The Movement* vol. 5, no. 6 (July 1969).

559. Douglas, E. "Legal Gain by GIs Fighting Transfer." *The Militant* vol. 34, no. 31 (7 Aug. 1970).

560. Drumm, Lt. Col. Robert H. "The Air Force Man and the Cultural Value Gap." *Air University Review* vol. 19 (May-June 1968). Advice to senior air force officers on how to deal with the "new" Air Force breed.

561. Eberle, P. "Levy on GI Repression." *L.A. Free Press* vol. 7, no. 20 (15 May 1970). Dr. Levy was imprisoned for refusing to train medics.

562. "GIs Rebel at Ft. Dix and Ft. Ord." *Old Mole* vol. 1, no. 6 (3 July 1969).

563. "Hawaii GIs Protest." *Old Mole* vol. 1, no. 21 (11 Sept. 1969).

564. Hays, Col. Samuel H. (USA, Ret.). "The Soldier's Rights in a Free Society." *Army* vol. 20 (May 1970). In order to produce the reliability and group solidarity needed to "win" in battle, the individual soldier's "rights" and "needs" must be subordinated, and thus the soldier has no "inherent rights."

565. Heilbroner, B. "Dix Brass Plot Vengeance." *Fifth Estate* vol. 4, no. 7 (20 Aug. 1969).

566. King, Lt. Col. Edward L. (USA. Ret.). "The Death of the Army: A Pre-Mortem." See no. 200.

567. "Know Your Rights." *The Ally* no. 29 (Aug. 1970).

568. Mataxis, Brig. Gen. Theodore C. (USA). "This Far, No Farther —How Army Handles Dissenters in Uniform." *Military Review* vol. 50 (Mar. 1970).

569. Murphy, Maj. Arthur A. "The Soldier's Right to a Private Life." *Military Law Review* vol. 24 (1964). Military lawyer urges colleagues to inform commanders of GI privacy rights.

570. "Navy Marines Move against GI Paper." *Old Mole* vol. 1, no. 22 (26 Sept. 1969).

571. Quinn, Robert E. "The U. S. Court of Military Appeals and Individual Rights in the Military." *Notre Dame Lawyer* vol. 34 (1960): 491.

572. Rivkin, Robert. *GI Rights and Army Justice.* See no. 260.

573. Schwartz, W. "WRL Benefactor Faces Navy Charges." *WIN* vol. 5, no. 14 (Aug. 1969). War Resister's League.

574. Sherrill, Robert. "Must the Citizen Give up His Civil Liberties When He Joins the Army?" *New York Times Magazine* (18 May 1969), p. 25.

575. Stapp, Andy. "Army Brass Moves on GI Dissent." *The Guardian* vol. 21, no. 50 (27 Sept. 1969).

576. Stickgold, M. "The New Action Army." *Ann Arbor Argus* vol. 1, no. 12 (2 Oct. 1969).

577. U. S. Department of Defense. DoD Directive no. 1325.6. "Guidelines for Handling Dissent and Protest Activities Among Members of the Armed Forces." (12 Sept. 1969).

578. Wingate, J. "Wittels: Advice for COs in the Armed Services." *WIN* vol. 6, no. 15 (15 Sept. 1970).

579. Wittels, Mike. *Advice for Conscientious Objectors in the Armed Forces.* Philadelphia: Central Committee for Conscientious Objectors, 1970. A handbook.

3. Blacks and Black Protest

580. "Alaskan Exile for Black GI." *Helix* vol. 9, no. 1 (31 Sept. 1969).

581. "Black and Puerto Rican GIs Resist." *The Bond* vol. 4, no. 8 (26 Aug. 1970).

582. "Black GIs in Ft. Hood Confrontation." *The Guardian* vol. 22, no. 44 (29 Aug. 1970).

583. "Black GIs in Germany." *Fatigue Press* no. 25 (July 1970).

584. "Black GIs in Germany—Mass Meeting." *The Bond* vol. 4, no. 7 (22 July 1970).

585. "Black GIs Organize." *The Ally* no. 28 (July 1970).

586. "Black Power in Vietnam." *Time* (19 Sept. 1969).

587. "Black Solidarity Illegal Says Brass." *Peoples World* vol. 33, no. 39 (26 Sept. 1970).

588. "Black Unity." *Fifth Estate* vol. 5, no. 10 (17 Sept. 1970).

589. "Blacks Flee U.S." *Amex—Canada* vol. 2, no. 3 (Apr. 1970).

590. Cleaver, Eldridge. "Statement to GIs in South Vietnam." *Black Panther* vol. 5, no. 13 (26 Sept. 1970).

591. "Draft Rulings Hit Blacks." *Guardian* vol. 22, no. 44 (29 Aug. 1970).

592. *Ebony* vol. 23 (Aug. 1968). The entire issue is devoted to the black soldier with articles on the black officer, blacks in Vietnam, black reenlistment, blacks and the draft, etc.

593. Elkan, D. "Black GIs in Germany." *The Militant* vol. 34, no. 30 (31 July 1970).

594. Fletcher, E. "Black Refugee Organization," *Amex-Canada*, vol. 2, no. 4 (June 1970).

595. Halstead, Fred. "Ft. Jackson GIs United against War." *International Socialist* vol. 30, no. 4 (Aug. 1969). Halstead was Socialist Worker's Party candidate for president.

596. "Message to Black GIs." *Fatigue Press* no. 23 (May 1970).

597. Morris, Steven. "How Blacks Upset the Marine Corps." *Ebony* (Dec. 1969).

598. "Pigs Harass GIs at Ft. Carson." *Black Panther* vol. 5, no. 10 (5 Sept. 1970).

599. Schechter, D. "The CIA Is an Equal Opportunity Employer." *Ramparts* vol. 7, no. 13 (June 1969). Activities in Africa.

600. Seale, Bobby. "Black Soldiers as Revolutionaries." *Black Panther* vol. 3, no. 22 (20 Sept. 1969).

601. Stapp, Andy. "Black Marines against the Brass." American Serviceman's Union interview with William Harvy and George Daniels, two black Marines imprisoned for their war opposition. Available from Radical Education Project (REP), Box 561A Detroit, Michigan 48232.

602. Stillman, Richard J., Jr. *Integration of the Negro in the U. S. Armed Forces*. New York: Praeger, 1968. Broad historical view.

603. "Struggles against Racism." *Second City* vol. 2, no. 9 (Sept. 1970).

604. Terry, Wallace. "The Angry Blacks in the Army." In Banning Garrett and Katherine Barkeley, eds., *Two, Three, . . . Many Vietnams*. See no. 693. Survey of black opinions in Vietnam.

605. "Third World People Unite against the War." *Fatigue Press* no. 23 (May 1970).

606. "The War at Home." *The Ally* no. 27 (June 1970).

607. Young, M. "Brothers, Sisters, Comrades." *Black Panther* vol. 5, no. 11 (12 Sept. 1970).

608. Young, Whitney M., Jr. "When the Negroes in Vietnam Come Home." *Harper's Magazine* (June 1967).

609. See also IE2, "Race Relations."

4. Disobedience and Desertion

610. "Americong." *Berkeley Tribe* vol. 2, no. 13 (3 Apr. 1970).

611. "A Company Won't Go." *Fifth Estate* vol. 4, no. 9 (17 Sept. 1969).

612. Cooney, John, and Spitzer, Dana. "Hell No, We Won't Go!" In Martin Oppenheimer, ed. *The American Military*. See no. 12. Resisters and deserters.

613. Coyle and Smith. "Resistance across the Country." *Plain Rapper* vol. 1, no. 5 (Jan. 1969).

614. Digia, R. "Canada: Our Loss Is Their Gain." *WIN* vol. 6, no. 7 (15 Apr. 1970).

615. Durbin, K. "AWOL from Columbia." *WIN* vol. 5, no. 21 (1 Dec. 1969).

616. Erlich, R. "Deserter Scene in Vancouver." *Amex-Canada* vol. 1, no. 16 (Sept. 1969).

617. "Ex-Marine Arrested." *WIN* vol. 5, no. 13 (July 1969). Conscientious objection.

618. Farrell, R. "Deserter." *L.A. Free Press* vol. 7, no. 15 (10 Apr. 1970), p. 42.

619. Gardner, Fred. "The Future of Desertion," *Hard Times* no. 76 (4 May 1970).

620. "Presidio Mutiny." *The Movement* vol. 5, no. 6 (July 1969).

621. Gaynes, D. "Escape and Evasion." *Fifth Estate* vol. 4, no. 10 (1 Oct. 1969).

622. "GIs Refuse Vietnam Duty." *Guardian* vol. 22, no. 38 (4 July 1970).

623. Halstead, Fred. *GIs Speak out against the War: The Case of the Ft. Jackson 8.* New York: Pathfinder Press, 1970. Interviews of participants.

624. Hayes, Thomas Lee. *American Deserters in Sweden: The Men and Their Challenge.* New York: Associated Press, 1971. Personal histories by a clergyman who worked with the deserters.

625. Karpel, C. "Don't Look Back." *WIN* vol. 5, no. 21 (1 Dec. 1969). Deserters in Canada.

626. Linden, Eugene. "The Demoralization of an Army: Fragging and Other Withdrawal Symptoms." *Saturday Review* (8 Jan. 1972). "Fragging" (killing the commander) comes from seeing all enemies as less than human. Describes type of officer who gets fragged.

627. Liberation News Service. "80,000 GIs Missing." *Chinook* vol. 2, no. 28 (30 July 1970).

628. _____. "AWOLS Threat to U. S. Army." *Old Mole* vol. 1, no. 17 (17 July 1969).

629. _____. "Desertions up 300 Percent." *Philadelphia Free Press* vol. 2, no. 27 (8 Dec. 1969).

630. _____. "GI Stays on the Run." *L.A. Free Press* vol. 6, no. 78 (16 Nov. 1969).

631. _____. "GIs Desert to NLF." *Old Mole* vol. 1, no. 24 (23 Oct. 1969).

632. Lyons, I. "But So Much More." *WIN* vol. 5, no. 16 (15 Sept. 1969).

633. "Marines Rebel in Iwakuni." *The Bond* vol. 4, no. 7 (22 July 1970).

634. Peck, J. "Canada Policy on Deserters." *WIN* vol. 5, no. 13 (July 1969).

635. Rigg, Col. Robert B. (USA, Ret.). "Future Military Discipline." *Military Review* vol. 50 (Sept. 1970).

636. Romano, M. "I Am Curious Sweden." *WIN* vol. 5, no. 21 (1 Dec. 1969). Deserters.

637. Sigal, C. "Travelers Aid, Sweden." *WIN* vol. 6, no. 10 (1 June 1970).

638. "Six GIs Wouldn't Invade Cambodia." *Guardian* vol. 22, no. 43 (22 Aug. 1970).

639. "USS Hancock Resistance." *The Ally* no. 28 (July 1970).

640. "Where the Guys Go." *Amex-Canada* vol. 2, no. 5 (Aug. 1970).

641. Articles on deserters will be found regularly in *Amex-Canada* as well as in the GI press. For "disobedience," see also IC2, "Protest," and IC5, "Military Justice. . . ."

5. Military Justice, Military Prisons and the Uniform Code of Military Justice (UCMJ)

642. Adelsberger, D. "Military Injustice." *WIN* vol. 5, no. 21 (1 Dec. 1969).

643. Allan, S. "Military Injustice." *Peoples World* vol. 34, no. 36 (5 Sept. 1970).

644. "Antiwar GI on Trial for Opinons." *Peace News* vol. 17, no. 23 (4 July 1969).

645. "Anti-War Sailor on Trial." *Old Mole* vol. 1, no. 25 (6 Nov. 1969).

646. Barnes, Peter. "The Presidio Mutiny." *New Republic* (5 July 1969).

647. Bourdow, Joseph A. "Dissent and the Code." See no. 554.

648. Brodsky, Stanley L., and Eggleston, Norman E. eds. *The Military Prison: Theory, Research, and Practice.* Carbondale, Ill.: Southern Illinois University Press, 1970. Articles, many scholarly, with good bibliography.

649. Brown, Kenneth H. *The Brig: A concept for Theatre or Film.* New York: Hill and Wang, 1965. A play.

650. Calley, Lt. William L. *Lieutenant Calley/His Own Story* as told to John Sack. New York: Viking, 1971. A good deal of court transcript is reproduced with commentary.

651. Donovan, Brian. "The Man Who Beat the Army." *New Republic* (31 Jan. 1970). A CO's fight for release.

652. Ervin, Senator Sam, Jr. "The Military Justice Act of 1968." *Military Law Review* vol. 45 (1969). Cf. Mounts no. 662.

653. "Fort Lewis 61—Revolt Brews." *Willamette Bridge* vol. 3, no. 33 (14 Aug. 1970).

654. Frederick, B. "Fort Lewis 35." See no. 527.

655. Gardner, Fred. *The Unlawful Concert: An Account of the Presidio Mutiny Case.* New York: Viking, 1970. Narrative account.

656. Glines, C. V. "Military Justice: On Trial." *Armed Forces Management.* vol. 16 (Feb. 1970).

657. Hammer, Richard. *The Court-Martial of Lt. Calley.* New York: Coward, McCann, & Geoghegan, 1971.

658. Heinze, F. "GI Convicted in Ft. Dix Uprising." *Guardian* vol. 22, no. 7 (15 Nov. 1969).

659. Jussel, Peter. "A Day in the Life of an Army Jail." *Liberation* vol. 15, no. 10 (Winter 1971). Poem.

660. Kester, John G. "Soldiers Who Insult the President: An Uneasy Look at Article 88 of the UCMJ." *Harvard Law Review* vol. 81 (1969): 1697.

661. McClellan, V. "War at Fort Devens." *Phoenix* vol. 2, no. 23 (8 Aug. 1970).

662. Mounts, Lt. Col. James A., and Sugarman, Capt. Myron G. "The Military Justice Act of 1968." *American Bar Association Journal* (May 1969). Cf. Ervin no. 652.

663. Murphy, Maj. Arthur A. "The Army Defense Counsel: Unusual Ethics for an Unusual Advocate." *Columbia Law Review.* vol. 61 (1961).

664. Orreck, C. "Ft. Knox GIs Win Court Victory." *Southern Patriot* vol. 28, no. 4 (Apr. 1970).

665. Ponicsan, Darryl. *The Last Detail.* New York: Dial, 1970. Novel. A "stunning indictment" of military justice.

666. "Rebellion at Ford Ord." *Willamette Bridge* vol. 3, no. 37 (11 Sept. 1970).

667. Richardson, F. O. *The GIs Handbook on Military Injustice: Why Rank and File GIs Need an Organization of Their Own.* New York: Committee for GI Rights, 1968. Pamphlet.

668. Rivkin, Robert S. *GI Rights and Army Justice.* See no. 260.

669. Schiesser, Capt. Charles W. "Trial by Peers: Enlisted Members on Courts-Martial." *Catholic University Law Review* vol. 15 (1966).

670. Sherman, Edward F., and Robinson, O. Everett. "Court-Martial: How Good Is Military Justice? Two Views." *Family* (16 June 1971). Semimonthly magazine supplement to the *Army/*

Navy/Air Force/Times weekly newspapers. Laudatory and critical views by two law professors formerly military lawyers.

671. Sherrill, Robert. *Military Justice Is to Justice as Military Music Is to Music.* New York: Harper & Row, 1969. Dislikes the music also.

672. ———. "Justice, Military Style." *Playboy* vol. 17, no. 2 (Feb. 1970).

673. ———. "The Pendleton Brig: Andersonville-by-the-Sea." *The Nation* vol. 209 (15 Sept. 1969).

674. Stapp, Andy. "Roger on Trial." *The Bond* vol. 4, no. 4 (22 Apr. 1970).

675. "Strangest Court Martial." *Peace News* vol. 17, no. 66 (1 May 1970).

676. Ulmer, S. Sidney. *Military Justice and the Right to Counsel.* Lexington: University Press of Kentucky, 1970. Reviews *USS Pueblo* incident and U. S. military justice system's interplay with politics and public opinion.

677. United States. *Manual for Courts-Martial, United States 1969*, rev. ed. Washington, D. C.: USGPO, 1969. Includes rules of procedure, offenses, punishments, etc.

678. U. S. Court of Military Appeals. Law Library. *Bibliography on Military Justice and Military Law.* See no. 2461.

679. United States. Department of the Army. Special Civilian Commission for the Study of the U. S. Army Confinement System. *Report.* Washington, D.C.: USGPO, 1970. Tables, charts, plans.

680. U. S. Department of Defense. Committee on a Uniform Code of Military Justice. *Report to Hon. Wilber M. Brucker, Secretary of the Army.* Washington, D. C.: USGPO, 1960.

681. United States. House. Committee on Armed Services. Special Subcommittee to Probe Disturbances on Military Bases. *Inquiry into the Reported Conditions in the Brig, Marine Corps Base, Camp Pendleton, Calif.: Report, Feb. 25, 1970.* 91st Congress, 2d session. Washington, D.C., 1970. HASC no. 91–43.

682. "Victory for Ft. Jackson 8." *WIN* vol. 5, no. 13 (July 1969).

683. Volz, Joseph. "The Rights of Free Men—Military vs. Civilian Courts." *Armed Forces Journal* vol. 107 (21 Feb. 1970).

684. "War GIs vs. the Brass." *Old Mole* vol. 1, no. 37 (17 Apr. 1970).

685. West, Luther Charles. *The Command Domination of the Military Judicial Process.* Ph.D. thesis, George Washington University Law School (1970).

686. Wiener, Col. Frederick B. (USA). "The Perils of Tinkering with Military Justice." *Army,* vol. 20 (Nov. 1970).

D. ASSAULT ON MILITARY INSTITUTIONS
AND VALUES: OUTSIDE THE MILITARY
1. The Movement in General

687. Arbona, C. "Decentralizing the Anti-War Movement." *Liberation* vol. 15, no. 5 (July, 1970).

688. Averyt, Ens. William F. (USN). "The Philosophy of the Counterculture." *Naval War College Review* vol. 23 (Mar. 1971).

689. Chicago 8. *Contempt.* Chicago: Swallow Press, 1970. Contains complete transcript of contempt citations.

690. Davidson, C. "New Mobe Undecided on Program." *Guardian* vol. 22, no. 38 (4 July 1970).

691. "End Army Blacklist of Civilian Demonstrators." *WIN* vol. 6, no. 6 (1 Apr. 1970).

692. Fernandez, Benedict. *In Opposition: Images of American Dissent in the Sixties.* New York: DaCapo Press, 1968. Pictures.

693. Garrett, Banning, and Barkley, Katherine, eds. *Two, Three . . . Many Vietnams: A Radical Reader on the Wars in Southeast Asia and the Conflicts at Home.* San Francisco: Canfield Press, 1971. A collection of articles from *Ramparts.*

694. Ginsburgh, Brig. Gen. Robert N. (USAF). "Anti-Militarism in Perspective." *Air Force Policy Letter for Commanders.* Supplement no. 10 (Oct. 1970).

695. Haltham, G. "History of the Peace Symbol." *WIN* vol. 5, no. 17 (1 Oct. 1969).

696. Haskins, Jim. *The War and the Protest: Vietnam.* Garden City, N. Y.: Doubleday, 1971. Includes bibliography.

697. Hoffman, Paul. *Moratorium: An American Protest.* New York: Tower, 1970.

698. Horowitz, Irving L. *The Struggle Is the Message: The Organization and Ideology of the Anti-War Movement.* Berkeley: Glendessary Press, 1970.

699. Kaplan, Morton A. *Dissent and the State in Peace and War: An Essay on the Grounds of Public Morality.* New York: Dunnellen, 1970.

700. Kempton, Murray. "Washington after Dark." *New York Review of Books* vol. 13, no. 11 (18 Dec. 1969).

701. "Lawyers Lobby for Peace." *Progressive* vol. 34, no. 7 (July 1970).

702. Liebert, Robert. *Radical and Militant Youth: A Psychoanalytical Inquiry.* New York: Praeger, 1971.

703. Liston, Robert A. *Dissent in America.* New York: McGraw-Hill, 1971.

704. Liberation News Service. "Anti-War Demonstration in Saigon."
      Chinook vol. 2, no. 29 (6 Aug. 1970).

705. Lund, C. "PL & SDS Attack Anti-War Strategy." *The Militant*
      vol. 34, no. 26 (3 July 1970). Progressive Labor Party and Stu-
      dents for a Democratic Society.

706. Mailer, Norman. *The Armies of the Night: History as a Novel, The
      Novel as History.* New York: New American Library, 1968.

707. Mitford, Jessica. *The Trial of Dr. Spock, the Rev. William Sloane
      Coffin, Jr., Michael Ferber, Mitchell Goodman, and Marcus Raskin.*
      New York: Knopf, 1969. Appendices include text of indictment
      and various "overt acts" (speeches, etc.).

708. Morey and Calvert. "Truth Speaks at the Pentagon." *WIN* vol.
      6, no. 12 (July 1970).

709. "Protests Disrupt Military College." *Southern Patriot* vol. 28, no.
      5 (May 1970).

710. Sheffield, L. "Mobe Widens Anti-War Movement." *Second City,*
      vol. 2, no. 8 (July 1970).

711. Socialist Workers. "The American Anti-War Movement." *Inter-
      national Socialist Review* vol. 30, no. 6 (Dec. 1969). Treats
      demonstrations particularly.

712. Thorstad, D. "Parley Maps Anti-War Program." *The Militant*
      vol. 34, no. 26 (3 July 1970).

713. Young, B. "How to Stop the War by Ending the Draft." *Peace-
      maker* vol. 23, no. 9 (18 July 1970).

714. The periodicals listed in section IVD regularly carry articles on
      this topic. *Liberation* is particularly good at carrying internal
      movement communications.

            2. Coffeehouses, Rapping with GIs, Base Demonstrations

715. "8,000 Demonstrate at Ft. Dix." *Old Mole* vol. 1, no. 24 (23 Oct.
      1969).

716. "Alice's Restaurant." *Vocations for Social Change* no. 17 (June
      1970), p. 43.

717. "Antiwar Coffeehouse Vexes Town Near Fort Knox." *New York
      Times* (8 Nov. 1969), p. 13.

718. "Army Moves on GI Coffeehouse." *Veterans Stars and Stripes for
      Peace* vol. 3, no. 1 (Jan. 1970).

719. "Coffee House Busted." *Fifth Estate* vol. 4, no. 15 (10 Dec.
      1969).

720. "Coffeehouse Shuts Down." *Liberated Guardian* vol. 1, no. 8 (11
      Aug. 1970).

721. Dane, B. "The GIs Cheer Peoples Songs." *Peoples World* vol. 33,
      no. 19 (9 May 1970).

722. Chinn, R. "Battle of Muldraugh." *WIN* vol. 6, no. 11 (15 June 1970).

723. "Fort Dix Coffee House Bombed." *Philadelphia Free Press* vol. 3, no. 6 (16 Feb. 1970).

724. Gardner, Fred. "Down among Sheltering Half." *Hardtimes* no. 63 (9 Feb. 1970). Coffeehouse in Tacoma, Wash.

725. ———. "GI Coffeehouses—America Is Very Uptite." *Dock of the Bay* vol. 1, no. 2 (12 Aug. 1969).

726. ———. "No Vacancy for GI Coffee Houses." *Plain Rapper* vol. 1, no. 6 (Sept. 1969).

727. Garson, B. "GI Morale—Take Back Your Life." *Village Voice* vol. 15, no. 5 (29 Jan. 1970).

728. "GIs March in Augusta." *Southern Patriot* vol. 28, no. 7 (Sept. 1970).

729. "Guard at Fort Lewis." *Willamette Bridge* vol. 3, no. 34 (21 Aug. 1970).

730. "List of GI Coffee Houses." *WIN* vol. 5, no. 21 (1 Dec. 1969).

731. Liberation News Service. "Army Attacks Coffeehouse." *Fifth Estate* vol. 4, no. 18 (21 Jan. 1970).

732. ———. "Evictions at Dix." *Philadelphia Free Press* vol. 2, no. 22 (3 Nov. 1969).

733. ———. "GI Coffeehouse Bust Set Up." *Fifth Estate* vol. 4, no. 8 (3 Sept. 1969).

734. McClellan, V. "War at Fort Devens." *Phoenix* vol. 2, no. 23 (8 Aug. 1970).

735. "Military Claw Reaches Out." *The Bond* vol. 4, no. 2 (18 Feb. 1970).

736. Moody, K. "Sand in the Machine." *International Socialist* vol. 1, no. 12 (Sept. 1969).

737. "Pentagon—GI Coffee House, Oakland, Calif." *Black Panther* vol. 5, no. 10 (5 Sept. 1970).

738. SCEF. "Coffeehouse Shuts Down." *Liberated Guardian* vol. 1, no. 8 (11 Aug. 1970).

739. "Shelterhalf." *Fatigue Press* no. 21 (Feb. 1970).

740. Thorstad, D. "Brass in New Moves against GI Right." *The Militant* vol. 34, no. 2 (23 Jan. 1970).

741. Townley, R. "Alice's Restaurant." *Liberation* vol. 14, no. 9 (Jan. 1970).

742. "Twenty-Five Invade Army Base." *Peacemaker* vol. 22, no. 10 (19 Sept. 1969).

743. "UFO Bust." *Fatigue Press* no. 23 (May 1970). UFO, located in Columbia, S. C., was one of the first GI coffeehouses.

744. Vlasits, G. "UFO Sentences—Six Years." *Southern Patriot* vol. 28, no. 5 (May 1970).

745. Wingate, J. "GI Coffeehouse Busted." *WIN* vol. 6, no. 3 (15 Feb. 1970).

746. _____. "Southern Fried Justice." *WIN* vol. 6, no. 10, (1 June 1970).

747. See Appendix A in Rivkin, no. 260, for list of coffeehouses.

*3. Conscientious Objection, Draft Resistance, Civil Disobedience,
Violent Protest, Exile*

748. Aiken, D. "We Did It." *Plain Rapper* vol. 1, no. 5 (Jan. 1969). Direct action against the draft.

749. "Akron Draft Files Are Destroyed." *Peacemaker* vol. 22, no. 14 (18 Oct. 1969).

750. "Attacks on Draft Files Continue." *Peacemaker* vol. 22, no. 9 (28 June 1969).

751. Bedau, Hugo A., ed. *Civil Disobedience: Theory and Practice.* New York: Pegasus, 1969.

752. Berrigan, Daniel. *The Dark Night of Resistance.* Garden City, N. Y.: Doubleday, 1971. Personal narrative, poetry, and prose.

753. _____. "Letter from the Underground." *New York Review of Books* vol. 15, no. 3 (13 Aug. 1970).

754. Cohen, Carl. *Civil Disobedience: Conscience, Tactics, and the Law.* New York: Columbia University Press, 1971.

755. Column, M. "Oh Happy Day Chicago." *WIN* vol. 5, no. 15 (1 Sept. 1969).

756. "Conscience and Conscription." *Progressive* vol. 34, no. 8 (Aug. 1970).

757. Cooney, John, and Spitzer, Dana. "Hell No, We Won't Go!" See no. 612.

758. "Draft Board Raids Continue." *Peacemaker* vol. 23, no. 9 (18 July 1970).

759. "Draft File Rip Off." *WIN* vol. 5, no. 15 (1 Sept. 1969).

760. "Draft Resistance Spreads." *Plain Rapper* vol. 1, no. 6 (Sept. 1969).

761. Elmer, J. "Boston and Beaver 55." *WIN* vol. 5, no. 22 (15 Dec. 1969).

762. _____. "Draft Board Rip Off." *WIN* vol. 6, no. 13 (Aug. 1970).

763. _____. "Me and My Draft Board." *WIN* vol. 5, no. 18 (15 Oct. 1969).

764. "Exiled Yankees in Toronto Picket." *Amex-Canada* vol. 2, no. 1 (Dec. 1969).

765. Ferber, Michael, and Lynd, Staughton. *The Resistance.* Boston:

Beacon Press, 1971. A history of recent noncooperation with the draft. Card turn-ins, etc., by two of the early organizers.

766. Finn, James, ed. *A Conflict of Loyalties: The Case for Selective Conscientious Objection.* New York: Pegasus, 1968.

767. Forest, L. "Milwaukee 14." *WIN* vol. 5, no. 13 (July 1969).

768. Furst, R. "Definition of CO Status." *The Militant* vol. 34, no. 26 (3 July 1970).

769. Gaylin, Willard, M.D. *In the Service of Their Country: War Resisters in Prison.* New York: Viking, 1970. Case histories by a sympathetic observer.

770. "Guerilla Raids Destroy Draft Files." *Old Mole* vol. 1, no. 18 (31 July 1969).

771. Harris, David. "Jail Jail Jail." *Dock of the Bay* vol. 1, no. 2 (12 Aug. 1969). Harris is the founder of the Resistance.

772. Hayden, Thomas. *Trial.* New York: Holt, Rinehart and Winston, 1970.

773. ———. "Inside the Conspiracy." *The Guardian* vol. 22, no. 5 (1 Nov. 1969). Hayden wrote many articles in *The Guardian* during the trial.

774. Hipps, S. "Sanctuary." *WIN* vol. 5, no. 14 (Aug. 1969).

775. Kilmer, Richard L.; Lecky, Robert S.; and Wiley, Debrah S. *They Can't Go Home Again: The Story of America's Political Refugees.* Philadelphia: Pilgrim Press, 1971. With appendices on draft-age emigrants and aid centers in Canada.

776. Lens, Sidney. "Notes on the Chicago Trial." *Liberation* vol. 14, no. 8 (Nov. 1969).

777. Liberation News Service. "Draft Resisters Clog Courts." *Space City* vol. 1, no. 7 (11 Oct. 1969).

778. ———. "N. Y. Induction Bldg. Bombed." *L.A. Free Press* vol. 6, no. 75 (24 Oct. 1969).

779. Lynd, Alice. *We Won't Go—Personal Accounts of War Objectors.* Boston: Beacon Press, 1968.

780. Lyttle, Brad. "Stopping." *Liberation* vol. 15, no. 5 (July 70).

781. Milwaukee 14. Statements by J. Bayless, L. Forest, and M. Levock. *WIN* vol. 5, no. 13 (1 Aug. 1969).

782. "Minnesota Draft Boards Raided." *Second City* vol. 2, no. 9 (Sept. 1970).

783. Mitford, Jessica. *The Trial of Dr. Spock.* See no. 707.

784. National Interreligious Service Board for Conscientious Objectors. *Religious Statements on Conscientious Objection.* Washington, D. C.: 1970. Pamphlet.

785. *The Peacemaker.* Articles almost every issue on draft resistance.

786. Peck, J. "Hiroshima Week at the Pentagon." *WIN* vol. 5, no. 16 (15 Sept. 1969).

787. ———. "Right of Non-Religious CO Reaffirmed." *WIN* vol. 6, no. 12 (July 1970).

788. Pekelis, C. "Women Wreck 1–A Files in New York." *Guardian* vol. 21, no. 40 (12 July 1969).

789. Pittsburgh Resistance. *Resistance and Beyond: A Handbook Prepared by the Pittsburgh Resistance and Their Friends.* Pittsburgh, Pa.: The Victory Press, 1970. Articles, letters, poems, pictures, etc. on "living at war, living in America, living at school, alternatives."

790. Salant, A. "Bread not Bombs." *Catholic Worker* vol. 37, no. 7 (Sept. 1970).

791. Schlissel, Lillian, ed. *Conscience in America: A Documentary History of Conscientious Objection in America, 1757–1967.* New York: Dutton, 1968.

792. Seven Mighty Anvils. "Shaft the Draft." See no. 368.

793. Stevens, Franklin. *If This Be Treason: Your Sons Tell Their Own Stories of Why They Won't Fight for Their Country.* New York: Wyden, 1970. How they avoided the army.

794. "Ten Quakers Arrested." *WIN* vol. 5, no. 13 (July 1969).

795. *Trials of the Resistance.* New York: Random House, 1970. Essays on civil disobedience and resistance from *New York Review of Books.*

796. Tychonievich, W. "I Refuse." *San Francisco Bay Guardian* vol. 3, no. 6 (10 July 1969).

797. "U. S. Draft Resisters—Sentences Up." *Peace News* vol. 17, no. 47 (19 Dec. 1969).

798. Velvel, Lawrence R. *Undeclared War and Civil Disobedience: The American System in Crisis.* New York: Dunellen, 1970.

799. "Views from Allenwood." *WIN* vol. 5, no. 15 (1 Sept. 1969).

800. Waskow, A. "American-Cambodia Crisis." *Liberation* vol. 15, no. 5 (July 1970).

801. Webb, M. "They Burn Draft Boards." *Amex-Canada* vol. 1, no. 16 (Sept. 1969).

802. Williams, Roger. *The New Exiles: American War Resisters in Canada.* New York: Liveright, 1971.

803. Draft exiles are treated regularly in *Amex-Canada.*

4. Veterans Against The War

804. Another Mother for Peace. List of Vietnam Veterans Against the War Coordinators. Also VVAW Tapes & Films. Write: Another Mother for Peace. See section IVD for address.

805. Duncan, Donald. *The New Legions.* New York: Random House,

1967. Memoirs of the ex-Green Beret now military editor for *Ramparts.*

806.   ———. "I Quit: Memoirs of a Special Forces Hero." In Banning Garrett and Katherine V. Barkeley, eds., *Two Three . . . Many Vietnams.* See no. 693.

807.   Faith, M. "Portland Braces for Vets Meeting." *Guardian* vol. 22, no. 43 (22 Aug. 1970).

808.   Fendrich, James, and Pearson, Michael. "Black Veterans Return." In Martin Oppenheimer, ed., *The American Military.* See no. 12. Survey of black veterans in Jacksonville, Fla.

809.   Halstead, Fred. *GIs Speak Out against the War.* See no. 623.

810.   Hayes, Thomas L. *American Deserters in Sweden.* See no. 624.

811.   Kerry, John, and Vietnam Veterans Against the War. *The New Soldier.* See no. 250. Includes survey of background and opinions of antiwar veterans.

812.   McCusker, M. "Vets Who Say No." *Willamette Bridge* vol. 3, no. 32 (7 Aug. 1970).

813.   Mayers, Pa. "Ex-Berets Attack Military at Rally." *L.A. Free Press* vol. 6, no. 79 (21 Nov. 1969).

814.   Pew, T. "Terrible Crippler." *Progressive* vol. 34, no. 8 (Aug. 1970).

815.   Pinderhughes, C. "Vietnam Vet Hounded by Pig." *Black Panther* vol. 5, no. 4 (1 Aug. 1970).

816.   Polner, Murray. *No Victory Parades: The Return of the Vietnam Veteran.* New York: Holt, Rinehart and Winston, 1971. Nine in-depth interviews. Not all "doves."

817.   Ramsdell, S. "Soldiers of Peace at Valley Forge." *Peoples World* vol. 33, no. 38 (19 Sept. 1970).

818.   Vets for Peace. "Letters." *Second City* vol. 2, no. 8 (July 1970).

819.   "Viet Vets Bring It All Back Home." *Old Mole* vol. 1, no. 46 (11 Sept. 1970).

820.   See also all of IC, "Assault on Military Institutions and Values: Inside the Military."

821.   See IE5, "Veterans," for more general works on the topic.

E. SPECIAL PROBLEMS AND ISSUES
1. Drug Abuse

822.   "Drug Abuse in the Air Force." *Air Force Information Policy Letter for Commanders.* Supplement no. 1 (Jan. 1970). Official paper.

823.   "Fresh Disclosures on Drugs and GIs." *U.S. News and World Report* vol. 68 (6 Apr. 1970). Senate study.

824. Halleck, S. "Great Drug Education Hoax." *Progressive* vol. 34, no. 7 (July 1970).

825. Knoll, Erwin. "Our Junkies in Vietnam." *Progressive* vol. 35 (July 1971).

826. "Mai Lai Dope." *Helix* vol. 2, no. 14 (2 Apr. 1970).

827. "Marijuana—the Other Enemy in Vietnam." *U.S. News and World Report* vol. 68 (27 Jan. 1970). The "crackdown" and its difficulties.

828. "The New Opium War." *Ramparts* (May 1971). Exposé of American and Saigon involvement in Asian drug traffic.

829. Pursch, Comdr. J. A. (USN). "Drug Abuse in the Navy." *U.S. Naval Institute Proceedings* vol. 96 (July 1970).

830. Szasz, Thomas S. "Scapegoating 'Military Addicts': The Helping Hand Strikes Again." *Trans-action* vol. 9, no. 3 (Jan. 1972). Attack on addicts veils failure in war.

831. United States. Senate. Committee on the Judiciary. Subcommittee to Investigate Juvenile Delinquency. Hearings: pt. 21, Mar. 24–Oct. 30, 1970, pursuant to SR 342, Investigation of Juvenile Delinquency in the U.S. Washington D.C.: USGPO, 1971. Considers the relationship of drug abuse and delinquency in the armed forces.

832. United States. Senate. Committee on Labor and Public Welfare. Special Subcommittee on Alcoholism and Narcotics. *Drug and Alcohol Abuse in the Military.* Hearings, Nov. 17–Dec. 3, 1970, on examination of drug abuse and alcoholism in the armed forces. 91st Congress, 2d session. Extensive.

833. ――――. *Military Drug Abuse, 1971.* Hearings, June 9–22, 1971. 92d Congress, 1st session.

2. Race Relations

834. "The Angry Black Soldiers." *Progressive* vol. 34 (Mar. 1970). Racial conflict at military bases.

835. "Black GIs in Ft. Hood Confrontation." *Guardian* vol 22, no. 44 (29 Aug. 1970).

836. "Blood on Whose Hands, Kent, My Lai." *Peoples World* vol. 33, no. 25 (20 June 1970). Editorial.

837. Boyd, Maj. George M. "A Look at Racial Polarity in the Armed Forces." *Air University Review* vol. 21 (Sept.–Oct. 1970).

838. Cameron, Colin, and Blackstone, Judith. *Minorities in the Armed Forces: A . . . Bibliography.* See no. 2441.

839. Choy, S. "Long Way from Home." *Black Panther* vol. 5, no. 4 (1 Aug. 1970).

840. "Chronological History of the Black Soldier." *Black Panther* vol. 5, no. 4 (1 Aug. 1970).
841. Davenport, R. K. "The Negro in the Army: A Subject of Research." *Journal of Social Issues* vol. 3, no. 4 (1947).
842. "Defense Extends 'Open Housing' Ban to Pentagon Area." *Commanders Digest* vol. 3 (30 Dec. 1967).
843. Dwyer, R. J. "The Negro in the United States Army: His Changing Role and Status." *Sociology and Social Research* vol. 38 (1953).
844. *Ebony.* See no. 592.
845. "Freak the Army." *Good Times* vol. 3, no. 38 (25 Sept. 1970).
846. Jackson, Comdr. George L. (USN). "Constraints of the Negro Civil Rights Movement on American Military Effectiveness: A Survey." *Naval War College Review* vol. 22 (Jan. 1970). Loss of South African ports, etc.
847. Johnson, Jesse, Jr. *Ebony Brass: An Autobiography of Negro Frustrations Amid Aspirations.* New York: William-Frederick Press, 1967.
848. Lee, Irvin H. *Negro Medal of Honor Men.* 3d ed. New York: Dodd, Mead, 1969.
849. "Marine Corps Still Building Men." *Street Journal* vol. 2, no. 34 (6 Aug. 1970).
850. Marshall, S. "Racial Fights on Southern Bases." *L.A. Free Press* vol. 7, no. 39 (25 Sept. 1970).
851. "Message to Black GIs." *Fatigue Press* no. 23 (May 1970).
852. Moskos, Charles C., Jr. "Racial Integration in the Armed Forces." *American Journal of Sociology* vol. 72 (Sept. 1966). Assignment of Negroes and degree of integration in on-duty and off-duty behavior.
853. "Newer Negro Marines Are Looking for Identity with Blackness." *New York Times* (21 Dec. 1969), p. 44.
854. Orreck, C. "Ft. Knox GIs Win Court Victory." *Southern Patriot* vol. 28, no. 4 (Apr. 1970).
855. "Racism." *Fatigue Press* no. 25 (July 1970).
856. "Racism in the Military." *Fifth Estate* vol. 5, no. 9 (3 Sept. 1970).
857. "Sec-Def Orders End to Discrimination in the Military." *Armed Forces Journal* vol. 108 (4 Jan. 1971).
858. Stillman, Richard J., II. *Integration of the Negro in the U.S. Armed Forces.* See no. 602.
859. U. S. Army. *Equal Opportunity and Treatment of Military Personnel.* Regulation no. 600–6. Ft. Mead, N. J.: First Army Headquarters (14 Nov. 1966).
860. United States. U. S. Army Military History Research Collection,

Historical Research and Reference Division. *The U. S. Army and the Negro.* Bibliography. See no. 2470.

861. U. S. Assistant Secretary of Defense (Manpower, Personnel, and Reserve). *Integration and the Negro Officer in the Armed Forces of the United States of America.* Washington, D.C.: USGPO, 1962.

862. U. S. Commission on Civil Rights. South Dakota Advisory Committee. *Negro Airmen in a Northern Community: Discrimination in Rapid City, S. D.: A Report.* Washington, D. C.: USGPO, 1963.

863. United States. Congress. House. Committee on Armed Services. Special Subcommittee to Probe Disturbances on Military Bases. *Inquiry into the Disturbances at Marine Corps Base, Camp Lejeune, N.C. on July 20, 1969: Report, Dec. 15, 1969.* 91st Congress, 1st session. H.A.S.C. no. 91–32.

864. Vance, Samuel. *The Courageous and the Proud.* New York: Norton, 1970. Personal narratives of blacks in battle.

865. Weil, F. E. G. "The Negro in the Armed Forces." *Social Forces,* vol. 26 (1947).

866. Westmoreland, Gen. William C. "Westmoreland: Facing Up to the External and Internal Challenges." See no. 267.

867. White, Lt. Col. James S. "Race Relations in the Army." *Military Review* vol. 50 (July 1970).

868. See also IC3, "Blacks and Black Protest."

3. War Crimes and Atrocities

869. *The American Crime of Genocide in South Vietnam.* South Vietnam: Giai Phong Publishing House, 1968.

870. Burchett, Wilfred. "New Details on Songmy Massacre." *Guardian* vol. 22, no. 10 (6 Dec. 1969).

871. _____. "Songmy Will Be Avenged." *Guardian* vol. 22, no. 9 (22 Nov. 1969).

872. Calley, Lt. William L. *Lieutenant Calley/His Own Story,* See no. 650.

873. Chomsky, Noam. *At War with Asia.* New York: Pantheon, 1970. U. S. presence in Vietnam is absurd and immoral; accuses U. S. of premeditated genocide.

874. Coburn, Judith, and Cowan, Geoffrey. "Training for Terror: A Deliberate Policy?" *The Village Voice* (11 Dec. 1969).

875. _____. "The War Criminals Hedge Their Bets." *Village Voice* vol. 14, no. 60 (14 Dec. 1969). Atrocities.

876. Commission for Investigation of the American Imperialists' War Crimes in Vietnam. *American Crimes in Vietnam.* Hanoi: Democratic Republic of Vietnam, 1966.

877. Committee to Denounce the United States Puppets' War

Crimes in South Vietnam. *U. S. Puppet Massacres of the Population in South Vietnam* (from 1965–1969). Issued Dec. 1969. See also communiqués issued 30 Sept. 1969, 5 Jan. 1970, and later.

878. D'Amato, Anthony A. "War Crimes and Vietnam: The 'Nuremberg Defense' and the Military Service Resister." *California Law Review* vol. 57 (Nov. 1969). Soldier cannot be forced into a position where he may be asked to commit war crimes.

879. Dougall, I. "Why We Need a Vietnam." *Peace News* vol. 17, no. 84 (4 Sept. 1970).

880. Ellison, H. "The Glass Teat." *L.A. Free Press*, vol. 6, no. 81 (5 Dec. 1969).

881. Falk, Richard A.; Kolko, Gabriel; and Lifton, Robert J., eds. *Crimes of War*. New York: Random House, 1971. Anthology, with many well-known contributors. Documentary indictment of U. S. policy, covering legal, political, and psychological aspects of the Vietnam War. Has controversial eye-witness accounts of atrocities. Primarily anti-Vietnam, but some attention to more general question of responsibility.

882. Garsse, Y. "Bibliography of Crimes." *Peace News* vol. 17, no. 75 (3 July 1970).

883. Goldblat, J. "Are Tear Gas and Herbicides Permitted Weapons?" *Bulletin of Atomic Scientists* vol. 26, no. 4 (1970).

884. Grajewski, J. "Love." *Liberation* vol. 15, no. 6 (1970).

885. Hammer, Richard. *The Court-Martial of Lt. Calley*, New York: Coward, McCann, & Geohegan, 1971. Written in tone of outrage over MyLai tragedy, but humane and incisive analysis of trial.

886. _____. *One Morning in the War: The Tragedy at Sonmy*. New York: Coward, McCann, & Geohegan, 1970. MyLai account, includes Vietnamese side of the event.

887. Herman, Edward S. *Atrocities in Vietnam: Myths and Realities*. Philadelphia: Pilgrim, 1970. Examines and compares claims of atrocities on both sides.

888. Hersh, Seymour M. *MyLai 4: A Report on the Massacre and Its Aftermath*. New York: Random House, 1970. As seen through American eyes.

889. International War Crimes Tribunal, Stockholm and Roskilde, Denmark, 1967. *Against the Crime of Silence: Proceedings of the Tribunal, Stockholm (and) Copenhagen*. Edited by John Duffett. New York: Simon & Schuster, 1970. Proceedings of the "Bertrand Russell Tribunal" of 1967.

890. Knoll, Erwin, and McFadden, Judith N. *War Crimes and the Ameri-*

can Conscience. New York: Holt, Rinehart and Winston, 1970. Edited transcript of Congressional Conference on War and National Responsibility. Over 40 contributors, all critical of U. S. policy.

891.   Kunen, James Simon. *Standard Operating Procedure* and *Notes of a Draft-Age American.* New York: Avon, 1971. Includes transcripts of inquiry and interviews with veterans. Produced with cooperation of Citizen's Commission of Inquiry on U. S. War Crimes in Indochina.

892.   Lane, Mark. *Conversations with Americans.* New York: Simon and Schuster, 1970. Interviews of former soldiers who witnessed or participated in alleged atrocities in Vietnam.

893.   Lang, Daniel. *Casualties of War.* New York: McGraw-Hill, 1969. Account of a murder-rape and surrounding events. British version titled *Incident on Hill 192.*

894.   *Liberation Magazine.* Special issue on Indochina War, vol. 15, no. 11; vol. 16, no. 1 & 2 (single issue Spring 1971). Includes testimony from Winter Soldier Investigation on war crimes.

895.   Melman, Seymour (Research Director). *In the Name of America: The Conduct of the War in Vietnam by the Armed Forces of the U.S. as Shown by Published Reports, Compared with the Laws of War Binding on the U.S. Government and on Its Own Citizens.* New York: Clergy and Laymen Concerned about Vietnam, 1968. Uses news dispatches to make war crimes accusations.

896.   Morris, G. "Someday I'll be a War Criminal." *WIN* vol. 5, no. 21 (1 Dec. 1969).

897.   "MyLai Massacre: Grim Details, Unanswered Questions." *Congressional Quarterly Weekly Report* vol. 27 (5 Dec. 1969).

898.   Rigg, Col. Robert B. (USA, Ret.). "Where Does Killing End and Murder Begin in War?" *Military Review* vol. 51 (Mar. 71). Asserts that the double standard which prosecutes for MyLai but ignores saturation fires and bombing must be changed—but how?

899.   Russell, Bertrand. *War Crimes in Vietnam.* London: Allen and Unwin, 1967.

900.   Salant, A. "Bread not Bombs." *Catholic Worker* vol. 36, no. 7 (Sept. 70).

901.   Sartre, Jean Paul. *On Genocide.* Boston: Beacon Press, 1968. With a summary of the evidence and the judgment of the International War Crimes Tribunal, by Arlette El Kaim-Sartre.

902.   Schell, Jonathan. *The Military Half: An Account of the Destruction of*

Quang Ngai and Quang Tin. New York: Knopf, 1968. The destruction of Quang Ngai province (where MyLai is) from the air.

903. _____. *The Village of Ben Suc.* New York: Knopf, 1967. Military operations in a single village.

904. Schemmer, Benjamin F. "Thundering Silence, Instead of Public Accounting." *Armed Forces Journal* vol. 108 (15 Feb. 1971).

905. Stanford Biology Group. *"The Destruction of Indochina."* San Francisco: *California Tomorrow,* June 1970.

906. Stone, I. F. "Atrocities Nixon Condoned." *I. F. Stone's Bi-Weekly* vol. 17, no. 23 (15 Dec. 1969).

907. Syme, Anthony. *Vietnam: The Cruel War.* London: Horwitz, 1966.

908. Taylor, Telford. *Nuremberg and Vietnam: An American Tragedy.* Chicago: Quadrangle Books, 1970. A minimalist indictment, by the former Chief U. S. Prosecutor at Nuremberg.

909. *They Are Even More Ruthless than Hitler!* South Vietnam: Liberation Editions, 1966.

910. Thomas, Ann Van Wynam, and Thomas, A. J., Jr. *Legal Limits on the Use of Chemical and Biological Weapons.* See no. 485.

911. U. S. Department of the Army. *The Law of Land Warfare.* (Department of the Army Field Manual No. 27–10). Washington, D.C.: Headquarters Department of the Army, July 1956.

912. United States. House. Committee on Armed Services. Armed Services Investigation Subcommittee. *Investigation of the MyLai Incident: Report,* under authority of H. Res. 105. Washington, D.C.: USGPO, 1970.

913. *U.S. Imperialists' "Burn All, Destroy All, Kill All" Policy in South Vietnam.* South Vietnam: Giai Phong (Liberation) Editions, 1967. "Published by the South Vietnam Committee for Denunciation of the Crimes of the U.S. Imperialists and Their Henchmen."

914. "U. S. Practices Shock Torture." *L.A. Free Press.* vol. 6, no. 84 (26 Dec. 1969).

915. *U.S. War Crimes in Vietnam.* Juridical Sciences Institute under the Vietnam State Commission of the Social Sciences, Hanoi, 1968.

916. "Vietnam and Women." *Rat* (23 Aug. 1970).

917. "War Crimes." *Hardtimes* vol. 1, no. 56 (16 Dec. 1969).

918. Wasserstrom, Richard. "Criminal Behavior." *New York Review of Books* vol. 16, no. 10 (3 June 1971). Review of Telford Taylor's *Nuremberg and Vietnam* with amplification.

919. _____. "The Relevance of Nuremberg." *Philosophy and Public Affairs* vol. 1, no. 1 (Fall 1971).

920. Weisberg, Barry, ed. *Ecocide in Indochina.* See no. 494.

921. See also IB3, "CBW: Chemical and Biological Warfare," IIF2, "Ecology," and IIIF3, "Fighting Insurgency."

4. Prisoners of War (POWs)

922. Albee, L. "Vietnam Idyll." *WIN* vol. 5, no. 17 (1 Oct. 1969).

923. Dellinger, David. "Dave Dellinger Speaks from Chicago." *Freedom News* vol. 4, no. 1 (Jan. 70).

924. ———. "The Prisoner of War Hoax." *Liberation* vol. 15, no. 10 (Winter 1971).

925. ———. "Those Reports of Torture," *Liberation.* vol. 14, no. 7 (Oct. 1969).

926. Dudman, Richard. *Forty Days with the Enemy.* New York: Liveright, 1971.

927. Duncan, Donald. "The Prisoner." *Ramparts* vol. 8, no. 3 (Sept. 1969).

928. Emerson, G. "Vietnam Mujeres." *Rat* (4 Apr. 1970).

929. Havens, Charles W., III. "Release and Repatriation of Vietnam Prisoners." *American Bar Association Journal* vol. 57 (Jan. 1971). Legal obligations on both sides.

930. Hill, H. "Vietnam: Racist Red Cross." *Distant Drummer* vol. 2, no. 53 (10 Oct. 1970).

931. "Info on POWs." *Guardian* vol. 22, no. 17 (24 Jan. 1970).

932. "International Conference of the Red Cross Calls for Observance of the Geneva Conventions on Prisoners of War." *Department of State Bulletin* vol. 61 (13 Oct. 1969).

933. Krone, Col. Robert M. "Politics and Prisoners of War." *Air University Review* vol. 21 (Mar.–Apr. 1970). Historical perspective.

934. Liberation News Service. "Bringing the Boys Back." *Ann Arbor Argus* vol. 1, no. 11 (29 Aug. 1969).

935. McGrath, K. "South Vietnamese Political Prisoners in Cages." *Peace News* vol. 17, no. 76 (10 July 1970).

936. Marti, J. "Hanoi Answers U. S. Slanders about POWs." *Eyewitness* vol. 2, no. 4 (Apr. 1970).

937. Paley, D. "Report from the DRV." *WIN* vol. 5, no. 16 (15 Sept. 1969).

938. Richardson, Col. Walton K. "Prisoners of War as Instruments of Foreign Policy." *Naval War College Review* vol. 23 (Sept. 1970).

939. Ripple. "Living with the Viet Cong." *Fifth Estate* vol. 5, no. 7 (6 Aug. 1970).

940. Salaff, S. "The Role of U. S. Airmen Prisoners." *Freedom News* vol. 4, no. 4 (Apr. 1970).

941. Schwartz, W. "Well, It Beats the YMCA." *WIN* vol. 5, no. 21 (1 Dec. 1969).

942. Smith, George E. *POW: Two Years with the Vietcong.* Berkeley: Ramparts Press, 1971. Sympathetic prisoner.

943. Sullivan, William H. "Department Gives Views on Proposed Congressional Resolution on U. S. Prisoners of War in Southeast Asia." *Department of State Bulletin* vol. 62 (25 May 1970). This journal carries many articles on POWs, e.g., 8 Sept. 1969, 13 Oct. 1969, 1 Dec. 1969 and 22 Dec. 1969.

944. "Tell It to Hanoi." *Street Journal* vol. 2, no. 34 (31 July 1970).

945. United States. Congress. House. Committee on Armed Services. *Hearings on Problems of Prisoners of War and Their Families, March 6, 1970.* Washington, D. C.: USGPO, 1970. 91st Congress, 2d session.

946. United States. Congress. House. Committee on Armed Services. Special Subcommittee on the U.S.S. *Pueblo. Inquiry into the U.S.S.* Pueblo *and EC–121 Plane Incidents: Report.* H.A.S.C. no. 91–12 (28 July 1969).

947. United States. Congress. House. Committee on Foreign Affairs. Subcommittee on National Security Policy and Scientific Developments. *American Prisoners of War in Southeast Asia, 1970: Hearings, April 29–May 6, 1970.* Washington, D. C.: USGPO, 1970. 91st Congress, 2d session.

948. ———. *American Prisoners of War in Vietnam: Hearings, November 13–14, 1969.* Washington, D.C.: USGPO, 1969. 91st Congress, 1st session.

949. United States Department of Defense. Advisory Committee on Prisoners of War. *POW: The Fight Continues after the Battle; a Report.* Washington, D.C.: USGPO, 1955. Includes bibliography.

950. United States Embassy. Saigon, Vietnam. "Public Presentation of U. S. Prisoners of War." *Viet-Nam Documents and Research Notes.* Document no. 65 (Aug. 1969).

951. "War Prisoners Speak Out." *Good Times* vol. 3, no. 21 (22 May 1970).

952. Ward, R. "Committee of Liaison." *Guardian* vol. 22, no. 18 (31 Jan. 1970).

953. Wolfkill, Grant F. with Rose, Jerry A. *Reported to Be Alive.* New York: Simon & Schuster, 1965. Autobiographical account of former prisoner of the Pathet Lao.

954. "Women Bring News of War Prisoners." *Freedom News* vol. 4, no. 1 (Jan. 1970).

5. *Veterans: Economic and Psychological Problems of Returning to Civilian Society*

955. "ASU Aids Wounded GIs." *The Bond* vol. 4, no. 6 (17 June 1970).

956. Clemons, Neil C. "Johnny Marches Home, 1970 Style." *Wall Street Journal* (24 Feb. 1970), p. 22. Mood of Vietnam vets in middle America.

957. "Conditions in Veterans Hospitals." *Guardian* vol. 22, no. 43 (22 Aug. 1970).

958. Fendrich, James, and Pearson, Michael. "Black Veterans Return." See no. 808.

959. "How They Take Care of Vietnam Dead." *Eyewitness* vol. 1, no. 8 (Sept. 1969).

960. "I'd Rather Be Dead." *The Ally* no. 27 (June 1970).

961. Lifton, Robert J. "Testimony." *Radical Therapist* vol. 1, no. 1 (May 1970).

962. _____. "Vietnam: Betrayal and Self-Betrayal." *Trans-action* vol. 6, no. 11 (Oct. 1969).

963. Liberation News Service. "Viet Vets Harrassed." *Liberated Guardian* vol. 1, no. 3 (23 May 1970).

964. Louviere, Vernon. "What We're Doing for Vietnam Vets." *American Legion Magazine* vol. 84 (Mar. 1968).

965. Morris, G. "Someday I'll Be a War Criminal." See no. 896.

966. Oakland, O. "War on Black Vets." *Berkeley Tribe* vol. 2, no. 17 (May 1970).

967. Pew, T. "Terrible Crippler." *Progressive* vol. 34, no. 8 (Aug. 1970).

968. Pinderhuges, C. "Vietnam Vet Hounded by Pig." *Black Panther* vol. 5, no. 4 (1 Aug. 1970).

969. Polner, Murray. *No Victory Parades.* See no. 816.

970. _____. "Vietnam War Stories." *Trans-action* vol. 6, no. 1 (Nov. 1968).

971. Rappoport, Leon, and Cvetkovich, George. "Opinion on Vietnam, Some Findings from Three Studies." *Proceedings,* Seventy-Sixth Annual Convention, American Psychological Association vol. 3 (1968).

972. Robbyelee. "Vietnam—Wounds Far Worse." *Second City* vol. 2, no. 5 (Apr. 1970).

973. Spivak, Jonathan. "Vietnam to Campus: Administration Views College for Veterans as Easing City Unrest." *Wall Street Journal* (17 Sept. 1969), p. 1.

974. Steif, William. "GI Bill Failing to Attract Vietvets." *College and University Business* vol. 47 (Sept. 1969).

975. United States. Congress. House. Committee on Veterans' Affairs. This committee regularly publishes information, hearings, etc. on this topic.

976. United States. Congress. Senate. Committee on Labor and Public Welfare. Subcommittee on Veterans' Affairs. *Unemployment and Overall Readjustment Problems of Returning Veterans: Hearings, Nov. 25 and Dec. 3, 1970.* Washington, D.C.: USGPO, 1971. This committee regularly publishes information, hearings, etc. on this topic.

977. United States. President's Committee on the Vietnam Veteran. *Report.* Washington, D.C.: Veterans Adminstration, 1970. Recommendations on access to educations, jobs and job training.

978. "Veterans: Economic and Social Costs on the Rise." *Congressional Quarterly Weekly Report* vol. 29 (9 Apr. 1971).

979. "Viet Vets Bring It All Back Home." *Old Mole* vol. 1, no. 46 (11 Sept. 1970).

980. "Why Vietnam Veterans Feel Like Fogotten Men." *U. S. News and World Report* vol. 70 (29 Mar. 1971).

981. See also ID4 "Veterans against the War."

6. The Volunteer Army

982. Alger, Maj. John (Ret.). "The Objective Was a Volunteer Army." *U. S. Naval Institute Proceedings* vol. 96 (Feb. 1970).

983. "Barracks Life Now a Little Brighter, to Attract Volunteers." See no. 238.

984. Bass, H. "Cost of Ending the Draft—A Preview." *WIN* vol. 5, no. 18 (15 Oct. 1969).

985. Brooks, Lt. Leon P. "Vital Interests and Volunteer Forces." *U. S. Naval Institute Proceedings* vol. 97 (Jan. 1971).

986. Brown, George E., Jr. "For an All-Volunteer Military." *War/Peace Report* vol. 9 (Apr. 1969). A congressman analyzes many sides of the picture.

987. "Congressional Battle: Draft or All Volunteer Army." *Congressional Quarterly Weekly Report* vol. 29 (2 Apr. 1971).

988. Davis, Vincent. "Universal Service: An Alternative to the All-Volunteer Armed Services." *Naval War College Review* vol. 23 (Oct. 1970).

989.   Ford, William F., and Tollison, Robert. "Notes on the Color of the Volunteer Army." *Social Science Quarterly* vol. 50 (Dec. 1969). Discusses claim that volunteer army would be mostly black.

990.   Friedman, Milton. "Why Not a Volunteer Army?" *New Industrialist Review* vol. 4, no. 9 (Spring 1967).

991.   Holbrook, Capt. James R. (USA). "Volunteer Army: Military Caste." See no. 163.

992.   Killebrew, Capt. Robert B. (USA). "Volunteer Army: How It Looks to a Company Commander." *Army* vol. 21 (Mar. 1971).

993.   Kim, K. H.; Farrell, Susan; and Clague, Ewan. *The All-Volunteer Army: An Analysis of Demand and Supply.* New York: Praeger, 1971. A technical economic analysis carried out for the army.

994.   Miller, James C., III, ed. *Why the Draft? The Case for a Volunteer Army.* See no. 364.

995.   Moore, John L. "Draft, Volunteer Army Proposals Head for Showdown in Congress." *National Journal* vol. 3 (6 and 13 Mar. 1971). Zero draft program.

996.   Nichols, Col. Robert L. et. al. "The Officer Corps in an All-Volunteer Force: Will College Men Serve?" *Naval War College Review* vol. 23 (Jan. 1971). A group research project.

997.   Oi, Walter T. "The Economic Cost of the Draft." *American Economic Review* vol. 57, nos. 48–49 (May 1967).

998.   "The Question of an All Volunteer Armed Force." *Congressional Digest* (May 1971). Views pro and con.

999.   Rhode, Alfred S.; Gelke, John J.; and Cooke, Francis X. *Impact of an All Volunteer Force on the Navy in the 1972–1973 Time Frame.* Washington, D.C.: Office of the Chief of Naval Operations, Analysis and Long Range Objectives Division (Staff Paper), Dec. 1970.

1000.   Sorensen, Maj. Neal G. (USAF). "Implications of a Volunteer Force." *Air University Review* vol. 22 (Mar.–Apr. 1971). Social implications adumbrated, appropriate adaptations of military to insure responsiveness to society are noted.

1001.   Stockstill, Louis R. "The All-Volunteer Force: Its Cloudy Pros and Cons." *Air Force and Space Digest* vol. 53 (June 1970). Brief analysis of Gates Commission report, barely deals with social effects of volunteer force.

1002.   United States. *Studies Prepared for the President's Commission on an All-Volunteer Armed Force.* 2 vols. Washington, D.C.: USGPO, 1970.

1003.   United States. President's Commission on an All-Volunteer

Armed Force. *Report.* Washington, D.C.: USGPO, 1970. "Gates Commission Report."

1004. Tobis, D. "Future Domination May Rely on Volunteer Army." *Guardian* vol. 22, no. 10 (6 Dec. 1969).

1005. Truscott, L. "The Troops Can't Dig It." *Village Voice* vol. 14, no. 59 (27 Nov. 1969).

1006. "Volunteer Army Gains Support but Passage Is Doubtful." *Congressional Quarterly Weekly Report* vol. 28 (3 Apr. 1970).

1007. "A Volunteer Army-Pro and Con." *Dissent* vol. 16 (Sept.-Oct. 1969). Articles by R. Hoffman, A. Lenchek and H. Rabasseire.

1008. See also IA5, "Military Life," and IA8, "The Selective Service System."

7. Other Special Problems and Issues

1009. "AFA's Industrial Associate Program." *Air Force Magazine* vol. 54 (Feb. 1971). About the Air Force Association.

1010. Fitch, Morgan L., Jr. "Objectives and Influence of the Navy League." *Naval War College Review* vol. 23 (Sept. 1970).

1011. Fox. H. "Group Getting Shafted, Then Drafted." *L.A. Free Press* vol. 7, no. 33 (14 Aug. 1970).

1012. Hardy, George D. "AFA's Mission: Power for Peace." *Air Force Magazine* vol. 54 (Feb. 1971). About the Air Force Association.

1013. Lien, Lt. Col. Maurice L. (USAF. Ret.). "The Independent Spokesman." *Airman* vol. 15 (Mar. 1971): 16–20. About the Air Force Association.

1014. McDonnell, James. "Education: AFA's Basic and Continuing Mission." *Air Force Magazine* vol. 54 (Feb. 1971). About the Air Force Association.

1015. "Military Morale in America." *Army Quarterly* vol. 101 (Oct. 1970).

1016. "Military Policies on Gays." *Advocate* vol. 4, no. 10 (8 July 1970).

1017. Moon, Col. Gordon A., II (Ret.). "A Matter of Integrity." *Army Digest* vol. 25 (June 1970).

1018. Rehn, Lt. Col. Thomas A. "Ethics and the Military Establishment." *Military Review* vol. 50 (Sept. 1970).

1019. Williams, Colin J., and Weinberg, Martin S. *Homosexuals and the Military: A Study of Less Than Honorable Discharge.* New York: Harper & Row, 1971. Kinsey researchers argue that military policy on homosexuals is "unwise, unjust and in essence unenforceable."

II. National Security and American Society

1020. Andreski, Stanislav. *Military Organization and Society*. See no. 1.

1021. Barber, Cmdr. James A., Jr. (USN). "War: Limitations and National Priorities." *Naval War College Review* vol. 23 (Jan. 1971).

1022. Barnet, Richard J. *The Economy of Death*. New York: Atheneum, 1969. Wide-ranging criticism of foreign and military policies. Clique of "National Security Managers" has set the country on a course which is dangerous and absurd.

1023. Boulding, Kenneth E. et al. *National Priorities: Military, Economic, and Social*. Washington, D.C.: Public Affairs Press, 1969. Compilation of statements made at the hearings of the Senate Subcommittee on Economy in Government of the Joint Economic Committee, chaired by Senator William Proxmire.

1024. Coats, Charles H., and Pellegrin, Roland. *Military Sociology*. See no. 2.

1025. Cook, Fred J. *The Warfare State*. New York: Macmillan, 1962. Historical development of the MIC, and its effects on all major social and economic groups and on foreign policy.

1026. Donovan, Col. James A. (USMC, Ret.). *Militarism, U.S.A.* See no. 3.

1027. Duscha, Julius. *Arms, Money and Politics*. New York: Ives Washburn, 1965. Journalistic account of backscratching, etc.

1028. Galbraith, John K. *How to Control the Military*. See no. 42.

1029. Giddings, Col. Ralph L., Jr. (USAF, Ret.). "Power, Strategy, and Will." *Air University Review* vol. 22 (Jan.-Feb. 1971). —And propaganda. National power depends on both material wealth and national creeds and values.

1030. Ginsburgh, Brig. Gen. Robert N. (USAF). "U. S. Goals, Priorities, and Means." *Air Force Policy Letter for Commanders* supplement no. 3 (Mar. 1971).

1031. Glick, Edward B. *Soldiers, Scholars, and Society: The Social Impact of the American Military*. Pacific Palisades, Calif.: Goodyear, 1971. Moderately promilitary analysis of racial integration, civic action, ROTC, civilian education, R & D, the draft, etc.

1032. Hanks, R. J. "Against All Enemies." See no. 5.

1033. Hays, Col. Samuel H. (USA, Ret.), and Rehm, Lt. Col. Thomas A. "The Military in a Free Society." *U.S. Naval Institute Proceedings* vol. 95 (Feb. 1969). The US' military constabulary role in maintaining world order may make it easier to acculturate youth in the military in the future.

1034. Howard, Michael, "Civil-Military Relations in Great Britain and the United States, 1945–1958." See no. 52.
1035. Huntington, Samuel P. *The Common Defense.* See no. 56.
1036. ———. *The Soldier and the State.* See no. 6.
1037. Lasswell, Harold D. *National Security and Individual Freedom.* New York: McGraw-Hill, 1950. How to achieve security without seriously impairing individual liberty.
1038. ———. "The Garrison State." *American Journal of Sociology* vol. 46, no. 4 (Jan. 1941). Seminal article on the militarized society. See his updating of the theory in Huntington, ed. *Changing Patterns of Military Politics.* See no. 1346.
1039. Lens, Sidney. *The Military Industrial Complex.* See no. 10.
1040. Mills, C. Wright. *The Power Elite.* See no. 210.
1041. *Report from Iron Mountain on the Possibility and Desirability of Peace.* New York: Dial Press, 1967. Satirical "official study" which argues war is economically and socially necessary to prevent national disintegration.
1042. Rodberg, Leonard S. and Shearer, Derek, eds. *The Pentagon Watchers.* See no. 13.
1043. Sargent, Clyde B. "National Cultural Characteristics and National Power." *Naval War College Review* vol. 23 (Jan. 1971).
1044. Shoup, Gen. David M. (USMC, Ret.). "The New American Militarism." See no. 14.
1045. Swomley, John M. *The Military Establishment.* See no. 88.
1046. van Doorn, Jacques, ed. *Armed Forces and Society: Sociological Essays.* See no. 17.
1047. Velvel, Lawrence R. *Undeclared War and Civil Disobedience; The American System in Crisis.* New York: Dunellen, 1970. Legal discussion.
1048. Weigley, Russell F., ed. *The American Military.* See no. 18.
1049. Yarmolinsky, Adam. *The Military Establishment.* See no. 19.

A. THE NATIONAL ECONOMY

1050. Adams, Walter. *The Brain Drain.* New York: Macmillan, 1968. Impact on the country of current priorities.
1051. ———, and Gray, Horace. *Monopoly in America: The Government as Promoter.* New York: Macmillan, 1955. Military spending is just a manifestation of the larger partnership between politics and economics.
1052. Abshire, David M., ed. *National Security: Political, Military & Economic Strategies in the Decade Ahead.* New York: Hoover Institute

on War, Revolution, and Peace, 1963. A large collection of writings showing the thinking of the mid-1960s.

1053. Barnet, Richard J. *The Economy of Death*, See no. 1022.

1054. Baran, Paul. *The Political Economy of Growth*. New York: Monthly Review Press, 1957.

1055. _____, and Sweezy, Paul. *Monopoly Capital: An Essay on the American Economic and Social Order*. New York: Monthly Review Press, 1966. A must for radical economics; includes analysis of imperialism and the MIC.

1056. Barber, Richard. *The American Corporation: Its Power, Its Money, Its Politics*. New York: Dutton, 1970. A good survey basis for understanding both American security needs and military procurement politics.

1057. Boulding, Kenneth E. *The Meaning of the 20th Century: The Great Transition*. New York: Harper & Row, 1964. The economics of security in historical perspective.

1058. Christoffel, Tom; Finkelhor, D; and Gilbarg, D. eds. *Up against the American Myth*. New York: Holt, Rinehart and Winston, 1971. Critiques of capitalism.

1059. Clark, John J. *The New Economics of National Defense*. New York: Random House, 1966. Microeconomics and national security politics.

1060. Galbraith, J. K. *The New Industrial State*. Boston: Houghton Mifflin, 1967. The last few chapters especially explore security and its economic implications.

1061. Hitch, Charles, and McKean, Roland. *The Economics of Defense in the Nuclear Age*. Cambridge, Mass.: Harvard University Press, 1969. Systems approach.

1062. Horowitz, David, ed. *Corporations and the Cold War*. New York: Monthly Review Press, 1970. Mixed collection—includes data on corporate ties of foreign policy establishment.

1063. Lieberson, Stanley. "Military-Industrial Linkages." *American Journal of Sociology* vol. 76, no. 4 (Jan. 1971). Explores several theories of defense spending and decision making, using quanitative data.

1064. McKean, Roland N., ed. *Issues in Defense Economics*. New York: National Bureau of Economic Research, 1967.

1065. Magdoff, Harry. *The Age of Imperialism: The Economics of U.S. Foreign Policy*. New York: Monthly Review Press, 1969. Brings variety of data to bear on his argument. Shows mechanisms of U. S. control of foreign economies.

1066. Mansfield, Edwin, ed. *Defense, Science, and Public Policy: An Introduction.* New York: Norton, 1968. A reader containing articles by several economists.

1067. Melman, Seymour. *Our Depleted Society.* New York: Dell, 1966. The impact of our military priority.

1068. ———. *Pentagon Capitalism: The Management of the New Imperialism.* New York: McGraw-Hill, 1970.

1069. ———. *The War Economy of the United States.* New York: St. Martin's Press, 1971.

1070. ———, ed. *The Defense Economy: Conversion of Industries and Occupations to Civilian Needs.* New York: Praeger, 1970. A text.

1071. ———, ed. *The War Economy of the United States: Readings in Military Industry and Economy.* New York: St. Martin's Press, 1971.

1072. Mollenhoff, Clark R. *The Pentagon: Politics, Profits and Plunder.* New York: Putnam, 1967. Critical investigative reporting—but recommended by *Armed Forces Journal!*

1073. Okun, Arthur. *The Political Economy of Prosperity.* Washington, D. C.: The Brookings Institution, 1970.

1074. Perlo, Victor. *Militarism and Industry.* New York: International Publishers, 1963. A Marxist view of military economics.

1075. Pilisuk, Marc, and Hayden, Thomas. "Is There a Military Industrial Complex Which Prevents Peace?: Consensus and Countervailing Power in Pluralistic Systems." *Journal of Social Issues* vol. 21, no. 3 (July 1965). Seminal theoretical and review article. Concludes the U.S. *is* a military-industrial complex.

1076. Schlesinger, James R. *The Political Economy of National Security: A Study of the Economic Aspects of the Contemporary Power Struggle.* New York: Praeger, 1960.

1077. URPE (Union for Radical Political Economics). Ad Hoc Committee on the Economy and the War. *The War and Its Impact on the Economy.* Special issue of *The Review of Radical Political Economics* (Aug. 1970). Political economic data and analysis of the war: an organizer's guide.

1. The Military Budget: Causes and Effects

1078. Ames, William. "Seattle Payroll Fattened by War." *Christian Science Monitor* (23 May 1969).

1079. Barnet, Richard. *The Economy of Death.* See no. 1022.

1080. Becker, Eugene M. "Economy vs. Defense." *Ordnance* vol. 55 (Mar.-Apr. 1971).

1081. Benoit, Emile. "The Monetary and Real Costs of National Defense." *American Economic Review* vol. 58 (May 1968). Budgetary expenditure is only part of the cost.

1082. Benson, Robert S. "How the Pentagon Can Save $9,000,000,-000." *Washington Monthly* vol. 1 (Mar. 1969).

1083. Bingham, Jonathan. "Can Military Spending Be Controlled?" *Foreign Affairs* vol. 48 (Oct. 1969). Political constraints.

1084. "Budget: A Calculated Risk." *Armed Forces Management* vol. 16 (Mar. 1970).

1085. Chapman, W. "Senate's Five Runaway Freshmen." *Progressive* vol. 33, no. 8 (Aug. 1969).

1086. Clayton, James L. "Defense Spending: Key to California's Growth." *Western Political Quarterly* vol. 15 (June 1962).

1087. _____, comp. *The Economic Impact of the Cold War: Sources and Readings.* New York: Harcourt Brace Jovanovich, Inc., 1970.

1088. Clotfelter, James. "The South and the Military Dollar." *New South* vol. 25 (Spring 1970). Impact of spending in the South.

1089. Congress of Peace through Law. Military Spending Committee. *The Economics of Defense: A Bipartisan Review of Military Spending.* New York: Praeger, 1971.

1090. Crecine, John P. *Defense Budgeting: Organizational Adaptation to External Constraints.* Santa Monica, Calif.: RAND, 1970. Budgetary process in DoD, 1952–1969.

1091. Davidson, C. "Doves Win in Senate." *Guardian* vol. 22, no. 39 (18 July 1970).

1092. Davis, Kenneth S., ed. *Arms, Industry and America.* New York: H. W. Wilson, 1971. Pro and con on the MIC.

1093. "Defense Spending: Military Critics Win Some Battles on Defense Costs." *Congressional Quarterly Weekly Report* vol. 27 (19 Dec. 1969).

1094. Duscha, Julius. *Arms, Money, and Politics.* New York: Ives, Washburn, Inc., 1965. Journalistic exposé of political-military-industrial linkages and waste.

1095. _____. "The Pentagon under Fire." *Progressive* vol. 33 (Sept. 1969).

1096. Galper, Harvey. "The Impacts of the Vietnam War on Defense Spending: A Simulation Approach." *Journal of Business* vol. 42 (Oct. 1969).

1097. Gordon, Bernard K. "The Military Budget: Congressional Phase." *Journal of Politics* vol. 23 (Aug. 1961). A case study.

1098. Halverson, Guy. "Air Power Propels Ft. Worth's Upward Economic Spiral." *Christian Science Monitor* (28 Mar. 1969).

1099. Heilbroner, Robert. "Military America." *New York Review of Books* vol. 15, no. 2 (23 July 1970).

1100. Hessman, James D. "Behind the Budget Decisions: Five Years of Constant Change." *Armed Forces Journal* vol. 108 (15 Feb. 1971).

1101. Hitch, Charles J. "The Military Budget and Its Impact in the Economy." In Thomas K. Hitch, ed. *Economics for the 1960s.* Honolulu: First National Bank of Hawaii, 1961.

1102. _____, and McKean, Roland N. *The Economics of Defense in the Nuclear Age.* Cambridge: Harvard University Press, 1960. Economic analysis of problems and choices of national defense.

1103. Hollenhorst, Jerry, and Ault, Gary. "An Alternative Answer to Who Pays for Defense?" *American Political Science Review* vol. 65, no. 3 (Sept. 1971). Reanalysis of Russett's data. See no. 1138.

1104. Isard, Walter, and Ganschow, James. *Awards of Prime Military Contracts by County, State and Metropolitan Area of the United States, Fiscal Year 1960.* Philadelphia: Regional Science Research Institute, 1962.

1105. _____, and Karaska, Gerald J. *Unclassified Defense and Space Contracts: Awards by County, State, and Metropolitan Area of the United States, Fiscal Year 1962.* Philadelphia: World Friends Research Center, 1964.

1106. _____. *Unclassified Defense Contracts: Awards by County, State, and Metropolitan Area of the United States, Fiscal Year 1964.* Philadelphia: World Friends Research Center, 1966.

1107. _____, and Schooler, Eugene. "An Economic Analysis of Local and Regional Impacts of Reduction of Military Expenditures." *Peace Research Society (International) Papers* vol. 1 (1964).

1108. Javits, Jacob; Hitch, Charles J.; and Burns, Arthur F., eds. *The Defense Sector and the American Economy.* New York: New York University Press, 1968. Defense employment; ABM; etc.

1109. Kaufman, Richard. "Billion Dollar Grab Bag." *The Nation* (17 Mar. 1969). Kaufman was on the staff of the Proxmire Subcommittee.

1110. _____. "The Usury of War." *The Nation* (26 Mar. 1969).

1111. Knoll, E. "Who Stole the Peace Dividend?" *Progressive* vol. 34, no. 5 (May 1970).

1112. Kolodziej, Edward A. *The Uncommon Defense and Congress, 1945–1963.* Columbus, O.: Ohio State University Press, 1966. Notes inadequacy of the Congress to control the defense establishment.

1113. *LeMonde.* "U. S. Can't Vietnamize the Dollar." *Guardian* vol. 22, no. 45 (5 Sept. 1970).

1114. Leontief, Wassily et al. "The Economic Impact—Industrial and

Regional—of an Arms Cut." In Leontief, ed. *Input-Output Economics.* New York: Oxford University Press, 1966.

1115. Lieberson, Stanley. "Military Industrial Linkages." See no. 1063.

1116. Magdoff, Harry. "Militarism and Imperialism." *Monthly Review* (Feb. 1970). Defense spending necessary for capitalist economy.

1117. May, Donald. "Pentagon, White House Wrestling to Control Defense Budget." *National Journal* vol. 2 (4 July 1970).

1118. Melman, Seymour. *Our Depleted Society.* See no. 1067.

1119. ———. *Pentagon Capitalism.* See no. 1068.

1120. "The Military-Industrial Complex: A Problem for the Secretary of Defense." *Congressional Quarterly Weekly Report* Special report (24 May 1968). Defense spending by district, key committees, etc.

1121. "The Military Lobby—Its Impact." *Congressional Quarterly Weekly Report* (24 Mar. 1961).

1122. "Military Spending: Another Heated Debate in Congress." *Congressional Quarterly Weekly Report* vol. 28 (4 Dec. 1970).

1123. Mollenhoff, Clark. *The Pentagon.* See no. 1072.

1124. Moore, John L. et al. "Inflation, Pressure for Weapons, Promise Rise in Pentagon's Fiscal 1972 Budget." *National Journal* vol. 3 (23 Jan. 1971).

1125. Moorer, Adm. Thomas H. (USN). "Budget and National Security." *Review* vol. 50 (Jan.-Feb. 1971).

1126. Moot, Robert C. "The Defense Budget." *Defense Management Journal* vol. 6 (spring 1970).

1127. National Industrial Conference Board. *The Federal Budget: Its Impact on the Economy.* New York: annual.

1128. "Nixon's Sorry Speech." *People's World* vol. 33, no. 5 (31 Jan. 1970). War costs.

1129. Novick, David, ed. *Program Budgeting: Program Analysis and the Federal Budget.* 2d ed. Cambridge, Mass.: Harvard University Press, 1967. DoD Planning, Programming, and Budgeting.

1130. Nutter, G. Warren. "Defense and the Economy." *Air Force Policy Letter for Commanders* supplement no. 2 (Feb. 1971).

1131. Oliver, Richard P. "The Employment Effect of Defense Expenditures." *Monthly Labor Review* (Sept. 1967).

1132. "The Peace Bonanza That Went Bust." *Business Week* (5 Sept. 1970).

1133. Proxmire, Senator William. *Report from the Wasteland: America's Military Industrial Complex.* New York: Praeger, 1970. Inefficiency, cost-overruns, backscratching, etc. Especially good on congressional role.

1134. ———. "The Military—Who Controls It?" *Carillion* vol. 3, no. 1 (Sept. 1969).

1135. "Proxmire and Goldwater on Priorities." *People's World* vol. 33, no. 6 (7 Feb. 1970).

1136. RAND Corporation. *Competition & Complementarity between Defense and Development—A Preliminary Approach.* Santa Monica, Calif.: RAND, 1969.

1137. Roberts, D. "Why Senate Can't Curb Nixon." *The Militant* vol. 34, no. 26 (3 July 1970).

1138. Russett, Bruce M. *What Price Vigilance? The Burdens of National Defense.* New Haven, Conn.: Yale University Press, 1970. Opportunity costs (education, welfare, etc.), political system costs of defense spending; arms races, alliances, senate roll calls and state defense spending.

1139. ———. "The Price of War." *Trans-action* (Oct. 1969).

1140. ———. "Some Decisions in the Regression Analysis of Time-Series Data." In James Herndon and Joseph Bernd, eds., *Mathematical Applications in Political Science,* vol. 5. Charlottesville, Va.: University of Virginia Press, 1971. Further analysis of data on opportunity costs of military spending.

1141. Schilling, Warner R.; Hammond, Paul Y; and Snyder, Glenn H. *Strategy, Politics, and Defense Budgets.* See no. 81.

1142. Schultze, Charles L. "Reexamining the Military Budget." *The Public Interest* (Winter 1970).

1143. Simmons, Erwin H. "Planners, Programmers and Budgeteers: A Critical Review of the Planning, Programming, and Budgeting System as Practiced by the Department of Defense." *Federal Accountant* vol. 18 (Sept. 1969).

1144. Smith, Senator Margaret Chase. "Defense Spending: Changing Attitudes." *Defense Management Journal* vol. 6 (Winter 1970).

1145. "Status of Funds." *Defense Industry Bulletin* vol. 6 (Feb., May, July, Dec. 1970). Quarterly report of DoD military functions and Military Assistance Program funds' status.

1146. Stone, I. F. *I. F. Stone's Weekly* (and, more recently, *Bi-Weekly*) regularly published pieces on the defense budget. The newsletter has now been discontinued, but Mr. Stone writes often in the *New York Review of Books.*

1147. ———. "Hoax That Cost a Trillion Dollars." *I. F. Stone's Bi-Weekly* vol. 17, no. 15 (28 July 1969).

1148. ———. "Nixon's Blackout on Military Spending." *I. F. Stone's Bi-Weekly* vol. 18, no. 5 (9 Mar. 1970).

1149. _____. "Nixon's Iron Curtain on War Cost." *I. F. Stone's Bi-Weekly* vol. 18, no. 4 (23 Feb. 1970).

1150. _____. "Peace Dividend." *I. F. Stone's Bi-Weekly* vol. 18, no. 6 (23 Mar. 1970).

1151. Stromberg, John L. *The Internal Mechanisms of the Defense Budget Process—Fiscal 1953–1968.* Santa Monica, Calif.: RAND, 1970.

1152. "That Time of Year Again." *Progressive* vol. 34, no. 6 (June 1970). Budget.

1153. United States. Congress. Joint Economic Committee. Subcommittee on Economy in Government. *The Military Budget and National Economic Priorities: Hearings.* Washington, D. C.: USGPO, 1969. See also the committee's *Report.*

1154. _____. *Economic Effects of Vietnam Spending.* Washington, D. C.: USGPO, 1967.

1155. URPE (Union for Radical Political Economics). *The War and Its Impact on the Economy.* See no. 1077. URPE's *Review* often carries articles on government spending. See no. 1262.

1156. Webb, L. "New Defense Budget for War Economy." *Guardian* vol. 22, no. 24 (14 Mar. 1970).

1157. Weidenbaum, Murray. "Adjusting to a Defense Cutback: Public Policy Toward Business." *Quarterly Review of Economics and Business* (Spring 1964).

1158. _____. "Defense Expenditures and the Domestic Economy." In Enke, *Defense Management.* See no. 36.

1159. Winchester, Edward E. "Economic Analysis—Ordering Spending Priorities." *Defense Industry Bulletin* vol. 6 (May 1970).

2. Procurement, Military Contractors, the Military-Industrial Complex (MIC)

1160. Adams, P. "The Defense Firms vs. the Engineers." *Probe* vol. 2, no. 8 (Nov. 1969).

1161. Adams, Walter. "The Military-Industrial Complex and the New Industrial State." *American Economic Review, Papers and Proceedings* vol. 58, no. 2 (May 1968). Describes some of the government's deliberate "giveaway" policies for business.

1162. _____, and Gray, Horace M. *Monopoly in America: The Government as Promoter.* See no. 1051.

1163. Arkhangelsky, N. "Sword and Dollar Alliance." *Soviet Military Review* no. 10 (Oct. 1970). Soviet perspective.

1164. Baldwin, William L. *The Structure of the Defense Market, 1955–1964.* Durham, N. C.: Duke University Press, 1967. Formal economic analysis.

1165. Barnet, Richard. *The Economy of Death.* See no. 1022.

1166. Baumgartner, John Stanley. *The Lonely Warriors.* Los Angeles: Nash Publishing, 1970. Defense of the MIC.

1167. Bingham, Jonathan. "Can Military Spending Be Controlled?" See no. 1083.

1168. "Boeing Boeing." *Williamette Bridge* vol. 3, no. 16 (23 Apr. 1970).

1169. Bosch, Juan. *Pentagonism, A Substitute for Imperialism.* Translated by Helen R. Lane. New York: Grove Press, 1968. A broad critique of the military-industrial-political-economic-academic-labor complex: claims U. S. needs foreign adventures to bolster domestic economy, and that American people support these adventures. Bosch is former President of the Dominican Republic.

1170. Boulding, Kenneth, ed. *Peace and the War Industry. Trans-action* (1970). Essays and articles from *Trans-action.*

1171. Burnham, Frank. "The Pentagon and Industry: Antagonism Replacing Trust." *Armed Forces Management* vol. 16 (Jan. 1970).

1172. Campbell, Lt. Gen. Levin H. *The Industry-Ordnance Team.* New York: McGraw-Hill, 1946. Interesting early account of military-industry symbiosis.

1173. Carey, Omer L., ed. *The Military-Industrial Complex and U. S. Foreign Policy.* Pullman, Wash.: Washington State University Press, 1969. Articles by Huntington, Lapp, Adams, Weidenbaum, and P. M. Morgan. Some are reprints.

1174. Coburn, J. "Pyrrhic Victory for the Military." *Village Voice* vol. 14, no. 54 (23 Oct. 1969). Aerospace Industries.

1175. Cochran, Bert. *The War System.* New York: Macmillan, 1965.

1176. Coffin, Tristram. *The Passion of the Hawks.* New York: Macmillan, 1964. Typical MIC critique. Originally published as *The Armed Society: Militarism in Modern America.*

1177. Cole, Edward N. "Efficiency in Defense." *Ordnance* vol. 55 (July-Aug. 1970).

1178. Colwell, V. Adm. J. B. "What Military Industrial Complex?" *Ordnance* (July-Aug. 1969).

1179. *Congressional Quarterly.* "The Military-Industrial Complex: A Problem for the Secretary of Defense." See no. 1120.

1180. _____. "The Military Lobby—Its Impact." See no. 1121.

1181. "Contractors Officers Favor GOP in Contributions." *Congressional Quarterly Weekly Report* vol. 28 (18 Sept. 1970). Campaign contributions of executives of top 25 defense contractors.

1182. Cook, Fred J. "Juggernaut: The Warfare State." *The Nation* (28 Oct. 1961). One of the earliest MIC critiques. Puts much of the blame on the military.

1183. ———. *The Warfare State.* See no. 1025.

1184. Danhof, Clarence H. *Government Contracting and Technological Change.* Washington, D. C.: The Brookings Institution, 1968.

1185. Davis, Kenneth S., ed. *Arms, Industry, and America.* See no. 1092.

1186. "Defense Procurement: Contracts of $1,000,000 and Over." *Defense Industry Bulletin.* Regular feature.

1187. Domhoff, G. William. *Who Rules America?* Englewood Cliffs, N. J.: Prentice-Hall, 1967. Includes discussion of the MIC in broader perspective.

1188. Donovan, Col. James A. (USMC, Ret.). *Militarism, U.S.A.* See no. 3.

1189. Duscha, Julius. *Arms, Money, and Politics.* See no. 1094.

1190. Engelbrecht, H. C. and Hanighen, F. C. *Merchants of Death: A Study of the International Armament Industry.* New York: Dodd, Mead, 1934. Ours is not the first MIC.

1191. "Facts for Critics of the 'Military-Industrial Complex': Defense Contract Profits 25% Below Commercial Business." *Armed Forces Journal* vol. 107 (18 Apr. 1970). Controversial study.

1192. Finan, William F. "Defense Industry Profits?" *Ordnance* vol. 55 (Sept.-Oct. 1970).

1193. Fitzgerald, A. Ernest. "Gilbert Fitzhugh's Golden Fleece." *Washington Monthly* vol. 2 (Nov. 1970). The government procurement study is a whitewash.

1194. "Fitzhugh (Blue Ribbon Defense) Panel Recommends Competitive Prototypes, Sweeping Organizational Changes." See no. 38.

1195. Galbraith, John K. *How to Control the Military.* See no. 42.

1196. Gallagher, T. "Cancer as Highest Stage of Imperialism." See no. 431.

1197. Goulden and Singer. "Dial-A-Bomb—AT&T and the ABM," *Ramparts* vol. 8, no. 5 (Nov. 1969).

1198. Harr, Karl G., Jr. "The Arsenals of Peace." *Air Force and Space Digest* vol. 53 (Sept. 1970). Lauds technological progress of aerospace industry.

1199. "Has America Become a Militarized Society." *Center Magazine* vol. 3, no. 1 (Jan. 1970). See also other articles in same issue.

1200. Heilbroner, Robert. "Military America." *New York Review of Books* vol. 15, no. 2 (23 July 1970).

1201. Hitch, Charles J. "The Defense Sector: Its Impact on American Business." In Jacob K. Javits et al. *The Defense Sector and the American Economy.* See no. 1108.

1202. Horowitz, David, ed. *Corporations and the Cold War.* See no. 1062.

1203. "The Industrial College and the AOA Are Partners in Preparedness." See no. 113.
1204. Isard, Walter, et al. Defense Contracts by Region. See nos. 1104–1106.
1205. Javits, Jacob; Hitch, Charles J.; and Burns, Arthur F. eds. *The Defense Sector and the American Economy.* See no. 1108.
1206. Kaufman, Richard. "As Eisenhower Was Saying, . . ." *New York Times Magazine* (22 June 1969). "Unwarranted influence."
1207. ———. "Billion Dollar Grab Bag." See no. 1109.
1208. ———. "The Usury of War." See no. 1110.
1209. ———. *The War Profiteers.* Indianapolis, Ind.: Bobbs-Merrill, 1970. Waste and aggrandizement.
1210. "Knowledge for Defense." See no. 120.
1211. Lapp, Ralph E. *Arms Beyond Doubt.* See no. 397.
1212. ———. *The Weapons Culture.* See no. 400.
1213. Lasley, John W. *The War System and You.* Chapel Hill, N. C.: Institute for International Studies, 1965. Pacifist view of the MIC.
1214. Lens, Sidney. *The Military Industrial Complex.* See no. 10.
1215. Lieberson, Stanley. "Military-Industrial Linkages." See no. 1063.
1216. Lyle, Adm. J. M. (USN, Ret.). "If We Didn't Have a Military-Industrial Complex, We Would Have to Invent One." *National Security Industrial Association Newsletter* (June, 1969).
1217. McGaffin, W. "Making It in Marietta." *Progressive* vol. 33, no. 11 (Nov. 1969).
1218. Madsen, Maj. Gen. Frank M., Jr. "The Social Implications of Military Education and Training." See no. 123.
1219. Magdoff, Harry. "Militarism and Imperialism." See no. 1116.
1220. Mann, Forbes. "Military-Industrial Strength: Vital to National Defense." *Army* vol. 20 (Nov. 1970).
1221. Melman, Seymour. *Pentagon Capitalism.* See no. 1068.
1222. ———. *The War Economy of the United States.* See No. 1069.
1223. Mills, C. Wright. *The Power Elite.* See no. 210.
1224. Mollenhoff, Clark. *The Pentagon.* See no. 1072.
1225. Nossiter, Bernard. "Arms Firms See Postwar Spurt." *Washington Post* (8 Dec. 1968).
1226. ———. "Defense Firms Leery of Civilian Work." *Washington Post* (9 Dec 1968). Highly interesting interviews with defense firm executives.
1227. ———. *The Mythmakers.* Boston: Beacon Press, 1964. Investigative journalism on the armsmakers.

1228. "Overseas Expansion and Government Contracting: The Story of Kaiser's Global Empire." *NACLA Newsletter* vol. 2, no. 2 (Apr. 1968).

1229. Pace, Dean F. *Negotiation and Management of Defense Contracts.* New York: Wiley-Interscience, 1970.

1230. Peck, Merton J., and Scherer, Frederic M. *The Weapons Acquisition Process: An Economic Analysis.* Boston: Harvard University School of Business Administration, 1962. The most thorough research on the economics of procurement. A second volume, *The Weapons Acquisition Process: Economic Incentives,* was written by Sherer alone.

1231. "Pentagon Socialism." *Progressive* vol. 34, no. 5 (May 1970).

1232. Perlo, Victor. *Militarism and Industry: Arms Profiteering in the Missile Age.* New York: International Publishers, 1963. Importance of weapons to the economy is examined.

1233. Pilisuk, Marc, and Hayden, Thomas. "Is There a Military Industrial Complex which Prevents Peace?" See no. 1075. Seminal; argues that U. S. *society* is a military-industrial complex.

1234. Powell, Craig. "A Troubled Industry Views Buying Defense for the 70s." *Armed Forces Management* vol. 16 (Jan. 1970).

1235. Prokosch, E. "Military-Industrial Reading List." *WIN* vol. 5, no. 5 (1 Sept. 1969).

1236. Proxmire, Senator William. *Report from the Wasteland: America's Military Industrial Complex.* See no. 1133.

1237. Rankin, A. "War-Related Research." *L.A. Free Press* vol. 7, no. 21 (22 May 1970).

1238. Raymond, Jack. "The Growing Threat of Our Military-Industrial Complex." *Harvard Business Review* vol. 46, no. 3 (May-June 1968).

1239. Reich, Michael, and Finkelhor, David. "Capitalism and the 'Military-Industrial Complex': The Obstacles to Conversion." *Review of Radical Political Economics* vol. 2, no. 4 (fall 1970). Capitalist economics requires government spending; capitalist ideology requires military spending.

1240. *Report from Iron Mountain.* See no. 1041.

1241. *San Francisco Bay Guardian* vol. 4, no. 4 (11 June 1970). Numerous articles on bay area defense contractors.

1242. Sarkesian, Sam C., ed. *The Military-Industrial Complex: A Reassessment.* Beverly Hills: Sage, 1972.

1243. Schemmer, Benjamin F. et al. "Where the Defense Industry Is Headed." pt. 1. "What Did the Assault on the 'MIC' really cost?" *Armed Forces Journal* vol. 108 (1 Mar. 1971).

1244. Schiller, Herbert I., and Phillips, Joseph D., eds. *Superstate: Readings in the Military Industrial Complex.* Urbana, Ill.: University of Illinois Press, 1970. Comprehensive. Thirty-one contributors (mostly national political figures) including pro-MIC views. Selections largely abstracted from congressional testimony.

1245. Shloss, Leon. "Government Procurement under the Microscope." *Government Executive* vol. 3 (Mar. 1971). Work of the Commission on Government Procurement explained.

1246. Schmalz, Anton B. *Insights into the Changing Government Marketplace.* North American Rockwell: Canoga Park, Calif., n.d. Procurement process.

1247. Shoup, David. "The New American Militarism." See no. 14.

1248. Sims, David E. "Spoon-Feeding the Military—How New Weapons Come to Be." In Rodberg and Shearer. *The Pentagon Watchers.* See no. 13.

1249. Soper, W. "ABM Risks Atom War to Aid the Rich." *Old Mole* vol. 1, no. 20 (28 Aug. 1969).

1250. Stackhouse, Max L. *The Ethics of Necropolis: An Essay on the Military-Industrial Complex and the Quest for a Just Peace.* Boston: Beacon Press, 1971.

1251. Staley, Eugene. *War and the Private Investor.* Garden City, N. Y.: Doubleday, 1935. To put the problem in historical perspective.

1252. Stone, I. F. "Scandalous Costs of C–5A." *I. F. Stone's Bi-Weekly* vol. 17, no. 17 (28 July 1969).

1253. Swomley, John. *The Military Establishment.* See no. 88.

1254. Tansik, David A., and Wasko, Frank J. "Dimensions of the Military-Industrial Complex." *Arizona Review* vol. 20 (June 1971).

1255. "Top Fifty War Profiteers." *Guardian* vol. 22, no. 16 (17 Jan. 1970).

1256. Tyrrell, C. Merton. *Pentagon Partners, The New Nobility.* See no. 91.

1257. United States. Congress. House. Committee on Banking and Currency. *Hearings on HR 15683, To Renew the Defense Production Act of 1950, As Amended.* April 1968. See especially the testimony of Adm. Hyman Rickover.

1258. United States. Congress. Joint Economic Committee. Subcommittee on Economy in Government. 91st Congress, 1st session. *Acquisition of Weapons Systems, Hearings.* Washington, D.C.: USGPO, pt. 1, 29–31 Dec. 1969 (1970); pt. 2, 20–23 May 1970 (1970). See also the committee's *Report: Economics of Military Procurement* (May 1969).

1259. United States. Congress. Senate. Committee on the Judiciary.

Subcommittee on Antitrust and Monopoly. *Hearings: Competition in Defense Procurement.* Washington, D.C.: USGPO, 1968.

1260. United States Department of Commerce. Bureau of the Census. *Current Industry Reports: Shipments of Defense-Oriented Industries.* Washington, D.C.: USGPO, various years.

1261. U. S. Department of Defense. *100 Companies and Their Subsidiaries Listed According to Net Value of Military Prime Contract Awards.* Published annually by the Directorate for Statistical Services of the Office of the Secretary of Defense and Printed in *Defense Industry Bulletin.* Also available from the Office of the Assistant Secretary of Defense for Public Affairs, Washington, D.C.

1262. URPE (Union for Radical Political Economics) Ad Hoc Committee on the Economy and the War. "Political Power and Military Spending." In URPE. *The War and Its Impact on the Economy.* See no. 1077. Very concise discussion of the MIC.

1263. Wald, George. "Corporate Responsibility—War Crimes." *New York Review of Books* vol. 15, no. 1 (2 July 1970).

1264. Wallace, Henry J. "Industrial Mobilization." *Ordnance* vol. 55 (Sept.-Oct. 1970).

1265. Weidenbaum, Murray. "Adjusting to the Defense Cutback." See no. 1157.

1266. ———. "Arms and the American Economy: A Domestic Convergence Hypothesis." *American Economic Review, Papers and Proceedings* vol. 58, no. 2 (May 1968). Pentagon exercises such control over operation of defense industries that they no longer function like private enterprises.

1267. ———. "Concentration and Competition in the Military Market." *Quarterly Review of Economics and Business* vol. 8 (Spring 1968).

1268. ———. *The Military Market in the United States.* Chicago: American Marketing Association, 1963.

1269. Weissman, S. Review of Galbraith's *How to Control the Military* in *Ramparts* vol. 8, no. 6 (Dec. 1969).

1270. Wilson, George C. "Proxmire and the Pentagon." *Armed Forces Management* vol. 16 (Feb. 1970).

1271. "World's Most Experienced Peacemaker." *WIN* vol. 6, no. 7 (15 Apr. 1970).

1272. Yale, Col. Wesley W. (USA, Ret.). "The Military Industrial Complex." *Military Review* vol. 50. (Sept. 1970).

1273. See also IB, "Weapons," IIB2, "Congress" and IIC, "The Scientific and Intellectual Community."

3. The Economics of Disarmament and Conversion

1274. Baldwin, William L. *The Structure of the Defense Market, 1955–1964.* See no. 1164.

1275. Benoit, Emile, ed. *Disarmament and World Economic Interdependence.* Oslo: Universitetsforlaget, 1967.

1276. _____, and Boulding, Kenneth. eds. *Disarmament and the Economy.* New York: Harper & Row, 1963.

1277. Berkowitz, Marvin. *The Conversion of Military-Oriented Research and Development to Civilian Uses.* New York: Praeger, 1970. One of a series.

1278. Bolton, Roger E., ed. *Defense and Disarmament: The Economics of Transition.* Englewood Cliffs, N. J.: Prentice-Hall, 1966.

1279. _____. *Defense Purchases and Regional Growth.* Washington, D.C.: The Brookings Institution, 1966.

1280. Cox, Donald W. *The Perils of Peace: Conversion to What?* Philadelphia: Chilton Books, 1965. Critical.

1281. Daicoff, Darwin W. et al. *Economic Impact of Military Base Closings.* 2 vols. Lawrence, Kan.: University of Kansas, 1970. A government research document which deals in detail with particular communities and cities near closed bases.

1282. Gilmore, John S.; Ryan, John J.; and Gould, William S. *Defense Systems Resources in the Civil Sector: An Evolving Approach, An Uncertain Market.* Washington, D. C.: USACDA, 1967.

1283. Clark, John J. *The New Economics of National Defense.* New York: Random House, 1966.

1284. Copps, John A., ed. *The Cost of Conflict.* Ann Arbor, Mich.: University of Michigan (Bureau of Business Research), 1969.

1285. Falk, Richard A., and Mendlovitz, Saul H. eds. *The Strategy of World Order.* 4 vols. New York: World Law Fund, 1966. Volume 4 is entitled *Disarmament and Economic Development.*

1286. Isard, Walter, and Schooler, Eugene. "An Economic Analysis of Local and Regional Impacts of Reduction of Military Expenditures." See no. 1107.

1287. Leontief, Wassily et al. "The Economic Impact—Industrial and Regional—Of an Arms Cut." See no. 1114.

1288. Melman, Seymour, ed. *The Defense Economy.* See no. 1070.

1289. National Planning Association. *Community Information System: A Method for Evaluation of Community Dislocation Sensitivity and Adjustment Potential.* (10 vols.) Washington, D.C.: USACDA, 1967. Volumes 2–10 are each devoted to a particular city.

1290. Reich, Michael, and Finkelhor, David. "Capitalism and the 'Military-Industrial Complex': The Obstacles to 'Conversion'." See no. 1239.

1291. *Report From Iron Mountain.* See no. 1041.

1292. Ullman, John E., ed. *Conversion Prospects of the Defense Electronics Industry.* Hempstead, N. Y.: Hofstra, 1965.

1293. U. S. Arms Control and Disarmament Agency. *Economic Impacts of Disarmament.* Washington, D.C.: USACDA, 1965.

1294. U. S. Committee on the Economic Impact of Defense and Disarmament. *Report.* Washington, D.C.: USGPO, 1965.

1295. United States. Congress. Senate. Committee on Foreign Relations. Subcommittee on Disarmament. "The Economic Impact of Arms Control Agreements." *Congressional Record* (5 Oct. 1962): pp. 2139–2194.

1296. Weidenbaum, Murray. "Adjusting to a Defense Cutback." See no. 1157.

4. Other Economic Effects

1297. Bloice and Stevens. "The Postman's Revolt—Nixon's Army." *Peoples World* vol. 33, no. 13 (28 Mar. 1970).

1298. Cabbell, P. "Pan Am Helps Win War." *L.A. Free Press* vol. 6, no. 78 (14 Nov. 1969). Defense contracting by commercial airliners.

1299. *Channelling,* an official publication of the Selective Service System. Original version reprinted in Reeves and Hess, *The End of the Draft.* See no. 366. Use of the draft to control the occupations and activities of all American males.

1300. "Channelling, 1969—The Draft as a Weapon." *Plain Rapper* vol. 2, no. 7 (Nov. 1969). Channelling is the process of influencing *all* registrants in their career choices and activities through the draft and deferrment system.

1301. Doyle, T. "Rapping with Reservists." *The Bond* vol. 4, no. 4 (22 Apr. 1970). About postal strike.

1302. "GI Slaves Used as Strikebreakers." *The Ally* no. 25 (Apr. 1970). Postal strike.

1303. "Government Buys Grapes, Hurts Strikers." *Peacemaker* vol. 22, no. 11 (9 Aug. 1969).

1304. Janowitz, Morris. "American Democracy and Military Service." *Trans-action* vol. 4, no. 4 (1967). Manpower procurement policies.

1305. Meisler, Stanley. "Meddling in Latin America: The Dubious Role of the AFL-CIO." *The Nation* (10 Feb. 1964).

1306. "Pax Americana and the U. S. Balance of Payments." *New England Economic Review* (Jan.-Feb. 1969).

1307. Radosh, Ronald. *American Labor and United States Foreign Policy.* New York: Random House, 1970. Takes us back to Gompers vs. the Kaiser.

1308. Schultze, Charles L. "Budget Alternatives after Vietnam." In Kermit Gordon, ed. *Agenda for the Nation.* Washington D.C.: The Brookings Institution, 1968.

1309. "Standing Army of Scabs." *Helix* vol. 11, no. 13 (26 Mar. 1970). Postal strike breakers.

1310. Thayer, George. *The War Business.* New York: Simon & Schuster, 1969. International arms trade.

1311. Weixel, G. "ASU Fights Back—For Postal Strike." *The Bond* vol. 4, no. 4 (22 Apr. 1970).

1312. Wheaton, D. "No Troops vs. Workers on Strike." *The Bond* vol. 4, no. 4 (22 Apr. 1970).

1313. "When the Guard Carried the Mail." *National Guardsman* vol. 24 (May 1970).

1314. Wool, Harold. *The Military Specialist: Skilled Manpower for the Armed Forces.* Baltimore: Johns Hopkins Press, 1968.

B. POLITICAL INSTITUTIONS
1. General: Presidency, Bureaucracy, Parties, Localities

1315. Abt, John J. *Who Has the Right to Make War? The Constitutional Crisis.* New York: International Publishers, 1970.

1316. Allison, Graham T. *Essence of Decision: Explaining the Cuban Missile Crisis.* Boston: Little, Brown, 1971. Three systematic analytical frameworks for evaluation of foreign and military decision. Provocative.

1317. Armacost, Michael H. *The Politics of Weapons Innovation: The Thor-Jupiter Controversy.* New York: Columbia University Press: 1969.

1318. Art, Robert J. *The TFX Decision.* See no. 20.

1319. Barnet, Richard. "How Hanoi Sees Nixon." *New York Review of Books* vol. 14, no. 2 (29 Jan. 1970).

1320. Barrett, Raymond J. "Partners in Policy Making." *Military Review* vol. 45 (Oct. 1965).

1321. _____. "Politico-Military Expertise." *Military Review* vol. 46 (Nov. 1966).

1322. Bowman, Capt. J. C. "The Post and the Community." *Military Review* vol. 35, no. 3 (June 1955).

1323. Caraley, Demetrios. *The Politics of Military Unification.* See no. 30.

1324. Clark, Keith C., and Legere, Laurence J., eds. *The President and the Management of National Security; a report by the Institute for Defense Analysis.* New York: Praeger, 1969. Good introductory text on the functioning of the national foreign policy making machinery.

1325. "Confidential Memorandum to Rand." *Seed* vol. 5, no. 9 (n.d.).

1326. de Rivera, Joseph H. *The Psychological Dimension of Foreign Policy.* (James N. Rosenau, Consultant). Columbus, O.: Charles E. Merrill, 1968. Comprehensive; applies contemporary psychology to the behavior of foreign and military policy-makers. Useful as a text.

1327. Dower, J. "Asia and the Nixon Doctrine." *Bulletin of Concerned Asian Scholars* vol. 2, no. 4 (1970).

1328. Edinger, Lewis J. "Military Leaders and Foreign Policy-Making." *American Political Science Review* vol. 57, no. 2 (June 1963).

1329. Enthoven, Alain C., and Smith, K. Wayne. *How Much Is Enough?* See no. 4.

1330. Falk, Richard A.; Kolko, Gabriel; and Lifton, Robert J. *Crimes of War.* See no. 881.

1331. Fitch, B. "Nixon—With a Little Help from His Friends." *Ramparts* vol. 8, no. 9 (Mar. 1970).

1332. Fox, William T. R. "Representativeness and Efficiency: Dual Problems of Civil-Military Relations." See no. 40.

1333. Garvey, Capt. Gerald. "The Changing Management Role of the Military Departments Reconsidered." See no. 44.

1334. Halperin, Morton H. "The President and the Military." *Foreign Affairs* vol. 50, no. 2 (Jan. 1972).

1335. Hansen, J. "Nixon's Vietnam Gamble." *Militant* vol. 34, no. 20 (22 May 1970).

1336. Hoopes, Townsend. *The Limits of Intervention.* See no. 51.

1337. Huntington, Samuel. *The Common Defense.* See no. 56.

1338. _____. "Interservice Competition and the Political Roles of the Armed Services." See no. 57.

1339. _____. "The Defense Establishment: Vested Interests and the Public Interest." In Omer Carey, ed. *The Military-Industrial Complex and U.S. Foreign Policy.* See no. 1173. The military's new role as a "vested interest" will bring a new outlook and new strategies. Thought-provoking piece.

1340. Janis, Irving. "Groupthink." *Psychology Today* (Nov. 1971). Political decision making.

1341. Kempton, Murray. "From the City of Lies." *New York Review of Books* vol. 14, no. 11 (4 June 1970).

1342. Kissinger, Henry A., ed. *Problems of National Strategy; A Book of Readings.* New York: Praeger, 1965.

1343. Knebel, Fletcher, and Bailey, Charles W., II. *Seven Days in May.* See no. 201.

1344. Kolko, Gabriel. *The Roots of American Foreign Policy.* Boston: Beacon, 1969. Not military, but pervasive "business" ideology and personnel control foreign policy.

1345. Kurth, Ronald J. "The Military and Power in the U.S." See no. 62.

1346. Lasswell, Harold D. "The Garrison State Hypothesis Today." In Samuel P. Huntington, ed. *Changing Patterns of Military Politics.* Glencoe, Ill.: Free Press, 1962. Finds ambivalent trends in the U.S. regarding "the domination of the specialists on violence" (both police and military).

1347. Lerche, Charles O. "The Professional Officer and Foreign Policy." *U.S. Naval Institute Proceedings* vol. 90, no. 7 (July 1964).

1348. Lyons, Gene M. "The New Civil-Military Relations." See no. 64.

1349. ———. "The Pressures of Military Necessity," In Gene M. Lyons, ed. *America: Purpose and Power.* Chicago: Quadrangle, 1965. New technology has affected traditional civil-military relations.

1350. Mansfield, Harvey C. "Civil-Military Relations in the United States." See no. 67.

1351. Maxey, D. R. "The Decision to Invade Cambodia." *Look Magazine* (11 Aug. 1970). Hour by hour run-down of whom Nixon saw.

1352. May, Ernest R. *The Ultimate Decision: The President as Commander-in-Chief.* New York: Braziller, 1960.

1353. Mollenhoff, Clark R. *The Pentagon.* See no. 1072.

1354. Nixon, Richard. "Duties of the Commander-in-Chief." *Weekly Compilation of Presidential Documents* vol. 6 (8 June 70). Letter to Senator Hugh Scott on Byrd amendment to Cooper-Church amendment.

1355. "Nixon and the War Crisis." *International Socialist Review* vol. 31, no. 4 (June 1970).

1356. Paige, Glenn D. *The Korean Decision, June 24–30, 1950.* New York: The Free Press, 1968. An excellent detailed narrative of the key U.S. decisions following the Korean invasion. Also an attempt to analyze these decisions systematically.

1357. Peck, J. "Write Nixon—Reply from the Pentagon." *WIN* vol. 5, no. 13 (July 1969).

1358. Peters, Charles, and Adams, Timothy J., eds. *Inside the System.* New York: Praeger, 1970. Journalistic, but presents some useful insights into internal functioning of U.S. government. Not cohesive.

1359. *The Politics of Military Policy: Seminars on the Politics of Policy-Making.* Los Angeles: UCLA Security Studies Project, 1965.

1360.   Powell, Craig. "Arms Sales Is More Than Just a Military Question." *Armed Forces Management* vol. 14 (Jan. 1968). DoD presents its case to Congress—the rationale behind arms sales.

1361.   Rovere, Richard H. and Schlesinger, Arthur M., Jr. *The General and the President, and the Future of American Foreign Policy.* See no. 80.

1362.   Russett, Bruce. "Making Defense Defensible." *Virginia Quarterly Review* vol. 66, no. 4 (Autumn 1970). Summary of no. 1138.

1363.   Schilling, Warner R.; Hammond, Paul Y; and Snyder, Glenn H. *Strategy, Politics and Defense Budgets.* See no. 81.

1364.   Schurman, Franz. "Is Nixon Winning?" *Liberation* vol. 14, no. 10 (Feb. 1970).

1365.   Scott, Peter D. "Cambodia—Why the Generals Won." *New York Review of Books* vol. 14, no. 12 (18 June 1970).

1366.   Simons, Lt. Col. William E. "Military Professionals as Policy Advisors." *Air University Review* vol. 20 (Mar.-Apr. 1969).

1367.   Smith, Maj. Mark E. and Johns, Maj. Claud J., Jr. *American Defense Policy.* See no. 15.

1368.   Stone, I. F. "Nixon, Inflation and the War." *I. F. Stone's Bi-Weekly* vol. 18, no. 3 (9 Feb. 1970).

1369.   Taylor, Gen. Maxwell (USA). *The Uncertain Trumpet.* New York: Harper & Row, 1960. The weakness of massive retaliation, with considerable description of executive processes.

1370.   Taylor, Telford. *Nuremberg and Vietnam: An American Tragedy.* See no. 908.

1371.   Tracey, William R. "Politico-Military Involvement—A Functional Imperative." *Military Review* vol. 49 (Apr. 1969).

1372.   United States. Congress. Senate. Committee on Government Operations. Subcommittee on National Security and International Operations. *The State-Defense Officer Exchange Program: Analysis and Assessment.* Washington, D.C.: USGPO, 1969.

1373.   Vought, Lt. Col. Donald B. "Soldiers Must Be Statesmen." *Military Review* vol. 48 (Oct. 1968).

1374.   Waskow, Arthur. "American-Cambodia Crisis." *Liberation* vol. 15, no. 5 (July 1970).

1375.   Wells, John M., and Wilhelm, Maria, comp. and eds. *The People vs. Presidential War.* New York: Dunellen, 1970. The Massachusetts Shea Bill.

1376.   "Why There Is a Real Need for Political Advisors in the Military," *Armed Forces Management* vol. 12 (Jan. 1966).

1377.   Wilcox, Francis O. "President Nixon, the Congress, and Foreign Policy." *Michigan Quarterly Review* vol. 9 (Winter 1970).

1378. Yarmolinsky, Adam. "How the Pentagon Works." *Atlantic* (Mar. 1967).

1379. _____."Bureaucratic Structures and Political Outcomes." See no. 101.

1380. "'72 Elections Off." *Old Mole* vol. 1, no. 40 (29 May 1970). Study on the possibilities of a presidential coup.

1381. See also IA1, "Organization. Decision Making, Civilian Control," for political impact within the executive branch. IIA1, "The Military Budget," and IIA2, "The Military-Industrial Complex," both deal with political institutions: as does IIIC, "Foreign Policy Politics and Processes." In a larger sense, nearly all categories in this bibliography deal with politics.

2. Congress

1382. Bader, William B. "Congress and National Strategy." *Naval War College Review* vol. 22 (Feb. 1970).

1383. Batten, James K. "Why the Pentagon Pays Homage to John Cornelius Stennis." *New York Times Magazine* (23 Nov. 1969).

1384. Becker, Eugene M. "Economy vs. Defense." See no. 1080.

1385. Braden, C. "ABM-Southerners Vote Yes." *Southern Patriot* vol. 27, no. 7 (Sept. 1969).

1386. Brogan, D. W. "U.S.: Civil and Military." See no. 28.

1387. Byrd, Harry F., Jr. "The Outlook in the Senate for Advice and Consent." *Naval War College Review* vol. 23 (Oct. 1970).

1388. Clotfelter, James. "Senate Voting and Constituency Stake in Defense Spending." *Journal of Politics* vol. 32, no. 4 (Nov. 1970).

1389. Cobb, Stephen A. "Defense Spending and Foreign Policy in the House of Representatives." *Journal of Conflict Resolution* vol. 13, no. 3 (Sept. 1969). Finds no evidence of relationship between defense spending and House Roll Call voting in 89th Congress.

1390. *Congressional Quarterly.* "The Military Industrial Complex." See no. 1120.

1391. _____."The Military Lobby." See no. 1121.

1392. _____."Military Spending." See no. 1122.

1393. Cossaboom, Bruce. "1970 Congressional Elections: Their Impact on Defense." *Armed Forces Journal* vol. 108 (19 Oct. 1970).

1394. Davidson, C. "Doves Win in Senate." *Guardian* vol. 22, no. 39 (11 July 1970).

1395. _____."Liberals Defeat War Amendment." *Guardian* vol. 22, no. 36 (20 June 1970).

1396. Davis, Vincent. *The Admirals Lobby.* See no. 148.

1397. Dawson, R. H. "Congressional Innovation and Intervention in Defense Policy: Legislative Authorization of Weapons Systems." *American Political Science Review* vol. 56, no. 1 (1962).

1398. Duscha, Julius. *Arms, Money, and Politics.* See no. 1094.

1399. "Fathers and Sons, The Draft." *Peoples World* vol. 33, no. 14 (4 Apr. 1970).

1400. Garvey, Capt. Gerald. "The Changing Management Role of the Military Departments Reconsidered." See no. 44.

1401. Gordon, Bernard K. "The Military Budget: Congressional Phase." See no. 1097.

1402. Gray, Charles H., and Gregory, Glenn W. "Military Spending and Senate Voting: A Correlational Study." *Journal of Peace Research* no. 1 (1969).

1403. Harrison, Stanley L. "Military Challenge in the 1970s." *Marine Corps Gazette* vol. 55 (Jan. 1971). Congress and the Soviet threat.

1404. Heiman, Grover. "Congressional Management—An Outrage for Change." *Armed Forces Management* vol. 16 (June 1970).

1405. Hersh, Seymour. "The Military Committee." *Washington Monthly* (Apr. 1969).

1406. Hessman, James D. "Behind the Budget Decisions: Five Years of Constant Change." *Armed Forces Journal* vol. 108 (15 Feb. 1971).

1407. Hillsman, Roger. "Congressional Executive Relations and the Foreign Policy Consensus." *American Political Science Review* vol. 52, no. 3 (Sept. 1958).

1408. "House Armed Services Committee Transcript." *Hardtimes* no. 59 (12 Jan. 1970).

1409. Huntington, Samuel P. "Equilibrium and Disequilibrium in American Military Policy." *Political Science Quarterly* vol. 76 (Dec. 1961).

1410. _____. *The Common Defense.* See no. 56.

1411. Huzar, Elias. *The Purse and the Sword: Control of the Army by Congress through Military Appropriations, 1933–1950.* Ithaca, N. Y.: Cornell University Press, 1950. Comprehensive for the period, based on committee hearings and other documents.

1412. Kanter, Arnold. "Congress and the Defense Budget, 1960–1970." *American Political Science Review* vol. 66, forthcoming 1972.

1413. Kaufman, Richard. "Who Won the Debate?" *The Nation* (17 Feb. 1970).

1414. Kolodziej, Edward A. *The Uncommon Defense and Congress, 1945–1963.* See no. 1112.

1415. Lieberson, Stanley. "Military-Industrial Linkages." See no. 1063.

1416. Morgenthau, Hans J. "Congress and Foreign Policy," *New Republic* (14 Jan. 1969). Congressional power has declined.

1417. Nelson, Garrett. "Nixon's Silent House of Hawks." *Progressive* vol. 34, no. 8 (Aug. 1970). Statistics on House voting.

1418. Oberdorfer, Don. "Rivers Delivers." *New York Times Magazine* (29 Aug. 1965).

1419. Pearson, Drew, and Anderson, Jack. *The Case against Congress.* New York: Pocket Books, 1969.

1420. Powell, Craig. "Arms Sales Is More Than Just a Military Question." See no. 1360.

1421. Proxmire, Senator William. *Report from the Wasteland.* See no. 1133.

1422. Rivers, L. Mendel. "If War Can Be Morally Justified, Victory Is Morally Justified." *Officer* vol. 46 (July 1970).

1423. Roberts, D. "McGovern-Hatfield Amendment." *The Militant* vol. 34, no. 21 (26 May 1970).

1424. _____. "Senate Bloc against Nixon." *The Militant,* vol. 34, no. 22 (5 June 1970).

1425. _____. "Why Senate Can't Curb Nixon," *The Militant* vol. 34, no. 26 (3 July, 1970).

1426. Robinson, James A. *Congress and Foreign Policy-Making.* Homewood, Ill.: Dorsey, 1962.

1427. Russett, Bruce M. "Communication." *Journal of Conflict Resolution* vol. 14, no. 2 (June 1970). Critique of Cobb (no. 1389). See also Russett, no. 1138.

1428. Schiller, Herbert I., and Phillips, Joseph D. *Superstate.* See no. 1244. Many of the articles in this volume concern Congress.

1429. Sherrill, Robert. "Military Mountain." *The Nation* (9 Feb. 1970).

1430. Stone, I. F. "The Supineness of the Senate." *New York Review of Books* (13 Feb. 1969).

1431. Starbird, Gen. Alfred D. *Sentinel System Public Affairs Plan.* Dept. of Defense Memorandum OASD (PA) 22/1, 15 March 1968. Reproduced in *Congressional Record,* pt. 15, 115 (91st Congress, 1st session, July 25, 1969): 20831–20833.

1432. Webb, L. *"ABM and the Liberals."* *Guardian* vol. 21, no. 44 (16 Aug. 1969).

1433. _____. "Liberals May Save Nixon's ABM." *Guardian* vol. 21, no. 41 (19 July 1969).

1434. Westerfield, H. Bradford. "Congress and Closed Politics in National Security Affairs." *Orbis* vol. 10, no. 3 (fall 1966).

1435. _____. *Foreign Policy and Party Politics: Pearl Harbor to Korea.* New

294 THE NEW POLITICS OF NATIONAL SECURITY

Haven: Yale University Press, 1955. Nonpartisanship and "extrapartisanship" in Congress.

1436. "Who Feeds the MIC? The ABM Fiasco and Congressional Politics." *The Public Life* vol. 1, no. 11 (2 May 1969).

1437. Wilson, Geroge C. "Proxmire and the Pentagon." See no. 1270.

1438. Witze, Claude. "Is the Enemy in Hanoi?" *Air Force and Space Digest* vol. 53 (July 1970). Attack on Congress' doves.

1439. ———. "The Senate's Watchdog for Defense." *Air Force and Space Digest* vol. 51 (Dec. 1968). The Preparedness Investigating Subcommittee.

1440. ———. "Who Said the Cold War Is Over?" *Air Force and Space Digest* vol. 53 (Oct. 1970). Attack on Senate doves, especially Fulbright and Proxmire.

1441. "1965 Selden Resolution and Excerpts from House Debate." *NACLA Newsletter* vol. 1, no. 7 (Nov. 1967).

1442. See also IIB1 and the note which follows that section.

C. THE SCIENTIFIC AND INTELLECTUAL COMMUNITY
1. General: Research and Development (R&D), Funding, University Complicity

1443. Allen, Jonathan, ed. *March 4: Scientists, Students, and Society.* Cambridge, Mass.: MIT Press, 1970. Transcripts of MIT symposium on misuse of science.

1444. American Assembly (of Columbia University). *The Federal Government and Higher Education.* Englewood Cliffs, N. J.: Prentice-Hall, 1960. A general survey.

1445. Barber, Richard J. *The Politics of Research.* Washington, D.C.: Public Affairs Press, 1966. R & D spillover into civilian market.

1446. Blum, J. "The University Enlists, . . ." *Plain Rapper* vol. 1, no. 5 (Jan. 1969).

1447. Brown, Martin, ed. *The Social Responsibility of the Scientist.* New York: Free Press, 1971. Includes bibliography.

1448. Butler, Thomas W., Jr. "The Continuing Role of Universities in Electronic Warfare." *Electronic Warfare* vol. 3 (winter 1971).

1449. Caldwell, Lynton K., ed. "Science, Technology, and Public Policy: A Selected and Annotated Bibliography." See no. 2440.

1450. Chomsky, Noam. *American Power and the New Mandarins.* New York: Patheon Books, 1969. Articles on the relationship of scholars to Vietnam and the cold war.

1451. *Correlation Index to Current Department of Defense Research Reports.* Cambridge, Mass.: MIT Press, quarterly. From Aug. 1963.

1452. Crawford, Elizabeth T. *The Social Sciences in International and Military Policy: An Analytical Bibliography.* See no. 2443.

1453. Debaggio, T. "CBW Research at University of Delaware." *Heterodoxical Voice* vol. 1, no. 15 (Sept. 1969).

1454. Gilpin, Robert. *American Scientists and Nuclear Weapons Policy.* Princeton, N.J.: Princeton University Press, 1962. Moral questions.

1455. Glick, Edward B. "Scholars, Soldiers, and Society." *Air Force/Space Digest* (Nov. 1969). Favors academic involvement in government research.

1456. _____. *Soldiers, Scholars, and Society.* See no. 1031. See especially chap. 6, "The Professor and the Pentagon."

1457. Goldner, G. "Labs Kill." *Old Mole* vol. 1, no. 24 (23 Oct. 1969).

1458. Government Data Publications, Inc. *R & D Contracts Monthly.* Monthly cumulative list of contract awards. Also publishes *R & D Directory,* an annual cumulative list.

1459. Greer, Edward. "The Public Interest University." *Viet-Report* (Jan. 1968).

1460. "Harvard Overseas—Retooling the Peasantry." *Old Mole* vol. 1, no. 24 (23 Oct. 1969).

1461. Henderson, B. "$400,000 Project Themis Contract." *L.A. Free Press* vol. 6, no. 82 (12 Dec. 1969).

1462. Hersh, Seymour. "20,000 Guns under the Sea." See no. 433.

1463. Hinckle, Warren, in conjunction with Stern, Sol, and Scheer, Robert. "MSU: The University on the Make." *Ramparts* vol. 4, no. 12 (Apr. 1966). Exposé of CIA-MSU support of Diem regime.

1464. Horowitz, David. "Sinews of Empire." *Ramparts* vol. 8, no. 4 (Oct. 1969).

1465. Howze, Gen. Hamilton H. "In Defense of Academic Ignorance." *Army* vol. 19 (June 1969).

1466. Klare, Michael. "The New Radicals in the Multiversity." *Viet-Report* (June-July 1967).

1467. _____. "Universities in Vietnam." *Viet-Report* (Jan. 1968).

1468. _____. *The University-Military-Police Complex: A Directory and Related Documents.* See no. 1475.

1469. Knorr, Klaus, and Morgenstern, Oskar. *Political Conjecture in Military Planning.* Princeton: Center of International Studies, 1968.

1470. _____. *Science and Defense: Some Critical Thoughts on Military Research and Development.* Princeton: Center of International Studies, 1965.

1471. Levine, Robert. *The Arms Debate.* Cambridge, Mass.: Harvard University Press, 1963.

1472. Lyons, Gene M., and Morton, Louis. *Schools for Strategy.* See no. 122.

1473. Maguire, M. "Stanford-Campaign against Research." *The Movement* vol. 5, no. 5 (June 1969).

1474. NACLA. "Subliminal Warfare—The Role of Latin American Studies." NACLA Pamphlet, c. 1970. Cultural imperialism and counterinsurgency research. Includes charts and tables. Available directly from NACLA (address in section IVD).

1475. _____, and Klare, Michael. "The University-Military-Police Complex: A Directory and Related Documents." Tabulation of military and policy research on U. S. campuses. Mostly from official data: Highly useful. Available directly from NACLA. See section IVD for address.

1476. _____. "Who Rules Columbia?" NACLA Pamphlet, n.d. Documents the university's complicity and describes its power structure. Data-packed. Available directly from NACLA. See section IVD for address.

1477. National Science Foundation. *Federal Funds for Research, Development, and Other Scientific Activities.* Washington, D.C.: USGPO, annually. NSF publishes much information on this topic, e.g. *Federal Support to Universities and Colleges.* Washington, D.C.: USGPO, periodically.

1478. _____. *Research and Development in Industry, 1965: Basic Research, Applied Research, and Development in American Industry, 1965, A Final Report on a Survey of R & D Funds, 1965, and R & D Scientists and Engineers, Jan. 1966.* Washington, D.C.: USGPO, 1967.

1479. Nelson, William R., ed. *The Politics of Science.* New York: Oxford University Press, 1968.

1480. Nicolaus, Martin. "The Professor, the Policeman and the Peasant." *Viet-Report* (Mar.-Apr. 1966).

1481. Nieburg, H.L. *In the Name of Science.* See no. 404.

1482. Ober, John David, and Carradi, Juan Eugenio, "Pax Americana and Pax Sociologica: Remarks on the Politics of Sociology." *Catalyst* (Summer 1966).

1483. Orlans, Harold. *The Effects of Federal Programs on Higher Education.* Washington, D.C.: The Brookings Institution, 1962.

1484. Packard, David. "R & D: Key to Our Nation's Strength." *Signal* vol. 25 (Mar. 1971).

1485. Palmer, A. M., and Kruzas, A. T. *Research Centers Directory.* 2d ed. Detroit, Mich.: Gale Research Co., 1966. Semiautonomous research centers and foundations, cross-indexed by university, with information about each. See also the periodic supplement, *New Research Centers.*

1486. "Pentagon Foreign Policy Research." *NACLA Newsletter* vol. 3, no. 4 (Aug. 1969); no. 6 (Oct. 1969). Includes official statistics.

1487. Pohl, C. "U. of W. Business in Exploitation." *Kaleidoscope—Madison* vol. 1, no. 3 (22 July 1969).

1488. Pool, Ithiel de Sola. "The Necessity for Social Scientists Doing Research for Governments." *Background* (now called *International Studies Quarterly*) vol. 10 (Aug. 1966). Social science as "The only hope for humane government."

1489. Price, William J. "Defense Research and the University." *Defense Industry Bulletin* vol. 6 (July 1970).

1490. _____. "Some Aspects of Air Force-University Relations." *Air University Review* vol. 21 (Jan.-Feb. 1970). R & D—the need to explicate and clear the air around existing programs.

1491. "The Research Apparatus of U. S. Imperialism." *NACLA Newsletter* vol. 1, no. 10 (Feb. 1968).

1492. Ridgeway, James. *The Closed Corporation: America's Universities in Crisis.* New York: Random House, 1968.

1493. "The Rise and Fall of Project Camelot." *NACLA Newsletter* vol. 1, no. 7 (Nov. 1967).

1494. Rivlin, Alice M. *The Role of the Federal Government in Financing Higher Education.* Washington, D.C.: The Brookings Institution, 1961.

1495. *San Francisco Bay Guardian.* See no. 1241.

1496. Shapiro and Shalom. "MIT Moves into Cambridge, . . ." *Old Mole* vol. 1, no. 25 (6 Nov. 1969).

1497. "Social Research and Counterinsurgency—The Science of Neocolonialism." *NACLA Newsletter* pt. 1: vol. 3, no. 10 (Feb. 1970); pt. 2: vol. 4, no. 1 (Mar. 1970).

1498. Stanford Research Institute. "R & D Study Series." separate reports on R & D, including *The Structure and Dynamics of the Defense R & D Industry: The Los Angeles and Boston Complexes* (1965); *The Role of the University in R & D* (1966); and others. Menlo Park, Calif.: SRI Publications Department.

1499. Stern, Sol. "NSA and the CIA." *Ramparts* vol. 5, no. 9 (Mar. 1967). CIA support of student groups.

1500. Tobey, T. "University & Draft Counseling." *Prarie Primer* vol. 2, no. 7 (15 Dec. 1969).

1501. United States Congress. "Pentagon Foreign Policy Research." *Congressional Record* (1 May 1969), p. S4417. Listing includes project description, contract amount, and name of researcher.

298   THE NEW POLITICS OF NATIONAL SECURITY

1502. United States. Congress. House. Committee on Foreign Affairs. *Behavioral Sciences and the National Security.* House Report no. 1224. 89th Congress, 2d session. Washington, D. C.: USGPO, 1966.

1503. United States. Congress. House. Committee on Government Operations. Subcommittee on Research and Technical Programs. *Conflicts between the Federal Research Programs and the Nation's Goals for Higher Education: Hearings,* 89th Congress, 1st session (14, 15, 17 June 1965). See also "Responses. . . ." (Aug. 1965) and "18th Report of the Committee on Government Operations" (13 Oct. 1965), same title.

1504. United States. Congress. House. Committee on Science and Astronautics. *Centralization of Federal Science, Research, and Development.* 91st Congress, 1st session Washington, D.C.: USGPO, 1969. See also other *Reports* to the Subcommittee, e.g. *Mission Agency Support of Basic Research,* 91st Congress, 2d session (1970) and *Technical Information for Congress,* 91st Congress, 1st session (1969). This latter contains a description of Project Camelot. See also various Subcommittee *Hearings,* e.g. *Government and Science.* 88th Congress, 1st session (1964).

1505. United States. Congress. Senate. Committee on Government Operations. Subcommittee on Government Research. *Inventory of Congressional Concern with Research and Development: A Bibliography* 2 vols. Washington, D.C. (15 Dec. and 23 Sept. 1966).

1506. United States. Department of Commerce. Clearinghouse for Federal Scientific and Technical Information. *U. S. Government Research and Development Reports.* Springfield, Va.: semimonthly. Lists nonclassified studies commissioned by the government and sold through the Clearinghouse.

1507. United States. Department of Defense. Office of the Director of Defense Research and Engineering. *Project Themis: A Program to Strengthen the Nation's Academic Institutions.* Washington, D. C. (Nov. 1968). Directs funds to smaller institutions.

1508. U. S. Department of Defense. Office of the Secretary of Defense. Directorate of Statistical Services. *500 Contractors Listed According to Net Value of Military Prime Contract Awards for Research, Development, Test, and Evaluation Work.* Available from the office of the Assistant Secretary of Defense for Public Affairs, The Pentagon.

1509. "The University Arsenal." *Look* (26 Aug. 1969).

1510. "Why Smash MIT." *Old Mole* vol. 1, no. 26 (21 Nov. 1969).

2. Think Tanks

1511. "Flying Thinktank over the Amazon." *NACLA Newsletter,* vol. 1, no. 8 (Dec. 1967). South American research.

1512. Green, Philip. "Science, Government, and the Case of RAND, A Singular Pluralism." *World Politics* vol. 20 (Jan. 68). Review of B. L. R. Smith's *The RAND Corporation.* Critical of role of think-tanks in national security policy.

1513. Horowitz, Irving Louis. *The War Game: Studies of the New Civilian Militarists.* New York: Balantine, 1963. Civilian planners in general.

1514. Klare, Michael. *The University-Military-Police Complex.* See no. 1468 and no. 1475.

1515. Licklider, Roy E. *The Private Nuclear Strategists.* Columbus, O.: Ohio State University Press, 1972. Sociological study of academic and thinktank analysts.

1516. Smith, Bruce L. R. *The Rand Corporation: Case Study of a Nonprofit Advisory Corporation.* Cambridge, Mass.: Harvard University Press, 1966. Chronological study of Rand as an aid to management and decision making. Should be read in conjunction with article by Green. See no. 1512.

1517. United States. Department of Commerce. Clearinghouse for Federal Scientific and Technical Information. *U. S. Government Research and Development Reports.* See no. 1506.

1518. See also IIC1, "R & D . . . University Complicity."

3. ROTC and Other Military Education Programs in Civilian Universities

1519. "Army Upgrading Junior ROTC." *Guardian* vol. 22, no. 26 (4 Apr. 1970).

1520. "Behind the Drive to Destroy ROTC." *U. S. News and World Report* (29 June 1970).

1521. Blumenfeld, Col. C. H. "The Case for ROTC." *Military Review* vol. 43, no. 3 (Mar. 1963).

1522. "Brother Arrested in Fight against ROTC." *The Bond* vol. 4, no. 4 (22 Apr. 1970).

1523. "Case Resolution to Abolish ROTC." *The Militant* vol. 34, no. 19 (15 May 1970).

1524. Clanton, I. "Insurrection." *Berkeley Tribe* vol. 2, no. 15 (17 Apr. 1970).

1525. Elliot, Ward. "The Assault on ROTC: Are We Trying to Stop the War Machine by Getting Rid of the Brakes?" *Army* vol. 21 (Feb. 1971).

1526. "GAO Scores Military Graduate Education Programs." *Armed Forces Journal.* See no. 108.

1527. Gibson, Col. Baylor. "The Universities: Trial by Fire." *U. S. Naval Institute Proceedings* vol. 96 (Apr. 1970). The removal of ROTC from campuses is a violation of academic freedom. General prescription for vigilance against further "encroachment."

1528. Glick, Edward B. "ROTC: From Riot to Reason." *Air Force and Space Digest* vol. 53 (Oct. 1970). Prussianization of officer corps would result without ROTC. See also chapter of same name in his book, *Soldiers, Scholars, and Society.* See no. 1031.

1529. Goldrich, Robert L. "The Art of Winning Friends on Campus, Though Uniformed." *Army* vol. 21 (Jan. 1971).

1530. Homan, Richard. "High School ROTC Growing." *Washington Post* (3 Aug. 1969).

1531. Joulwan, Maj. George A. (USA). "ROTC: An Academic Focus." *Military Review* vol. 51 (Jan. 1971).

1532. Kaufman, B. "Cops Make War in Berkeley." *Peoples World* vol. 33, no. 17 (25 Apr. 1970).

1533. Leavitt, William. "The Keys to Survival Are Reform and Relevance." *Air Force and Space Digest* vol. 53 (Apr. 1970). ROTC should be tailored by military and colleges to improve academically; more money incentives need to be added in the future.

1534. Liberation News Service. "ROTC Takes . . . Beating." *Chinook* vol. 2, no. 27 (23 July 1970).

1535. Lyons, Gene M., and Masland, John W. *Education and Military Leadership: A Study of the ROTC.* Princeton, N.J.: Princeton University Press, 1959. Some of the conflicts which now plague ROTC were noted in this early study.

1536. Marsh, John J. "One of Our Social Sciences Is Missing." *Air University Review* vol. 22 (Jan.-Feb. 1971). All colleges and universities ought to have courses in "The Study of National Defense" or "Military Science."

1537. Moberg, D. "Melee Erupts in Chicago Courtroom." *Guardian* vol. 22, no. 44 (29 Aug. 1970).

1538. "No More ROTC." *Helix* vol. 10, no. 5 (6 Nov. 1969).

1539. Padilla, M. "Year of Major Student Struggles." *The Militant* vol. 34, no. 28 (17 July 1970).

1540. Scott, Joseph W. "ROTC Retreat." In Martin Oppenheimer, ed., *The American Military.* See no. 12.

1541. Swomley, John M., Jr. et al. *Militarism in Education.* Washington, D. C.: National Council against Conscription, 1950. An early attack on ROTC.

1542. Trager, Frank N. "ROTC on Campus: Challenge and Response." *American Legion Magazine* vol. 87 (Dec. 1969).

1543. United States. Department of the Army. *Army ROTC Scholarship Program*. Washington, D. C.: 1969.

1544. ———. *Educational Scholarships, Loans, and Financial Aids*. (Department of the Army Pamphlet no. 352–1). Washington, D.C.: Headquarters, Department of the Army, 1969.

1545. ———. *Fifth Annual ROTC/NDCC Conference, 5 to 8 September 1967*. Fort Monroe, Va.: Continental Army Command Headquarters, 1967.

1546. U. S. Department of Defense. Office of the Assistant Secretary of Defense for Manpower and Reserve Affairs. *Report of the Special Committee on ROTC to the Secretary of Defense*. Washington, D. C.: Sept. 1969.

1547. Wyche, Richard C. "Why ROTC?" *Military Engineer* vol. 63 (Mar.-Apr. 1971). First prize essay.

D. CIVIL DISTURBANCE ROLES:
CITIES, CAMPUS, DOMESTIC INTELLIGENCE

1548. "Army Rushes Riot Training and Gear." *National Guardsman* vol. 25 (Feb. 1971).

1549. Beaumont, Roger A. "Must the Guard Be a Police Force?" *Army* vol. 20 (Sept. 1970).

1550. "Big Brother Bigger Than Ever." *The Ally* no. 25 (Apr. 1970). Spies.

1551. Childs, F. "61 Imprisoned for Opposing Riot Training." *Philadelphia Free Press* vol. 2, no. 28 (16 Dec. 1969).

1552. Coble, Donald W. "DoD Establishes a 'Watch' on the 'Battle at Home.'" *Armed Forces Management* vol. 15 (Sept. 1969). The Pentagon's Directorate of Civil Disturbance Planning and Operations—DCDPO.

1553. Cochran, Charles L. "Student Activism: Civilian and Military Institutions." *U. S. Naval Institute Proceedings* vol. 96 (Oct. 1970).

1554. "Civil Disturbance Planning." *The Inspector General Brief* vol. 22 (19 June 1970).

1555. Donner, Frank. "The Theory and Practice of American Political Intelligence." *New York Review of Books* vol. 16, no. 7 (22 Apr. 1971). Not just military, but CIA, FBI and local police.

1556. Duerr, Edwin C. "Campus Violence: Actions, Reactions, and Alternatives." *Naval War College Review* vol. 23 (Dec. 1970).

1557. Farmer, David J. *Civil Disorder Control: A Planning Program of Municipal Coordination and Cooperation*. Chicago: Public Administration Service, 1968. Based in part on the Report of the National Advisory Commission on Civil Disorders.

1558. Fisher, Maj. Richard B. "Keeping the Lid on Is Not Enough." *Military Review* vol. 49 (Sept. 1969).

1559. Gibson, Col. Baylor. "The Universities: Trial by Fire." See no. 1527.

1560. "The Guard on Campus." *National Guardsman* vol. 24 (Nov. 1970). Critique of the report of the President's Commission on Campus Unrest.

1561. "The Guard vs. Disorder." *National Guardsman* vol. 24 (June 1970). Army and Air National Guard.

1562. Higham, Robin D., ed. *Bayonets in the Streets: The Use of Troops in Civil Disturbances.* Lawrence, Kan.: University Press of Kansas, 1969. The most important collection on the subject so far.

1563. Hoover, J. Edgar. "Battlefield." *Army Digest* vol. 23 (Oct. 1968). FBI cooperation with the armed forces.

1564. ———. "Partners in Protecting America—The FBI and the Army." *Army Digest* vol. 25 (Dec. 1970).

1565. "How to Control Riot Control." *The Movement* vol. 5, no. 5 (June 1969).

1566. "Intelligence: The Lagging Function." *Armed Forces Management* vol. 16 (May 1970).

1567. "Judge Allows Army to Witch-Hunt," *Peacemaker* vol. 23, no. 7 (23 May 1970).

1568. Kent, Lt. Col. Irvin M. "A National Security Corps." *Military Review* vol. 47 (July 1967).

1569. Lane, Maj. Gen. Thomas A. "The Right to Intelligence." *New York Times* (11 Jan. 1971). If the army is asked to do this job, it must have information.

1570. Leber, Lt. Comdr. Theodore T., Jr., (USN). "The Genesis of Antimilitarism on the College Campus: A Contemporary Case Study of Student Protest." *Naval War College Review* vol. 23 (Nov. 1970). Long article.

1571. Long, Col. William F. "Urban Insurgency War Game." *Naval War College Review* vol. 21 (May 1969).

1572. Liberation News Service. "Berkeley Life with the Guard." See no. 278.

1573. "More Posts Test VOLAR." *Army Times* (3 Feb. 1971).

1574. National Guard Association of the U. S. "The Role of the National Guard in an Age of Unrest." *National Guardsman* vol. 24 (Sept. 1970).

1575. Ney, Col. Virgil (USA, Ret.). "Tactics and Techniques of Riot Warfare." *Military Review* vol. 50 (May 1970).

1576. Peers, Lt. Gen. William R. "Army Reserve and National Guard Meet the Test at Home and Abroad." See no. 284.

1577. "Pentagon-GI Coffeehouse, Oakland, Calif." *Black Panther* vol. 5, no. 10 (5 Sept. 1970).

1578. Pyle, Christopher. "CONUS Intelligence: The Army Watches Civilian Politics." *Washington Monthly* (Jan. 1970). Award-Winning article. Stimulated Ervin committee investigations. See no. 1591.

1579. Quigley, Carroll. "Dissent: Do We Need It?" *Perspectives in Defense Management* (Jan. 1971).

1580. Reston, J. "Can Nixon Trust the Army?" *L.A. Free Press* vol. 7, no. 26 (26 June 1970).

1581. Rigg, Col. Robert F. (USA, Ret.). "Made in USA (Urban Guerrilla Warfare)." *Army* vol. 18 (Jan. 1968).

1582. "Riot Duty." *Willamette Bridge* vol. 3, no. 35 (28 Aug. 1970).

1583. Schlotterbeck, Col. Walter B., and Mansinne, Lt. Col. Andrew, Jr. *National Security Management: The Role of the Department of Defense in Civil Disturbances.* Washington, D.C.: U.S. Industrial College of the Armed Forces, 1970. Surveys legal basis, historical examples, and current plans, organization and method of operations.

1584. Sears, Lt. Edward (USA). "Riotsville, U.S.A." *Army Digest* vol. 23 (Aug. 1968). The Civil Disturbance Orientation Course, Fort Gordon, Ga.

1585. "Spider Webs in Ivory Towers." *Old Mole* vol. 1, no. 24 (23 Oct. 1969).

1586. "Spies." *Long Beach Free Press* vol. 2, no. 1 (2 Apr. 1970).

1587. Stone, I. F. *The Killings at Kent State.* See no. 286.

1588. Stoner, Maj. John K., Jr. (USA). "Riot Control Doctrine." *Military Review* vol. 45 (Feb. 1965). Brief history of riot control doctrine since nineteenth century; pre-Watts, superficial affirmation of minimum force doctrine.

1589. *Supplemental Studies for the National Advisory Commission on Civil Disorders.* Washington, D.C.: USGPO, 1968. These studies were conducted independently of the Commission and of each other by research groups at three universities.

1590. United States Army Military History Research Collection, Historical Research and Reference Division. *The U.S. Army and Domestic Disturbances.* (Bibliography). See no. 2469.

1591. United States. Congress. Senate. Committee on the Judiciary.

Subcommittee on Constitutional Rights (92d Congress, 1st session). Subcommittee chairman Senator Sam J. Ervin. *Federal Data Banks, Computers, and the Bill of Rights. Hearings,* Feb. 23, 24 and 25 and Mar. 2, 3, 4, 9, 10, 11, 15 and 17. Washington, D.C.:USGPO, 1971. Includes army surveillance hearings.

1592. United States. National Advisory Commission on Civil Disorders. *Report.* Washington, D.C.: USGPO, 1968.

1593. ———. *Report. New York Times* ed. New York: Dutton, 1968. The *Times* edition has an interesting introduction by Tom Wicker.

1594. United States. President's Commission on Campus Unrest. *Report of the President's Commission on Campus Unrest.* Including special reports: The Killings at Jackson State, The Kent State Tragedy. New York: Arno, 1970.

1595. "Urban Guerilla." *Berkeley Tribe* vol. 2, no. 24 (19 June 1970). Espionage.

1596. Walters, Robert. "Army Sets up Riot Center." *Washington Star* (24 Mar. 1969).

1597. Weiss, George. "DoD Tightens Civilian Control over Intelligence, But No Reorganization." *Armed Forces Journal* vol. 108 (1 Mar. 1971). Results of the Senator Sam J. Ervin subcommittee investigations of army domestic surveillance activities.

1598. Yarmolinsky, Adam. *The Military Establishment.* See no. 19. Data-packed chapter on civil disturbance roles.

1599. See also IB4, "Weapons of Counterinsurgency," and IA6, "The National Guard."

E. THE PUBLIC CONSCIOUSNESS
1. Public Opinion

1600. Aptheker, Herbert. "Workers and the War." *Peoples World* vol. 33, no. 28 (11 July 1970).

1601. Armbruster, Lt. Comdr. William A. (USN). "The Pueblo Crisis and Public Opinion." *Naval War College Review* vol. 23 (Mar. 1971).

1602. Barrett, Raymond J. "The Military Image." *Ordnance* vol. 54 (May-June 1970).

1603. Bletz, Col. Donald F. (USA). "After Vietnam: A Professional Challenge." *Military Review* vol. 51 (Aug. 1971). Post-Vietnam antimilitary isolationism is the challenge.

1604. Bobrow, Davis B., ed. *Weapons Systems Decisions.* See no. 381.

1605. Caspary, William. "The Mood Theory: A Study of Public Opinion and Foreign Policy." *American Political Science Review* vol. 64 (June 1970). Contends that public support for internationalist foreign policy has been stable.

1606. Cherne, Leo. "State of the Nation." *Perspectives in Defense Management* (Jan. 1971).

1607. Clotfelter, James. "Vacillation and Stability in American Public Opinion toward Military and Foreign Policy." *Naval War College Review* vol. 23 (Feb. 1971).

1608. Cohen, C. B. "The Military Policy Public." *Public Opinion Quarterly* vol. 30 (1966). Size and characteristics.

1609. Coleman, J. "The Silent Majority and the War." *Workers Power* no. 21 (11 Sept. 1970).

1610. Drucker, Peter F. *The Age of Discontinuity: Guidelines to Our Changing Society.* New York: Harper & Row, 1969.

1611. Flint, Lt. Col. Roy K. (USA). "Army Professionalism for the Future." *Military Review* vol. 51 (Apr. 1971). Professional soldiers must not succumb to "Stab-in-the-Back Complex" due to civilian criticism; must patiently accommodate social change.

1612. Free, Lloyd A. "Political Beliefs and Public Opinion." *Naval War College Review* vol. 23 (Mar. 1971).

1613. Frisbee, John L. "The Mythical Menace of Militarism." *Air Force and Space Digest* vol. 53 (Mar. 1970). Real danger not militarism (which author claims does not exist in U.S.) but antimilitary clamor which risks alienating the military from society just when foreign threat is growing.

1614. Gardner, Fred. "Poll Axed." *Seed* vol. 5, no. 1 (1970).

1615. Ginsburgh, Brig. Gen. Robert N. (USAF). "Anti-Militarism in Perspective." *Air Force Policy Letter for Commanders* supplement no. 10 (Oct. 1970).

1616. Hahn, H. "Dove Sentiments among Blue Collar Workers." *Dissent* vol. 17, no. 3 (June 1970). Poll.

1617. Hartly, Eugene. "Prediction of U.S. Public Response to Damage Limiting Programs." In Bobrow, ed. *Weapons Systems Decisions.* See no. 381.

1618. Hays, Col. Samuel H., and Rehm, Lt. Col. Thomas A. "The Military in the Free Society." *U.S. Naval Institute Proceedings* vol. 95 (Feb. 1969).

1619. Knoll, Erwin, and McFadden, Judith N. *War Crimes and the American Conscience.* See no. 890.

1620. Liferstein, I. "Psychological Habituation to War." *Long Beach Free Press* vol. 2, no. 5 (24 June 70).

1621. Mills, C. Wright. *The Causes of World War Three.* New York: Simon and Schuster, 1958.

1622. Moskos, Charles C., Jr., ed. *Public Opinion and the Military Establishment.* Beverly Hills, Calif.: Sage, 1971. Also deals with military education.

1623. Mueller, John E. "Presidential Popularity from Truman to Johnson." *American Political Science Review* vol. 64 (1970). No clear evidence that decline in popularity attributable to wars.

1624. "Organization of American National Security Opinions." *Public Opinion Quarterly* vol. 33, no. 2 (Summer 1969).

1625. Roberts, D. "Suppressed Poll—South Vietnamese Antiwar Mood." *The Militant* vol. 34, no. 3 (7 Aug. 1970).

1626. Rosenau, James. *Public Opinion and Foreign Policy.* New York: Random House, 1961.

1627. Rosenberg, Milton J.; Verba, Sidney; and Converse, Philip E. *Vietnam and the Silent Majority: A Dove's Guide.* New York: Harper & Row, 1970. Recent Vietnam opinion research.

1628. Russett, Bruce M. "The Revolt of the Masses: Public Opinion on Military Expenditures." In Russett, ed., *Peace, War, and Numbers.* Beverly Hills, Calif.: Sage, 1972. Documents the precipitous and unprecedented decline in public support for military spending.

1629. Seamans, Robert C., Jr. "Public Management of National Security." *Air Force Information Policy Letter for Commanders* supplement no. 2 (Feb. 1971).

1630. Taylor, A. "Surprise Party." *New York Review of Books* vol. 15, no. 3 (13 Aug. 1970).

1631. Verba, Sidney et al. "Public Opinion and the War in Vietnam." *American Political Science Review* vol. 61 (June 1967). Shows majority support potentially available for escalation or deescalation.

1632. Wells, John M., and Wilhelm, Maria, eds. *The People vs. Presidential War.* See no. 1375.

1633. Williams, R. M., Jr. "Are Americans and Their Cultural Values Adaptable to the Concept and Techniques of Unconventional Warfare?" *Annals of the American Academy of Political and Social Science* vol. 341 (1962).

1634. Zubkoff, Harry M. "The Press and Public Opinion." *Air University Review* vol. 22 (Nov. and Dec. 1970).

2. Patriotism, Nationalism, Anticommunism

1635. Brennan, Charles D. "New Left Threatens Internal Security, FBI Official Tells Mid-Winter Meeting." *Officer* vol. 46 (May 1970).

1636. Brucan, S. "Nationalism Runs Deeper than Class." *Center Magazine* vol. 3, no. 4 (Aug. 1970).

1637. Camejo, A. "Marxism and Nationalism." *The Militant* vol. 34, no. 32 (4 Sept. 1970).

1638. Cleverdon, S. "Counterinsurgency in the Schools." *Old Mole* vol. 1, no. 18 (31 July 1969).

1639. Freeland, Richard M. *The Truman Doctrine and the Origins of McCarthyism.* See no. 1886.

1640. Galbraith, John K. "Bureaucratic Truth." *Progressive* vol. 33, no. 7 (July 1969). From *How to Control the Military.*

1641. "Honor America—Remember the Revolution." *The Ally* no. 28 (July 1970).

1642. Kazin, A. "Our Flag." *New York Review of Books* vol. 15, no. 1 (2 July 1970).

1643. Lasch, Christopher. *The Agony of the American Left.* New York: Knopf, 1969. The growth of liberal anticommunism.

1644. LeMay, Gen. Curtis E. (USAF, Ret.) with Smith, Maj. Gen. Dale O. *America Is in Danger.* See no. 204.

1645. Lester, Julius. "Aquarian Notebook." *Liberation* vol. 15, no. 5 (July 1970). On patriotism.

1646. McNamara, Robert S. *The Essence of Security.* New York: Harper & Row, 1969. Speeches, etc., many of which reveal the man behind the machine.

1647. North, J. "The Spirit of 1970." *Peoples World* vol. 33, no. 27 (4 July 1970).

1648. "On Patriotism." *Northern Patriot* vol. 1, no. 2 (Sept. 1970).

1649. Ottosen, M. "Dear WIN." *WIN* vol. 6, no. 8 (1 May 1970).

1650. Parenti, Michael. *The Anti-Communist Impulse.* New York: Random House, 1969. An excellent portrayal of Americans, their self-image, and practical consequences for the rest of the world.

1651. Pilisuk, Marc, and Hayden, Thomas. "Is There a Military Industrial Complex Which Prevents Peace?" See no. 1075.

1652. Power, Gen. Thomas S. (USAF, Ret.). *Design for Survival.* See no. 217.

1653. Prokosch, . "On Vigils and Radicalization." *WIN* vol. 6, no. 7 (15 Apr. 1970).

1654. Reynolds, Stanley. *Better Dead Than Red.* New York: Ballantine Books, 1965.

1655. Ryan, S. "Christian Anti-Communist Crusade." *Kaleidoscope—Madison* vol. 1, no. 3 (22 July 1969).

1656. Stone, I. F. "China Menace-American Hallucination." *I. F. Stone's Bi-Weekly* vol. 17, no. 18 (8 Sept. 1969).

1657. Such, R. "Honoring the Paper Tiger." *Guardian* vol. 22, no. 39 (11 July 1970).

1658. Twining, Gen. Nathan F. (USAF, Ret.). *Neither Liberty nor Safety.* See no. 226.

1659. Wilcox, H. "Leadership Training—Hitler Youth." *Philadelphia Free Press* vol. 2, no. 26 (1 Dec. 1969).

3. Secrecy, Loyalty, Security, Repression

1660. Barth, Alan. *Loyalty of Free Men.* New York: Viking, 1951. History of early loyalty program.

1661. Bontecon, Eleanor. *The Federal Loyalty-Security Program.* Ithaca, N.Y.: Cornell University Press, 1953.

1662. Brown, Ralph S. *Loyalty and Security: Employment Tests in the United States.* New Haven, Conn.: Yale University Press, 1958. Excellent survey.

1663. Cook, Fred J. *The Nightmare Decade: The Life and Times of Senator Joe McCarthy.* New York: Random House, 1971. The most recent and vivid description of an ideological legacy.

1664. Coser, L. A. "The Dysfunctions of Military Secrecy." *Social Problems* vol. 11 (1963).

1665. "Disclosure of Information Pertaining to Military Assistance." *The Inspector General Brief* vol. 22 (22 May 1970).

1666. Epstein, J. "The Trial of Bobby Seale." *New York Review of Books* vol. 13, no. 10 (4 Dec. 1969).

1667. Freeland, Richard M. *The Truman Doctrine and the Origins of McCarthyism.* See no. 1886.

1668. Hanks, Capt. Robert J. (USN). "Against All Enemies." See no. 5.

1669. Hayden, Tom. "Inside the Conspiracy." See no. 773.

1670. Kim, Young Hum. *The Central Intelligence Agency: Problems of Secrecy in a Democracy.* See no. 310.

1671. Lens, Sidney. "Notes on the Chicago Trial." See no. 776.

1672. Liberation News Service. "Concentration Camps USA." *Philadelphia Free Press* vol. 2, no. 19 (13 Oct. 1969).

1673. McGuire, Martin C. *Secrecy and the Arms Race: A Theory of the Accumulation of Strategic Weapons and How Secrecy Affects It.* Cambridge, Mass.: Harvard University Press, 1965.

1674. Moon, Col. Gordon A., II. "Military Security vs. the Right to Know." *Army* vol. 18 (July 1968).

1675. "A National Security State." *Progressive* vol. 33, no. 7 (July 1969).

1676. Packer, H. "The Conspiracy Weapon." *New York Review of Books* vol. 13, no. 8 (6 Nov. 1969).

1677. Quigley, Carroll. "Dissent: Do We Need It?" *Perspectives in Defense Management* (Jan. 1971).

1678. "Release of Information Concerning Military Installations." *The Inspector General Brief* vol. 22 (11 Sept. 1970).

1679. Rubin, Jerry. "Inside the Great Pigasus Plot." *Ramparts* vol. 8, no. 6 (Dec. 1969).

1680. "Scholars and Secrecy." *NACLA Newsletter* vol. 1, no. 8 (Dec. 1967). From the *Wall Street Journal.*

1681. Smith, Robert B. "Rebellion and Repression and the Vietnam War." *Annals of the American Academy of Political and Social Science* vol. 391 (Sept. 1970). Empirical study of public opinion on the war, tolerance and background factors.

1682. "Stamp of Secrecy." *Progressive* vol. 33, no. 12 (Dec. 1969).

4. Militarism, Violence

1683. Armando. "Sundance and the Bunch." *Seed* vol. 4, no. 10 (c. 1969).

1684. Bell, Daniel. "The Dispossessed—1962." In Bell, ed. *The Radical Right.* New York: Doubleday, 1963.

1685. Camara. "Violence—The Only Option." *Catholic Worker* vol. 35, no. 6 (Aug. 1969).

1686. Cameron, J. "Special Supplement—On Violence." *New York Review of Books* vol. 15, no. 1 (2 July 1970).

1687. Coffin, Tristram. *The Passion of the Hawks: Militarism in Modern America.* New York: Macmillan, 1964. Satirical critique of the American military establishment and the American spirit.

1688. Cottrell, Alvin J., and Dougherty, James E. *Western and Communist Attitudes towards Conflict: A Study in Strategic Theory and Practice.* Ann Arbor, Mich.: Ann Arbor University Microfilms, 1961.

1689. Dellinger, David. "Time to Look at Ourselves." *Liberation* vol. 15, no. 6 (1970).

1690. Demming, Barbara. "Need to Liberate Minds." *Liberation* vol. 15, no. 6 (1970).

1691. Drinan, Robert F., S. J. *Vietnam and Armageddon: Peace, War, and the Christian Conscience.* New York: Sheed and Ward, 1970.

1692. Eisenhower, Chairman Milton Stover. *The Rule of Law: An Alternative to Violence.* The Report of the National Commission on the Causes and Prevention of Violence. Nashville, Tenn.: Aurora Publications, 1970.

1693. Ekirch, Arthur A., Jr. *The Civilian and the Military.* New York: Oxford University Press, 1956. Proestablishment historical analysis of antimilitarism in the U. S.

1694. Elliot, Ward. "The Assault on ROTC: Are We Trying to Stop the War Machine by Getting Rid of the Brakes?" *Army* vol. 21 (Feb. 1971).

1695. Frank, Jerome D. *Sanity and Survival; Psychological Aspects of War and Peace.* New York: Random House, 1967.

1696. Frisbee, John L. "The Mythical Menace of Militarism." See no. 1613.

1697. Fulbright, Senator J. William. *The Arrogance of Power.* New York: Random House, 1966.

1698. Glusman, P. "Stone Drag." *Seed* vol. 4, no. 10 (1969).

1699. Hallinan, C. "Who Uses Violence?" *Peoples World* vol. 33, no. 38 (26 Sept. 1970).

1700. Heilbroner, Robert. "Military America." *New York Review of Books* vol. 15, no. 2 (23 July 1970).

1701. Hoffman, H. "View from the Hell Book." *Center Magazine* vol. 2, no. 4 (June 1969).

1702. McDonald, D. "Militarism in America." *Center Magazine* vol. 3, no. 1 (Jan. 1970).

1703. Montesano, G. "In Quest of Justice." *Catholic Worker* vol. 36, no. 6 (July 1970).

1704. Nelson, Garrett. "Nixon's Silent House of Hawks." See no. 1417.

1705. Plastrik, J. "Backlash, Violence, Politics." *Dissent* (Oct. 1969).

1706. Radway, Lawrence I. "Militarism." *International Encyclopedia of the Social Sciences* vol. 10. New York: Macmillan, 1968.

1707. Rumin, M. "Violence and Democracy." *Dissent* vol. 17, no. 4 (July 1970).

1708. "Vietnam Students against Militarism." *Peace News* vol. 17, no. 86 (18 Sept. 1970).

1709. Walzer, M. "Corporate Authority and Civil Disobedience." *Dissent* (Oct. 1969).

1710. Wolin, Sheldon. "Is a New Politics Possible?" *New York Review of Books* vol. 15, no. 4 (3 Sept. 1970).

5. Public Information, Propaganda, Public Deception, Credibility Gap

1711. Ashmore, H. "Policy of Illusion." *Center Magazine* vol. 3, no. 3 (May 1970).

1712. Austin, Anthony. *The President's War.* Philadelphia: Lippincott, 1971. Indicts excess executive power.

1713. Brown, George W. *Generals and the Public: Recent Policy-Making in Civil-Military Relations.* Lawrence, Kan.: Governmental Research Center, University of Kansas, 1964. Covers the problem of the armed forces informing or "propagandizing" the public about the "enemy," etc.

1714. Fisher, L. "A Case Study in Deception." *Progressive* vol. 33, no. 11 (Nov. 1969). Lying about armaments.

1715. Fritchev, C. "Communist Terrorism in Vietnam." *New America* vol. 9, no. 12 (31 Aug. 1970).

1716. Fulbright, Senator J. William. *The Pentagon Propaganda Machine.*

New York: Liveright, 1970. A survey of the activities, funding, and institutional arrangements of the Public Affairs Section of the DoD and various services. For greater detail, see the material Senator Fulbright placed in *The Congressional Record* 1, 2, 4, and 5 Dec. 1969.

1717. "GI's in War to Be Told About 'Silent Majority.' " *New York Times* (18 Dec. 1969), p. 14.

1718. Goulden, Joseph C. *Truth Is the First Casualty: The Gulf of Tonkin Affair—Illusion and Reality.* Chicago: Rand McNally, 1969.

1719. Goulding, Phil G. *Confirm or Deny: Informing the People on National Security.* New York: Harper & Row, 1970. Interesting and anecdotal, by a former DoD Public Affairs official.

1720. Holloway, Gen. Bruce K. (USAF). "The Telling Is as Important as the Doing." *Air Force and Space Digest* vol. 53 (Dec. 1970). Strategic Air Command Commander-in-Chief cites need for better public relations effort to convince public of worth of military operations, etc.

1721. Kempton, Murray. "From the City of Lies." *New York Review of Books* vol. 14, no. 11 (4 June 1970).

1722. Kraslow, David, and Loory, Stuart H. *The Secret Search for Peace in Vietnam.* New York: Random House, 1968. Evidence that U. S. did not want to negotiate as it publicly claimed.

1723. "Laird Lies 11 Times in One Speech." *Old Mole* vol. 1, no. 20 (28 Aug. 1969).

1724. Madsen, Maj. Gen. Frank M., Jr. "The Social Implications of Military Education and Training." See no. 123.

1725. McDonnell, James. "Education: AFA's Basic and Continuing Mission." See no. 1014.

1726. Marshall, S. L. A. "Politicians and the Military." *The New Leader* vol. 45 (5 Feb. 1962). Against General Edwin A. Walker's activities but cites need for military to indoctrinate its soldiers.

1727. Moon, Col. Gordon A., II. "Military Security vs. the Right to Know." *Army* vol. 18 (July 1968).

1728. Morey and Calvert. "Truth Speaks at the Pentagon." *WIN* vol. 6, no. 12 (July 1970).

1729. Murphy, Lt. Dan P. (USA). "CRACs mend the cracks." *Army Digest* vol. 26 (Jan. 1971). About Community Relations Advisory Councils.

1730. "National Security Seminars." *Air Force and Space Digest* (Sept. 1969).

1731. Navy Legislative Liaison Office. "FDL Public Affairs." Paper

(Jan. 1967). Reprinted as an appendix to the report of the Summer National Security Research Project, in the *Congressional Record* (6 Nov. 1969), pp. E–9417–23. Lobbying effort by the navy in behalf of the Fast Deployment Logistics Ship. Highly revealing.

1732. "OSD Gives Rules on Military Political Activity." *Air Force Policy Letter for Commanders* supplement no. 9 (Sept. 1968).

1733. Palma, Capt. Henry. "Motivating the 'Now' Generation." *U. S. Air Force Instructors Journal* vol. 8 (Summer 1970).

1734. "Presidential Propaganda." *Progressive* vol. 34, no. 9 (Sept. 1970).

1735. "Review, Clearance of Department of the Air Force Information." *The Inspector General Brief* vol. 23 (12 Mar. 1971).

1736. Roberts, D. "Revelation of U. S. Pnompenh Support." *The Militant* vol. 34, no. 33 (11 Sept. 1970).

1737. Rosen, M. "The Weapon Called Television." *Liberated Guardian* vol. 1, no. 7 (28 July 1970).

1738. Schurmann, Franz; Scott, Peter Dale; and Zelnik, Reginald. *The Politics of Escalation in Vietnam.* Boston: Beacon Press/Fawcett, 1966. Contrasts "diplomatic initiatives" with escalation that followed.

1739. Shearer, Derek. "The Pentagon Propaganda Machine." In Leonard Rodberg and Derek Shearer, eds. *The Pentagon Watchers.* See no. 13.

1740. Stanley, Maj. David L. "Getting through to Youth." *Infantry* vol. 60 (May-June 1970).

1741. Stone, I. F. "Fulbright Exposes the Pentagon's Multi-Million-Dollar Operation Brainwash." *I. F. Stone's Bi-Weekly* (15 Dec. 1969).

1742. ———— "Pentagon Poisons Public Mind on SALT." *I. F. Stone's Bi-Weekly* vol. 18, no. 15 (27 July 1970).

1743. Sturm, Ted. "Building Better Men Together." *The Airman* (Nov. 1967). About military citizenship education through the Boy Scouts.

1744. Swomley, John. *Press Agents of the Pentagon.* League against Conscription, 1953. Military propaganda in the postwar period. Available directly from Swomley, St. Paul School of Theology, St. Louis, Mo.

1745. U. S. Congress. House. Committee on Government Operations. Subcommittee on Military Operations. (91st Congress, 1st session). *Military Assistance to Commercial Film Projects: Staff*

Memorandum (with Department of Defense commentary.) Washington, D.C.: Committee print, Dec. 1969.

1746. U. S. Congress. Senate. Committee on Armed Services. Special Preparedness Subcommittee (87th Congress, 2d session). *Military Cold War Education and Speech Review Policies: Report on the Use of Military Personnel and Facilities to Arouse the Public to the Menace of the Cold War and to Inform and Educate Armed Forces Personnel on the Nature and Menace of the Cold War* (including individual views). Washington, D. C.: Committee print, USGPO, 1962.

1747. United States Department of the Army. *The Information Officer's Guide. (Department of the Army Pamphlet No. 360–5).* Washington D.C.: Headquarters, Department of the Army, August 1968.

1748. United States. Department of Defense. Office of the Assistant Secretary of Defense for Public Affairs. "Catalogue of Current Information Materials Produced by the Armed Forces Information Services."

1749. _____. "Selected list of Armed Forces Films for Public Exhibition." Both available directly from the Office of the Assistant Secretary of Defense for Public Affairs.

1750. United States. Industrial College of the Armed Forces. *Information Guide for the Conduct of National Security Seminars.* Washington D. C.: Industrial College of the Armed Forces, May 1964. Contains program authority, mission, methods of operation, funding, detailed outlines, etc.

1751. "War, What War?" *The Militant* vol. 34, no. 33 (11 Sept. 1970).

1752. Ward, R. "Truth Shrouded in Thai Agreement." *Guardian* vol. 21, no. 46 (30 Aug. 1969).

1753. Williams, R. M., Jr. "Are Americans and Their Cultural Values Adaptable to the Concept and Techniques of Unconventional Warfare?" See no. 1633.

F. OTHER ROLES AND IMPACTS
*1. Social Engineering: Project Transition, Project 100,000,
Domestic Action Council, Police Recruiting,
Aid to Civil Authorities, Others*

1754. Anderson, William A. "Military Organizations in Natural Disaster: Established and Emergent Norms." *American Behavioral Scientist* vol. 13, no. 3 (Jan.-Feb. 1971). Military disaster relief, where wholehearted civilian support is lacking.

1755. "Can the Fired Find Jobs?" *Government Executive* vol. 2 (Sept. 1970). Project Transition.

1756. Clark, Harold F., and Sloan, Harold S. *Classrooms in the Military.*

New York: Bureau of Publications, Teachers College, Columbia University, 1964.

1757. Clarke, Lt. Col. Mary E. (USA). "Your Army Cares and Shares." *Army Digest* vol. 25 (Sept. 1970). Domestic Action Program.

1758. Clifford, Clark M. "Defense's Responsibility to the Nation: More Than Just Arms." *Air Force and Space Digest* vol. 51 (Nov. 1968). Genesis of the Domestic Action Council.

1759. "Contributing in Many Ways." *Army Digest* vol. 25 (Oct. 1970).

1760. "Cooperative Education Program." *Army Digest* vol. 22 (Nov. 1967).

1761. "DoD Amends Program for College Early Release." *Commanders Digest* vol. 4 (27 Jan. 1968).

1762. "DoD Domestic Action Program." *The Inspector General Brief* vol. 22 (28 Aug. 1970).

1763. Engelhardt, Lt. Robert W. "Policing up Recruits." *Army Digest* vol. 24 (Jan. 1969). Early release for soldiers entering police work.

1764. "Equal Opportunity Office—A Total Involvement." *Army Digest* vol. 25 (Apr. 1970). Equal opportunity and treatment of military personnel; Project Transition.

1765. Erickson, Col. James L. "Bringing the School to the Man." *Army Digest* vol. 22 (Nov. 1967).

1766. Fisher, Allan, and Brown, George. *Army "New Standards" Personnel. Vol. 1: Relationship between Literacy Level and Indices of Military Performance. Vol. 2: Effect of Remedial Literacy Training on Performance in Military Service.* Alexandria, Va.: Hum RRO, Apr. 1971. Statistical analysis of Project 100,000 data.

1767. Forbes, Allan L. "Military Forces in the War on Hunger." *Military Review* vol. 50 (Jan. 1970).

1768. Glick, Edward Bernard. "Alaskan Civic Action." *Military Review* vol. 46 (Dec. 1966).

1769. _____. *Peaceful Conflict: The Non-military Use of the Military.* Harrisburg, Pa.: Stackpole, 1967. Proposes using armies for social and economic development needs.

1770. Hays, Col. Samuel H. (USA, Ret.). "The Soldier's Rights in a Free Society." *Army* vol. 20 (May 1970).

1771. Hill, Forest G. *Roads, Rails, and Waterways: The Army Engineers and Early Transportation.* Norman, Okla.: University of Oklahoma Press, 1957. Nonmilitary activities of the U. S. Army.

1772. Hogue, James. "Project Transition: Training for Tomorrow." *Army* vol. 18 (Oct. 1968).

1773. Johnston, Chief Journalist Thomas A. "Helping Others Help

Themselves." COMCBPAC Reports, Seabee Teams, special ed. (Oct. 1959–July 1968). Pearl Harbor, Ha.: Navy Publications and Printing Service Office, 1969.

1774. Kerr, Lt. Col. James W. "Military Support of Civil Authority." *Military Review* vol. 50 (July 1970).

1775. Leavitt, William. "Project 100,000: An Experiment in Salvaging People." *Air Force and Space Digest* (Jan. 1968).

1776. Little, Roger W. "Basic Education and Youth Socialization in the Armed Forces." *American Journal of Orthopsychiatry*, vol. 38 (July 1968). Using the army to instill primary learning. Cf. no. 1779.

1777. Maas, Arthur. *Muddy Waters: The Army Engineers and the Nation's Rivers.* Cambridge, Mass.: Harvard University Press, 1951. A study of the strong position attained by the Corps of Engineers in handling its civil functions as a result of its special relationships with certain groups in Congress. See also review by James H. Rowe, Jr., *American Political Science Review,* vol. 46 (June 1952).

1778. McLucas, John L. "Domestic Action—A New Challenge for the Air Force." *Air Force and Space Digest* vol. 53 (Feb. 1970). USAF helps attack social problems, construction of low-cost housing, recreation projects, Project Transition, Project 100,000, etc.

1779. Pilisuk, Marc. "A Reply to Roger Little: Basic Education and Youth Socialization Anywhere Else?" *American Journal of Orthopsychiatry* vol. 38 (July 1968). Compares Little's notion to that in Nazi Germany. Cf. no. 1776.

1780. Resor, Stanley R. "Project One Hundred Thousand." *Defense Management Journal* vol. 3 (Fall 1967). Former Secretary of the Army.

1781. Sharp, Laure M., and Biderman, Albert D. "Out of Uniform." *Monthly Labor Review* (Feb. 1967).

1782. Sturm, Ted R. "Building Better Men Together." *The Airman* (Nov. 1967). Military citizenship education through the Boy Scouts.

1783. _____. "Domestic Action—What It Is and How It Works." *The Airman* vol. 14 (July 1970).

1784. Tamburello, Capt. Gaspare B. "Education: A Reciprocal Civic-Military Objective." *U. S. Naval Institute Proceedings* vol. 95 (Oct. 1969).

1785. Tarr, Curtis W. "The Air Force as a National Resource." *Air University Review* vol. 21 (May-June 1970).

1786. U. S. Department of the Army. *Military Assistance to Civil Authori-*

ties. (*Department of the Army Pamphlet no. 27–11*). Washington D.C.: Headquarters, Department of the Army, December 1966.

1787.   ———. *Personnel Separations: Civilian Police Recruiting Program.* Circular no. 635–3. Washington, D. C.: 17 Apr. 1968.

1788.   U. S. Department of Defense. *Project Transition (Fact Sheet). (Department of Defense Fact Sheet no. 50.)* Washington D.C.: Department of Defense, May 1968.

1789.   United States. Department of Defense. Office of the Assistant Secretary of Defense for Manpower and Reserve Affairs. *Project One Hundred Thousand: Characteristics and Performance of "New Standards" Men.* Washington, D. C.: Sept. 1968. See also the updated report of the same title, March 1969.

1790.   ———. *Summary Statistics on Project One Hundred Thousand.* Washington, D. C.: Oct. 1967.

1791.   ———. *The Transition Program.* Washington, D. C.: Jan. 1969.

1792.   Wigner, Eugene, ed. *Who Speaks for Civil Defense?* New York: Scribners, 1968. An up-to-date account of the status of Civil Defense in the U. S.

1793.   See also IIIF2, ". . . Civic Action."

2. Ecology

1794.   "Birth Control: A Plot or a Beneficence?" *NACLA Newsletter* vol. 2, no. 1 (Mar. 1968).

1795.   Boyd, Max B. "Defense's War on Pollution." *Government Executive* vol. 2 (Sept. 1970).

1796.   "Deadly Chemicals Poison Vietnam." *Guardian* vol. 22, no. 8 (22 Nov. 1969).

1797.   "Defoliation, Dow, and Vietnam." *Peace News* vol. 17, no. 29 (15 Aug. 1969).

1798.   Earthworm. "Radioactive Death." *Rat* vol. 2, no. 17 (9 Sept. 1969).

1799.   Eggington, J. "Atom Death." *Kaleidoscope—Madison* vol. 1, no. 3 (22 July 1969).

1800.   Gallagher, T. "Cancer Highest Stage of Imperialism." *Old Mole* vol. 1, no. 20 (28 Aug. 1969).

1801.   Gitlin, Tod. "A Review—Earth and Politics." *Space City* vol. 1, no. 4 (28 Aug. 1969).

1802.   Inglis, D. "Nuclear Pollution and the Arms Race." *Progressive* vol. 34, no. 4 (Apr. 1970).

1803.   Jacobs, Paul. "The Coming Atomic Blast in Alaska." *New York Review of Books* vol. 17, no. 1 (22 July 1971).

1804. Lampe, K. "Ecology and the Movement." *WIN* vol. 5, no. 14 (Aug. 1969). Bibliography in same issue.
1805. Liberation News Service. "Vietnamese Ecology Battered." *Chinook* vol. 2, no. 26 (16 July 1970).
1806. Maas, Arthur. *Muddy Waters: The Army Engineers and the Nations Rivers.* See no. 1777.
1807. McGrath, K. "War Is Pollution." *Peace News* vol. 17, no. 43 (21 Nov. 1969).
1808. Maxson, R. "Peace-Ecology Coalition." *L.A. Free Press* vol. 7, no. 34 (21 Aug. 1970).
1809. Mayers, P. "U. S. CBW Deforms Viet Babies." *L.A. Free Press* vol. 6, no. 83 (19 Dec. 1969).
1810. Peck, J. "Nerve Gas Gets on World's Nerves." *WIN* vol. 5, no. 15 (1 Sept. 1969).
1811. "Population Control in the Third World." *NACLA Newsletter* vol. 4, no. 8 (Dec. 1970).
1812. Stanford Biology Group. *The Destruction of Indochina.* See no. 905.
1813. "UN—No Chemicals in Vietnam." *Guardian* vol. 22, no. 12 (20 Dec. 1969).
1814. Wagner, T. "Winged Pollution." *WIN* vol. 5, no. 17 (1 Nov. 1969). Airline boycott.
1815. Weisberg, Barry, ed. *Ecocide in Indochina.* See no. 494.
1816. Whiteside, Thomas. *Defoliation.* New York: Ballantine, 1970.
1817. *WIN* vol. 5, no. 14 (Aug. 1969). Articles on ecology by K. Lampe, T. Wagner and Ecology Action.
1818. See also IB3, "CBW," and IE3, "War Crimes and Atrocities."

III. American Security and the World

1819. Barnet, Richard J. *The Economy of Death.* See no. 1022.
1820. Bobrow, Davis B., ed. *Components of Defense Policy.* Chicago: Rand McNally, 1965. Various aspects.
1821. Donovan, Col. James A. (USMC, Ret.). *Militarism, U.S.A.* See no. 3.
1822. Fulbright, J. William. *The Arrogance of Power.* New York: Random House, 1967. America's new world role and its limitations.
1823. Gerberding, William P., and Brodie, Bernard. *The Political Dimension in National Strategy: Five Papers.* (Security Studies, Paper no. 13). Los Angeles: University of California, 1968. Brief articles critical of an anti-China ABM, student antimilitary protest and U. S. defense policies (including Vietnam and limited war).

1824. Hays, Col. Samuel H. (USA, Ret.), and Rehm, Lt. Col. Thomas A. "The Military in a Free Society." *U. S. Naval Institute Proceedings* vol. 95 (Feb. 1969). The U. S.'s military constabulary role in maintaining world order may make it easier to acculturate youth in the military in the future.

1825. Hilsman, Roger, and Good, Robert C., eds. *Foreign Policy in the Sixties: The Issues and the Instruments.* Baltimore: Johns Hopkins Press, 1965. Essays on the cold war, foreign policy processes, "orchestrating the instrumentalities" of foreign policy (in SE Asia), the U. N., statecraft and moral issues.

1826. Huntington, Samuel P. *The Common Defense.* See no. 56.

1827. _____. *The Soldier and the State.* See no. 6.

1828. Lens, Sidney. *The Military-Industrial Complex.* See no. 10.

1829. Ransom, Harry Howe. *The Intelligence Establishment.* See no. 327.

1830. Rodberg, Leonard S. and Shearer, Derek, eds. *The Pentagon Watchers.* See no. 13.

1831. Shoup, Gen. David M. (USMC, Ret.). "The New American Militarism." *Atlantic* vol. 223 (Apr. 1969). "America has become a militaristic and aggressive nation."

1832. United States. Arms Control and Disarmament Agency (ACDA). *Control of Local Conflict.* 4 vols. ACDA/WEC–98, Washington, D. C.: USGPO, 1967. Vol. 1: *Design Study on Arms Control and Limited War in the Developing Areas,* summary report by Lincoln P. Bloomfield et al.; vol. 2: *Design Study on Arms Control and Limited War in the Developing Areas* (defining problem, design study, and preliminary findings) by Lincoln P. Bloomfield et al.; vol. 3: *Design Study on Arms Control and Limited War in the Developing Areas: Studies of Conflict,* by Amelia C. Leiss et al.; vol. 4: *Design Study, The Relevance of Factor Analysis to the Study of Arms Control and Limited War,* by Thomas C. O'Sullivan.

1833. United States. *Collective Defense Treaties.* Prepared by Helen Mattas. Washington, D. C.: USGPO, 1969. Maps, texts of treaties, a chronology, status of forces agreement and comparative chart.

1834. Westerfield, H. Bradford. *The Instruments of America's Foreign Policy.* New York: Crowell, 1963. Historical; wide range of "instruments" covered. See no. 1920.

1835. Yarmolinsky, Adam. *The Military Establishment.* See no. 19.

1836. _____ et al. "No More Vietnams? The War and the Future of American Foreign Policy." (A Symposium) *Atlantic* vol. 222, no. 5 (Nov. 1968). With many well-known participants.

A. STRATEGIC IDEOLOGIES AND DOCTRINES

1837. Acheson, Dean G. *Present at the Creation: My Years in the State Department.* New York: Norton, 1969. Memoirs of a chief architect of the cold war. See the review by Ronald Steel. "Commissar of the Cold War." *New York Review of Books* (12 Feb. 1970).

1838. Aron, Raymond. *The Evolution of Modern Strategic Thought.* Adelphi Papers no. 54. London: Institute for Strategic Studies, 1969.

1839. Baldwin, Hanson. *Strategy for Tomorrow.* New York: Harper & Row, 1970. Conservative.

1840. Bell, Cora. *Negotiation from Strength: A Study in the Politics of Power.* New York: Knopf, 1963. Critical of many common assumptions.

1841. Brodie, Bernard, ed. *The Future of Deterrence in U. S. Strategy.* Los Angeles: Security Studies Project, 1968. Broad discussion of nuclear strategy.

1842. Dulles, John F. "The Doctrine of Massive Retaliation." *Department of State Bulletin* vol. 30 (25 Jan. 1954).

1843. Erickson, John et al., eds. *The Military-Technical Revolution.* See no. 386.

1844. Forrestal, James. *The Forrestal Diaries.* See no. 39.

1845. Frank, Jerome D. "Deterrence—For How Long?" *War/Peace Report* vol. 7 (Feb. 1968).

1846. Gavin, Lt. Gen. James M. *War and Peace in the Space Age.* New York: Harper & Row, 1958.

1847. Halperin, Morton H. *Limited War in the Nuclear Age.* New York: Wiley, 1963. Annotated bibliography, pp. 133–184.

1848. Harriman, W. Averell. *America and Russia in a Changing World: A Half Century of Personal Observation.* Garden City, New York: Doubleday, 1971.

1849. Hilsman, Roger. *To Move a Nation: The Politics of Foreign Policy in the Administration of John F. Kennedy.* New York: Dell, 1967. Comprehensive, if ideological.

1850. ———, ed. *Foreign Policy in the Sixties.* See no. 1825.

1851. Jackson, Henry M. "Senator Jackson in War College Lecture Warns of Pitfalls in Dealing with· Reds—Negotiate from Strength." *Officer* vol. 46 (May 1970).

1852. Kahn, Herman. *On Escalation: Metaphors and Scenarios.* Baltimore: Penguin, 1965. Contingency planning at its most frightening.

1853. ———. *On Thermonuclear War.* Princeton, N. J.: Princeton University Press, 1961.

1854.   ———. *Thinking about the Unthinkable*. New York: Avon Books, 1962. Important thinktank analyst.

1855.   Kaufmann, William W. *The McNamara Strategy*. New York: Harper & Row, 1964.

1856.   Kennan, George F. *Memoirs, 1925–1950*. Boston: Little, Brown, 1967. Good especially for its picture of the U.S.S.R.

1857.   Kissinger, Henry A. *American Foreign Policy: Three Essays*. New York: Norton, 1969. See review by Fritchy. *New York Review of Books* vol. 13, no. 5 (25 Sept. 1969).

1858.   ———. *The Necessity for Choice: Prospects of American Foreign Policy*. New York: Harper & Row, 1961.

1859.   Leckie, Robert. *The Wars of America*. New York: Harper & Row, 1968. Historical treatment of strategic doctrine.

1860.   LeMay, Gen. Curtis E. (USAF, Ret.). *America Is in Danger*. See no. 204.

1861.   McNamara, Robert S. *The Essence of Security: Reflections in Office*. See no. 1646.

1862.   Nixon, Richard. *Setting the Course, The First Year: Major Policy Statements by President Richard Nixon*. Commentaries by Richard Wilson. New York: Funk & Wagnalls, 1970.

1863.   ———. *U. S. Foreign Policy for the 1970s: A New Strategy for Peace. A Report to the Congress by Richard Nixon, President of the United States*. Washington, D. C.: USGPO, 1970.

1864.   Payne, James. *The American Threat*. Chicago: Markham, 1971. Hardline containment advocacy.

1865.   Power, Gen. Thomas (USAF, Ret.). *Design for Survival*. See no. 217.

1866.   Raser, J. "ABM and the Mad Strategy." *Ramparts* vol. 8, no. 5 (Nov. 1969).

1867.   *Report from Iron Mountain on the Possibility and Desirability of Peace*. See no. 1041.

1868.   Rivers, L. Mendel. "If War Can Be Morally Justified, Victory Is Morally Justified." *Officer* vol. 46 (July 1970).

1869.   Schelling, Thomas C. *Arms and Influence*. New Haven, Conn.: Yale University Press, 1966. Using force for bargaining and blackmail.

1870.   Taylor, Gen. Maxwell (USA, Ret.). *The Uncertain Trumpet*. See no. 1369.

1871.   Truman, Harry S. *Memoirs*. 2 vols. Vol. 1: *Year of Decisions;* vol. 2: *Years of Trial and Hope*. Garden City, N. Y.: Doubleday, 1956. Important source of early cold war thinking.

1872. Twining, Gen. Nathan (USAF, Ret.). *Neither Liberty nor Safety.* See no. 226.

1873. Westerfield, H. Bradford. *The Instruments of America's Foreign Policy.* See no. 1920.

1874. See also IIIJ, "National and Military Policies and Strategies; The Future."

B. THE COLD WAR
AND FOREIGN POLICY AS HISTORY

1875. Acheson, Dean G. *Present at the Creation.* See no. 1837.

1876. Alperovitz, Gar. *Atomic Diplomacy: Hiroshima and Potsdam.* New York: Simon and Schuster, 1965. Early cold war. Revisionist.

1877. ———. *Cold War Essays.* Garden City, N. Y.: Doubleday, 1969.

1878. Ambrose, Stephen E. *The Rise to Globalism: American Foreign Policy Since 1938.* Baltimore: Penguin, 1971. According to Ronald Steel, among the best surveys of cold war history yet to appear.

1879. Bernstein, Barton J., ed. *Politics and Policies of the Truman Administration.* Chicago: Quadrangle, 1970. Bernstein has edited this and other revisionist interpretations of the Truman period.

1880. Clemens, Diane S. *Yalta.* New York: Oxford, 1970. Well-researched reconstruction of the conference.

1881. Donnelly, Desmond. *Struggle for the World: The Cold War, 1917–1965.* New York: St. Martin's Press, 1965. Traditional.

1882. Draper, Theodore. *Abuse of Power.* New York: Viking, 1967. Reevaluation brought on in part by the Vietnam involvement.

1883. Etzioni, Amitai. "The Kennedy Experiment." *Western Political Quarterly* vol. 20 (June 1967). Discusses Kennedy's attempt to initiate reduction of tensions in 1963.

1884. Feis, Herbert. *From Trust to Terror: The Onset of The Cold War, 1945–1950.* New York: Norton, 1970. In-depth history.

1885. Fleming, D. F. *The Cold War and Its Origins, 1917–1960.* 2 vols. Garden City, N. Y.: Doubleday, 1961. The standard revisionist treatise, stimulated much new scholarship on the period.

1886. Freeland, Richard M. *The Truman Doctrine and the Origins of McCarthyism: Foreign Policy, Domestic Politics, and Internal Security 1946–1948.* New York: Knopf, 1972. Alleges Truman whipped up anticommunist emotion to gain domestic support for aid programs.

1887. Gamson, William, and Modigliani, Andre. *Untangling the Cold War.* Boston: Little, Brown, 1971. A quantitative analysis of Soviet-American relations, testing hypotheses about initiation of hostility and response.

1888.   Gardner, Lloyd C. *Architects of Illusion: Men and Ideas in American Foreign Policy.* Chicago: Quadrangle, 1970. American policymakers in the 1940s.

1889.   ———; Schlesinger, Arthur, Jr.; and Morgenthau, Hans J. *The Origins of the Cold War.* Waltham, Mass.: Ginn-Blaisdell, 1970. A liberal history.

1890.   Gittings, John. "Peanuts and the Good Soldier." *New York Review of Books* vol. 17, no. 1 (22 July 1971). Review of Tuchman's biography of Stilwell. See no. 1917.

1891.   Graebner, Norman A. *Cold War Diplomacy: American Foreign Policy, 1945–1960.* Princeton, N. J.: Van Nostrand, 1962. Traditional survey.

1892.   Herz, Martin F. *Beginnings of the Cold War.* Bloomington, Ind.: Indiana University Press, 1966. A traditional interpretation.

1893.   Horowitz, David. *Empire and Revolution: A Radical Interpretation of Contemporary History.* New York: Random House, 1969. Marxist interpretation of history since the October Revolution. Overview and synthesis. See also review by B. Fitch. *Monthly Review* vol. 21, no. 7 (Dec. 1969).

1894.   ———. *The Free World Colossus: A Critique of American Foreign Policy in the Cold War.* Rev. ed. New York: Hill and Wang, 1971. An important revisionist synthesis, intended specifically to refute traditional interpretation.

1895.   ———, ed. *Containment and Revolution.* Boston: Beacon Press, 1967. A collection of essays on the history of the cold war from 1917 to the present. Revisionist.

1896.   Houghton, N. D., ed. *Struggle against History: United States Foreign Policy in an Age of Revolution.* New York: Simon & Schuster, 1968.

1897.   Kennan, George F. *Memoirs, 1925–1950.* See no. 1856.

1898.   Kolko, Gabriel. *The Politics of War: The World and United States Foreign Policy, 1943–45.* New York: Random House, 1970. A major revisionist statement of the origins of the cold war in the World War II period.

1899.   LaFeber, Walter. *America, Russia, and the Cold War, 1945–1967.* New York: Wiley, 1967. LaFeber has also edited several revisionist works on the cold war.

1900.   Luard, Evan, ed. *The Cold War, A Re-appraisal.* New York: Praeger, 1964.

1901.   Lukacs, John. *A New History of the Cold War.* 3d ed., Garden City, N. Y.: Anchor Books, 1966.

1902.   Morgenthau, Hans J. "Historical Justice and the Cold War." *New York Review of Books* vol. 13, no. 1 (10 July 1969).

1903. Morray, Joseph P. *From Yalta to Disarmament: Cold War Debate.* New York: Monthly Review Press, 1961. Revisionist.

1904. Osgood, Robert, Tucker, Robert, et al. *America and the World: From the Truman Doctrine to Vietnam.* Baltimore: Johns Hopkins Press, 1970. Authors associated with Washington Center of Foreign Policy Research. Liberal interpretation.

1905. Parenti, Michael, ed. *Trends and Tragedies in American Foreign Policy.* Boston: Little, Brown, 1971. A radical critique.

1906. Pfaff, William. *Condemmed to Freedom: The Breakdown of Liberal Society.* New York: Random House, 1971. Sees Vietnam as liberal internationalism pushed to its logical extreme.

1907. Pope, D. "Radical Academic Guide: American History." *Liberation* vol. 15, no. 6 (1970).

1908. Quester, George. *Nuclear Diplomacy: The First Twenty-Five Years.* New York: Dunellen, 1970.

1909. Rostow, W. W. *The United States in the World Arena: An Essay in Recent History.* New York: Harper & Row, 1960. By one of L.B.J.'s chief cold warriors.

1910. Russett, Bruce M. *No Clear and Present Danger: A Skeptical View of the United States Entry into World War II.* New York: Harper & Row, 1972. Entry in World War II perhaps not necessary for American security; served as precedent to cold war acts and assumptions.

1911. Schlesinger, Arthur M., Jr. "Origins of the Cold War." *Foreign Affairs* vol. 46 (Oct. 1967). Shows influence of revisionism.

1912. Schilling, Warner et al. *Strategy, Politics and Defense Budgets.* See no. 81.

1913. Starobin, Joseph R. "Origins of the Cold War: The Communist Dimension." *Foreign Affairs* vol. 4 (July 1969).

1914. Steel, Ronald. "Commissar of the Cold War." *New York Review of Books* (12 Feb. 1970). Review of Acheson's memoirs.

1915. _____. "Did Anyone Start the Cold War?" *New York Review of Books* vol. 17, no. 3 (2 Sept. 1971). A useful comparison of liberal and revisionist cold war historians.

1916. Stillman, Edmund O., and Pfaff, William. *Power and Impotence; The Failure of America's Foreign Policy.* New York: Random House, 1966. Liberal critique.

1917. Tuchman, Barbara. *Stilwell and the American Experience in China, 1911–1945.* New York: Macmillan, 1971. A military biography which puts in perspective the U. S. involvement in China.

1918. Tucker, Robert W. *The Radical Left and American Foreign Policy.*

Baltimore: Johns Hopkins Press, 1971. Traces influence of new historiography and criticism.

1919. Truman, Harry S. *Memoirs.* See no. 1871.

1920. Westerfield, H. Bradford. *The Instruments of America's Foreign Policy.* New York: Crowell, 1963. "An analysis of the ways—military, economic, informational and undercover—in which America's foreign policy functions to secure America's survival."

1921. Williams, William Appleman. *The Tragedy of American Diplomacy.* Cleveland, O.: World Publishing Co., 1959. Important interpretation by one of the earliest of the revisionists.

1922. See also IIIE, "Intervention" and other related sections.

C. FOREIGN POLICY POLITICS AND PROCESSES

1923. Allison, Graham T. *Essence of Decision.* Boston: Little, Brown, 1971. An important study of crisis decision making, especially in Cuban missiles crisis. Contrasts various analytical models.

1924. Bauer, Raymond A., and Gergen, Kenneth J., eds. *The Study of Policy Formation.* New York: Macmillan, 1968. Epistemology and theory with applications to foreign aid.

1925. Bowles, Chester. *Promises to Keep: My Years in Public Life, 1941–1969.* New York: Harper & Row, 1971. Memoirs with much inside information.

1926. California, University of (Los Angeles). Security Studies Project. *The Politics of Military Policy; Seminars on Politics of Policy-Making.* Los Angeles: UCLA, 1965.

1927. Campbell, John F. *The Foreign Affairs Fudge Factory.* New York: Basic Books, 1971. Incisive critique of "bumbling" foreign policy bureaucracy.

1928. Carey, Omer L., ed. *The Military-Industrial Complex and U. S. Foreign Policy.* See no. 1173.

1929. Cooper, Chester L. *The Lost Crusade: America in Vietnam.* New York: Dodd, Mead & Co., 1970. The war as seen from inside the national security bureaucracy.

1930. de Rivera, Joseph H. *The Psychological Dimension of Foreign Policy.* Columbus, O.: Charles E. Merrill, 1968. Comprehensive; applies contemporary psychology to the behavior of foreign and military policymakers. Useful as a text.

1931. Drachman, Edward R. *U. S. Policy toward Vietnam, 1940–1945.* Rutherford, N. J.: Fairleigh Dickinson University Press, 1970.

1932. Edinger, Lewis. "Military Leaders and Foreign Policy-Making." See no. 34.

1933. Ellsberg, Daniel. "Laos: What Nixon Is Up To." *New York Review of Books* vol. 16, no. 4 (11 Mar. 1971). Connects Indochina policy to domestic politics.

1934. ———. "The Quagmire Myth and the Stalemate Machine." *Public Policy* vol. 19, no. 2 (spring 1971).

1935. Erickson, John, ed. *The Military-Technical Revolution: Its Impact on Strategy and Foreign Policy.* New York: Praeger, 1966.

1936. Galbraith, John K. "Opinion: The Plain Lessons of a Bad Decade" (guest editorial). *Foreign Policy* no. 1 (Winter 1970–1971). Organizational momentum in the Pentagon blamed for much of U. S. Vietnam policy.

1937. Gelb, Leslie. "Vietnam: The System Worked." *Foreign Policy* no. 3 (Summer 1971).

1938. Hilsman, Roger. *To Move a Nation.* See no. 1849.

1939. Hoffmann, Stanley. *Gulliver's Troubles: Or, The Setting of American Foreign Policy.* New York: McGraw-Hill, 1968. MIC doesn't dominate foreign policy; its members, as technical specialists, "share a commitment to a certain way of thinking with other public officials that leads to the selection of essentially technological solutions to policy problems." Best exposition of the "engineering approach" to foreign policy problems.

1940. Hoopes, Townsend. *The Limits of Intervention.* See no. 51.

1941. Johnson, Richard A. *The Administration of American Foreign Policy.* Austin, Tex.: University of Texas Press, 1971.

1942. Kolko, Gabriel. *The Roots of American Foreign Policy: An Analysis of Power and Purpose.* Boston: Beacon Press, 1969. The ideology and personnel of business dictate this country's policies.

1943. Lefever, Ernest W. *Ethics and U. S. Foreign Policy.* New York: Meridian Books, 1957.

1944. Lerche, Charles O., Jr. "The Professional Officer and Foreign Policy." See no. 167.

1945. Liska, George. *Imperial America: The International Politics of Primacy.* Baltimore: Johns Hopkins Press, 1967. Accepts—even hails—American empire.

1946. Magdoff, Harry. *The Age of Imperialism: The Economics of U. S. Foreign Policy.* See no. 1065.

1947. Morgenthau, Hans J. *A New Foreign Policy for the United States.* New York: Praeger, 1969. Thought-provoking recommendations for dealing with fundamental national security problems.

1948. Neustadt, Richard E. *Alliance Politics.* New York: Columbia University Press, 1970.

1949. Nutter, G. Warren. "Foreign Policy and the DoD." *Air Force Policy Letter for Commanders* supplement no. 9 (Sept. 1970).

1950. *The Pentagon Papers (The Senator Gravel Edition): The Defense Department History of United States Decisionmaking on Vietnam.* Boston: Beacon Press, 1971. In four volumes the most complete version available.

1951. Reischauer, Edmund O. *Beyond Vietnam: The United States and Asia.* New York: Vintage Books, 1968.

1952. Sapin, Burton M. *The Making of United States Foreign Policy.* New York: Praeger, 1966. Includes discussion of the role of the military in the foreign policy process.

1953. Smith, Maj. Mark E., and Johns, Maj. Claude J., Jr., eds. *American Defense Policy.* See no. 15.

1954. Stavins, Ralph, ed. *Warmakers: The Men Who Made the Vietnam War and How They Did It.* New York: Outerbridge and Dienstfrey, 1971.

1955. _____ et al. *Washington Plans an Aggressive War.* New York: Random House, 1971. Detailed account of decisions.

1956. Swomley, John M. *The Military Establishment.* See no. 88.

1957. Trask, David F. *Victory without Peace: American Foreign Relations in the Twentieth Century.* New York: Wiley, 1968.

1958. Vagts, Alfred. *Defense and Diplomacy.* See no. 94.

1959. Yarmolinsky, Adam. *United States Military Power and Foreign Policy.* Chicago: Center for Policy Study, University of Chicago, 1967. Argues that often the military's action-orientation and a "short-range, time-buying military program tends to obscure the need for a detailed, long-range non-military program."

1960. See also IA1, ". . . Decision-making. . . ." All of Section III, "American Security and the World," deals with one aspect or another of American foreign policy politics and processes.

D. MILITARISTIC INFLUENCES ON POLICY: WITHIN GOVERNMENT, FROM FIELD OPERATIONS, CONTINGENCY PLANNING

1961. Barrett, Raymond J. "Politico-Military Expertise: A Practical Program." See no. 137.

1962. _____. "The Role of the Military Attache." *Military Review* vol. 51 (May 1971). Appeal for "revitalizing" the attaché system to make it less a channel of contact with foreign armies and more a source of "politico-military advice in the Country Teams at our Embassies abroad."

1963. Benjamin, Roger W., and Edinger, Lewis J. "Conditions for Military Control over Foreign Policy Decisions in Major States." See no. 25.

1964. Bobrow, Davis B., ed. *Weapons Systems Decisions.* See no. 381.

1965. Bramson, Leon, and Goethals, George W., eds. *War: Studies from Psychology, Sociology, Anthropology.* New York: Basic Books, 1964.

1966. Carey, Omer L., ed. *The Military-Industrial Complex and U. S. Foreign Policy.* See no. 1173.

1967. Cochran, Bert. *The War System.* New York: Macmillan 1965.

1968. Cooper, Chester L. *The Lost Crusade.* See no. 1929.

1969. Drinan, Robert F., S. J. *Vietnam and Armageddon: Peace, War and the Christian Conscience.* New York: Sheed and Ward, 1970.

1970. Green, Philip. "Science, Government, and the Case of RAND." See no. 1512.

1971. Hilsman, Roger. *Strategic Intelligence and National Decisions.* Glencoe, Ill.: Free Press, 1956.

1972. Hoffmann, Stanley. *The State of War: Essays in the Theory and Practice of International Politics.* New York: Praeger, 1965. The international system operates under a continuous threat of violence.

1973. Horowitz, Irving L. *The War Game: Studies of the New Civilian Militarists.* New York: Ballantine Books, 1963.

1974. "The Imperial Team/Latin America." *NACLA Newsletter* vol. 3, no. 7 (Nov. 1969). Includes information on U. S. ambassadors, etc.

1975. Kahn, Herman. *On Escalation.* See no. 1852.

1976. Kyre, Martin, and Martin, Joan. *Military Occupation and National Security.* Washington, D. C.: Public Affairs Press, 1968.

1977. Lasswell, Harold D. "The Garrison State Hypothesis Today." See no. 1346.

1978. Metcalf, Lt. Col. Ramsey N. (USA). "The Continuing Requirement for the Professional Military Man in Diplomatic Roles." *Armor* vol. 74 (Jan.-Feb. 1965). Cold war has blurred peace-war distinction; need more people with military background in diplomacy to prevent "diplomatic weakness and unnecessary compromise tantamount to appeasement."

1979. Miles, Lt. Col. Jack L. (USMC). "The Fusion of Military and Political Considerations: Threat or Challenge to the Military." *Marine Corps Gazette* pt. 1, vol. 52 (Aug. 1968); pt. 2, vol. 52 (Sept. 1968).

1980. Mills, C. Wright. *The Power Elite.* See no. 210.

1981. Nelson, Lt. Comdr. Andrew G. (USN). "Politics and the Naval Officer." See no. 172.

1982. "Nixon's Latin America Team." *NACLA Newsletter* vol. 3, no. 1 (Mar. 1969).

1983. "Open Precedent by Hermano Alves." *NACLA Newsletter* vol. 1, no. 1 (Mar. 1967).

1984. "OSD Gives Rules on Military Political Activity." *Air Force Policy Letter for Commanders* supplement no. 9 (Sept. 1968).

1985. Paige, Glenn D. *The Korean Decision, June 24–30, 1950.* See no. 1356.

1986. *The Pentagon Papers.* See no. 1950.

1987. Pfeffer, Richard M., ed. *No More Vietnams? The War and the Future of American Foreign Policy.* New York: Harper & Row, 1968. The utility of power in foreign policy, and in Vietnam in particular.

1988. Sapin, Burton M. *The Making of United States Foreign Policy.* See no. 1952.

1989. Schlossberg, Maj. Arnold, Jr. "Key Men for the Politico-Military Arena." *Army Digest* vol. 25 (Aug. 1970).

1990. Simons, Lt. Col. William E. "Military Professionals as Policy Advisors." *Air University Review* vol. 20 (Mar.-Apr. 1969).

1991. Stavins, Ralph, ed. *Warmakers.* See no. 1954.

1992. _____ et al. *Washington Plans an Aggressive War.* See no. 1955.

1993. Swomley, John M. *The Military Establishment.* See no. 88. Includes discussion of foreign policy, military influence and the radical right.

1994. United States. Congress. Senate. Committee on Government Operations. Subcommittee on National Security and International Operations. *The State-Defense Officer Exchange Program: Analysis and Assessment* (pursuant to S. res. 24, 91st Congress). Washington, D. C.: USGPO, 1969. Exchange of personnel since 1961.

1995. Vagts, Alfred. *Defense and Diplomacy.* See no. 94.

1996. _____. *The Military Attaché.* Princeton, N. J.: Princeton University Press, 1967. Cross-cultural analysis.

1997. Wheeler, Gen. Earle G. (USA), and Parsons, J. Graham. "The Politico-Military Relationship." *Perspectives in Defense Management* (Mar. 1970).

1998. "Why There Is a Real Need for Political Advisors in the Military." *Armed Forces Management* vol. 12 (Jan. 1966).

1999. Wilson, Andrew. *The Bomb and the Computer: Wargaming from Ancient Chinese Mapboard to Atomic Computer.* New York: Delacorte Press, 1969.

2000.   Yarmolinsky, Adam. "Bureaucratic Structures and Political Outcomes." See no. 101.

2001.   ———. *United States Military Power and Foreign Policy.* See no. 1959.

2002.   See also IA1, "Decision-Making," IIA2, ". . . MIC," IIIC, "Foreign Policy Politics and Processes" and IIIF, "Counterinsurgency."

E. INTERVENTION
1. Intervention in General and in Specific Regions

2003.   Ackerman, Frank. "Industry and Imperialism in Brazil" *Review of Radical Political Economics* vol. 3, no. 4 (spring 1971). Relates Brazil's position in international economy to internal economic and social development. Good tabular data.

2004.   Barnet, Richard J. *Intervention and Revolution: The United States in the Third World.* New York: World Publishing Co., 1968. Argues intervention is the outcome of the policies of a near-autonomous group of "national security managers." Describes U. S. involvement and interest in Third World.

2005.   Bloomfield, Lincoln P. "Future Small Wars: Must the United States Intervene?" *Orbis* vol. 12 (Fall 1968). U. S. national interests in local conflicts.

2006.   Brown, Sam, and Ackland, Len. *Why Are We Still in Vietnam?* New York: Random House, 1970.

2007.   Caldwell, Malcolm, and Tan, Lek. *Cambodia in the Southeast Asian War.* New York: Monthly Review Press, 1971. U. S. foreign policy in the perspective of Cambodian history.

2008.   The Committee of Concerned Asian Scholars. *The Indochina Story.* New York: Pantheon, 1970. Detailed and documented account of American involvement.

2009.   Cooper, Chester L. *The Lost Crusade.* See no. 1929.

2010.   Countell, R. "U. S. Military Policy in Latin America." *Guardian* vol. 21, nos. 39–46 (June–Aug. 1969). Eight-part series.

2011.   Dommen, Arthur J. *Conflict in Laos.* New York: Praeger, 1964. Good example of prevailing ideological orientation toward intervention—high information content.

2012.   Fall, Bernard. *Anatomy of a Crisis.* Garden City, N. Y.: Doubleday, 1969.

2013.   ———. *Vietnam Witness.* New York: Praeger, 1966.

2014.   ———. *Street without Joy.* Harrisburg, Pa.: Stackpole, 1964.

2015.   Frank, Andre Gunder. *Capitalism and Underdevelopment in Latin*

America: Historical Studies in Chile and Brazil. New York: Monthly Review Press, 1967.

2016. ————. *Latin America: Underdevelopment or Revolution?* New York: Monthly Review Press, 1970.

2017. Gall, Norman. "Santo Domingo: The Politics of Terror." *New York Review of Books* vol. 17, no. 1 (22 July 1971). Exposé of Balaguer regime which U. S. helped establish in 1965.

2018. George, Alexander L.; Hall, David K.; and Simons, William E. (USAF). *The Limits of Coercive Diplomacy: Laos, Cuba, Vietnam.* Boston: Little, Brown, 1971. Claims to combine scholarly rigor and policy relevance.

2019. Gerassi, J. *The Great Fear in Latin America.* 2d ed. rev. New York: Collier Books, 1965.

2020. Goulden, Joseph C. *Truth Is the First Casualty.* See no. 1718.

2021. Halberstam, David. *The Making of a Quagmire.* New York: Random House, 1964. Vietnam.

2022. Hassler, Alfred. *Saigon, U.S.A.* New York: Richard W. Baron, 1970. Exposé of Thieu regime.

2023. Hoopes, Townsend. *The Limits of Intervention.* See no. 51.

2024. Horowitz, David. *Containment and Revolution.* See no. 1895.

2025. Johnson, Russell. "Is the Philippines Next?" *Liberation* vol. 15, no. 9 (Nov. 1970). Wide-ranging summary of the Philippines' internal development and relationship to U. S.

2026. Lieuwen, Edwin. *The United States and the Challenge to Security in Latin America.* Columbus, O.: Ohio State University Press, 1966.

2027. Moreno, José A. *Barrios in Arms: Revolution in Santo Domingo.* Pittsburgh, Pa.: University of Pittsburgh, 1970. The 1965 revolution, an inside view.

2028. Morgenthau, Hans J. "To Intervene or Not to Intervene." *Foreign Affairs* vol. 45 (Apr. 1967). Intervention only where our national interest requires it and where our power gives us a chance to succeed.

2029. NACLA. "U. S. Military and Police Operations in the Third World." New York: NACLA Pamphlet, 1971.

2030. Oglesby, Carl, and Shaull, Richard. *Containment and Change.* New York: Macmillan, 1967. Critique of U. S. foreign policy by a Marxist and a theologian.

2031. Paige, Glenn D. *The Korean Decision.* See no. 1356.

2032. *The Pentagon Papers.* See no. 1950.

2033. Parenti, Michael. *The Anti-Communist Impulse.* See no. 1650.

2034. Ravenal, Earl C. "The State of Nixon's World: The Political-Military Gap." *Foreign Policy* no. 3 (Summer 1971). Critique of the Nixon Doctrine; forsees U. S. controlling "a more consolidated empire."

2035. "Revolutionary War: Western Response." *Journal of International Affairs* (May 1971). America's third world policy in perspective.

2036. Salinger, Pierre. *On Instructions of My Government.* Garden City, N. Y.: Doubleday, 1971. Novel about a U. S.–China missile crisis in fictional "Santa Clara" whose theme is that U. S. policy is counterproductive in "stopping Communism."

2037. Schiller, Herbert I. "The Use of American Power in the Post-Colonial World." *Massachusetts Review* vol. 9, no. 4 (Autumn 1968).

2038. Scott, Peter Dale. "Laos: The Story Nixon Won't Tell." *New York Review of Books* vol. 14, no. 7 (9 Apr. 1970). Well documented, historical treatment of U. S. involvement in Laos.

2039. Slater, Jerome. *Intervention and Negotiation: The United States and the Dominican Revolution.* New York: Harper & Row, 1970. Based on classified and off-the-record sources. Somewhat apologetic.

2040. Stivers, William. "The Will to Intervene." In Leonard Rodberg and Derek Shearer. *The Pentagon Watchers.* See no. 13.

2041. Stone, I. F. *The Hidden History of the Korean War.* New York: Monthly Review Press, 1969. One of the original critiques of the Korean intervention. (First published in 1952).

2042. _____. Review of Hoopes's *Limits of Intervention. New York Review of Books* vol. 13, no. 10 (4 Dec. 1969).

2043. Toye, Hugh. *Laos: Buffer State or Battleground?* New York: Oxford, 1968. Includes history of U. S. involvement.

2044. "The U. S. Military and Economic Invasion of Thailand." *Pacific Research & World Empire Telegram* vol. 1, no. 1 (3 Aug. 1969).

2045. "U. S. Military Intervention: 1798–1945," and "U. S. Naval Activity 1946–1969." *NACLA Newsletter* vol. 3, no. 5 (Sept. 1969). From *Congressional Record.*

2046. "U. S. Military Operations/Latin America." *NACLA Newsletter* vol. 2, no. 6 (Oct. 1968).

2047. Warner, Dennis. *The Last Confucian: Vietnam, Southeast Asia and the West.* Sidney, Australia: Angus and Robertson, 1964.

2048. _____. *Reporting Southeast Asia.* Sidney: Angus and Robertson, 1966.

2. Imperialism

2049. Africa Research. "Ventures in Africa." *Old Mole* vol. 1, no. 16 (3 July 1969).

2050. Alavi, Hamza. "Imperialism, Old and New." In Ralph Miliband and John Saville, eds., *Socialist Register*. New York: Monthly Review Press, 1964.

2051. Baran, Paul. *The Political Economy of Growth*. See no. 1054.

2052. _____, and Sweezy, Paul. *Monopoly Capital*. See no. 1055.

2053. Bell, Peter F. "On the Theory of Imperialism." *Review of Radical Political Economics* vol. 3, no. 4 (Spring 1971). Outline summary of theoretical approaches with bibliography.

2054. Bodenheimer, Susanne. "Dependency and Imperialism: The Roots of Latin American Underdevelopment." *NACLA Newsletter* vol. 4, no. 3 (May-June 1970). Theoretical discussion.

2055. Bosch, Juan. *Pentagonism, A Substitute for Imperialism*. See no. 1169.

2056. Caspary, William. "American Economic Imperialism: A Survey of the Literature." Radical Education Project. See section IVD for address. Pamphlet. Very useful outline-bibliographic report.

2057. Daniels, E. "From Mercantilism to Imperialism." *NACLA Newsletter* vol. 4, no. 4 (July-Aug. 1970).

2058. Dos Santos, Theotonio. "The Structure of Dependence." *American Economic Review, Papers and Proceedings* vol. 60 (May 1970).

2059. Eakins, David. "The Modern American Empire: Origins and Ideology." *Socialist Revolution* vol. 2, no. 3 (May 1971).

2060. Frank, Andre Gunder. "The Development of Underdevelopment;" "Exploitation or Aid?" "Imperialism in Brazil;" "On the Mechanisms of Imperialism." Available directly from the Radical Education Project. See section IVD for address. Pamphlets.

2061. Garrett, B. "Final Solution For Indo-China." *Pacific Research & World Empire Telegram* vol. 1, no. 6 (Aug. 1970).

2062. Horowitz, David. *Empire and Revolution*. See no. 1893.

2063. _____. "Sinews of Empire." See no. 1464.

2064. Jalée, Pierre. *The Pillage of the Third World*. New York: Monthly Review Press, 1968.

2065. _____. *The Third World in World Economy*. New York: Monthly Review Press, 1971. Neo-colonialism, with much statistical data.

2066. Jones, G. Stedman. "The Specificity of U. S. Imperialism." *New Left Review* no. 60 (1970). Historical roots of imperialism from American Revolution to World War I.

2067. Kolko, Gabriel. *The Roots of American Foreign Policy.* See no. 1942.

2068. Katerinich, Lt. Col. V. (USSR). "Imperialist Military Blocs and Peace." *Soviet Military Review* no. 7 (July 1968).

2069. Lichtheim, George. *Imperialism.* New York: Praeger, 1971. Historical perspective. Holds Marxist theory not applicable to modern day.

2070. Magdoff, Harry. *The Age of Imperialism.* See no. 1065.

2071. _____. "Militarism and Imperialism." See no. 1116.

2072. Mandel, Ernest. "Where Is America Going." *Philadelphia Free Press* vol. 2, no. 21 (27 Oct. 1969).

2073. Min, L. "U. S. Imperialism's Disease." *Peking Review* vol. 12, no. 33 (15 Aug. 1969).

2074. O'Connor, James. "The Meaning of Economic Imperialism." Pamphlet published by New England Free Press, n.d. See section IVD for address. Excellent short theoretical treatment.

2075. Ogelsby, Carl. "Vietnamese Crucible." In Carl Oglesby and Richard Shaull. *Containment and Change.* New York: Macmillan, 1967. Argues a Leninist position. Concise.

2076. Pachter, H. "The Problem of Imperialism." *Dissent* vol. 17, no. 5 (Sept. 1970).

2077. Perrucci, Robert, and Pilisuk, Marc, eds. *The Triple Revolution: Social Problems in Depth.* 2d ed. Boston: Little, Brown, 1971.

2078. Rhodes, Robert. "Bibliography: On Studying Imperialism." *Review of Radical Political Economics* vol. 3, no. 4 (spring 1971). Also in Rhodes, ed. *Imperialism and Underdevelopment: A Reader.* New York: Monthly Review Press, 1971.

2079. Schiller, Herbert I. *Mass Communications and American Empire.* Boston: Beacon Press, 1969.

2080. Steel, Ronald. *Imperialists and Other Heroes: A Chronicle of the American Empire.* New York: Random House, 1971. Critical review of American foreign policy since World War II.

2081. _____. *Pax Americana.* New York: Viking, 1967. Very critical, but doesn't accept Marxist theory of imperialism.

2082. Stein, B. "Colonial Heritage of Latin America." *Monthly Review* vol. 22, no. 4 (Sept. 1970).

2083. Tucker, Robert. *Nation or Empire? The Debate over American Foreign Policy.* Baltimore: Johns Hopkins Press, 1969. A useful analysis of the issues.

2084. _____. *The Radical Left and American Foreign Policy.* See no. 1918.

2085. "U. S. Military and Economic Invasion." *Pacific Research & World Empire Telegram* vol. 1, no. 1 (3 Aug. 1969).

2086. Wolff, Richard. "Economics of Imperialism." *American Economic Review, Papers and Proceedings* vol. 60 (May 1970).

2087. Yuriev, N. "Imperialism, the Source of Wars and Violence." *Soviet Military Review* no. 7 (July 1970).

3. Economic Penetration

2088. Africa Research Group. Publishes information on U. S. economic penetration into Africa. See IVD for address.

2089. American Friends Service Committee. "Oil and Vietnam." AFSC White Paper, available directly. See IVD for address.

2090. Another Mother for Peace. "Are Our Sons Dying for Off-shore Oil?" AMP Paper. See IVD for address.

2091. "Are Our Boys Dying in Vietnam for Offshore Oil?" *Coronet Magazine* (July 1971). Article stimulated by Another Mother for Peace disclosures.

2092. Berry, W. "Congo's Mobutu Seeks U. S. Investments." *Guardian* vol. 22, no. 43 (22 Aug. 1970).

2093. Bishop, S. "The Imperial Team—Latin America." *NACLA Newsletter* vol. 3, no. 7 (Nov. 1969).

2094. Caldwell, Malcolm. "Oil and the War." *Liberation* vol. 15, no. 11; vol. 16, no. 1 and 2 (Spring 1971—single issue).

2095. Frappier, J. "Advertising—Latin America." *NACLA Newsletter* vol. 3, no. 4 (Aug. 1969).

2096. Goff, F. "Bank of America Has Mom on the Spot." *NACLA Newsletter* vol. 4, no. 5 (Sept. 1970).

2097. "Indonesia: The Making of a Neo-Colony." *Pacific Research & World Empire Telegram* vol. 1, no. 1 (3 Aug. 1969). Includes tables of investments.

2098. "Indonesia Wide Open to Imperialists." *Guardian* vol. 22, no. 41 (8 Aug. 1970).

2099. Lillis, B. "Investment as Aggression." *Punch* vol. 3, no. 5 (Dec. 1969).

2100. Liberation News Service. "Foreign Aid Kickback to U. S. Exporter." *Old Mole* vol. 1, no. 16 (3 July 1969).

2101. Locker, M. "Perspective on the Peruvian Military." *NACLA Newsletter* vol. 3, no. 5 (Sept. 1969).

2102. "The Moneymen and Their War." *The Bond* vol. 4, no. 7 (22 July 1970).

2103. Morris, D. "The Bolivian Colony." *Hard Times* no. 50 (3 Nov. 1969).

2104. NACLA. "The Hanna Industrial Complex." *NACLA Pamphlet*, n.d. See IVD for address. Includes description of Hanna Mining's activities in Brazil after 1964 coup.

2105.   _____. "The Rockefeller Empire/Latin America." *NACLA Pamphlet*, n.d. A striking catalogue of holdings and operations. Includes description of Rockefeller's 1969 trip. See IVD for address.

2106.   *NACLA Newsletter* carries much information about U. S. economic penetration in Latin America and elsewhere.

2107.   "Oil—Hidden Factor in the Vietnam Equation?" *Forbes Magazine* vol. 107, no. 6 (15 Mar. 1971).

2108.   *Pacific Research & World Empire Telegram* regularly carries information on U. S. investments in Asia and the Pacific.

2109.   Roberts, D. "U. S. Investments in Chile." *The Militant* vol. 34, no. 35 (25 Sept. 1970).

2110.   Sweezy, Paul, and Magdoff, Harry. "Notes on the Multinational Corporation." *Monthly Review* vol. 21, no. 5 (Oct. 1969); no. 6 (Nov. 1969).

2111.   Vernon, Raymond. *Sovereignty at Bay: The Multinational Spread of U. S. Enterprises.* New York: Basic Books, 1971. Comprehensive data from Harvard's Multinational Enterprise Project.

4. The Peace Corps, CIA, Green Berets, Political Meddling, Cultural Contacts

2112.   Alarcao, H. D. "Peace Corps Spying in Cuba." *Guardian* vol. 21, no. 47 (6 Sept. 1969).

2113.   "Che's Assassins Revealed." *NACLA Newsletter* vol. 2, no. 1 (Mar. 1968).

2114.   Gall, Norman. "How Trujillo Died." *The New Republic* (13 Apr. 1963). CIA role in the assassination.

2115.   Gott, Richard. "Guevara, Debray and the CIA" (The Bolivian Guerilla Movement). Available from Radical Education Project. See IVD for address.

2116.   "Harvard Overseas—Retooling the Peasantry." See no. 1460.

2117.   Hill, H. "CIA Terror." *Eyewitness* vol. 1, no. 10 (Dec. 1969). Assassination.

2118.   _____. "Interview." *Eyewitness* vol. 1, no. 9 (Oct. 1969). Green Beret murder case.

2119.   _____. "Wanted for Murder—The Green Berets." *Eyewitness* vol. 1, no. 8 (Sept. 1969).

2120.   Prouty, Fletcher. "Green Berets and the CIA." See no. 325.

2121.   NACLA. Special Issue: "The Politics of Cultural Exchange: An Analysis of the Institute for International Education." *NACLA Newsletter* vol. 1, no. 9 (Jan. 1968).

2122.   _____. "Subliminal Warfare: The Role of Latin American Studies." See no. 1474.

2123. "Rockefeller Trip under Armed Guard." *Guardian* vol. 21, no. 39 (5 July 1969).

2124. Schechter, D. "CIA Is Equal Opportunity Employer." *Ramparts* vol. 7, no. 13 (June 1969). Hiring Blacks for CIA operations.

2125. Scott, Peter Dale. "Air America: Flying the U. S. into Laos." *Ramparts* (Jan. 1970). CIA.

F. COUNTERINSURGENCY WARFARE AND ITS TECHNIQUES

2126. "Bibliography on Guerilla Warfare." See no. 2439.

2127. Bjelajac, Slavko N. "Unconventional Warfare in the Nuclear Era." *Orbis* vol. 4 (Fall 1960).

2128. Eckstein, Harry, ed. *Internal War, Problems and Approaches.* New York: Free Press, 1964.

2129. Eliot, Maj. George Fielding (Australian Army, Ret.). "Next Time We'll Have to Get There Faster." *Army* vol. 20 (Apr. 1970). Argues for lightening-fast intervention with enough force for quick victory.

2130. Ginsburgh, Col. Robert N. "Damn the Insurrectos." *Military Review* vol. 44, no. 1 (Jan. 1964).

2131. Hoopes, Townsend. *The Limits of Intervention.* See no. 51.

2132. Jacobs, Walter D. "This Matter of Insurgency." *Military Review* vol. 44, no. 10 (Oct. 1964).

2133. Klare, Mike. "The Great South Asian War: U. S. Imperial Strategy in Asia." NACLA reprint of two articles, available directly. See IV D for address.

2134. Ladd, Lt. Col. Jonathan F. "Some Reflections on Counterinsurgency." *Military Review* vol. 44, no. 10 (Oct. 1964).

2135. Long, Col. William F., Jr. (USA). "A Perspective of Counterinsurgency in Three Dimensions—Tradition, Legitimacy, Visibility." *Naval War College Review* vol. 22 (Feb. 1970). Argues U. S. policy has been contrary to U. S. traditions, has degraded army and government legitimacy; and high visibility has made it worse.

2136. Martínez Codo, Enrique. "Continental Defense and Counterinsurgency." *Military Review* vol. 50 (Apr. 1970). Emphasis on Latin America.

2137. Ney, Col. Virgil. "Guerilla Warfare and National Strategy." *Orbis* (Spring 1958).

2138. _____. "Guerilla Warfare: Annotated Bibliography." See no. 2452.

2139. Pratt, Maj. T. M., III. "Population and Resources Control." *Marine Corps Gazette* vol. 54 (Sept. 1970).

2140. Pustay, Maj. John S. *Counterinsurgency Warfare.* See no. 513.

2141. Rhyne, Russell F. "Victory in Vietnam." *Military Review* vol. 50 (Feb. 1970).

2142. Speier, Hans. *Revolutionary War.* Santa Monica: RAND Corporation, Sept. 1966. The various forms of a low intensity warfare.

2143. Stivers, William. "The Will to Intervene." In Leonard Rodberg and Derek Shearer. *The Pentagon Watchers.* See no. 13.

2144. U. S. Department of the Army. *Counterguerrilla Operations.* Department of the Army Field Manual no. 31–16. Washington, D.C.: Headquarters, Department of the Army, Mar. 1967.

2145. _____. *U. S. Army Counterinsurgency Forces.* Department of the Army Field Manual no. 31–22. Washington, D.C.: Headquarters, Department of the Army, Nov. 1963.

2146. _____. *Special Forces Operational Techniques.* Department of the Army Field Manual no. 31–20. Washington, D.C.: Headquarters, Department of Army, Feb. 1971.

2147. _____. *Special Forces Operations—U. S. Army Doctrine.* Department of the Army Field Manual no. 31–21. Washington, D.C.: Headquarters, Department of the Army, Feb. 1969.

2148. _____. *Stability Operations—Intelligence.* Department of the Army Field Manual no. 30–31. Washington, D.C.: Headquarters, Department of the Army, Jan. 1970.

2149. _____. *Stability Operations—U. S. Army Doctrine.* Department of the Army Field Manual no. 31–23. Washington, D.C.: Headquarters, Department of the Army, Dec. 1967.

1. Military Aid and Mercenarization: Money, Arms, Training, Advisors

2150. "AID Supports the Local Police." *Guardian* vol. 22, no. 4 (25 Oct. 1969).

2151. Atkinson, James D. "Arms for the Third World." *Ordnance* vol. 54 (May-June 1970).

2152. Barrett, Raymond J. "The Role of the Military Attaché." See no. 1962.

2153. "Chemical Warfare Training in the U. S. for Foreign Military Personnel." *NACLA Newsletter* vol. 4, no. 1 (Mar. 1970).

2154. Clifford, Clark M. "The Military Assistance Program." *Air Force Policy Letter for Commanders* supplement no. 7 (July 1968).

2155. Countell, R. "U. S. Military Policy in Latin America." See no. 2010.

2156. Denno, Col. Bryce F. "Advisor and Counterpart." *Army* vol. 15, no. 12 (July 1965).

2157. "Disclosure of Information Pertaining to Military Assistance." *The Inspector General Brief* vol. 22 (22 May 1970).

2158. Dougall, I. "Arms for the Love of Allah," "Arms Across the Sea —Military Statistics." *Peace News* vol. 17, nos. 33–34 (19–26 Sept. 1969).

2159. Eliasson, Col. Arne H. "Senior Army Officers Asignment to Developing Areas." *Military Review* vol. 48 (Nov. 1968).

2160. "Exclusive: How U. S. AID Shapes the Dominican Police." *NA-CLA Newsletter* vol. 5, no. 2 (Apr. 1971). See also vol. 4, no. 7 (Nov. 70).

2161. Fairchild, David. "U. S. AID in the Dominican Republic: An Inside View." *NACLA Newsletter* vol. 4, no. 7 (Nov. 1970). Transcript of taped interview with former official in the Dominican Republic. Reveals CIA activity.

2162. Furniss, Edgar S. *Some Perspectives on Military Assistance.* Memorandum no. 13. Princeton, N. J.: Center of International Studies, Princeton University (18 June 1957).

2163. Gall, Norman. "Slaughter in Guatemala." *New York Review of Books* vol. 16, no. 9 (20 May 1971). Terror by police and the military, following years of U. S. aid and advice.

2164. Hayward, Vice Adm. John T. (USN, Ret.). "The Second-Class Military Advisor: His Cause and Cure." *Armed Forces Management* vol. 15 (Nov. 1968).

2165. Heymont, Col. Irving (USA, Ret.). "U. S. Military Assistance Programs." *Military Review* vol. 48 (Jan. 1968).

2166. Hughes, Lt. Col. David R. "The Myth of Military Corps and Military Assistance." *Military Review* vol. 47 (Dec. 1967).

2167. "The Inter-American Defense College." *Military Review* vol. 50 (Apr. 1970).

2168. Jordan, Amos A., Jr. "Foreign Aid and Defense: United States Military and Related Economic Assistance to Southeast Asia." Ph.D. thesis, Columbia University, 1961.

2169. Katzenbach, Nicholas deB. "U. S. Arms for the Developing World: Dilemmas of Foreign Policy." *Air Force Policy Letter for Commanders* supplement no. 2 (Feb. 1968).

2170. Kemp, Geoffrey. "Dilemmas of the Arms Traffic." *Military Review* vol. 50 (July 1970).

2171. Kent, Col. Irvin M. "Political Warfare for Internal Defense." *Military Review* vol. 50 (Aug. 1970).

2172. Klare, Michael. "The Mercenarization of the Third World: Documents on U. S. Military and Police Assistance Programs." *NACLA Newsletter* vol. 4, nos. 7–9 (Nov. 1970–Jan. 1971). Extensive documentation—tables, etc. Klare coined the word "mercenarization."

2173. ———. "U. S. Police Assistance Programs in Latin America." *NACLA Newsletter* vol. 4, no. 3 (May–June 1970), vol. 4, no. 5 (Sept. 1970). AID Public Safety Programs.

2174. NACLA. "Exclusive: AID Police Programs for Latin America 1971–1972. *NACLA Newsletter* vol. 5, no. 4 (July-Aug. 1971). Includes complete Project Data documents by country, curriculum of OPA Police Academy and AID police plan for 1971–72.

2175. ———. "U.S. Military Assistance Programs: Combined Totals from All Sources, 1950–1969." *NACLA Newsletter* vol. 5, no. 2 (Apr. 1971).

2176. "NATO Bombs in Nigeria." *Peace News* vol. 17, no. 41 (10 Nov. 1969).

2177. Nihart, Brooke. "Increased Foreign Military Sales Inescapable under Nixon Doctrine." *Armed Forces Journal* vol. 108 (2 Nov. 1970).

2178. Powell, Craig. "The Drumbeat Is Muffled for U. S. Arms Sales Abroad." *Armed Forces Management* vol. 16 (Feb. 1970).

2179. President's Committee to Study the United States Military Assistance Program. *Report.* Washington, D.C.: USGPO, 1959. (Draper Report) See esp. Annexes.

2180. Ray, Capt. James F. "The District Advisor." *Military Review* vol. 45, no. 5 (May 1965).

2181. "Senate Panel Hits Overseas Commitments." *Armed Forces Journal* vol. 108 (4 Jan. 1971).

2182. SIPRI. *The Arms Trade with the Third World.* New York: Humanities Press, 1971. Basic data.

2183. Stepan, Alfred C. *The Military in Politics: Changing Patterns in Brazil.* Princeton, N. J.: Princeton University Press, 1971. Notes contact with U. S. Military advisors.

2184. "Supplying the Latin American Military." *NACLA Newsletter* vol. 3, no. 3 (May-June 1969).

2185. Thayer, George. "American Arms Abroad." *The Washington Monthly* vol. 1, no. 12 (Jan. 1970).

2186. "U. S. Army School of the Americas." *Military Review* vol. 50 (Apr. 1970).

2187. United States. Congress. House. Committee on Foreign Affairs. Subcommittee on National Security Policy and Scientific Developments. (91st Congress, 2d session). *Military Assistance Training: Hearings, Oct. 6, 7 and 8 and Dec. 15, 1970.* Washington, D.C.: USGPO, 1970.

2188. ———. *Reports of the Special Study Mission to Latin America on Military Assistance Training, Developmental Television, May 7, 1970, Pursuant to the Provisions of House Resolution 143, 91st Congress.* Committee print. Washington, D.C.: USGPO, 1970.

2189. U. S. Congress. House Committee on Government Operations. (86th Congress, 1st session). *United States Aid Operations in Laos: Seventh Report.* June 15, 1959. Exposé of aid scandal at time of military crisis.

2190. Ward, R. "Bangkok Fears Loss of U. S. Support." *Guardian* vol. 21, no. 40 (12 July 1969).

2191. Windle, Charles, and Vallance, T. R. "Optimizing Military Assistance Training. *World Politics* vol. 15, no. 1 (Oct. 1962). U. S. Military aid program as a potential modernizing force.

2. Nation Building, Civic Action, Pacification, Economic Aid.

2192. Alavi, Hamza. "U. S. Aid to Pakistan." *Economic Weekly* (Bombay) Special Number (July 1963).

2193. ———, and Khusro, Amir. "Pakistan: The Burden of U. S. Aid." *New University Thought* (Autumn 1962).

2194. Bentz, Maj. Harold F., Jr. "Psychological Warfare and Civil Action." *Army* vol. 13, no. 12 (July 1963).

2195. Burke, Maj. Robert L. "Military Civic Action." *Military Review* vol. 44, no. 10 (Oct. 1964).

2196. Frank, Andre Gunder. "Brazil: Exploitation or Aid?" *The Nation* (16 Nov. 1963).

2197. Glick, Edward Bernard. "And the Builders Had Every One His Sword." *Jewish Frontier* vol. 35 (Mar. 1968).

2198. ———. "Conflict, Civic Action and Counterinsurgency." *Orbis* vol. 10 (Fall 1966).

2199. ———. "Military Civic Action: Thorny Art of the Peace Keepers." *Army* vol. 17 (Sept. 1967).

2200. ———. "The Nonmilitary Use of the Latin American Military." In Norman A. Baily, ed. *Latin America: Politics, Economics, and Hemispheric Security.* New York: Praeger (Center for Strategic Studies, Georgetown University), 1965.

2201. _____ "The Nonmilitary Use of the Latin American Military: A More Realistic Approach to Arms Control and Economic Development." *Background* (since renamed *International Studies Quarterly*) vol. 8 (Nov. 1964).

2202. _____. *Peaceful Conflict: The Non-Military Use of the Military.* Harrisburg, Pa.: Stackpole, 1967. Historical survey and recommendations.

2203. _____. *United States Navy Civic Action: Its Status and Outlook.* Ann Arbor, Mich.: Office of National Security Studies of the Bendix Corporation, for the Office of Naval Research and the Naval Research Laboratory, Mar. 1967.

2204. _____. with Lawrance, Maj. Edward J. "Combat and Civic Action: Are They Compatible?" *Army* vol. 17 (Aug. 1968).

2205. Hanning, Hugh. *The Peaceful Uses of Military Forces.* New York: Praeger, 1967.

2206. Heymont, Col. Irving. "Armed Forces and National Development." *Military Review* vol. 49 (Dec. 1969).

2207. Janowitz, Morris. *The Military in the Political Development of New Nations.* Chicago: University of Chicago Press, 1964.

2208. Johnson, Lt. Col. Ross L. "Rebuilding a Nation." *Army Digest* vol. 25 (July 1970).

2209. Johnston, Chief Journalist Thomas A. "Helping Others Help Themselves." See no. 1773.

2210. Jones, Capt. Richard A. (USA). "The Nationbuilder: Soldier of the Sixties." *Military Review* vol. 45 (Jan. 1965). Frantic account of early confusion in civic action and counterinsurgency operations; notes the U. S. soldier-advisor must amass nonmilitary expertise to fulfill his mission.

2211. Leighton, Richard M., and Sanders, Ralph. "Military Civic Action." In Lewis P. Fickett, Jr., ed. *Problems of the Developing Nations.* New York: Crowell, 1966.

2212. Liberation News Service. "Foreign Aid Kickback to U. S. Exporters." See no. 2100.

2213. Melo, Hector, and Yost, Israel. "Funding the Empire: Part 1—U. S. Foreign Aid: Part 2—The Multinational Strategy." *NACLA Newsletter* vol. 4, no. 2 (Apr. 1970), no. 3 (May-June 1970). AID and business policy. Tables and charts.

2214. Middleton, Comdr. W. D. "Seabees in Vietnam." *United States Naval Institute Proceedings* vol. 93 (Aug. 1967).

2215. Montgomery, John D. *The Politics of Foreign Aid: American Experience in Southeast Asia.* Englewood Cliffs, N. J.: Prentice-Hall, 1963.

2216.   _____. *Foreign Aid in International Politics.* Englewood Cliffs, N.J.: Prentice-Hall, 1967.

2217.   Platt, Maj. Gen. Jonas M. "Military Civic Action." *Naval War College Review* vol. 22 (Apr. 1970).

2218.   Rouch, Col. Maurice D. "Master Plans for Nation-Building." *Military Review* vol. 49 (Nov. 1969).

2219.   Saalberg, Lt. Col. John J. "Army Nationbuilders." *Military Review* vol. 47 (Aug. 1967).

2220.   Sansom, Robert L. *The Economics of Insurgency in the Mekong Delta of Vietnam.* Cambridge, Mass.: MIT Press, 1970. Thorough study of economy of area, including V.C. and U. S.–Saigon policies.

2221.   Schwartz, W. "Mekong River Project." *WIN* vol. 5, no. 14 (Aug. 1969).

2222.   Tippin, Lt. Col. Garold L. "The Army as a Nationbuilder." *Military Review* vol. 50 (Oct. 1970).

2223.   Trainor, James L. "What Business Does the Military Have in Pacification/Nation Building?" *Armed Forces Management* vol. 13 (Aug. 1967).

2224.   U. S. AID (Agency for International Development) "Aids to Business Overseas Investment." Circular (Sept. 1966).

2225.   Wagner, Joe H. "Pacification: At an End—Or a New Beginning?" *Armed Forces Management* vol. 14 (Mar. 1968).

2226.   Waterhouse, Harry F. *A Time to Build: Military Civic Action: Medium for Economic Development and Social Reform.* Columbia, S. C.: University of South Carolina Press, 1964.

3. Fighting Insurgency: Covert War, Air War, Strategic Hamlets, Other Accounts

2227.   Adams, Nina S., and McCoy, Alfred W., eds. *Laos: War and Revolution.* New York: Harper & Row, 1970. Includes the U. S.'s overt and covert war activities.

2228.   American University. Special Operations Research Office. *Case Studies in Insurgency and Revolutionary Warfare.* 4 vols. Washington, D. C.: American University SORO, 1963–1964. Includes Cuba, Algeria, Vietnam and Guatemala.

2229.   American University. Special Operations Research Office. *Casebook on Insurgency and Revolutionary Warfare: 23 Summary Accounts.* Washington, D. C.: American University SORO, 1962.

2230.   Caine, Maj. Philip D. "Urban Guerrilla Warfare." *Military Review* vol. 50 (Feb. 1970).

2231.   Chomsky, Noam. *At War with Asia.* See no. 873.

2232.   "CIA's Navy Seals." *Old Mole* vol. 1, no. 24 (23 Oct. 1969).

2233. The Committee of Concerned Asian Scholars. *The Indochina Story: A Fully Documented Account.* See no. 2008.

2234. Cooper, Chester L. *The Lost Crusade.* See no. 1929.

2235. Felix, Christopher. *A Short Course in the Secret War.* New York: Dutton, 1963. The principles of secret operations by a former agent.

2236. "The Green Berets." *Progressive* vol. 33, no. 10 (Oct. 1969).

2237. Halberstam, David. *The Making of a Quagmire.* See no. 2021.

2238. Harvey, Frank. *Air War—Vietnam.* New York: Bantam Books, 1967. While Harvey was prointervention, his accounts were so vivid that they became important references for antiwar groups.

2239. Kahin, George McT., and Lewis, John W. *The United States in Vietnam.* Rev. ed. New York: Dial Press, 1969. Presents both sides of the war.

2240. Lane, Mark. *Conversations with Americans.* See no. 892.

2241. Lane, Gen. Thomas A. (USA, Ret.). *America on Trial: The War for Vietnam.* New Rochelle, N. Y.: Arlington, 1971.

2242. *Liberation Magazine.* Special issue on Indochina War. See no. 894.

2243. Long, Col. William F., Jr. (USA). "Counterinsurgency Revisited." *Naval War College Review* vol. 21 (Nov. 1968). Very critical of U. S. policy.

2244. Lorish, Robert E. "No More Vietnams: Ridiculous! Possible?" *Military Review* vol. 50 (Mar. 1970).

2245. Liberation News Service. "How They Take Care of Vietnam Dead." *Eyewitness* vol. 1, no. 8 (Sept. 1969).

2246. McAlister, John T., and Mus, Paul. *The Vietnamese and Their Revolution.* New York: Harper & Row, 1970.

2247. Miller, Comdr. Roger J. (USN). "Internal Defense and Development—'Idealism' or 'Realism?' " *Air University Review* vol. 19 (Jan.-Feb. 1968).

2248. Russell, Charles A., and Hildner, Maj. Robert E. "The Role of Communist Ideology in Insurgency." *Air University Review* vol. 22 (Jan.-Feb. 1971). Finds that neither Communist ideology nor a national variant has been a significant motivating force; instead, insurgent cadres are motivated by belief that only violence can cause change and that change is needed for a better life.

2249. Russett, Bruce M. "Vietnam and Restraints on Aerial Warfare." *Bulletin of the Atomic Scientists* vol. 26 (Jan. 1970).

2250. Schell, Jonathan. *The Military Half: An Account of Destruction in Quang Ngai and Quang Tin.* See no. 902.

2251. _____. *The Village of Ben Suc.* See no. 903.

2252. Shaplen, Robert. *The Road from War: Vietnam 1965–1970.* New York: Harper & Row, 1970.

2253. Sharp, Adm. U. S. Grant, and Westmoreland, Gen. W. C. *Report on the War in Vietnam, as of 30 June 1968.* Section I: Report on air and naval campaigns against North Vietnam and Pacific Command-wide support of the war, June 1964-July 1968, by U.S.G. Sharp (USN), Commander in Chief, Pacific. Section II: Report on operations in South Vietnam, January 1964–June 1968, by W. C. Westmoreland (USA), Commander, U.S. Military Assistance Command, Vietnam. Washington, D.C.: USGPO, 1969. An official brief account.

2254. Sights, Col. A. P., Jr. (USAF, Ret.). "Graduated Pressure in Theory and Practice." *U.S. Naval Institute Proceedings* vol. 96 (July 1970). Author claims theory failed in Vietnam; details why.

2255. Simpson, Howard R. "Counter-Guerrilla Operations." *U.S. Naval Institute Proceedings* vol. 96 (June 1970).

2256. _____. "Terror." *U.S. Naval Institute Proceedings* vol. 96 (Apr. 1970).

2257. Stavins, Ralph L. "Kennedy's Private War." *New York Review of Books* vol. 17, no. 1 (22 July 1971). Detailed account of early Kennedy intervention, based on interviews and documents.

2258. Thompson, Sir Robert G. K. *Defeating Communist Insurgency: The Lessons of Malaya and Vietnam.* New York: Praeger, 1966. A description of the bases for and strategy of Communist insurgency using Vietnam and Malaya as examples.

2259. _____. *Revolutionary War in World Strategy, 1945–1969.* London: Decker & Warburg, 1970. Supports U. S. on Vietnam.

2260. Weisberg, Barry, ed. *Ecocide in Indochina: The Ecology of War.* See no. 494.

2261. Westmoreland, Gen. William C. (USA). "The Army of the Future." See no. 417.

2262. Whiting, Allen S. "What Nixon Must Do to Make Friends in Peking." *New York Review of Books* vol. 17, no. 5 (7 Oct. 71). Historical account of U. S supported threats to security of mainland China.

2263. See also IE3, "War Crimes and Atrocities" and IIIE, "Intervention."

G. LIMITED WAR, FLEXIBLE RESPONSE

2264. Barber, Comdr. James A., Jr. (USN). "War: Limitations and National Priorities." *Naval War College Review* vol. 23 (Jan. 1971).

2265. Beavers, Comdr. Roy (USN). "A Doctrine for Limited War." *U. S. Naval Institute Proceedings* vol. 96 (Oct. 1970).

2266. Bloomfield, Lincoln P., and Leiss, Amelia C. *Controlling Small Wars: A Strategy for the 1970s.* New York: Knopf, 1969.

2267. Bratton, Joseph K. "Regional War Strategy in the 1970's." *Military Review* vol. 47 (July 1967).

2268. Brodie, Bernard. *Escalation and the Nuclear Option.* Princeton, N. J.: Princeton University Press, 1966.

2269. Collins, Gen. J. Lawton (USA, Ret.). *War in Peacetime: The History and Lessons of Korea.* Boston: Houghton Mifflin, 1969.

2270. Deitchman, Seymour J. *Limited War and American Defense Policy: Building and Using Military Power in a World at War.* 2d ed. Cambridge, Mass.: MIT Press, 1969.

2271. Gavin, Lt. Gen. James M. *War and Peace in the Space Age.* See no. 1846.

2272. Halperin, Morton. *Limited War in the Nuclear Age.* See no. 1847.

2273. Kissinger, Henry A. "Limited War: Conventional or Nuclear? A Reappraisal." In Donald Brennan, ed. *Arms Control, Disarmament, and National Security.* See no. 2288. Recants earlier advocacy of use of tactical nuclear weapons.

2274. ———. *The Necessity for Choice.* See no. 1858.

2275. ———. *Nuclear Weapons and Foreign Policy.* New York: Harper & Row, 1957. Early advocate of tactical use of nuclear weapons.

2276. LeGro, Col. William E. "The Why and How of Limited War." *Military Review* vol. 50 (July 1970).

2277. McClintock, Robert. *The Meaning of Limited War.* Boston: Houghton Mifflin, 1967.

2278. Osgood, Robert E. *Limited War: The Challenge to American Strategy.* Chicago: University of Chicago Press, 1957.

2279. Quester, George. *Deterrence before Hiroshima.* New York: Wiley, 1966. Counterpopulation targeting was not always the norm.

2280. Ridgeway, Gen. Matthew B. (USA, Ret.). *The Korean War.* See no. 78.

2281. Schelling, Thomas C. *Arms and Influence.* See no. 1869.

2282. Taylor, Gen. Maxwell D. (USA, Ret.). *The Uncertain Trumpet.* See no. 1369.

H. RUSSIA, EUROPE AND THE COLD WAR TODAY: ARMS RACE, DISARMAMENT, ALLIANCES

2283. Alperovitz, Gar. *Atomic Diplomacy.* See no. 1876.

2284. Bader, William B. *The United States and the Spread of Nuclear Weapons.* New York: Pegasus, 1968. History of U. S. Nuclear policy;

argues that an international nuclear nonproliferation treaty has drawbacks.

2285. Barnet, Richard J., and Raskin, Marcus G. *After Twenty Years: The Decline of NATO and the Search for a New Policy in Europe*. New York: Vintage Books, 1966. Critical of cold war policies.

2286. ———, and Falk, Richard A., eds. *Security in Disarmament*. Princeton, N. J.: Princeton University Press, 1965.

2287. Bell, Cora. *Negotiation from Strength*. See no. 1840.

2288. Brennan, Donald G., ed. *Arms Control, Disarmament, and National Security*. New York: Braziller, 1961.

2289. Bull, Hedley. *The Control of the Arms Race: Disarmament and Arms Control in the Missile Age*. 2d ed. New York: Praeger, 1965. A discussion of limiting war through control of manpower and conventional arms.

2290. Burdick, Eugene and Wheeler, Harvey. *Fail Safe*. New York: McGraw-Hill, 1962. A novel of accidental U. S. nuclear attack on U.S.S.R.

2291. Clark, Lt. Col. Donald L. "Soviet Srategy for the Seventies." *Air University Review* vol. 22 (Jan.-Feb. 1971).

2292. Coles, H. L., ed. *Total War and Cold War*. Columbus, O.: Ohio State University Press, 1962.

2293. Cottrell, A. J., and Hoehling, A. A. "Are We Courting Disaster? Cutback in U. S. Fleet Continues as Soviet Navy Builds and Builds." *Navy* vol. 14 (Jan. 1971).

2294. Damien, George D. "Arming through Disarmament." *Military Review* vol. 51 (Mar. 1971).

2295. Deagle, Maj. Edwin A., Jr. (USA). "The Politics of Missilemaking: A Dynamic Model." See no. 385.

2296. Eaker, Lt. Gen. Ira C. (USAF, Ret.). "Red Strategic Superiority." *Ordnance* vol. 55 (Jan.–Feb. 1971).

2297. Foster, John S., Jr. "The Growing Soviet Threat: A Sobering Picture." *Air Force and Space Digest* vol. 53 (Nov. 1970). U.S.S.R. ahead in weapons quantity; U. S. losing its lead in weapons quality, by Chief of Defense Research and Engineering.

2298. Giddings, Col. Ralph L., Jr. (Ret.). "Power, Strategy, and Will." See no. 1029.

2299. Green, Philip. *Deadly Logic; The Theory of Nuclear Deterrence*. Columbus, O.: Ohio State University Press, 1966. Very critical of deterrence theory.

2300. Harrison, Stanley L. "Military Challenge in the 1970s." See no. 1403.

2301. Hinterhoff, Maj. Eugene. "The Soviet Threat Since Czechoslovakia." *Military Review* vol. 50 (June, 1970).

2302. Howard, Michael. "Arms Control and Disarmament." *NATO's Fifteen Nations* vol. 15 (Dec.–Jan. 1971).

2303. Institute for Strategic Studies. *The Military Balance, 1971–1972.* London: International Institute for Strategic Studies, 1971. Basic data. Annual publication.

2304. Johnson, Maj. Gen. G. W. (USA) et al. "The Strategic Triad." *Ordnance* vol. 55 (Jan.–Feb. 1971).

2305. Kahn, Herman. *On Escalation.* See no. 1852.

2306. Karber, Phillip A. "MIRV: Anatomy of an Enigma." *Air Force Magazine* vol. 54 (Feb. 1971). Also deals with arms race.

2307. Kintner, William R. *Peace and the Strategy Conflict.* New York: Praeger, 1967. Should U. S. opt for strategic nuclear superiority over the Soviet Union? Discusses relative strengths and weaknesses of the U. S. and Soviet Union.

2308. Krulak, Lt. Gen. Victor H. (USMC, Ret.). "The Low Cost of Freedom." *U. S. Naval Institute Proceedings* vol. 96 (July 1970). A traditional exhortation to meet a great Soviet threat; cites lack of "guts" in "the vast bulk of our people."

2309. Laird, Melvin R. "Countering the Strategic Threat." *Air Force Policy Letter for Commanders* supplement no. 6 (June 1970).

2310. Lapp, Ralph E. "Can SALT Stop MIRV?" *New York Times Magazine* (1 Feb. 1970). MIRV technology and how it affects arms control.

2311. Lerner, Daniel, and Gorden, Morton. *Euratlantica: Changing Perspectives of the European Elites.* Cambridge, Mass.: MIT Press, 1969. Long-term interviews on defense and international relations.

2312. Meyer, Gen. John C. "The Changing Military Balance and Its Impact." *Air Force Policy Letter for Commanders* supplement no. 2 (Feb. 1970).

2313. Mills, C. Wright. *The Causes of World War Three.* See no. 1622.

2314. Moorer, Adm. Thomas H. (USN). "Challenge of Sea Power." *Ordnance* vol. 55 (Jul.–Aug. 1970).

2315. Morgenthau, Hans J. "Alliances and the Balance of Power." *Perspectives in Defense Management* (Jan. 1971).

2316. Nearing, S. "World Events—Present-Day Arms Race." *Monthly Review* vol. 21, no. 7 (Dec. 1969).

2317. Neustadt, Richard E. *Alliance Politics.* See no. 1948.

2318. Nihart, Brooke. "The Soviet Strategic Threat and U. S. Decisions." *Armed Forces Journal* vol. 107 (20 June 1970).

2319. "Our Friend Franco." *Progressive* vol. 33, no. 8 (Aug. 1969).

2320. Perle, Richard. "Arms Control Criteria." *Military Review* vol. 50 (Oct. 1970).

2321. Plate, Thomas G. *Understanding Doomsday: A Guide to the Arms Race for Hawks, Doves, and People.* New York: Simon and Schuster, 1971.

2322. Powers, Francis G., with Gentry, Curt. *Operation Overflight: The U–2 Spy Pilot Tells His Story for the First Time.* New York: Holt, Rinehart and Winston, 1970.

2323. Rapoport, Anatol. *The Big Two: Soviet-American Perceptions of Foreign Policy.* Indianapolis, Ind.: Pegasus, 1970. Asserts America and Russia still operate as if war were a live option.

2324. _____. *Strategy and Conscience.* New York: Harper & Row, 1964. Analyzes the presuppositions of military strategies and their moral attitudes; discusses the basic issues of the cold war.

2325. Raser, J. "ABM and the Mad Strategy." See no. 446.

2326. Rathjens, George W. *The Future of the Strategic Arms Race.* See no. 447.

2327. Russett, Bruce M. *What Price Vigilance? The Burdens of National Defense.* See No. 1138.

2328. _____, and Cooper, Carolyn. *Arms Control in Europe: Proposals and Political Restraints* vol. 4. Denver, Colo.: University of Denver Monograph Series in World Affairs, 1967. Comparative analysis of seventy-four proposals.

2329. Scanlan, James P. "Two Views on Disarmament—Disarmament and the USSR." *Military Review* vol. 50 (Mar. 1970).

2330. Seamans, Robert C., Jr. "The Growing Soviet Threat and What to Do about It." See no. 451.

2331. *SIPRI Yearbook of World Armaments and Disarmament, 1970–1971.* See no. 410.

2332. Stone, I. F. "A Century of Futility." *New York Review of Books* vol. 14, no. 7 (9 Apr. 1970); no. 8 (23 Apr. 1970). Historical review of disarmament.

2333. _____. "He couldn't Care Less—SALT-MIRV." *I. F. Stone's Bi-Weekly* vol. 17, no. 20 (3 Nov. 1969).

2334. _____. "How Much Is Enough?" *New York Review of Books* vol. 12, no. 6 (27 Mar. 1969).

2335. Stone, Jeremy J. *Containing the Arms Race: Some Specific Proposals.* Cambridge, Mass.: MIT Press, 1966.

2336. "Stop the Arms Trade." *Progressive* vol. 33, no. 10 (Oct. 1969).

2337. United States. Arms Control and Disarmament Agency. *World Military Expenditures, 1970.* See no. 414.

2338.   United States. Congress. Senate. Committee on Foreign Relations. Subcommittee on Arms Control, International Law and Organization. 91st Congress, 2d session. *ABM, MIRV, SALT, and the Nuclear Arms Race, Hearings, Mar. 16–Jan. 29, 1970.* Washington, D.C.: USGPO, 1970.

2339.   United States. Congress. Senate. Committee on Foreign Relations. Subcommittee on International Organization and Disarmament Affairs. 91st Congress, 1st session. *Strategic and Foreign Policy Implications of ABM (Antiballistic Missile Systems), Hearings.* Washington, D.C.: USGPO, 1969. pt. 1, Mar. 6–28, 1969; pt. 2, May 14–21, 1969; pt. 3, May 16–July 16, 1969. Also covers MIRV and antisubmarine warfare.

2340.   United States. Library of Congress. Arms Control and Disarmament Bibliography Section. See no. 2467.

2341.   Whiting, Kenneth R. *Soviet Reactions to Changes in American Strategy.* Maxwell Air Force Base, Ala.: Documentary Research Division, Aerospace Studies Institute, Air University, 1965. Air University documentary research study AU–296–62–RSI.

2342.   Witze, Claude. "Who Said the Cold War Is Over?" See no. 1440.

2343.   Wright, Quincy et al., eds. *Preventing World War III: Some Proposals.* New York: Simon and Schuster, 1962.

2344.   York, Herbert. *Race to Oblivion: A Participant's View of the Arms Race.* New York: Simon and Schuster, 1970. The absurdity of it all is the theme.

I. PROPAGANDA ABROAD AND PSYCHOLOGICAL WARFARE

2345.   "Agribusiness to Stress Propaganda Abroad." *NACLA Newsletter* vol. 1, no. 8 (Dec. 1967).

2346.   American University, Special Operations Research Office. *A Psychological Operations Bibliography.* See no. 2438.

2347.   Bentz, Maj. Harold F., Jr. "Psychological Warfare and Civil Action." *Army* vol. 13, no. 12 (July 1963).

2348.   Byfield, Robert C. *Fifth Weapon.* Linden, N.J.: Bookmailer, 1960.

2349.   Carroll, Wallace. *Persuade or Perish.* Boston: Houghton Mifflin, 1948. Propaganda.

2350.   Daugherty, William E. with Janowitz, Morris. *A Psychological Warfare Casebook.* Baltimore: Johns Hopkins Press, 1958. Wide-ranging with over seventy authors and contributors.

2351. Dyer, Murray. *The Weapon on the Wall: Rethinking Psychological Warfare*. Baltimore: Johns Hopkins Press, 1959.

2352. Frappier, Jon. "Advertising: Latin America." *NACLA Newsletter* vol. 3, no. 4 (July–Aug. 1969). Ties product advertising into a more theoretical discussion of imperialism. Tables.

2353. Heilbrun, Otto. *Warfare in the Enemy's Rear*. New York: Praeger, 1964.

2354. Holt, Robert T., and Van De Velde, Robert M. *Strategic Psychological Operations and American Foreign Policy*. Chicago: University of Chicago Press, 1960.

2355. Linebarger, Paul M. A. *Psychological Warfare* 2d ed. New York: Duell, Sloan and Pearce, 1960.

2356. MacCloskey, Monro. *Alert the Fifth Force*. New York: Rosen, Richards Press, 1969.

2357. Murphy, Gwendolyn E., and Angelo, Patricia W. *Psychological Warfare in Support of Military Operations*. Bibliography. See no. 2451.

2358. Schiller, Herbert I. *Mass Communications and American Empire*. See no. 2079.

2359. Speier, Hans. *Social Order and the Risks of War: Papers in Political Sociology*. Cambridge, Mass.: MIT Press, 1969.

2360. U. S. Department of the Army. *Psychological Operations—U. S. Army Doctrine*. Department of the Army Field Manual No. 33–1. Washington, D.C.: Headquarters, Department of the Army, Feb. 1971.

2361. "The U.S. Media Empire in Latin America." *NACLA Newsletter* vol. 2, no. 9 (Jan. 1969).

2362. Walters, H. C., Jr. *Military Psychology*. Dubuque, Iowa: Wm. C. Brown Co., 1968. Psychological warfare.

J. NATIONAL AND MILITARY POLICIES AND STRATEGIES: THE FUTURE

2363. Abshire, David M., ed. *National Security: Political, Military, & Economic Strategies in the Decade Ahead*. See no. 1052.

2364. Agan, Lt. Gen. Arthur A. "Aerospace Defense and National Security." See no. 420.

2365. Bader, William B. *The United States and the Spread of Nuclear Weapons*. See no. 2284.

2366. Baldwin, David A. "The Power of Positive Sanctions." *World Politics* vol. 24, no. 1 (Oct. 1971).

2367. Baldwin, Hanson W. *Strategy for Tomorrow*. See no. 1839.

2368. Barker, Charles A., ed. *Power and Law: American Dilemma in World Affairs.* Baltimore: Johns Hopkins Press, 1971. From the Conference for Peace Research, ten authors discuss contradiction between ideology of peace and reality of force in U. S. policy.

2369. Baudissin, Lt. Gen. Wolf Graf (German Army Ret.). "Teaching Strategy." *Survival* vol. 11 (Mar. 1969). A German view of current military strategy as related to Clausewitzian concepts.

2370. Beaufre, Andre. *An Introduction to Strategy, with Particular Reference to Problems of Defense, Politics, Economics, and Diplomacy in the Nuclear Age.* New York: Praeger, 1965. From the French.

2371. Bernardo, C. Joseph, and Bacon, Eugene H. *American Military Policy, Its Development Since 1775.* 2d ed. Harrisburg, Pa.: Stackpole, 1961.

2372. Bloomfield, Lincoln P., and Leiss, Amelia C. *Controlling Small Wars.* See no. 2266.

2373. Brodie, Bernard. *Escalation and the Nuclear Option.* See no. 2268.

2374. ———. *Strategy in the Missile Age.* Princeton: Princeton University Press, 1959. A RAND study for the USAF.

2375. Brooks, Lt. Leon P. "Vital Interests and Volunteer Forces." See no. 985.

2376. California, University of (Los Angeles). Security Studies Project. *The Politics of Military Policy: Seminars on Politics of Policy-Making.* See no. 1926.

2377. Cottrell, A. J., and Hoehling, A. A. "Are We Courting Disaster?" See no. 2293.

2378. Devan, S. Arthur. *Planning National Defense, 1950 to 1970.* Washington, D.C.: Legislative Reference Service, Library of Congress, Sept. 1949. Public Affairs Bulletin no. 75. Early analysis of future strategies now history.

2379. Erickson, John et. al. eds. *The Military-Technical Revolution; Its Impact on Strategy and Foreign Policy.* See no. 386.

2380. Friedman, Edward, and Selden, Mark, eds. *America's Asia: Dissenting Essays on Asian-American Relations.* New York: Pantheon, 1971. Twelve critiques of American ideology on Asia from the Korean War to teaching about Asia.

2381. Gavin, Lt. Gen. James M. *War and Peace in the Space Age.* 1st ed. See no. 1846.

2382. Ginsburgh, Brig. Gen. Robert N. (USAF). "U. S. Goals, Priorities, and Means." See no. 1030.

2383. Goldwin, Robert A., ed. *America Armed: Essays on United States Military Policy.* Chicago: Rand McNally, 1963. Various proposals, including disarmament.

2384.   Green, Philip. *Deadly Logic.* See no. 2299.

2385.   Gurtov, Melvin. *Southeast Asia Tomorrow: Problems and Prospects for US Policy.* Baltimore: Johns Hopkins Press, 1970.

2386.   Halperin, Morton H. *Defense Strategies for the Seventies.* Boston: Little, Brown, 1971.

2387.   Holloway, Gen. Bruce K. (USAF). "Strategic Quandary." *Ordnance* vol. 55 (July–Aug. 1970).

2388.   Huntington, Samuel P. "Equilibrium and Disequilibrium in American Military Policy." See No. 1409.

2389.   Institute for Strategic Studies. *Problems of Modern Strategy: Part One.* Adelphi Papers no. 54, vol. 1. London: Institute for Strategic Studies, 1969.

2390.   Intriligator, Michael D. "The Debate over Missile Strategy: Targets and Rates of Fire." *Orbis* vol. 1 (Winter, 1968). Nuclear strategy alternatives.

2391.   Jackson, Comdr. George L. (USN). "Constraints of the Negro Civil Rights Movement on American Military Effectiveness: A Survey." See no. 846.

2392.   Johnson, Maj. Gen. G. W. (USA) et al. "The Strategic Triad." See no. 2304.

2393.   Jordan, Amos A., Jr., ed. *Issues of National Security in the 1970s.* New York: Praeger, 1967. Collection of essays.

2394.   Kahn, Herman. *On Escalation.* See no. 1852.

2395.   ———. *On Thermonuclear War.* See no. 1853.

2396.   Karber, Phillip. "Deterrence, the ABM, and Stability in Asia." *Air Force and Space Digest* vol. 53 (Oct. 1970). ABM adds stability to U. S.-USSR and U. S.-Asia relationships.

2397.   Kaufmann, William W. *The McNamara Strategy.* See no. 1855.

2398.   Kaysen, Carl. "Keeping the Strategic Balance." *Foreign Affairs* vol. 46 (July 1968). Various force levels analyzed.

2399.   Kissinger, Henry A., ed. *Problems of National Strategy: A Book of Readings.* See no. 1342.

2400.   Knorr, Klaus E. *On the Uses of Military Power in the Nuclear Age.* Princeton, N. J.: Princeton University Press, 1966. Says use of military power (especially nuclear) is losing social legitimacy.

2401.   ———, and Morgenstern, Oscar. *Political Conjecture in Military Planning.* Princeton, N. J.: Princeton University Center of International Studies Policy Memo no. 35, 1968.

2402.   Komer, Robert W. "Perspectives on National Security in the 1970s." *Perspectives in Defense Management* (July 1970).

2403.   Laird, Melvin R. "Countering the Strategic Threat." See no. 2309.

2404. Lapp, Ralph E. *Kill and Overkill: The Strategy of Annihilation.* See no. 398.

2405. LeMay, Curtis E. *America Is in Danger.* See no. 204.

2406. Lorish, Robert E. "No More Vietnams: Ridiculous! Possible?" See no. 2244.

2407. McLucas, John L. "Security: Past, Present and Future." *Air Force Policy Letter for Commanders* supplement no. 7 (July 1970).

2408. McNamara, Robert S. *The Essence of Security: Reflections in Office.* See no. 1646.

2409. Maxwell, Stephen. *Rationality in Deterrence.* London: Institute for Strategic Studies, 1968. Adelphi Papers no. 50.

2410. Meyer, Gen. John C. "The Changing Military Balance and Its Impact." See no. 2312.

2411. Moorer, Adm. Thomas H. (USN). "Challenge of Sea Power." See no. 2314.

2412. ———. "Moorer: Viable Options, Purple Suit Questions and the Pendulum Theory." See no. 71.

2413. Nazzaro, Gen. Joseph J. "The Strategic Deterrent." *Ordnance* vol. 52 (Mar.-Apr. 1968).

2414. Nihart, Brooke. "Increased Foreign Military Sales Inescapable under Nixon Doctrine." See no. 2177.

2415. ———. "The Soviet Strategic Threat and U. S. Decisions." See no. 2318.

2416. Norman, Lloyd. "Mr. Laird and the No War Strategy for the 1970s." *Army* vol. 21 (Feb. 1971).

2417. O'Connor, Raymond G. "Current Concepts and Philosophy of Warfare." *Naval War College Review* vol. 20 (Jan. 1968). Review.

2418. Pfeffer, Richard M., ed. *No More Vietnams?* See no. 1987.

2419. Power, Gen. Thomas S. (USAF, Ret.). *Design for Survival.* See no. 217.

2420. ———. "Deterrence or Defeat." *Ordnance* vol. 53 (Nov.-Dec. 1968).

2421. Rapoport, Anatol. *Strategy and Conscience.* See no. 2324.

2422. Rathjens, George W. *The Future of the Strategic Arms Race: Options for the 1970s.* See no. 447.

2423. Roberts, Adam, ed. *The Strategy of Civilian Defense: Non-Violent Resistance to Aggression.* London: Faber, 1967.

2424. Ryan, Gen. John D. (USAF). "Aerospace—An Expanding Matrix for Deterrence." *Air Force Policy Letter for Commanders* supplement no. 11 (Nov. 1970).

2425. Sargent, Clyde B. "National Cultural Characteristics and National Power." See no. 1043.

2426. Schilling, Warner R.; Hammond, Paul Y.; and Snyder, Glenn H. *Strategy, Politics, and Defense Budgets.* See no. 81.

2427. Schratz, Paul R. "The Caesars, the Sieges, and the Anti-Ballistic Missile." See no. 450.

2428. Schwarz, Urs. *American Strategy: A New Perspective; The Growth of Politico-Military Thinking in the United States.* Garden City, N. Y.: Doubleday, 1966.

2429. Seamans, Robert C., Jr. "The Growing Soviet Threat and What to Do about It." See no. 451.

2430. "Senate Panel Hits Overseas Commitments." *Armed Forces Journal* vol. 108 (4 Jan. 1971).

2431. Smith, Edward C. "New Directions for National Defense." *Military Review* vol. 50 (Mar. 1970).

2432. Strausz-Hupé, Robert et al. *Protracted Conflict.* New York: Harper & Row, 1959.

2433. Taylor, Gen. Maxwell D. (USA, Ret.). *Responsibility and Response.* New York: Harper & Row, 1967.

2434. ———. *The Uncertain Trumpet.* See no. 1369.

2435. Twining, Gen. Nathan F. (USAF, Ret.). *Neither Liberty Nor Safety.* See no. 226.

2436. United States. Congress. Senate. Committee on Foreign Relations. Subcommittee on International Organization and Disarmament Affairs, 91st Congress, 1st session. *Strategic and Foreign Policy Implications of ABM (Antiballistic Missile Systems), Hearings.* See no. 2339.

2437. Westmoreland, Gen. William C. (USA). "Battlefield of the Future." *U. S. Army Aviation Digest* vol. 16 (Feb. 1970).

IV. Research Notes

A. BIBLIOGRAPHIES

2438. The American University. Special Operations Research Office. *A Psychological Operations Bibliography.* Carl Berger and Howard C. Reese, in collaboration with Charles A. Feder. Prepared under the general direction of D. M. Condit. Washington, D. C.: American University, Special Operations Research Office, 1960. Prepared under contract with the Department of the Army. 174 pages.

2439. "Bibliography on Guerrilla Warfare." *Military Affairs Journal of the American Military Institute* vol. 24, no. 3. Washington, D. C.: 1960.

2440. Caldwell, Lynton, K., ed. "Science, Technology, and Public Policy: A Selected and Annotated Bibliography." Bloomington, Ind.: University of Indiana, Dept. of Government, 1969. Published under the sponsorship of the National Science Foundation. Available on request.

2441. Cameron, Colin, and Blackstone, Judith. *Minorities in the Armed Forces: A Selected, Occasionally Annotated Bibliography.* Madison, Wis.: Institute for Research on Poverty, University of Wisconsin, Aug. 1970. 32 pages.

2442. Caspary, William. *American Economic Imperialism.* See no. 2056.

2443. Crawford, Elisabeth T. *The Social Sciences in International and Military Policy: An Analytical Bibliography.* Washington, D.C.: Bureau of Social Science Research, 1965. Prepared for the U.S. Air Force Office of Scientific Research. 67 pages.

2444. George Washington University. Human Resources Research Office. *Bibliography of Publications: As of 30 June 1966.* Washington, D.C.: George Washington University, Human Resources Research Office, Sept. 1966. Largely work done for the military: supplementary bibliographies of HumRRO reports are issued periodically. 237 pages.

2445. Graham, C. C., and Breese, Eleanor. *Publications of the Social Sciences Department of the RAND Corporation, 1948–1967.* (Memorandum RM–3600–4) Santa Monica, Calif.: The RAND Corporation, 1967.

2446. Halperin, Morton H. "Annotated Bibliography." In his *Limited War in the Nuclear Age.* New York: Wiley, 1963, pp. 133–184. Written under the auspices of the Center for International Affairs, Harvard University: 343 entries.

2447. Huntington, Samuel P. "Recent Writings in Military Politics—Foci and Corpora." In his (ed.) *Changing Patterns of Military Politics.* New York: Free Press, 1962, pp. 235–266.

2448. Lang, Kurt. "Military Sociology: A Trend Report and Bibliography." *Current Sociology* 13 (1965): 1–55.

2449. _____. "Military Sociology 1963–1969: A Trend Report and Bibliography." *Current Sociology* 16 (1968): 1–66. Prepared for the International Sociological Association under the auspices of the International Committee for Social Sciences Documentation. An international bibliography.

2450. _____. *Sociology of the Military: A Selected and Annotated Bibliogra-*

phy. n.p., 1969. Prepared for the Inter-University Seminar on Armed Forces and Society. 96 pages.

2451.   Murphy, Gwendolyn E., and Angelo, Patricia W. *Psychological Warfare in Support of Military Operations.* Washington, D.C.: Department of State, 1951. 25 pages, annotated.

2452.   Ney, Col. Virgil. "Guerrilla Warfare: Annotated Bibliography." *Military Review* vol. 41, no. 11 (Nov. 1961).

2453.   ———. "Military Sociology—A Selected Bibliography." *Military Affairs* vol. 30 (Winter 1966–1967), pp. 234–237.

2454.   North American Congress on Latin America (NACLA). "Bibliography." In NACLA's *Research Methodology Guide.* New York: NACLA, 1970. See no. 2563. Reprinted in Leonard Rodberg and Derek Shearer, eds., *The Pentagon Watchers.* See no. 13, pp. 399–409. A list of over 100 periodical and other official and private publications dealing with the military and national security affairs, with information on each.

2455.   *Political Science, Government, and Public Policy Series* vol. 3. See no. 2479.

2456.   Prokosch, E. *"Military-Industrial Reading List."* *WIN* vol. 5, no. 5 (1 Sept. 1969).

2457.   Rhodes, Robert. "Bibliography: On Studying Imperialism." *Review of Radical Political Economics* (URPE) vol. 3, no. 4 (Spring, 1971.) Also in Rhodes, ed., *Imperialism and Underdevelopment: A Reader.* New York: Monthly Review Press, 1971. 10 pages with sections on individual areas, giving precedence to recent but little-known works, often on rural structures.

2458.   Sica, Geraldine P. "A Preliminary Bibliography of Studies of the Economic Effects of Defense Policies and Expenditures." In Seymour Melman, ed., *The Defense Economy.* New York: Praeger, 1970.

2459.   Social Science Research Council. *Civil-Military Relations: An Annotated Bibliography, 1940–1952.* Prepared under the direction of the Committee on Civil-Military Relations Research of the Social Science Research Council. New York: Columbia University Press, 1954. Most comprehensive for the time period. 140 pages.

2460.   United States. Congress. Senate. Committee on Government Operations. Subcommittee on Government Research. *Inventory of Congressional Concern with Research and Development: A Bibliography.* 2 vols. Washington, D.C.: 15 Dec. and 23 Sept. 1966. Documents issued by the 88th, 89th, and 1st session of the 90th Congresses.

2461. United States Court of Military Appeals. Law Library. *Bibliography on Military Justice and Military Law*. Washington, D.C., 1960.

2462. United States. Department of the Army. *Civilian in Peace, Soldier in War: A Bibliographic Survey of the Army and Air National Guard* (Department of the Army Pamphlet no. 140–3). Washington, D.C.: Headquarters, Department of the Army, 1968. 119 pages.

2463. _____. Office of the Adjutant General. *The College Graduate and National Security: Utilization of Manpower by the U. S. Armed Services, A Bibliographic Survey*. Washington, D.C.: USGPO, 1968. 74 pages.

2464. _____. Office of the Adjutant General. Army Library. *Military Manpower Policy: A Bibliographic Survey*. Prepared by H. Moskowitz and J. Roberts for the Department of Defense. Washington, D.C.: USGPO, June 1965. 142 pages.

2465. United States. Industrial College of the Armed Forces. *Catalog of Publications, 1966–1968* (Publication no. R244). Washington, D.C.: Industrial College of the Armed Forces, 1970. 281 pages.

2466. United States. Library of Congress. *Civil Defense 1948–1951: A Subject Bibliography*. Washington, D.C.: Library of Congress, 1951. 1,700 items.

2467. _____. Arms Control and Disarmament Bibliography Section. *Arms Control and Disarmament*. Washington, D.C.: Library of Congress. A quarterly bibliography with abstracts and annotations.

2468. _____. Legislative Reference Service. *Organizing for National Security: A Bibliography*. Prepared for the Committee on Government Operations, United States Senate, and its Subcommittee on National Policy Machinery (pursuant to S. Res. 115, 86th Congress). Washington, D.C.: USGPO, 1959. 77 pages. Covers government (including military) organization, national security politics and civil-military relations.

2469. United States Army Military History Research Collection. Historical Research and Reference Division. *The US Army and Domestic Disturbances* (Special Bibliography 1), by John Slonaker. Carlisle Barracks, Pa.: U.S. Army Military History Research Collection, Oct. 1970. 56 pages. Lists the holdings on this subject in this collection.

2470. _____. *The US Army and the Negro* (Special Bibliography 2), by John Slonaker. Carlisle Barracks, Pa.: US Army Military History Research Collection, Jan. 1971. 102 pages. Lists the holdings on this subject in this collection.

B. INDEXES

2471. *Air University Library Index to Military Periodicals.* Published quarterly by the Air University Library, Maxwell Air Force Base, Ala. Includes most major U. S., international and foreign military journals (including English translations of USSR journals). Also indexes defense industry related journals. The best single source for tracing military thought.

2472. *Alternative Press Index.* Published quarterly by the Radical Research Center, Toronto, Ontario, Canada. Indexes most radical and new left periodicals, including GI antiestablishment publications. The only systematic compilation of much of the underground press, though dating back only to mid–1969.

2473. *Department of the Navy Directive Issuance System, Consolidated Checklist for Activities on Standard Navy Distribution List (Navy Publications Instruction no. 5215.3K).* Washington, D.C.: Headquarters, Department of the Navy, June 1970. This index may be used to find the date and the version of a basic document that is currently in effect.

2474. *Department of the Navy Directive Issuance System, Consolidated Subject Index of Unclassified Instructions (Navy Publications Instructions no. 5215.4J).* Washington, D.C.: Headquarters, Department of the Navy, June 1970. This index may be used to find titles and publication numbers of needed documents. Together, NAVPUBs 5215.4J and 5215.3K may be used to find the current official instructions or doctrine on any given subject.

2475. *Military Publications, Index of Administrative Publications* (Regulations, Circulars, Pamphlets, Posters, Joint Chiefs of Staff Publications and General Orders) (*Department of the Army Pamphlet* no. 310–1). Washington, D.C.: Headquarters, Department of the Army, June 1969. This index lists all the official documents of the type noted which are issued by Headquarters, Department of the Army, and are in effect at any given time. Most large army field headquarters and recruiting facilities have copies of this index.

2476. *Military Publications, Index of Doctrinal, Training, and Organizational Publications* (Field Manuals, Reserve Officers' Training Manuals, Training Circulars, Army Training Programs, Army Subject Schedules, Army Training Tests, Firing Tables and Trajectory Charts, Tables of Organization and Equipment, Type Tables of Distribution and Tables of Allowances) (*Department of the Army Pamphlet No. 310–3*). Washington, D.C.: Headquarters, Department of the Army, Aug. 1970. Same note as for *Pamphlet 310–1*.

2477. *Monthly Catalogue of United States Government Publications.* Washington, D.C.: Superintendent of Documents, USGPO, monthly. Indexed by issuing agency.

2478. *Numerical Index of Standard and Recurring Air Force Publications (Air Force Regulations 0–2).* Washington, D.C.: Headquarters, Department of the Air Force, Aug. 1971. This index lists all the official documents of the type noted that are issued by Headquarters, Department of the Air Force, that are in effect at any given time. Most large air force installations and recruiting facilities have copies of this index.

2479. *Political Science, Government and Public Policy Series.* 10 vols. Princeton, N.J.: Princeton Research Publishing Co., 1969. "An annotated and intensively indexed compilation of significant books, pamphlets and articles, selected and processed by the Universal Reference System—a computerized information retrieval service in the social and behavioral sciences." Annual supplements; vol. 3 is a bibliography of bibliographies. 925 pages.

2480. *Public Affairs Information Service Bulletin.* New York: PAIS, weekly (with periodic cumulations). "A selective subject list of the latest books, pamphlets, government publications, reports of public and private agencies and periodical articles, relating to economic and social conditions, public administration and international relations, published in English throughout the world."

2481. *Selected Rand Abstracts.* Santa Monica, Calif.: The Rand Corporation. "A Quarterly Guide to Publications of the Rand Corporation." Indexed both by subject and author, followed by abstracts of books, reports, memoranda and papers.

2482. *Social Science and Humanities Index.* New York: H. W. Wilson, quarterly (with annual cumulations). Formerly the *International Index.* "The periodicals indexed deal, on a scholarly level, with the social and cultural activities of man."

2483. *Subject Guide to Books in Print: An Index to the Publishers Trade List Annual.* 2 vols. New York: Bowker, annually. Useful for finding current books.

2484. *Union List of Military Periodicals.* Maxwell Air Force Base, Ala.: Air University Library, 1960. 121 pages, most comprehensive for the period.
See also more general indexes, such as the *Reader's Guide to Periodical Literature* and the *New York Times Index.*

C. MILITARY AND OTHER OFFICIAL AND
QUASI-OFFICIAL PERIODICAL PUBLICATIONS

The number of periodicals from which to choose is enormous. For example, the DoD and the individual services sponsor at least eighty-five, and possibly as many as 371, magazines with government funds. An authoritative overview of the scope of the Pentagon's publishing activities, and the source of our figures, is:

2485. Kopek, Bernadine, M., "The DoD Magazine Empire." *Armed Forces Journal* vol. 108 (Aug. 1971). Added to the journals published at taxpayers' expense are many published by private associations of active and retired servicemen and defense-related industries, and others published commercially but aimed at military and national security bureaucracy audiences. We have selected a small sample of journals which we have found to be especially prolific media for articles relevant to this bibliography. See the NACLA Bibliography, no. 2454 or *The Air University Library Index,* no. 2471 for a more complete list.

2486. *Air Force (Information) Policy Letter for Commanders.* Published by the Internal Information Division, Office of the Secretary of the Air Force. Contains many important policy speeches, announcements, explanations of actions, rationales—all from official sources. Published monthly.

2487. *Airman.* Monthly. Published by the "Internal Information Division, Directorate of Information, Office of the Secretary of the Air Force. As the official magazine of the U. S. Air Force, it is a medium of information for Air Force Personnel."

2488. *Air University Review* (Formerly *Air University Quarterly Review*). Published bi-monthly. "The Professional Journal of the United States Air Force." Published by the Air University, Maxwell Air Force Base, Ala., "to stimulate professional thought concerning aerospace doctrines, strategy, tactics, and related techniques. Its contents reflect the opinions of its authors or the investigations and conclusions of its editors and are not to be construed as carrying any official sanction of the Department of the Air Force or of Air University." Spanish and Portuguese editions are also published.

2489. *All Hands.* Monthly. "The Bureau of Naval Personnel Career Publication, is published . . . by the Bureau of Naval Personnel for the information and interest of the naval service as a whole.

. . . Opinions expressed are not necessarily those of the Navy Department."

2490. *Army Research and Development.* Monthly. Official publication for internal and army-industry-academia communication on R & D matters.

2491. *Commanders Digest.* Weekly. Published by the Armed Forces News Bureau for disseminating official information, news and policies from the highest Washington official sources to service personnel.

2492. *Defense Industry Bulletin.* "Published quarterly by the Defense Supply Agency for the Department of Defense. . . . The Bulletin serves as a means of communication between the Department of Defense, its authorized agencies, defense contractors and other business interests. It provides guidance to industry concerning DoD policies, programs and projects and seeks to stimulate thought on the part of the Defense-Industry team in solving problems allied to the defense effort."

2493. *Defense Management Journal.* "Published quarterly by the Directorate for Management Improvement Programs, Office of the Assistant Secretary of Defense (Installations and Logistics), for distribution within the Department of Defense" and "seeks to stimulate management improvement, promote cost consciousness, enhance understanding of efficiency programs and encourage excellence in the administration of governmental resources."

2494. *Military Review.* Monthly. "Published by the United States Army Command and General Staff College in close cooperation with the United States Army War College. It provides a forum for the expression of military thought on national and military strategy, national security affairs and on doctrine with emphasis at the division and higher levels of command." Spanish and Portuguese editions are published.

2495. *Naval War College Review.* Monthly. Published by the Naval War College, the *Review* includes the "forthright and candid views of the lecturers" at the War College "for the professional education of its readers. . . . Lectures are selected on the basis of favorable reception by Naval War College audiences, usefulness to servicewide readership and timeliness. Research papers are selected on the basis of professional interest to readers."

2496. *Perspectives in Defense Management.* Published at various intervals. Includes "a representative selection of presentations and papers drawn from the educational programs of the Industrial College of the Armed Forces. It is published by the college."

2497. *Soldiers.* (Formerly *Army Digest.*) Published monthly, *Soldiers* is designed to "provide timely factual information of professional interest to members of the United States Army. *Soldiers* is published under supervision of the Army Chief of Information to provide timely and authoritative information on policies, plans, operations and technical developments of the Department of the Army to the Active Army, Army National Guard, Army Reserve and Department of the Army civilian employees. It also serves as a vehicle for timely expression of the views of the Secretary of the Army and the Chief of Staff and assists in the achievement of information objectives of the Army."

D. RADICAL GROUPS AND PUBLICATIONS

A surprising number of radical and underground publications can now be found in large libraries, either because of their general interest or as part of an "American Studies" program [e.g. the "Movement (Protest) Collection" at Yale's Sterling Library]. The Radical Research Center (RRC) of Toronto, Ontario, Canada has begun indexing articles in over 100 such periodicals, so that radical contributions on a broad range of subjects can be better appreciated. The product of their endeavor is the *Alternative Press Index*, no. 2472, a quarterly beginning with articles from mid-1969. In preparing this bibliography we made extensive use of the *Alternative Press Index*. To aid in obtaining these writings, RRC has also begun a microfilming project and intends to make film copies of periodicals available to the public through the Inter-Library Loan system. In addition Bell and Howell, in cooperation with the Underground Press Syndicate, has produced a collection of underground papers dating from 1965. Libraries may purchase this Underground Newspaper Microfilm Collection from The Micropublishers, Micro Photo Division, Old Mansfield Road, Wooster, Ohio 44691.

Finally, much literature may be ordered directly from the groups which publish it. This is particularly necessary for pamphlets and other occasional literature which is not indexed, but which is often very good. Some of the groups will send price lists upon request, while others may be able to send back issues of periodicals. We include below the names and addresses of groups and periodicals which appear in the body of the bibliography but which may not be familiar to the reader.

2498. *Advocate.* A biweekly promoting gay liberation. Box 74695, Los Angeles, Calif. 90004.

2499. *Africa Research Group.* Publishes pamphlets and reprints with particular emphasis on imperialism in Africa. P.O. Box 213, Cambridge, Mass. 02138

2500. *The Ally.* A GI-oriented monthly. P.O. Box 9276, Berkeley, Calif. 94709.

2501. American Friends Service Committee (AFSC). A Quaker organization which carries much information on the draft, the war, prisons, etc. Numerous local offices. Mid-Atlantic office at 1500 Race St., Philadelphia, Pa.

2502. *Amex-Canada.* Published by the American exile community in Canada. Box 187, Station "D," Toronto 165, Ontario, Canada.

2503. Another Mother for Peace (AMP). Publishes a newsletter and its own research (e.g., on Vietnam oil) as well as mailing out literature of other groups. 407 North Maple Drive, Beverley Hills, Calif. 90210.

2504. *Berkeley Tribe.* Weekly. 1701 1/2 Grove, Berkeley, Calif. 94709.

2505. *Black Panther.* Weekly. Organ of the Black Panther Party. 3106 Shattuck Ave., Berkeley, Calif. 94705.

2506. *The Bond.* Monthly. Organ of the American Serviceman's Union. 156 Fifth Ave., Rm. 538, New York, N.Y. 10010.

2507. *Bulletin of Concerned Asian Scholars.* Published by the Committee of Concerned Asian Scholars, a group formed to educate the American public on Indochina and U. S. Asian policy. Philips Brook House, Cambridge, Mass. 02138.

2508. *Catholic Worker.* Published nine times per year. Radical pacifist Catholic orientation. 36 E. 1st St., New York, N.Y. 10003.

2509. *Center Magazine.* Bimonthly. Published by the Center for the Study of Democratic Institutions, which also puts out various occasional papers. P.O. Box 4068, Santa Barbara, Calif. 93103.

2510. Central Committee for Conscientious Objectors. Publishes excellent material on the draft. 2016 Walnut St., Philadelphia, Pa. 19103.

2511. *Chinook.* Weekly. 1458 Pennsylvania St., Office 12, Denver, Colo. 80203.

2512. Committee for Nonviolent Action (CNVA). Pacifist action group which stocks reprints of often hard to obtain literature and publishes its own newsletter. New England CNVA, RFD #1, Box 430, Voluntown, Conn. 06384.

2513. Committee of Concerned Asian Scholars. See *Bulletin of Concerned Asian Scholars*, no. 2507.

2514. *Direct from Cuba.* Biweekly. English edition of official Cuban information magazine. Available from Dept. Service Exterieur, 10 rue Talma, 75 Paris XVI, France.

2515. *Dissent.* Bimonthly. Socialist-Social Democratic orientation. Irving Howe is editor. 509 Fifth Ave., New York, N.Y. 10017.

2516. *Eyewitness.* Monthly. 343 Frederick St., San Francisco, Calif. 94117.

2517. *Fatigue Press.* A GI-oriented monthly. P.O. Box 1265, Killeen, Texas 76541.

2518. *Fifth Estate.* Weekly. 4403 Second, Detroit, Mich. 48201.

2519. *El Grito Del Norte.* Monthly Chicano oriented paper, published in English. Box 466, Fairview Station, Española, N.M. 87532.

2520. *The Guardian.* "An independent radical Newsweekly." 32 W. 22nd St., New York, N.Y. 10010.

2521. *Hard Times.* Now a feature of *Ramparts.* Editors Kopkind and others originally broke with *New Republic* to take a more radical position.

2522. *I. F. Stone's Bi-Weekly.* Originally *I. F. Stone's Weekly*, a "muckraking"-type newsletter with especially good coverage of congressional testimony. The *Bi-Weekly* has recently ceased publication, but Mr. Stone now writes a special supplement for the *New York Review of Books. I. F. Stone's Bi-Weekly*, 4420 29th St., N.W., Washington, D.C. 20008.

2523. *International Socialist Review.* A monthly journal of the Socialist Workers Party. 14 Charles Lane, New York, N.Y. 10014.

2524. *Kaleidoscope.* Biweekly. P.O. Box 881, Madison, Wis. 53701.

2525. *Liberated Guardian.* A biweekly publication of the Liberated Guardian Workers Collective, which split from the *Guardian* in an "anarchist" direction. 14 Cooper Square, New York, N.Y. 10003.

2526. *Liberation.* Monthly. While the editorial board is pacifist (in the tradition of A. J. Muste), *Liberation* sees itself as something of a forum for intramovement dialogues. 339 Lafayette St., New York, N.Y. 10012.

2527. Liberation News Service (LNS). 160 Claremont Ave., New York, N.Y. 10027.

2528. *Long Beach Free Press.* 1255 E. 10th St., Long Beach, Calif. 90813.

2529. *L.A. Free Press.* Weekly. 7813 Beverley Blvd., Los Angeles, Calif. 90036.

2530. *The Militant.* Weekly organ of the Socialist Worker's Party. 14 Charles Lane, New York, N.Y. 10014.

2531. *Monthly Review.* An independent socialist magazine. Monthly Review Press publishes many books on imperialism and related topics. See their price list. 116 W. 14th St., New York, N.Y. 10011.

2532. *NACLA Newsletter.* Published monthly by the North American Congress on Latin America, which also puts out excellent pamphlets on imperialism, university complicity and the MIC. NACLA's research publications always contain a considerable amount of tabular data. Box 57 Cathedral Station, New York, N.Y. 10026.

2533. National Action/Research on the Military-Industrial Complex (NARMIC). A Quaker project which publishes material on military contractors, weapons, etc., aimed at local action. 160 N. 15th St., Philadelphia, Pa. 19102.

2534. New England Free Press (NEFP). Publishes and distributes pamphlets, reprints, etc. on militarism, imperialism and related topics. 791 Tremont St., Boston, Mass. 02118.

2535. *New Left Review.* Bimonthly. The oldest "new left" journal. 7 Carlisle St., London W1, England.

2536. *New York Review of Books.* A biweekly magazine of left wing intellectuals, which often carries articles on political topics. 250 W. 57th St., New York, N.Y. 10019.

2537. *Nola Express.* Biweekly. Box 2342, New Orleans, La. 70116.

2538. North American Congress on Latin America. See *NACLA Newsletter,* no. 2533.

2539. *Old Mole.* Now *The Mole.* Triweekly. Media Center, 2 Brookline Center, Cambridge, Mass. 02139.

2540. *Pacific Research & World Empire Telegram.* Published bimonthly by the Pacific Studies Center, a research group concentrating on Asia and the Pacific. 1963 University Ave., East Palo Alto, Calif. 94303.

2541. Pacific Studies Center. See *Pacific Research & World Empire Telegram,* no. 2541.

2542. *Peace News.* A weekly British pacifist publication. 5 Caledonian Rd., London, N1, England.

2543. *People's World.* A West Coast Communist party weekly. 81 Clementina St., San Francisco, Calif. 94105.

2544. *Progressive.* A monthly in the tradition of Robert LaFollette. 408 West Gorham St., Madison, Wis. 53703.

2545. Radical Education Project (REP). Publishes and distributes a great many pamphlets, reprints, etc., on various topics, including militarism and imperialism. Box 561A, Detroit, Mich. 48232.

2546. Radical Research Center. Publishes the *Alternative Press Index.* Bag Service 2500, Postal Station E, Toronto, Ontario, Canada.

2547. *Ramparts.* Monthly. Excellent exposés on the CIA, etc. 1940 Bonita Ave., Berkeley, Calif. 94704.

2548. *Rat.* Biweekly. Far left-wing women's collective, last address 241 E. 14th St. New York, N.Y. 10003.

2549. *The Review of Radical Political Economics.* Published quarterly by the Union for Radical Political Economics (URPE), which also prints occasional special reports, organizes conferences and attempts generally to bring radicals in the discipline together. 2503 Student Activities Building, University of Michigan, Ann Arbor, Mich. 48104.

2550. *San Francisco Bay Guardian.* An occasional publication with particularly good coverage of military research and defense contractors in the Bay area.

2551. *Second City.* Monthly. Guild Book Store, 2136 Halsted, Chicago, Ill. 60614.

2552. *Seed.* Biweekly. 950 Wrightwood, Chicago, Ill. 60614.

2553. *Socialist Revolution.* Bimonthly formerly *Studies on the Left*, a new left journal. Agenda Publishing Co., 1445 Stockton St. San Francisco, Calif. 94133.

2554. *Southern Patriot.* Monthly. Aimed at southern whites, concerned with economic issues and with combatting racism. 3210 W. Broadway, Louisville, Ky. 40211.

2555. *Street Journal.* Biweekly. c/o MIC, 531 19th St., San Diego, Calif. 92102.

2556. Toronto Anti-Draft Programme. Publishes information on emmigration to Canada and aids those who flee the draft and the military. 2279 Yonge St., Suite 15, Toronto, 12, Ontario, Canada.

2557. Union for Radical Political Economics. See *Review of Radical Political Economics,* no. 2550.

2558. Vietnam Veterans against the War. Publishes irregular paper, *The First Casualty.* 25 W. 26th St., New York, N.Y. 10010.

2559. *Willamette Bridge.* Weekly. 6 6th St. S.W., Portland, Ore. 97204.

2560. *WIN* magazine. Published biweekly by the Workshop in Nonviolence and the War Resisters League. These groups also publish and distribute much more literature on war, the military, and related topics. Action-oriented. 339 Lafayette St., New York, N.Y. 10012.

2561. *Workers Power.* Biweekly. Formerly *International Socialist.* 14131 Woodward Ave., Highland Park, Mich. 48203.

E. RESEARCH GUIDES AND USEFUL HINTS

The most useful aid we have encountered to researching the military is:

2562. North American Congress on Latin America (NACLA). *The NA-CLA Research Methodology Guide.* New York: NACLA, 1971. The complete version of the guide is available directly from NACLA (P.O. Box 57, Cathedral Station, New York, N.Y. 10025) for $1.25. It is also carried in many libraries. A more limited version on the MIC (with bibliography) is in the back of *The Pentagon Watchers,* Leonard Rodberg and Derek Shearer, eds. (no. 13). *The Research Methodology Guide* contains very practical information on how to do research on corporations, the MIC, police, universities, U.S. imperialism and more. We have tried to duplicate as little as possible in the suggestions we present below.

Research on the U.S. national security establishment, especially when dealing with official military documents or publications, is often complicated by military jargon. There are two references that may be used in translating such writings into colloquial English:

2563. United States. Joint Chiefs of Staff. *Dictionary of United States Military Terms for Joint Usage* (short title: JD). With NATO and SEATO glossaries incorporated. *Joint Chiefs of Staff Publication No. 1.* Washington, D.C.: USGPO, 1968.

2564. United States. Department of the Army. *Dictionary of United States Army Terms* (short title: AD). *Department of the Army Regulation No. 310–25.* Washington, D.C.: Headquarters, Department of the Army, 1969.

The best source for uncovering or clarifying chains of authority and command on a general level, and for identifying activities and agencies in the federal bureaucracies is:

2565. United States. General Services Administration. National Archives and Records Service. Office of the Federal Register. *United States Government Organization Manual, 1971–1972.* Washington, D.C.: USGPO, 1971. This manual has sections entitled, "Sources of Information," which note whom to contact for further information about specific government agencies or offices. It is the "Official Handbook of the Federal Government" and contains descriptions of all branches, boards, commission, committees and quasi-official agencies. A facsimile of the "Freedom of Information Act" (5U.S.C. 552) of 1967 appears in the 1971–1972 edition, pp. 569–572.

Three other sources that may be used in the identification of specific military organizations, agencies, offices, or activities, and in some cases their commanders, are:

2566. *Army Green Book.* Annual, the October or November issue of *Army* contains a status report of all army major commands and activities with rosters of key commanders.

2567. United States. Department of the Army. *U. S. Army Installations and Major Activities in the Continental United States (Department of the Army Pamphlet 210–1).* Washington, D.C.: Department of the Army, 1970.

2568. United States. Organization Chart Service. *U.S. Military and Government Installation Directory.*

Original research materials are located in literally numberless depositories and libraries throughout the installations of the national security establishment, most of which are open to the public. Among the most important are the libraries of the formal service schools. Each service has catalogs of its service-level schools which may be used to locate both the schools and the courses taught there, as well as facilities and libraries maintained by these schools. We note here only the catalog for the army's schools; such catalogs are normally available in major recruiting facilities:

2569. United States. Department of the Army. *U.S. Army Formal Schools Catalog (Department of the Army Pamphlet No. 350–10, with 1971 Changes).* Washington, D.C.: Headquarters, Department of the Army, Feb. 1965.

Similarly, each service has its own historical division at the level of the department (Department of the Army, etc.). These agencies are staffed with professional historians that are more than willing to assist civilian researchers and in some instances may allow their substantial holdings of original materials to be examined. One of the most extensive such agency is:

2570. Office, Chief of Military History, Department of the Army, Washington, D.C.

Another very large collection of largely unclassified original materials on many phases of army activities is:

2571. U. S. Army Military History Research Collection, Carlisle Barracks, Pa.

Of course, the National Archives also maintain records of many of the highest-level military headquarters.

It is possible for civilian academic researchers to be granted access to classified government files. After identifying the type and location of the classified documents needed for research, interested parties should apply for clearance at the Office of Information for the particular service that originated the classified documents. Normally the manuscripts resulting from such research into classified documents must be submitted for review and clearance by the originating service before publication. In general the following list identifies the agencies responsible for public information in each of the services and an office that may be contacted for specific information. Telephone numbers noted are extracted from the *U. S. Government Organization Manual*'s "Sources of Information" sections for the respective services:

2572. United States Air Force, Office responsible for public information: Director, Office of Information, Department of the Air Force, The Pentagon. For information also: Directorate of Administration, Department of the Air Force, The Pentagon, Washington, D.C., 20330, Tel: 202–695–2246.

2573. Department of Defense, office responsible for public information: Directorate for Defense Information, Office of the Assistant Secretary of Defense (Public Affairs), The Pentagon, Washington, D.C. 20301, Tel: 202–697–5131.

2574. United States Army, office responsible for public information: Chief of Public Information, Department of the Army, The Pentagon. For information also: The Adjutant General, Department of the Army, The Pentagon, Washington, D.C. 20310 or Staff Management Division, Office of the Chief of Staff, Tel: 202–695–6700, ext. 78841.

2575. United States Navy, office responsible for public information: Chief of Information, Department of the Navy. For information also: Administrative Office, Department of the Navy, Room

580, Crystal Plaza #6, Arlington, Virginia (Mail: Washington, D.C. 20360), Tel: 202–692–7106.

2576. United States Marine Corps, Office responsible for Public Information: Director of Information, Headquarters, Marine Corps.

See also:

2577. "Army Military History Research Collection." *Armed Forces Journal* vol. 106. (12 Oct. 1968).

2578. "Keeping the Chronicles." *Airman* vol. 15 (Mar. 1971).

Most major military installations and activities have an individual designated to respond to queries from the general public (normally the Public Information Officer), and he is usually available to civilian researchers.

Another highly useful source is the *Congressional Record*. Many Congressmen insert miscellaneous studies, reports and information into the *Record* as a way of overcoming bureaucratic secrecy. For example, the most complete public version of the *Pentagon Papers* was first read into the *Record* by Senator Gravel. Sometimes these inserts go into great detail, as when Senator J. William Fulbright listed the names of all the individuals who were taken on Pentagon "public information" tours of scattered defense installations. The main difficulty with using this source is that information is not arranged in any logical order. The index is of some help for the bound volumes. One should usually begin by looking under the name of a specific official or agency, since subject coverage in the index is spotty.

A great deal of other information is produced each year by the government. Congress, of course, publishes not only the *Record* but voluminous materials in the form of committee hearings and reports. And Congress does not approach the executive branch in sheer quantity of output. Much of this information concerns national security in the broad sense we have used here. While some of the data are classified, the Freedom of Information Act is intended to assure that most will remain accessible, if not always readily so.

Nongovernmental groups have also contributed much to the discussion on national security. Here again, while secrecy is sometimes employed, the more usual objective of these groups is to reach as large an audience as possible.

It has thus occurred to us in preparing this bibliography that one cause of national security establishment's mysteriousness may be not a lack of information but rather a surfeit—that the difficulty of sorting through the vast mountain of data has given the military a certain amount of protection from scrutiny. At risk of simply adding more data, we have undertaken the task of sorting. It is our belief that an inscrutible military is ultimately harmful to itself, its society and the world.

973. Spivak, Jonathan. "Vietnam to Campus: Administration Views College for Veterans as Easing City Unrest." *Wall Street Journal* (17 Sept. 1969), p. 1.

974. Steif, William. "GI Bill Failing to Attract Vietvets." *College and University Business* vol. 47 (Sept. 1969).

975. United States. Congress. House. Committee on Veterans' Affairs. This committee regularly publishes information, hearings, etc. on this topic.

976. United States. Congress. Senate. Committee on Labor and Public Welfare. Subcommittee on Veterans' Affairs. *Unemployment and Overall Readjustment Problems of Returning Veterans: Hearings, Nov. 25 and Dec. 3, 1970.* Washington, D.C.: USGPO, 1971. This committee regularly publishes information, hearings, etc. on this topic.

977. United States. President's Committee on the Vietnam Veteran. *Report.* Washington, D.C.: Veterans Adminstration, 1970. Recommendations on access to educations, jobs and job training.

978. "Veterans: Economic and Social Costs on the Rise." *Congressional Quarterly Weekly Report* vol. 29 (9 Apr. 1971).

979. "Viet Vets Bring It All Back Home." *Old Mole* vol. 1, no. 46 (11 Sept. 1970).

980. "Why Vietnam Veterans Feel Like Fogotten Men." *U. S. News and World Report* vol. 70 (29 Mar. 1971).

981. See also ID4 "Veterans against the War."

6. The Volunteer Army

982. Alger, Maj. John (Ret.). "The Objective Was a Volunteer Army." *U. S. Naval Institute Proceedings* vol. 96 (Feb. 1970).

983. "Barracks Life Now a Little Brighter, to Attract Volunteers." See no. 238.

984. Bass, H. "Cost of Ending the Draft—A Preview." *WIN* vol. 5, no. 18 (15 Oct. 1969).

985. Brooks, Lt. Leon P. "Vital Interests and Volunteer Forces." *U. S. Naval Institute Proceedings* vol. 97 (Jan. 1971).

986. Brown, George E., Jr. "For an All-Volunteer Military." *War/Peace Report* vol. 9 (Apr. 1969). A congressman analyzes many sides of the picture.

987. "Congressional Battle: Draft or All Volunteer Army." *Congressional Quarterly Weekly Report* vol. 29 (2 Apr. 1971).

988. Davis, Vincent. "Universal Service: An Alternative to the All-Volunteer Armed Services." *Naval War College Review* vol. 23 (Oct. 1970).